Behavioral Risk Management

The Jossey-Bass Managed Behavioral Healthcare Library

Michael A. Freeman, General Editor

Behavioral Risk Management

How to Avoid Preventable Losses from Mental Health Problems in the Workplace

A VOLUME IN THE JOSSEY-BASS
MANAGED BEHAVIORAL HEALTHCARE LIBRARY

Rudy M. Yandrick

Foreword by Michael A. Freeman, General Editor

Jossey-Bass Publishers • San Francisco

A volume in the Jossey-Bass Managed Behavioral Healthcare Library.
Copyright © 1996 by Jossey-Bass Inc., Publishers, and CentraLink, 1110 Mar West, Suite E,
Tiburon, CA 94920 (415/435–9821), in cooperation with the Institute for Behavioral
Healthcare, 4370 Alpine Road, Suite 108, Portola Valley, CA 94028 (415/851–8411).

Figures 8.1 and 8.2, as well as other material in this book, are adapted or reprinted from
EAP Digest, published by Performance Resource Press of Troy, MI.

Substantial discounts on bulk quantities of Jossey-Bass books are available to
corporations, professional associations, and other organizations. For details and
discount information, contact the special sales department at Jossey-Bass Inc.,
Publishers (415) 433–1740; Fax (800) 605–2665.

For sales outside the United States, please contact your local Simon & Schuster
International Office.

 Manufactured in the United States of America on Lyons Falls Pathfinder
Tradebook. This paper is acid-free and 100 percent totally chlorine-free.

Library of Congress Cataloging-in-Publication Data

Yandrick, Rudy M.
  Behavioral risk management: how to avoid preventable losses from
mental health problems in the workplace/Rudy M. Yandrick; foreword by
Michael A. Freeman.
      p.   cm.—(The Jossey-Bass managed behavioral healthcare
library)
  Includes bibliographical references and index.
  ISBN 0-7879-0220-9 (alk. paper)
  1. Industrial psychiatry.   I. Freeman, Michael A.   II. Title.
III. Series.
RC967.5.Y36   1996
658.3'82—dc20
                                                        95-26783
                                                        CIP

FIRST EDITION
HB Printing 10 9 8 7 6 5 4 3 2 1

Contents

With love, to Roni, Greg, and Shelby

Foreword

Behavioral healthcare has changed. The old and once familiar professional landscape now seems altered and disorienting. The familiar landmarks that were well known to mental health administrators, clinicians, insurance executives, employee assistance program directors, and academic researchers are fading off the map. Vanishing or gone are the employers who did not pay attention to healthcare costs, the insurance plans that would reimburse on a fee-for-service basis, the hospitals with beds filled with patients whose coverage encouraged lengthy stays, the solo clinicians with full practices of affluent patients seeking long-term insight-oriented therapy, and the community mental health centers that worked in a system of their own.

The scenery of today is different. Health maintenance organizations and managed behavioral health plans have replaced the insurance companies. Employers and purchasing cooperatives are bypassing even these new organizations and purchasing directly from providers. Clinicians are forming group practices. Groups are affiliating with facilities. Facilities are forming integrated delivery systems. Integrated delivery systems are building organized systems of care that include insurance, care management, and service delivery functions. Information systems are linking payers, managers, and providers into coordinated and comprehensive systems with new levels of accountability. The boundaries of the public sector are eroding, and the distinction between public and private has become more difficult to perceive.

Adjusting to this "brave new world" is challenging, and many mental health professionals are being tempted to give up and opt out now. But for most of us, the challenge is worth facing. While this period is fraught with difficulty and risk, there are also a number of opportunities. Whenever a paradigm shifts, those having a stake in the previous paradigm risk losing their place in the one that emerges. The Jossey-Bass Managed Behavioral Healthcare

Library will help you identify and confront the challenges you will face as the prevailing healthcare paradigms change. Moreover, the volumes in this library will provide you with pragmatic strategies and solutions that you can call upon to sustain your importance in the healthcare systems of the future.

In spite of the upheavals transforming the behavioral healthcare enterprise in this country, many of its basic goals remain the same. In fact, managed behavioral healthcare has come about largely because our previous way of doing things failed to solve fundamental problems related to the cost, quality, accessibility, and outcomes of care. "Managed behavioral healthcare"—whatever this concept may eventually come to mean—holds out the promise of affordable, appropriate, and effective mental health and addiction treatment services for all. The various initiatives and efforts that are under way to reach this new service plateau will result in a vast array of professional opportunities for the behavioral healthcare specialists whose talents are required to make this promise come true.

By reading the books and reports in the Managed Behavioral Healthcare Library, you will learn how to respond to the perils and possibilities presented by today's shift to managed behavioral healthcare. The authors of this book and of the other volumes in this series recognize the need for direct and pragmatic solutions to the challenges posed by the changing paradigms of behavioral healthcare financing and services. To help you meet this need and obtain the resources and solutions you require, each chapter of each publication is written by an outstanding expert who can communicate in a pragmatic style to help you make a difference and meet each of the key challenges posed by the new landscape in behavioral healthcare.

This volume and the others planned for the series help you improve your effectiveness at pricing, financing, and delivering high-quality, cost-effective care. Future volumes will also provide straightforward solutions to the ethical challenges of managed behavioral healthcare and offer advice about practice management and marketing during a period of industry consolidation. You can look forward to still other books and reports about developing and managing a group practice, creating workplace-based behavioral healthcare programs, measuring outcomes, computerizing delivery systems, and ways of "benchmarking" in order to compare your organization or practice with others that face similar challenges.

Because the landscape of behavioral healthcare is in flux, professionals in the field need to be aware of alternative scenarios of the future and develop the skill sets for success within each one. For behavioral healthcare leaders, it is critical to have the vision to select the best options that accord with shared values and to have the skills to put these possibilities into practice. For this reason, the themes of vision, action, and results are incorporated into the volumes you read in the Managed Behavioral Healthcare Library.

Vision

In the context of the current debate and upheavals in healthcare, we have seen broad agreement regarding the importance of behavioral health scrutiny at an affordable price for all Americans. The Managed Behavioral Healthcare Library offers publications that show how universal coverage for affordable, appropriate, accessible, and effective mental health and addiction treatment benefits and services can be achieved.

Methods

How can we put into operation the new paradigms, the new models and systems of care needed to make the promise of managed care come true? New methods of benefit administration and health services delivery will be required to implement this vision within realistic financial limits.

At the broadest level, these methods include the core technologies used to manage benefits, care, and the health status of individuals and defined populations. At the level of frontline operations, these methods include continuous quality improvement, process reengineering, outcomes management, public-private integration, computerization, and delivery system reconfiguration in the context of capitation financing. These are the areas in which the Managed Behavioral Healthcare Library helps you build skill sets.

New methods of direct clinical care are also required. Instead of treating episodes of illness, clinicians in future managed and integrated behavioral healthcare systems will use disease-state management methods to reduce morbidity and mortality for individuals and for groups. The Managed Behavioral Healthcare Library provides frontline clinicians and delivery system managers with the skills that will enable our healthcare systems to truly provide scientifically validated bio-psycho-social treatment of choice in behavioral healthcare.

Action and Results

Knowing that we are in a period of change, and even having the desire to make the changes that are needed, makes little difference without actions based on methods that can produce results. Because you take action and produce results through day-in, day-out application of your professional expertise, the Managed Behavioral Healthcare Library is action oriented, to provide the greatest possible benefit to you and your colleagues.

∞∞∞

The management of workplace behavioral risk is an increasingly important concern for employee benefit managers, disability managers, and risk managers on the staff of self-insured employers. Health insurers share this risk because they absorb many of the costs that are produced when preventable risks are not prevented and unnecessary medical care results. Workplace behavioral risk management matters to labor unions, employee assistance programs, and employees as well, since these programs ultimately improve productivity, safety, and the quality of work life.

Downsizing, reengineering, outsourcing, and the implementation of new technologies across virtually every sector of the U.S. economy has contributed significantly to occupational stress and disability. Meanwhile, a host of new methods of measure for managing and reducing workplace behavioral risk have become broadly understood and available. This volume of the Managed Behavioral Healthcare Library was written in response to the critical need for concise information about behavioral risk management and for pragmatic examples of best practices that can be applied in a variety of occupational settings.

Given the increasingly competitive nature of the global marketplace, simply staying in business has become a compelling concern for many U.S. employers. The cost of production must be reduced to match global standards if U.S. products and services are to remain competitive. This volume helps employers find every opportunity to reduce direct and indirect costs associated with a company's most valuable resource—its people, or "human capital." The author, Rudy Yandrick, is an experienced management practices analyst who has spent years observing and reporting on the subject of this book and is uniquely qualified to bring the core concepts and strategies of behavioral risk management together in this pragmatic, effective volume.

We have designed this book, along with the other volumes in the Managed Behavioral Healthcare Library, to provide the information and inspiration essential for all professionals who want to understand the challenges and opportunities available today.

Tiburon, California   MICHAEL A. FREEMAN, M.D.
January 1996

Introduction:
The Paradigm Shift

After President Bill Clinton took office in 1993, the American public believed that decisive action would finally be taken to resolve the U.S. healthcare crisis. Employers wanting to contain costs, consumers wanting to retain their medical freedom of choice, and the uninsured wanting to acquire healthcare coverage, all awaited the administration's proposal and subsequent congressional action. When the 1,000-plus-page bill was finally submitted, the congressional leadership thumbed through its contents then splintered it into pieces for review by numerous committees and subcommittees. The lawmakers then proceeded to wrangle over its literally thousands of provisions.

Long before the end of the 103rd Congress—and the late 1994 deadline set for passage—it became apparent that this Godzilla of public policy issues was dying a slow intractable death. The eventual diagnosis was that healthcare reform had drowned in its own complexity.

This left employers, the primary payers for private healthcare, to assume leadership in restructuring the delivery system to provide higher-quality care for less money. Private-sector healthcare reform has actually been in process since the early 1980s, but its results have only begun to be realized during the last few years. Whereas the increase in private-sector healthcare cost was in the double digits in 1990, according to the actuarial firm Milliman & Robertson, it fell to only 2.6 percent for the twelve months ended in June 1994. Managed care both in medical and surgical areas and in behavioral health is credited for the impressive drop-off.

This is not to suggest that healthcare utilization is decreasing or that employers no longer feel they are paying excessively to cover employees. In fact, to sustain their progress, progressive employers have shifted their attention to reducing the *demand* for healthcare instead of merely seeking to contain costs. They are attacking those antecedents of healthcare utilization that come in the form of "people problems," including employee accidents, substance abuse, and unhealthy and dangerous life-styles and the similar problems of family members (who are usually covered under employees' healthcare plans). Some employers are even going after the systemic problems in their work organizations that can lead to these problems.

By reducing people and systemic problems, employers also often achieve the ancillary benefit of increasing productivity and reducing their financial losses from absenteeism, high turnover, employee and customer lawsuits, workers' compensation claims, and recruitment and training expenses. In order to curtail the problems, though, employers also have to take into account such additional factors as poor work attitudes, disharmony on work teams, and conflicts originating from ethnic and gender differences.

Since there are interrelationships among all these issues of health and problematic behavior, employers need a new paradigm, one that helps them devise solutions that are holistic and preventive. That new paradigm is behavioral risk management, that is, the global management of behavioral issues that affect work organizations.

Behavioral risk management is holistic and preventive because its interventions attack the causal links that turn nonhealth into health issues. For example, senior leadership problems in an organization might create an oppressive workplace that ultimately contributes to the stress-related illness of a night doorman's spouse. Or unmitigated problems among work team members might result in resentment, alienation, and emotional problems that then spin off as a variety of workplace losses. These losses can also be called *risk exposures.*

Let's shift gears now and consider how behavioral risk management relates to other changes that are occurring in U.S. business and industry. Work organizations are revolutionizing how they make products and deliver services. They are shedding old dogmas and sacred cows as though they were last year's coat of fur. Employers are becoming more willing to look at how they may be contributing to their own problems. They do not want stale formulas for resolving new problems. They are demanding newfound efficiency and teamwork, not insulated programs that perform redundant tasks.

This transformation—which is applying such concepts as Total Quality Management and reengineering to achieve its ends—has been called the biggest change in business and industry since the Industrial Revolution. One of the truly avant-garde aspects of the U.S. business transformation is the emergence of the work team concept, whose article of faith is that harnessing the full work and intellectual contributions of all employees will improve the productivity and profitability of the organization. Gone for the most part are rigid hierarchical management structures and adversarial labor unions, and in their place are "empowered" employees.

Behavioral risk management is the framework for reengineering what until recently have been the forgotten pieces of the U.S. workplace transformation: prevention of loss and management of people issues. Business decision makers have seen that the introduction of work teams is fraught with new behavioral risks, since interactions between employees and employees' relationships with managers are fundamentally altered. They now realize that better, more reliable equipment and processes mean little if the breakdowns in production and service delivery simply shift to the people involved.

What we now understand is that as businesses are transformed, *behavioral* issues need to be put on par with *structural* changes if the transformation is to be successful. This plain fact is one reason why behavioral risk management is a concept whose time has come.

Behavioral risk management includes the best strategies already offered by such workplace functions as employee assistance, conflict resolution, managed behavioral healthcare, wellness and health promotion, safety management, and organizational development. In this respect, behavioral risk management is an eclectic approach to business loss management.

In the thirteen chapters of this book, I offer a comprehensive explanation of how an employer can manage behavioral risks, including

- An introduction to the behavioral risk management concept
- A description of a comprehensive audit instrument with which employers can determine their individual and organizational behavioral risks
- An explanation of a variety of interventions including programs and services; supportive benefits; supportive policies and procedures; organizational interventions; and supervisor, work team, employee, executive, and board member training
- A discussion of a comprehensive strategy that incorporates these interventions
- An analysis of specialized issues in management and service delivery

This book is neither dense nor academic. Business generalists, for example, will find practical, understandable chapters on performing a behavioral risk audit that shows where productivity and financial losses occur and how to measure them.

Occupational managers and service providers will appreciate this book's bird's-eye view of behavioral risk management. In the everyday press of business, program specialists can become cloistered by the four walls of their jobs. This book takes a macroscopic look at how their work contributes to the advancement of the work organization.

Similarly, designers of workplace programs and services will find the content useful as the starting gate from which more detailed operating guidelines can be written and tailored to the needs of their work organizations.

The paradigm shift in healthcare is already under way, and more and more employers are beginning to use behavioral risk management strategies to stay (or become) competitive. *Behavioral Risk Management,* ultimately, is an idea book for employers who want to create a new infrastructure that will meet the needs of today's—and tomorrow's—work organization.

Acknowledgments

I owe a debt of gratitude to scores of people with whom I have become friends through my twelve-year association with the employee assistance, managed behavioral healthcare, and allied occupational professions. I have been fortunate to work with many visionaries having a canny sense of what lies on the horizon and, in writing this book, drew upon my memories of literally hundreds of conversations with such people. As a journalist who seeks the objective vantage point of a perch "above the din," from which to observe, take notes, and process information, I have also relied heavily upon many managers and professionals working in the trenches of U.S. business and industry.

Three special acknowledgments are in order. The first is to George T. Watkins, publisher and editor-in-chief of Troy, Michigan–based *EAP Digest* magazine. George gave me the opportunity to write a supplement titled "Behavior Risk Management" in each issue of the magazine during 1994 and 1995. That was the first launch of this concept. He has graciously granted me permission to use editorial material previously published in the *EAP Digest* in this book.

My second special acknowledgment is to Michael Freeman of the Institute for Behavioral Healthcare. Michael's appreciation for the growing importance of behavioral risk management in contemporary work organizations led to the development of the present comprehensive volume, which is published as part of the institute's Managed Behavioral Healthcare Library.

Last, I would like to thank Alan Rinzler, senior editor for Jossey-Bass Publishers, who worked with me throughout the drafting of this book. By setting high standards for editorial quality and content, he helped to ensure that *Behavioral Risk Management* would make an important contribution to employers' ability to address workplace problems.

Harrisburg, Pennsylvania　　　　　　　　RUDY M. YANDRICK
April 1996

Behavioral Risk Management

Chapter One

Behavioral Problems in the Workplace

Have you ever worked in a company that was awash in employee discontent? Or one that was continually mired down by heavy absenteeism that resulted in consistently missed production deadlines? How about one that was accident prone? Or one staffed mostly with physically unhealthy employees? Or one that seemed to harbor backbiters, complainers, and victims? Most of us have experienced these workplace problems at one time or another. And most of us noted that management was often either a part of the problem—by being oblivious to it or by contributing to it—or was groping in the dark for solutions.

Such problems are evidence of the systemic dysfunctional patterns of behavior that commonly take root and fester in work organizations. They tend to persist because management has a limited understanding of their origins and mutability. This should come as little surprise, considering that senior managers in most organizations typically devote their energies to solving tactile problems like meeting production schedules and staying within budget projections. They use "if-then" deductive schemes to reach their solutions: "if I make the production process more efficient by tweaking steps B, F, and Q, then I'll be able to reduce my costs." This type of problem solving has generally served them well throughout their careers.

Resolving "people problems," however, is another matter. Interpersonal communications and behavioral dynamics are seldom part of the requisite competency and knowledge base for executives on the fast track. Further, the untidy business of trying to

1

curtail mental health or behavioral problems may be neglected or, at least, placed lower on the priority list. If decision makers have only a limited understanding of where the people problems occur and how these problems siphon off financial resources, they are less likely to have insights on how to prevent or minimize their impact.

Seven Case Studies

Here are seven case studies of typical behavioral problems in work organizations. Although the employers' identities are confidential, the case studies are based on actual situations and, chances are, have been replicated many, many times over throughout U.S. business. They illustrate the reciprocity that can exist between individual and organizational behaviors, the way that a molehill of a problem can become a mountain, and the costs that are borne by the organization when it fails to make a timely appropriate intervention. While some of these problems are systemic and others are isolated events, every one of the work organizations involved incurred considerable financial or productivity loss because of them.

Case Study 1: The Restructuring Plan That Produced a Stress-Related Disability

An Eastern U.S. food-processing company had a district manager who had amassed an impressive sales record over ten years with the company. The following year, under a companywide restructuring plan, her district was merged with another to form a new area whose combined sales were more than 50 percent larger than those in her previous district. The prior management of the new territory had a history of poor performance. Consequently, the district manager's mop-up job following the merger included disposing of old stock, refurbishing ramshackle warehouses, healing the wounds of dissatisfied customers, and improving sales. She also had to hire and train new salespeople. As a result, her workweek increased from 55 to 70 hours.

Shortly after the consolidation, the district manager began experiencing somatic, that is physical, problems. Half a year later, she notified her supervisor that the new district was too large for her to manage, but the supervisor made no effort to accommodate her need for assistance or job restructuring. Several months after that, she was seen by a psychiatrist, who diagnosed what she was experiencing as a depressive episode. Although her mood improved briefly with therapy, she eventually relapsed, experiencing the same condition that had preceded her initial treatment. Suffering what was now deemed a psychiatric injury, she filed for workers' compensation benefits. The company challenged her claim before a workers' compensation appeal board, but since she proved that her condition was a reaction to abnormal working conditions, the award stood.

Consequently, the company's costs for its failure to make suitable accommodation included permanent workers' compensation benefits to the claimant, payment for her psychiatric treatment prior to the claim, legal fees, recruitment and training costs associated with filling her position, loss of revenue and loss of long-term customers due to disruptions in sales activity in her district, and adverse publicity generated by the case.

As this case illustrates, stress-related problems, whether manifested as physical injuries or as terminal stage psychological disorders, can result in costly workers' compensation claims for employers. Work-related stress can express itself as

- A mental disorder that leads to compensable physical injury
- A psychiatric disability that accompanies a primary physical injury (known as a secondary psychiatric disability)
- A short-term workers' compensation case that is protracted into a long-term or permanent case due to the onset of psychiatric malaise (which is common to workers out on relief)
- A work disability that is entirely psychological in nature

In any of these four circumstances, the employer pays in triplicate, through medical, rehabilitative, and wage-replacement benefits. Furthermore, a single claim won by an employee can have devastating consequences on employee relations throughout the firm

Case Study 2: An Exploitative Managed Behavioral Healthcare Plan

A large self-insured municipal government contracted with a managed behavioral healthcare vendor to provide preauthorization and case management of treatment to employees and their dependents with behavioral illnesses. Rather than pay for treatment on a case-by-case basis, though, it engaged in a full financial risk contract with the provider for a single prepaid fee. Significantly, this capitated system of managed care was separate and distinct from the one used to manage the employer's medical and surgical healthcare plan.

A consultant who was subsequently hired to audit the program at the end of the first year found extensive gaming by the managed care provider in the provision—and lack of provision—of treatment. He determined that the financial incentives in the contract led the vendor to use a chutes-and-ladders healthcare access and service delivery structure. For example, if the managed behavioral healthcare firm found that a beneficiary had two or more coexisting behavioral health problems, that person was usually "chuted" to treatment only for the least expensive one. The consultant also learned that, except in medical emergencies, beneficiaries with chemical dependency problems were directed only to outpatient services, even when the severity of the illness warranted inpatient or intensive-outpatient services. Those were typical chutes. The ladders were the laborious appeals processes that patients, their families, and referring doctors went through when they felt that more intensive care was warranted than the care provider was willing to certify.

Moreover, the numbers of reported substance abuse cases and of coexisting behavioral disorders (among the most expensive conditions to treat) were well below norms commonly accepted in the behavioral health industry. These data, too, led the consultant to conclude that many plan participants with behavioral illnesses were being treated only for the secondary medical and surgical symptoms of their primary behavioral health problems. They were, in effect, being passed off to the medical and surgical health plan. Finally, upon inspection of clinical charts, the consultant found diagnostic inaccuracy in 20 to 30 percent of the cases.

What confirmed that this was a system gone awry was the vendor's financial take: only one-third of the dollar value of its contract with the employer was spent on the actual provision of care. The remaining two-thirds was used to cover administrative costs and profit loading.

Most employers understand that workers cannot just check their psychological baggage at the front door, becoming mere automatons during working hours. Some mental health and substance abuse problems are going to manifest, that is, become apparent, no matter what steps are taken by an employer to prevent them. Therefore, interventions to control cost risk can be as critical as those that prevent behavioral problems from developing. All employers face this cost risk—especially those who do not offer behavioral healthcare benefits!—but some attempt in vain to transfer it to an outside source with a cash payment and the stroke of a pen. Employers need to manage their costs and managed behavioral healthcare, on the whole, has been effective in helping them do it. But employers also need to safeguard against unwittingly motivating external service providers to underdiagnose and undertreat healthcare plan participants.

Case Study 3: The Quality Improvement Program That Failed

In its pursuit of total quality awards, a large East Coast energy company zealously encouraged its newly formed work teams to make quality improvements. Individual and team compensation and recognition were based not just on introducing new efficiencies and fewer errors but also on producing promotable success stories.

The rewards were incentive enough to spawn some reprehensible actions by employees, with the tacit approval of team leaders. For example, some improvements made prior to implementation of the quality improvement (QI) program were rewritten in the corporate QI lexicon, backfit to the former problem, and claimed as QI success stories, thus giving a team a competitive advantage over the other work teams. Meanwhile, managers derisively labeled the "QI thought police" by employees and empowered to enforce the new controls were roaming the halls to spot infractions. Employees refusing to comply with onerous work rules had to consider the consequences of their career-limiting decisions.

In less than two years, many workers—including long-term employees whose pensions were not yet vested—began leaving the company because of the institutionalized unfairness they perceived. Other employees, unable to land jobs in greener pastures, remained with the company but carried chips on their shoulders.

From internal surveys, the company learned that employees felt the new system lacked intrinsic awards. Stated differently, employees had lost the warm and fuzzy sense of belonging and accomplishment they once got from their jobs. The work culture had become stark and regimented, almost like a boot camp.

Employees retaliated, no longer being willing to make an extra effort for the company when it was needed, failing to report violations of safe work procedures, and abstaining from contributing ideas to the QI process. Healthcare use went up for stress-related problems, as did the number of disability cases. Absenteeism increased. There were suspected incidents of sabotage and pilfering.

This company's problems were seeded in part by the failure of its organizational development consultants, on whose expertise the company relied, to take into account the ramifications that QI policies and practices would have on employees. There are three key concepts to consider when implementing team concepts: promoting a sense of fairness, holding people accountable, and providing and receiving feedback. This company's problems resulted primarily from a perception of unfairness, which was caused in part by new work-site behavioral codes. This perception obstructed the upward flow of feedback. Finally, the ability of less-than-ethical employees to exploit the process for personal gain was evidence of misguided accountability standards.

Companies usually have the best of intentions when they implement quality improvement initiatives. But frequently, conceptual flaws or oversights result in crossed lines of communication, ambition run amok, faulty compensation and reward systems, and unrealistic production goals, all of which can undermine the intended benefit of the QI initiative and invite unintended consequences.

Case Study 4: The Work-Team Concept That Ignored Behavioral Issues

A less dramatic but nonetheless telling example of a failed quality improvement initiative occurred in a 115-employee mechanical assembly company that implemented self-directed work teams. The owner of this company was an impatient man who kept abreast of management trends and saw himself as a visionary. When he noticed other employers "going horizontal" in their structures and operational strategies, he decided, without a second thought, that his company, too, should ride this wave.

Many management experts believe that a permanent transition to a horizontal structure and work format takes two to five years. This owner wanted it done in less than two, however, and replaced the plant operations manager with a Total Quality Management consultant who was to implement the new concept. Employees were very enthusiastic, although the departmental managers were threatened with job loss unless they could adapt to a training and coaching role.

The consultant arranged employees into ten work teams of between five and fifteen people. Job titles, descriptions, and policies and procedures were phased out. Each work team was responsible for establishing its own practices, such as creating its own schedule, dealing with customers, ordering production and related materials, taking responsibility for conforming to requirements, and preparing its own budget.

Enthusiasm about the novelty of the concept sustained it for the first year. However, after a short while, several teams began to have problems when, as the consultant explained, certain employees "didn't keep their egos in check." There was no process for effectively handling disagreements, a common deficiency in self-directed work team environments. When either the consultant or owner tried to act as arbiter in disputed daily operating decisions, however, the disputants, and often other employees, resisted out of concern that the company was reneging on its promise to "empower" employees.

These conflicts sometimes brought productivity grinding to a halt and ultimately caused the work team concept to require six years for implementation instead of the original goal of two. Even in the sixth year, though, employees felt they were still learning from the school of hard knocks.

This company lacked two essential ingredients for successful self-directed work team implementation. The first was long-term behavioral training to instruct employees in effective communication and interaction, skills that are particularly important when an authority figure is not present to make binding decisions. The second was a conflict-resolution process to help disagreeing employees negotiate solutions and to promote collegial decision making.

Case Study 5: The Alcoholic Who Was Enabled

Behavioral health problems can be ignored by employers for a time but not indefinitely. Consider the case of "Bill," an alcoholic. Bill worked for twenty-two years at a Midwest manufacturing company that was tolerant of heavy drinking and light on behavioral healthcare benefits. He worked himself up to senior lathe technician, a position he held for seven years. Although his job performance was usually at an acceptable level, he was prone to alternating periods of deteriorating and exceptional craftsmanship. Co-workers periodically worried that he teetered on losing control. Bill had seniority and was highly valued for his expertise, which in some cases made him more valuable to the company than were the people supervising him. So others in the department would compensate for his poor craftsmanship during his periodic bouts. At times, Bill's supervisor would attempt to confront him about poor work quality and no-shows, but Bill knew how to manipulate the conversation to exploit the supervisor's personal shortcomings or vulnerabilities.

Bill's family was also concerned but unable to change his drinking behavior. Then Bill's absences became more frequent and the level of his work plummeted. Eventually, the toxicity of the alcohol deteriorated his internal organs to the point that he could no longer meet the physical requirements of his job, and he was forced into early retirement.

Over the years, Bill's cost to the company was considerable. His absenteeism rate during his last few years was double the company average, and his healthcare costs were five times higher. As codependents of an alcoholic, Bill's family members also used their healthcare benefits excessively. Several of his on-the-job errors cost the company thousands of dollars over the last three years of his employment. Finally, he had several spats with management that cast a pall over the workplace for weeks at a time.

Bill's company had no system to document the impact of his problem, however. It lacked a progressive discipline policy, documentation procedures, supervisors with effective intervention skills, integrated record keeping to document employees' longitudinal attendance records and job performance, a means of referring Bill to help, and adequate treatment benefits. As a result, Bill's ultimate cost to the company was far greater than his contribution.

Case Study 6: The Corporate Diversity Plan That Backfired

A Southern division of a large appliance manufacturing company had a long history of racial tension. Blacks, especially women, often held hourly wage jobs on the lowest rungs of the corporate ladder, working in custodial, helper, and apprentice positions. In many cases, they were ineligible for advancement and deeply resented the two-tiered system that they felt exploited them.

Against this backdrop worked one black female in the position of "operator," making her an unqualified success among her demographic peers. However, the culture of the organization allowed her to be incessantly tormented as a woman in a man's domain. For example, she was exposed to pornographic photos and abusive remarks by male co-workers on an almost daily basis. On one occasion, she was tied to a chair, and on another, she was locked for hours in a room.

After eight years, she was the first female promoted to supervisor in the manufacturing group's history. At about the same time, the company began offering diversity training for employees, ostensibly to promote better racial harmony. This was intended to be a preventive step based on the projected hiring of more workers from ethnic minority groups. However, it became apparent after the program was implemented that management was not prepared to make hard decisions whenever unanticipated and divisive racial issues arose.

In the case of this supervisor, the training sessions opened a Pandora's box, as they brought to her conscious thought the hostility that she had accumulated over the course of her employment. What followed was one payback after another for anyone unfortunate enough to be her subordinate. She ignored the suggestions of workers for improving daily operations, refused to grant time off to employees for personal matters, and showed hostility toward any employee who did not address her in a manner that she felt she deserved. In short, employees feared being in her doghouse.

Eventually, a consultant hired to address her department's problems suggested that she undergo a psychiatric evaluation, a suggestion based on comments from subordinates about her frequent displays of anger and her hasty, ill-conceived, and often irrational decision making. Management refused the consultant's recommendation, however, feeling that if the company took adverse action against her, it risked a public relations fiasco. So it transferred her laterally to another department, where after only a short period of time, the same drama played out once more.

Some interventions intended to effect positive change in workplace behavior can backfire if they are applied as a quick fix. In this case, the diversity training program appeared to some employees to *enable* the supervisor to take her problems out on co-workers. To other employees, the lack of management commitment to creating a work culture more supportive of diversity made the training exercises seem disingenuous and inconsequential. It was clear, in any case, that the mission of the training was not commensurate with the size of the problem. In addition to management's goal of a reduction in the race-based anxieties of employees, it should have also had a plan for long-term healing and a method for measuring results. Ultimately, the outcome of the training was the opposite of its intent: it protected the status quo.

Case Study 7: The Social Service Agency That Overheated

A twenty-year-old nonprofit social service agency with seventy-five employees was fraught with internal problems. Since its inception, the agency had grown by fits and starts, expanding as revenue-generating opportunities arose instead of according to a clearly articulated mission and coherent strategic plan. The agency offered five sundry client services—adult education, vocational rehabilitation, energy assistance, transportation, and family planning—which filled certain community needs but could not be structured as a continuum from the clients' point of view. The agency's lack of an integrated service delivery system had also sown seeds of discontent at three operating levels: the board of directors, staff leadership, and staff members. In its fifteenth year, even as the agency started to prosper financially, these seeds were sprouting.

Many of the board members exclusively represented one of the five services, and during periods of budget negotiation, these members executed their duties more in the manner of professional lobbyists protecting special interests than of trustees concerned about the common welfare of the organization and community. Another factor contributing to conflict was the fact that many board members were appointed by the president instead of by vote of the board. On the one hand, this gave the president authority to stack the deck, but on the other hand, it made him a lightning rod for criticism. Jockeying occurred when meeting agendas were set and when the chief operating officer (COO), the agency's senior staff member, executed board decisions.

Lobbying occurred at the staff level, too, arising out of the COO's broad discretionary authority in executing board decisions. The COO, herself affiliated with one of the five services, had trouble making fair and dispassionate decisions. This led to ambiguous marching orders delegated to the associate staff director and individual staff members. The chaotic daily operation of the agency also made staff vulnerable to direct lobbying by board members.

Eventually, the organization overheated. Money was wasted as funding streams were unpredictably altered from one board meeting to the next. Projects were started but not completed. Decisions were tabled. Tempers flared.

All of these behaviors exacted their heaviest toll on staff, who had the least amount of control over the situation. An employee counseling service with whom the agency contracted became a revolving door. It was used by many staff members seeking help for personal problems, but despite its best efforts, the most that could be said about it was that it kept staff members from becoming emotionally submerged in the undertow of organizational problems. It provided a rope for employees to grab, but it was powerless to prevent crises from occurring in the first place.

Ultimately, the organization resembled a dysfunctional family more than a business, and it became a sieve for behavior-related financial losses. Healthcare benefits were constantly in use, absenteeism and tardiness were high, morale plunged, and the quality of customer service suffered. Because board and staff members were all, in effect, operating from bunkers, meaningful structural change was not made until several years later, when emotions were defused by a near-total turnover of board and staff members.

Some behavioral problems take root during periods of rapid organizational growth but do not manifest as problems until years later, during a period when a status quo is being maintained. Oftentimes management consultants are hired when the level of organizational pain becomes unbearable, but by then, the organization has usually experienced substantial losses of money, productivity, reputation, talent, and competitiveness. What this agency lacked was a pressure gauge for assessing organizational stress, which can be measured from productivity indicators, healthcare utilization data, periodic surveys of staff attitudes that might precede behavioral problems, and feedback from the counseling service. Had this agency measured its organizational stress from year to year, red flags would have been raised earlier and organizational development interventions could have been made.

Statistical Data on Behavioral Problems

Data have been said to be the plural of anecdote, and it is true that quantitative research that generates statistical information can provide revealing insights to behavioral problems. Specifically, quantitative research helps employers to understand that workplace behavioral problems are usually omnipresent, not isolated. Consider these findings:

• In a research project that studied socioeconomic variables, drinking behavior, and the likelihood of injury-related work absences, employees with low job satisfaction were found to have incurred multiple injuries more often than those with high job satisfaction (55 percent to 43 percent), and employees with a higher number of stressful life events were more likely to have had more than one injury than those with a lower number of such events (53 percent to 41 percent). Problem drinkers, compared with nonproblem drinkers, were 2.7 times more likely to have an injury-related absence. Subjects with low levels of job satisfaction were 2.2 times more likely than others to have an injury-related absence.

• Psychosocial and work environment factors have been shown to be far more accurate predictors of worker disability than physical factors. One panel of experts assigned them a combined 40.1 weighting out of a possible 100. In comparison, injury and diagnostic factors received only a 33.9 weighting. By far, psychological symptoms are the most important psychosocial factor (receiving a weighting of 8.6 out of a possible 20.0). Further, the presence of an attorney—who in many cases can sour an injured worker's attitude toward his or her employer—is also an important variable. Although 90 percent of injured workers without an attorney had returned to work, a lower percentage of individuals with an attorney returned. Also, if a worker is disabled for six months, the probability of return to work is 50 percent, whereas at the one-year mark, that probability falls to 20 percent.

• According to a study of one major U.S. corporation, the average annual cost of healthcare for a claimant with six or more health risk factors—most of which are behavioral—is $1,700. By contrast, the average cost for a claimant with three risk factors is $600 and the average for a claimant with no risk factors is only $200.

• One health risk factor that qualifies as an epidemic in the U.S. is obesity. Thirty-five percent of women and 31 percent of men are overweight, and these percentages are increasing every year. For example, in 1974, 23 percent of men aged sixty-five to seventy-four were overweight; in 1991, that figure was 43 percent. In 1974, 15 percent of women aged twenty to thirty-four were overweight; in 1991, that figure was 25 percent. Obesity—which is often related to behavioral problems—impairs an employee's ability to perform many workplace tasks; reduces stamina, which can lead to work defects; and results in greater healthcare use and, for that reason, more absenteeism.

• The major factors affecting truck-driver attitudes over the drivers' career stages were found to be due primarily to equipment, benefits, perceived advancement opportunities (both within and outside the company), and driver perceptions of the company's attitude toward its employees. Significantly, compensation was found to be less of a factor.

• Men with demanding jobs that give them little control over their work are three times as likely to have hypertension as co-workers. Conversely, men with demanding jobs that allow them to exercise control show no ill effects.

• An estimated one in three white-collar men and one in two white-collar women suffer a major depressive episode by age fifty, with the decline in productivity being an estimated 20 percent during each depressive episode.

• In a study of five clerical units, the structure of an absence policy was cited to explain the presence of an "absence culture" in a work organization. Individuals were shown to take as many paid absence days as was allowed by the policy if this behavior contributed to their personal happiness without penalty. The findings also showed that the longer the tenure of an employee with the organization, the less he or she was absent, possibly due to his or her greater awareness of the costs to both employee and employer.

• Unscheduled absences by U.S. employees rose 9 percent in 1993, costing work organizations as much as $750 per employee, according to a national survey of 380 employers. Governmental agencies reported the highest rate of unscheduled absences, averaging 2.98 hours of paid sick leave for every 100 hours of paid productive time. Manufacturing companies averaged 2.55 sick hours. Mean absenteeism increased to 2.7 percent from 2.5 percent in 1992, but was down from a four-year high of 3.1 percent in 1990.

• Losses to U.S. businesses due to employee fraud, primarily theft, range from $10 billion to $40 billion, although an estimated 90 percent of fraud goes undetected.

The case studies and data presented in this chapter illustrate how unresolved behavioral problems turn into financial and productivity losses and how interventions that are too narrow in scope allow the same problems to burst out again elsewhere. To prevent such losses, employers need a holistic strategy for addressing workplace mental health and behavioral problems, one that is consistent with prevailing management thought and responsive to organizational change. This strategy is behavioral risk management, the global management of behavioral risks that have a negative impact on work organizations.

Notes

P. 2, *An Eastern U.S. food-processing company:* Bittker, J. A. (ed.). "Can Sales Manager Recover Benefits for Stress-Induced Psychological

Problems?" *Workers' Compensation Law Bulletin*, 1995 (special issue).

P. 12, *research project that studied socioeconomic variables, drinking behavior:* Webb, G., and others. "The Relationships Between High-Risk and Problem Drinking and the Occurrence of Work Injuries and Related Absences," *Journal of Studies on Alcohol*, 1994, *55*(4), 441–442.

P. 12, *One panel of experts:* Frymoyer, J. W. "Predicting Disability from Low Back Pain," *Clinical Orthopaedics and Related Research*, 1992, *279*, 106.

P. 13, *the presence of an attorney:* Haddad, G. H. "Analysis of 2,932 Workers' Compensation Back Injury Cases: The Impact on the Cost to the System," *Spine*, 1987, *12*, 765.

P. 13, *if a worker is disabled for six months:* Frymoyer. "Predicting Disability from Low Back Pain," p. 105.

P. 13, *a study of one major U.S. corporation:* Edington, D. W. University of Michigan, 1991. Reported in Chenoweth, D. "Health Claims Data Analysis: Rx for Behavior Risk Management," *EAP Digest* (Behavior Risk Management supplement), 1994, *14*(5), 23–26.

P. 13, *an epidemic in the U.S. is obesity:* Institute of Medicine, National Center for Health Statistics. *Weighing the Options: Criteria for Evaluating Weight Management Programs.* Washington, D.C.: National Academy Press, 1994, pp. 46–53.

P. 13, *factors affecting truck-driver attitudes:* McElroy, J., and others. "Career Stage, Time Spent on the Road, and Truckload Driver Attitudes," *Transportation Journal*, 1993, *33*(1), 11–12.

P. 13, *Men with demanding jobs:* Schnall, P., and others. "The Relationship Between 'Job Strain,' Workplace Diastolic Blood Pressure, and Left Ventricular Mass Index," *Journal of the American Medical Association*, 1990, *263*, 1928–1935.

P. 13, *one in three white-collar men:* Greenberg, P., Stiglin, L., Finkelstein, S., and Berndt, E. "The Economic Burden of Depression in 1990," *Journal of Clinical Psychiatry*, 1993, *54*(11), 405–418.

P. 14, *In a study of five clerical units:* Martocchio, J. J. "The Effects of Absence Culture on Individual Absence," *Human Relations*, 1994, *47*(3), 256.

P. 14, *Unscheduled absences by U.S. employees:* Moskal, B. S. "Missing Persons," *Industry Week*, Aug. 15, 1994, p. 22.

P. 14, *Losses to U.S. businesses due to employee fraud:* Bourque, A. *Getting Smart About Getting Ripped Off.* Quincy, Mass.: Surveillance Specialties, 1994 (Press release).

Chapter Two

What Is Behavioral Risk Management?

As its name suggests, *behavioral risk management* is an applied risk management strategy. *Risk management* describes any of a variety of methods for making risk- and reward-based calculations. Risk management has traditionally been used by investors, businesspeople, and insurers in such endeavors as financial investments, mergers and acquisitions, and indemnity protection. In these cases, the risks include investment losses, environmental liabilities, and reduced market share. Similarly, behavioral risk management applies to the risks connected with workplace behaviors of employees and work organizations that have a negative impact on the productivity of an organization; behavioral healthcare episodes and the cost of treating these episodes; and life-style behaviors that lead to preventable healthcare conditions and the cost of treating these conditions.

All risk management seeks to avoid risk and prevent exposure to material loss. The fundamental premise of behavioral risk management is that defining certain workplace problems as behavioral will yield prevention-based solutions. The linear progression shown below gives employers a simple frame of reference for understanding how many internal problems develop as behavioral problems.

Social Issues	⟹	Psychological Problems	⟹	Behavioral Problems	⟹	Healthcare and Productivity Problems

Healthcare and productivity problems originate as social issues, or factors. These social issues may be related to the workplace as well as to nonwork environments. Furthermore, they may occur outside

16

of work but be exacerbated by conditions of work, or vice versa. (Note that preexisting medical and mental health problems are not included here as social problems. Generally these are problems to which employers can apply neither intervention nor prevention strategies. Indeed, each of us has predispositions that sometimes, but not always, will make us more vulnerable to developing personal problems if we are exposed to certain negative environmental stimuli.)

In the progression of events that leads to workplace problems, social issues manifest in individuals as psychological problems, including the negative attitudes that can prompt employees to behave in counterproductive ways. When these undesired behaviors of employees or dependents are not dealt with directly, they can then progress to healthcare and productivity problems, with their related risk exposures.

Employers have traditionally attacked such behaviors at the last stage, after healthcare and productivity problems have already taken root. This, however, is only damage control. The best behavioral risk management strategy is to try to arrest problem development earlier, in the behavioral stage.

The even earlier stage of psychological problems is off-limits for intervention outside of the therapeutic mental healthcare environment, since thoughts and attitudes are private and may never surface as workplace behavioral problems. Interventions by employers at this level that have job-related consequences—such as psychological testing in an effort to weed out "bad actors" among existing employees—are rife with legal problems and can be ineffective, too. For example, many employers have tried to blacklist or otherwise earmark workers felt to be most likely to manifest violent behavior. However, they have been thwarted by their low rate of predictive accuracy. Of course, observable behaviors—such as threats, menacing stares, mean-spirited practical jokes, and other forms of intimidation initiated by one employee against another—are cause for legitimate intervention.

An additional rationale for addressing problems at the earliest observable stage comes from behavioral modification research, which has shown that modification of an individual's behavior—including work-related behavior—is often followed by corresponding changes in that person's thoughts and attitudes.

Some employers seek to prevent behavioral problems through community-involvement activities that address educational problems and provide drug and alcohol avoidance education for teens and prenatal care programs and so on. This strategy is a nexus between the mission of the work organization and the best interests of the community at large. It may be done as altruistic community service or for the purpose of attracting a better talent pool to the organization. In either case, the focus in these activities is far beyond that of only managing behavioral risk.

Five-Step Behavioral Risk Management Process

The basic process of risk management is to identify risks, quantify them, and then seek to prevent some risks while assuming or transferring others. I recommend that employers use the following five-step adaptation of this process, which I devised after years of observing the ways business organizations solve (or fail to solve) their employee problems.

1. Identify the organization's behavior-related risks and determine what its risk exposures have been.
2. Take stock of current activities that affect risks and risk exposures. These might include programs and services, the benefits that support them, and relevant policies and procedures.
3. Gather two sets of data that indicate or suggest (a) the individual and organizational risks and risk exposures and (b) the effectiveness of behavioral risk management activities.
4. Correlate and analyze the data, looking for relationships between the two sets of measures.
5. Introduce new (or modify existing) interventions, such as programs, services, and benefits to emphasize (a) prevention of behavioral problems and (b) early-stage intervention following any problem's onset. This step is where the rubber meets the road.

I will discuss the steps in this process in detail beginning in Chapter Three. The remainder of this chapter will prepare for that discussion by describing the kinds of behaviors and risk exposures the audit taken in step 1 might reveal and by further defining behavioral risk management in the light of those behaviors and risk exposures.

Start With the Problems

The behavioral risk management process starts with the identification of behavioral problems, or risks. The following are generic behavioral risks that can occur in any workplace and should be audited for their impact. The employee risks lead to behavioral risk exposures, which are the actual productivity and financial losses to the work organization. The organizational risks are factors that can elevate the level of employee risk and, therefore, the probability of behavioral risk exposures. Each of these risks can vary significantly from one organization to another due to such factors as industry type, local culture, and socioeconomic variables.

Employee Risks

The following employee risks are associated with acting out behavior, particularly behaviors such as retaliation against an employer, manager, or co-worker; self-medicating and other coping actions; actions arising out of emotional instability; or actions borne of ignorance, due to a person's lack of socialization. The risks range from acts of people engaging in willful misconduct to the acts of people who are hapless victims of circumstance.

• *Problems associated with excessive work demands or high job stress.* Most work organizations have periods of bustle and of slack. Tax-preparation firms, for example, have a sharp line of demarcation known to all U.S. taxpayers as April 15th. In such firms, there is a cyclical, predictable drop-off in workload. Other companies have increased employee workloads over an indefinite period, however, and these are the ones that are particularly vulnerable to this risk—which can show up as various undesirable employee behaviors.

Job consolidation, downsizing, and employee empowerment are examples of workplace initiatives that can place excessive stress on employees that is not specifically related to workload. Common coping reactions include overeating (especially at the lunch table with co-workers), self-medication with either alcohol or drugs, and infighting. The possible risk exposures of excessive work demands or high job stress include excessive absenteeism and turnover, high use of behavioral healthcare benefits, and an unusually high rate of work defects.

• *Job-related problems resulting from an imbalance between work life and family life.* This is a separate category of job stress because it includes factors outside the workplace. The risk of these problems arises when work activities compete with life activities such as commuting, dependent care responsibilities, and marital relations, all of which impose time and energy demands on employees. Possible risk exposures include absenteeism, tardiness, early departures, and stress-related disorders.

• *Employee negligence, indifference, or premeditation that poses a safety risk.* An estimated 85 to 95 percent of all accidents have behavioral attributes. This risk includes those mishaps that suggest underlying attitudinal problems, but excludes those arising from factors such as the manual operation of machinery that can be addressed through job and equipment training. Possible risk exposures are the occurrence of preventable accidents, workers' compensation costs, and lost work time. Furthermore, lost work time and turnover may also incur costs for new employee recruitment and training.

• *Violence perpetrated by or on employees in the work setting.* Employers have to be aware of the potential for employee violence, especially during periods of organizational change. There are many forms of acting out behavior, but violence can be the most disruptive, costly, and deadly. Work organizations most vulnerable to violence are those which deal with the public at large, especially those involved with the transfer of money. That is why the banking industry has been heavily involved in violence prevention and early-stage intervention. Many academic institutions have also taken steps to curb student violence toward teachers and teacher-parent conflict. Possible risk exposures are the time expenditure and cost of critical incident stress debriefing interventions, delayed stress-related problems, healthcare costs, diminished loyalty, retaliation by employees against an organization, and disruptions in production.

• *Lawsuits filed by disgruntled employees.* The one prerequisite for a lawsuit filed by an employee is not an egregious act on the part of an employer; it is simply an employee who wants to sue the company. Courts in the United States are glutted with frivolous lawsuits against work organizations that cost employers hefty sums, even when the cases are thrown out of court. Possible risk exposures include legal fees, lost work time, and a damaged business reputation.

• *Sabotage and theft.* Risks of sabotage and theft occur as a result of employee desires for retaliation, weak morals, or behavioral disorders. Among the companies most vulnerable to these risks are ones providing accessibility to highly sensitive information; having expensive easily transported equipment; and using inadequate screening processes for job applicants. A computer software design company in Silicon Valley, for example, is especially vulnerable to unauthorized technology transfer, which can result from disloyalty. Possible risk exposures include loss of equipment, loss of competitive advantage, and loss of income.

• *Conflicts due to racial or gender disharmony.* These risks correlate highly with racial or gender biases and tensions in society at large. They are particularly detrimental when they infiltrate the ranks of management and supervision. Examples of workplace behaviors are use of racial epithets, sexual harassment, and outright discrimination during the hiring and promotion processes, all of which can result in a hostile work environment. Rarely do managers articulate their racial or gender biases, but when they do not proactively respond to evident tensions, they tacitly condone the disharmony that follows. Ultimately, these problems can traumatize and debilitate a company. Possible risk exposures are legal costs, turnover, disruptions in production, behavioral healthcare problems, and a damaged business reputation.

• *Problems arising from employee alcohol and drug abuse.* This is a risk that left unattenuated can dominate an organization's work culture. It arises most often in male-dominated blue-collar industries. The occupations with the highest prevalence of alcohol and drug problems are construction laborer, farmworker, waiter, mover of freight and stock, carpenter, and machine operator. Of special note is that public attention to this risk arose from the rash of drug- and alcohol-related accidents in the transportation industry during the 1980s, which resulted in death and injury to innocent people. With the incentive of tough federal antidrug and anti-alcohol laws and regulations, the airline, trucking, and other transportation industries—which are considered by Congress to hold the public trust—have taken the most extensive steps of any industry to prevent on-the-job impairment. Possible risk exposures from such impairment problems include increased accidents, healthcare costs, absenteeism, and disruptions in production.

•   *Malingering by employees on disability health insurance or workers' compensation.* This risk arises out of the fact that disgruntled employees may fabricate injuries to retaliate against an employer, attribute off-the-job injuries to the workplace in order to receive workers' compensation benefits, and protract short-term disabilities into long-term disabilities due to the feeling of alienation that often accompanies worker injury. Risk exposures include excessive workers' compensation and disability costs and lost work time. (Note that a company may determine "excessive" usage and costs by comparing its rates with industry or geographic averages or by determining its own acceptable levels.)

•   *Behavioral healthcare utilization.* As far as employees and their dependents are concerned, the risks in behavioral health problems are primarily the costs to the company of treating mental health and substance abuse problems. These risks arise due to emotional and psychological problems that employees (and their dependents) pose to the company—risks that employers *can't* control—as well as organizational stressors that may lead to these risks becoming risk exposures—which employers *can* control. Besides creating a more positive organizational culture (which is discussed in the next chapter), employers can seek to reduce the size of the risk exposure through cost-containment for behavioral health treatment.

•   *Preventable Physical Illnesses Among Employees and Dependents.* The risk of these illnesses arises from such behaviors as sedentary life-styles (the "couch-potato syndrome," for example), poor diet habits, and physical manifestations of stress disorders. This category also includes high-risk behaviors that may transmit communicable diseases such as acquired immunodeficiency syndrome (AIDS). Possible risk exposures are excessive behavioral healthcare utilization and costs, lost time, and turnover and diminished productivity.

Organizational Risks

Some organizational behaviors are risk factors that can lead to employee risk exposures. These organizational behaviors can occur in isolation—for example, in a single department where a dysfunctional manager disrupts the orderly work lives of his subordinates—or as a systemic dysfunction. Some troublesome systemic behaviors have been described as "addictive," "neurotic" or "anorexic" in nature, names that suggest that organizations can assume undesirable behavioral attributes typically ascribed to individuals or families.

Organizational dysfunction can take root during a firm's poorly managed transition from a small company with lax policies and standards to a larger one requiring more formalized practices to sustain orderly work activity. Dysfunction can also appear following a leadership transition or changes imposed on an affiliate organization by its parent or as a result of shifting market conditions or product obsolescence. The impetus for dysfunction can be sudden, springing from a single event, or gradual, occurring over years.

The remainder of this section describes the types of organizational behavioral risks.

- *Poor internal communications.* Many problems between people occur due to a lack of good communication. Poor communication can lead to the formation of cliques and backstabbing. One form of poor communication is triangulated communication, that is, communication through indirect and largely ineffective channels. Poor communication can occur on an organizationwide basis, too, when information does not freely flow downward from senior management or upward from the rank-and-file. The classic example is the company that keeps employees in the dark about major organizational changes being contemplated by upper management, offering them no opportunity for input. Think of the problems that are created inside a company whose employees learn of a major downsizing plan on the six o'clock news instead of through internal communication!

- *Lack of management-employee trust and cooperation.* This problem arises once trust between senior management and the rank-

and-file has been broken or once institutional unfairness is perceived toward particular groups of employees. Suspicion, blaming, and lack of mutual respect (employees believe management "doesn't know what it's doing," management believes employees are docile and dull-witted) are omnipresent. In unionized work environments, the result can be work stoppages, lockouts, and contentious labor negotiations. One need look no further than professional baseball, which had work stoppages in 1994 and 1995, to see the destructive effects. Play was discontinued late in 1994 and early in 1995, which alienated the fans who provide the income for both management and players.

- *Lack of a supportive organizational culture.* Organizational culture is summed up in the answer to the question, "What does it feel like to come to work?" That answer is distilled from a person's experience of a variety of phenomena, including ceremonies and rituals; taboos and violations; metaphors, myths, and stories; paradigms for handling employees and customers; and values, conflicts, dilemmas, and images presented by the organization. These are the "soft" issues in a work organization that, when they are not nurtured, invite hard-hitting behavioral risk exposures.

- *Lack of supportive programs, services, and benefits.* Essential to minimizing employee behavioral risk is the availability of programs and services, supported by benefit plans where appropriate, that can identify primary behavioral problems early and cost effectively restore people to health and productivity. Having these programs and services may run contrary to the philosophy of work organizations that view employees as interchangeable tools, preach a version of frontier self-reliance, or assume an overly paternalistic "we can take care of our own" attitude. The last form of organizational behavioral risk is especially common in family-run businesses, where management and employees circle the wagons when problems arise.

- *A sustained high level of organizational stress.* Companies that continually put heat on employees to perform better—whether that heat is occasioned by the struggles of an atrophying industry, excessive ambition, or impatient stockholders—invite organizational breakdowns. According to one study, three-quarters of employers say that their level of stress has increased over the past five years. Other research has shown that companies that dove headlong into the "excellence" movement of the 1980s experienced a rash of marriage failures, crumbled business partnerships, and unfulfilled business objectives.

• *Lack of controls in hiring and promotion.* Work organizations that are not discriminating suitors should not expect partnerships with employees that are made in heaven. Companies that do not have controls become dumping grounds for job applicants who were rejected by employers that exercise hiring and promotion controls.

• *Tolerance of confrontive or work avoidance behaviors.* It is commonly said by organizational psychologists that dysfunctional work organizations harbor dysfunctional employees. If employees can be hostile or confrontive to each other with no fear of retribution—in other words, if there are no standards of acceptable behavior for handling employee disputes—the workplace will favor bullies and become a hostile environment for others.

Work avoidance behaviors are those in which problems are not addressed, particularly by managers. Such behaviors protect troubled and poorly performing employees from interventions. They are usually accompanied by an enabling process in which the manager and other employees actually compensate for the troubled employee's shortcomings. Both of these work avoidance and enabling behaviors are associated with a lack of supervisory skills in such areas as interpersonal communication, documentation of employee work performance, and constructive confrontation techniques.

• *Dysfunctional work relationships among managers and employees.* These behavioral problems, often called "toxic" manager-employee relationships, are also born largely out of inadequate supervisory skills. The visible signs are open disputes between superiors and subordinates, defiance, and employee retaliation against a supervisor or company through any of a variety of inappropriate workplace behaviors.

• *Encouragement of pathological workplace behaviors.* On-the-job employee behavior is usually triggered by one or more of four motivations: self-interest, advancement of the organization, a desire to avoid getting into trouble, and revenge. Acting out of self-interest is, by itself, neither a positive nor negative behavior, because the action can help or hurt the organization. Behavior based on advancement of the organization is a sign of a healthy organization, except in situations where it is used in a game of one-upmanship that actually undercuts work relationships. However, employees who go to extremes to avoid getting into trouble or who are compelled to seek revenge on the organization are participants in a work system that has underlying pathological problems. They are indicators of abusive and subservient work relationships that can form links between employees. For example, a manager might have a domineering relationship with his secretary, in which the secretary acts as the manager's messenger to rank-and-file employees, bearing bad news that she would never consider conveying in her own household. The oppression that exists in this work environment may eventually lead to employee revenge arising out of an accumulation of put-downs and heavy-handed actions. This chain may originate and be perpetuated by harsh dictates from upper management that originate at company headquarters and are passed on to lower managers, who must execute them without rebuttal. In this case, the individual manager may simply lack the inclination to protect his employees from this oppression. Even if headquarters softens its productivity requirements or the manner in which they are communicated to managers later on, the established behavioral patterns among a manager and his underlings may remain intact.

These pathological behaviors are often reinforced by the company's reward system and a lack of managerial accountability, and perpetuated by benefits and other inducements that dissuade personnel from quitting. This chain of behavior may also extend to contractors.

• *Dysfunctional work teams.* Companies that adopt team concepts often dramatically change the way that employee responsibility is assigned, rewards are given, and decisions are made. The structural, operational, and task-performance portions of team development are often carried off without a hitch because of the enthusiasm that accompanies this empowerment-based and egalitarian concept. When transition to the team concept gets derailed, it is usually the result of behavioral issues, such as intergroup and intragroup confrontations.

• *Inattention to workplace safety.* Work produces anxiety for most people because they rely on it for their economic livelihoods, must perform according to the expectations of other people, and have to balance it with other obligations. These anxieties are amplified in a hazardous work environment that has inadequate safeguards against accidents. Social defense systems such as *splitting*—in which groups of employees take sides and enemies are created—are a means of channeling anxiety away from the dangerous situation. Ironically, this defensive reaction increases the potential for accidents because the hazard continues to exist and, at the same time, the employees' attention is directed toward enemies.

- *Continual crisis management.* Companies can live in perpetual crisis when company leadership is unable to anticipate external changes and prepare accordingly. Organizations that manage by crisis are usually not able to act preemptively, with promptness and agility—especially if their human resources have been trimmed to the bone. Instead, they react to events from a defensive posture, and employees typically work in a state of panic.

Focus on Problem Prevention

Problem prevention, where practical and cost effective, is the highest form of workplace intervention. The axiom that best fits is "An ounce of prevention is worth a pound of cure"—and it can be considerably less expensive, too. Table 2.1 illustrates the stages of the transition that a large company of 7,500 employees might make from a late-stage to a prevention-based intervention strategy and the accompanying change in costs. In the late-stage intervention model, little money is spent on preventive workplace-based programs, but there are high costs on the terminal end in the form of productivity losses and healthcare expenses. In the prevention model, more money is invested in preventive programs, but terminal costs are far lower. The financial goal of the strategy of behavioral risk management is to achieve lower overall costs. Clearly, employers who consistently address problems only after they have exacted a significant loss to the organization are presiding over ailing, reactive, and ultimately, uncompetitive systems.

In recent years, many employers have attacked late-stage, healthcare-related risk exposures by containing their costs and intervening earlier using managed care strategies. In the area of behavioral health treatment, managed care has made the

Table 2.1 Progression Toward Prevention and Related Costs.

	Late-Stage Intervention ⮕	Early Intervention ⮕	Prevention
Amount spent on workplace programs, services, and benefits	$1 million	$3 million	$5 million
Costs incurred following onset of behavioral risk exposures	$30 million	$15 million	$5 million
Characteristics	Hospitalizations Lawsuits Major accidents Excessive absenteeism, turnover Lack of policies and procedures that favor help seeking, program integration, support for management intervention, and the like Work culture that encourages inappropriate or destructive behaviors	Greater use of outpatient healthcare Managed care Some preventive programs Some attention to workplace issues and their impacts on employees Some integration of programs and services	Integrated behavioral risk management strategy Strategy supported by appropriate policies and procedures Workplace culture that conscientiously looks after employee need

treatment delivery system more efficient, accountable, flexible, and able to treat a wider variety of behavioral problems. Treatment providers now emphasize multiple levels of care (so that the level of care matches the severity of the illness); comprehensive treatment that encompasses biological, psychological, and social factors; and step-down transitions to less-intensive care. Managed behavioral healthcare was a swift and decisive move by employers to contain the portion of healthcare that had the highest cost escalation in the 1980s. Because of managed care's success in the private sector, state governments are now experimenting with it in their Medicaid systems.

As effective as managed behavioral healthcare has been, it still intervenes only after the onset of behavioral health problems. Therefore, employers should consider a prevention model that entails investing more resources up front in the form of workplace programs, services, and benefits. The trade-off is that a well-managed integrated risk management strategy will probably reduce the terminal costs of destructive employee behaviors, and do so by a substantial margin.

Realistically, not all behavioral problems can be eliminated from an organization, a fact reflected by the still-considerable sum of money ($5 million) spent for terminal costs in the large company's prevention strategy. A proportion of behavioral health problems—say, half the prevalence rate in the general community, with socioeconomic factors being equal—will manifest themselves regardless of the quality of the preventive activities. Similarly, a proportion of other behavior-related problems, such as workplace accidents due to human error, will occur regardless of an employer's efforts to prevent them. This arises out of a simple fact of human existence: people have good days and bad days, some people have better innate coping skills than others, and so forth. Nevertheless, employer efforts such as instilling an actively caring reward-based safety culture can dramatically reduce the number of preventable accidents.

Furthermore, some problems may be behavior-related in only some cases. For example, a portion of the people who have contracted AIDS could have prevented the disease by modifying their sexual or drug activity, but the portion that has contracted it though blood transfusions could not. The former case is an example of a condition related to life-style and therefore to behavior, while the latter is an example of a condition inflicted by environmental factors. Life-style is the greatest influence in 51 percent of all healthcare use. In comparison, only 19 percent is predominantly due to environmental factors (such as contaminated blood used for a transfusion).

These statistics underscore the need to retain a secondary focus on effective early-stage interventions, which are themselves preventions against more severe illnesses. Early-stage interventions can be almost as cost effective as prevention activities, especially since they can be tailored to the 10 to 20 percent of employees who manifest behavioral illnesses. In contrast, prevention activities, in order to be as widely preventive as possible, must target the entire workforce.

Efforts to prevent behavioral problems among dependents covered by an employee benefit plan are more difficult because these interventions require softer sell approaches and there are fewer of them available. Dependents do not come under the direct observation of workplace managers, supervisors, co-workers, and union stewards, the people who are critical to identifying incipient behavioral health problems of employees. Job-performance criteria and observation of inappropriate workplace behavior are effective parts of an intervention effort that are not available for use with dependents. In addition, the work organization cannot apply job-related incentives to motivate dependents toward help, as it can with employees. For example, an employer can confront an employee with his or her behavioral problems by threatening the troubled employee with termination, demotion, or disciplinary action but cannot take this same step with a family member having the same problem.

Therefore, a well-conceived behavioral risk management strategy builds a cushion into its risk projections for late-stage problems. For example, in the twelve months prior to implementation of a behavioral risk management strategy, the company may have made 50 percent of its interventions in the early stage and 50 percent in the late stage. There would be no percentage attributed to prevention in this period because there would be no baseline data against which to compare employees. A prevention goal might then be set for the current year of reducing by 20 percent the number of behavioral risk problems experienced in the prior year. The early-stage intervention goal might be set at 50 percent, and the late-stage intervention goal, then, would be no more than 30 percent. A sample long-range goal (for the third year) would be 50 percent problem prevention, 40 percent early-stage intervention, and 10 percent late-stage intervention.

Distinctive Characteristics of Behavioral Risk Management

In addition to the features of behavioral risk management already described in this chapter, there are six other distinctive characteristics that define the concept further.

- *A focus on behavioral, not healthcare, issues.* Consider, first, that physical, mental, and substance abuse problems that are rooted in behavior are preventable or have an impact that can be controlled. However, many support program staff from the helping professions treat their workplace activities as healthcare, as consistent with delivering care to people afflicted with many medical problems, but is not the primary focus in behavioral risk management. Healthcare is custodial, whereas behavioral risk management, ideally, is preventive.

Consider, second, that employers have an inherent vested interest in workplace behavior but have a direct interest in healthcare only because they are the primary payers for the private healthcare system in the United States. U.S. employers' involvement in creating more efficient healthcare delivery systems would quickly wane if national healthcare reform were implemented that featured either a single-payer (Canadian-style) scheme or a community rating scheme (under which each employer pays the same premium per individual as all other employers, regardless of its success at reducing employee healthcare costs). In either case, employers' interest in healthcare would be limited to the residual effects, such as absenteeism and diminished capacity to be productive. In contrast, employers will retain the risks they face from undesirable workplace behavior under any circumstances, and behavioral risk management will continue to be necessary.

- *A focus on tasks instead of functions.* Workplace functions or programs are really sets of tasks. What should be valued is the tasks performed, not the bureaucratic structures that execute them. Therefore, a procedure for considering the relative value of each task performed under the auspice of a particular program can be integrated into a five-part behavior risk management process. The task analysis can occur during the third step of the risk management process described earlier, when activities are evaluated for their effectiveness, and during the fifth step, when solutions are formulated. This is consistent with the activities of reengineering, which is to structural change what Total Quality Management is to process change. Thus, the steps of task analysis are essential to restructuring workplace functions, based on the organization's identified and quantified behavioral risks. This process, as discussed later, may lead to the dismantling of entrenched bureaucracies and privileged positions that do not reach an acceptable cost-benefit ratio.

- *Global management of behavioral risks.* A behavioral risk management strategy must be global, or holistic, in order to address behavioral risks in all their permutations. This means it must avoid efforts to suppress but not resolve a behavioral risk, since that risk is likely to resurface elsewhere or in another form. (A good illustration is provided in case study 3 in Chapter One.)

- *"Ownership" by the organization of its risks, and internal management of the solutions to them.* There is an important distinction to be made between management of services and actual service delivery. In a behavioral risk management paradigm, management responsibility must be retained by the company, not outsourced to a service provider, regardless of whether the tasks that diminish behavioral risk are performed by individuals outside or inside the organization. Additionally, the person assigned to manage the behavioral risks must be more than a point person, liaison, or reader of outcomes reports. She or he must be integrally involved with the daily operation of the internal *and external* processes.

- *Use of computerized information management.* Michael Hammer, the progenitor of reengineering, has defined data management as part and parcel of reengineering. Since behavioral risk management is consistent with reengineering, it is, ipso facto, a computer-based data-driven exercise. Given the amount of data needed for risk management task analyses, a manually performed analysis would be inherently inefficient.

- *Integration of individual behavior and organizational behavioral problems.* This integration confronts some of the turf wars that have traditionally existed between employee-oriented program personnel and organizational development specialists, who have historically often carried on as though their spheres of activity had no intersection. They do intersect, and management needs to be as concerned about organizational behaviors that affect employee well-being and productivity as it is about management decisions that affect marketplace positioning, capital expenditures, and the logistics of work units.

As the term behavioral risk management was coined only recently, few organizations have a function or use a process bearing that name or complying with all the principles discussed here. However, organizations that are ambitiously seeking to manage their "people problems" are probably using some variation of this process or have adopted at least a few of its underlying principles. For example, a company might have a function called Integrated Health Systems that is prevention-focused, has a carefully defined reporting structure, and is well integrated with other workplace activities, just as a behavioral risk management initiative would be. It might also use many of the same interventions that I will describe.

The different frame of reference, however, is bound to result in some operational variations. If Integrated Health Systems has a focus on healthcare, for instance, it probably places minimal importance on intervening in organizational behaviors since its mission is more likely to be custodial than preventive, there may be no apparent causal relationship between organizational factors and individuals' healthcare conditions, and a diagnosis of organizational dysfunction is not based on medical technology. As explained earlier, in the behavioral risk management paradigm, the causal relationship between organization and individual is important.

Street-Level Behavioral Risk Management

What does a behavioral risk management system look like to management, to employees, and to customers when it is taken off the drawing board and put on the street? First, it permeates the organization on five levels to produce

- Development of a supportive work culture
- Use of appropriate programs and services
- Implementation of benefits that facilitate the use of those programs and services
- Adoption of appropriate policies and procedures
- Use of periodic behavioral risk training for various work populations

Second, to decision makers in most work organizations, behavioral risk management resembles aspects of both human resource management and organizational development, as shown in the following figure.

Third, behavioral risk management is a malleable management concept that can conform to the organization. It can be structured as *inter-* or *intra*departmental. Its auditing and evaluation activities can be conducted internally or by an external consultant. (But the external consulting should *never* be done by an external firm that is also delivering services). Its services can be delivered internally, externally, or in some combination of both. It can direct the performance of substantially different tasks in different divisions of the same company in order to reflect different behavioral risks.

It can also be designed to suit the character of the organization. For example, behavioral risk management at a manufacturing site might be predicated on building a hard hat–style safety

Human Resource Management

／　　　　　　　　　　＼

Role: human potential enhancement

This IS NOT behavioral risk management.

Role: human loss management

This IS behavioral risk management.

Organizational Development

／　　　　　　　　　　＼

Role: externally focused business decision making

This IS NOT behavioral risk management.

Role: internally focused operational decision making

This IS behavioral risk management, with regard to employee behaviors.

culture. It might have as its underpinning breaking the heavy drinking patterns of employees and specifying proactive management intervention at the first sign of a problem. This approach has been applied successfully in the railroad industry. Operation Red-Block, a joint program of several railroads and their participating unions, has eroded the drinking culture that has existed for decades in the industry.

Companies can also promote the fundamental objectives in terms that express the employees' interests—rather than those of the employer—in the interventions. An office environment that is highly compartmentalized, leading to isolation and sagging morale, for example, may seek to "build esprit de corps." The strategic underpinning might be using peer pressure to encourage employees to seek help when they are troubled. A service company with a lot of sedentary jobs might focus on "wellness, fitness, and life-style management." This dyadic approach—packaging corporate loss management inside an upbeat promotional message that focuses on benefits to employees—can help the strategy meet rigorous business objectives while also appearing inviting to employees and family members.

To recap, identifying the behavioral sources of many workplace problems will yield new, and ultimately more effective, solutions. The renowned management expert Peter Drucker, in describing the approach to accident prevention of the Occupational Safety and Health Administration (OSHA), put the same point this way: "The most effective way to produce safety is to eliminate unsafe behavior. OSHA's definition of an accident—'when someone gets hurt'—is inadequate. To cut down on accidents, the definition has to be 'a violation of the rules of safe behavior, whether anyone gets hurt or not.'" Drucker also points out that the U.S. nuclear submarine program has used this philosophy to achieve a splendid safety record, despite the program's perilous high-risk work.

Behavioral safety management leads to fewer accidents, less healthcare utilization, fewer lost days, and less chance of lawsuits. Focusing first on behavioral risk exposures is, at last, getting the horse ahead of the cart.

Next, Chapter Three takes a close look at how a behavioral risk management strategy is built from the ground up, starting with the identification of problems and measurement of their severity.

Notes

P. 20, *An estimated 85 to 95 percent of all accidents:* Lenkus, D. "Safety Awareness Alone Not Enough to Sow the Seeds for Fewer Injuries." *Business Insurance,* Oct. 17, 1994, p. 3.

P. 21, *occupations with the highest prevalence of alcohol and drug problems:* Anthony, J., Eaton, W., Mandell, W., and Garrison, R. "Psychoactive Drug Dependence and Abuse: More Common in Some Occupations Than Others?" *Journal of Employee Assistance Research,* 1992, *1*(1), 148–186.

P. 24, *That answer is distilled from a person's experience:* Hampden-Turner, C. *Creating Corporate Culture: From Discord to Harmony.* Reading, Mass.: Addison-Wesley, 1990, p. 185.

P. 24, *According to one study, three-quarters of employers say:* Olsten Corporation. *Workplace Social Issues of the 1990s* (The Olsten Forum on Human Resource Issues and Trends). Westbury, NY: Olsten Corporation, 1992, p. 2.

P. 29, *people who have contracted AIDS:* U.S. Department of Health and Human Services, Centers for Disease Control, Office of Disease Prevention and Health Promotion. *National Survey of Worksite Health Promotion Activities.* Atlanta, Ga.: Centers for Disease Control, 1992.

P. 35, *"The most effective way to produce safety":* Drucker, P. F. "Really Reinventing Government," *Atlantic Monthly,* Feb. 1995, p. 56.

Chapter Three

Auditing Your Employees' Behavioral Risks

Now that the behavioral risk management process has been outlined and its distinctive characteristics described, we are ready to explore each of the five steps of the process in more detail. This chapter describes the first step: identify the organization's behavior-related risks and determine what its risk exposures have been. In preparation for this first step of auditing behavioral risks, consider the following example of how an accumulation of employee behavioral risk exposures affects a company.

A California banking establishment with 1,200 employees enjoyed a reputation for being family oriented, catering to long-term clients, and favoring personalized "shirt-sleeve" services in which customers dealt with tellers instead of automatic teller machines. The company was well established in its niche and had chosen to not take the path of the many competitors who had become full financial service institutions, offering trust services, employee benefit plans, investment management services, and the like. The company was stable, although it operated with a thin profit margin. Nevertheless, like other companies in the 1980s, it felt the brunt of healthcare cost escalation when its healthcare benefits costs increased at an average annual rate of 18 percent from 1987 to 1989.

Other problems also arose. The commercial banking industry, whose financial health fluctuates with the economy, hit a trough in 1987, taking this bank with it. The financial stress caused an elevated level of organizational stress. Several employee support programs were discontinued when the bank's operating budget was trimmed. Rumors crept into the branch offices about closures and layoffs. Shortly afterward, two major psychiatric disability claims filed by employees, one for $165,000 and another for $98,000, were awarded. (At the time, California's workers' compensation laws awarded mental-stress claims if employees could prove that their employer was even 10 percent responsible for the disability.)

The rate and size of financial shortfalls at the branch banks doubled in 1988 and 1989, although it was never clear whether the cause was theft or accounting error. These shortfalls created a scare among managers, causing some of them to begin lording over their branches. A few employees interpreted this autocratic management as a sign of lack of professionalism and trust, and they left the company.

Finally, two 1988 incidents of armed robbery—always a risk in the banking industry—traumatized several of the employees who were held at gunpoint. About three dozen other employees were witnesses. All those held at gunpoint received trauma interventions and none subsequently developed posttraumatic stress disorder. However, only a few of the witnesses received critical incident stress debriefings. Within six months, eight of them experienced medical problems including tension headaches, insomnia due to nightmares, and problems with anxiety. Three of them eventually needed psychotherapy, requiring access to their behavioral health benefit plans.

This example illustrates the many fronts on which behavioral risk occurs. Stress-related disorders, retaliation against the organization, and quitting one's job are among the behaviors that can all manifest from the same negative stimulus. This multiplicity explains why measuring and intervening in only one area of behavioral risk exposure (for example, utilization of workers' compensation) can obfuscate the true dimensions of risk.

Behavioral risk management uses a holistic systems approach to track a company's behavioral risk exposures and the organizational factors that may precipitate them. This audit enables you to quantify your risk exposures and assess your degree of risk, which is the functional equivalent of the amount of pressure in a human ecological system. Once you have established the dimensions of the problem in your organization and excavated the underlying factors causing the increased risk, you can determine appropriate solutions to remediate the situation and prevent the risks from reemerging later.

Introduction to Gathering and Analyzing the Data

To perform a behavioral risk audit, an organization obtains data from four primary sources. Objective data are derived from (1) personnel files and (2) healthcare utilization and cost figures. Subjective, supplemental data are derived from (3) "employee sensing" (performed through pencil-and-paper surveys, focus groups, and individual interviews) and (4) management surveys and interviews.

The subjective information in items 3 and 4 may, on management's first inspection, seem "soft" and therefore not substantial enough to warrant a formal response, but it is valuable in that it embellishes the personnel and healthcare data and may be able to indicate areas facing probable future increases in risk not presently reflected in the objective data.

The objective data in items 1 and 2 can both identify and measure the risk. These data may also identify some factors as contributors to stress while disqualifying others. For example, if personnel data show an elevated rate of absenteeism in one division of an organization, that result might be due to the severe behavioral health problems of only a few employees, excessive stress among most employees resulting from a major workplace development, or a seasonal pattern of inclement weather. Certain healthcare data, such as utilization for stress-related medical conditions, would reveal whether there was excessive organizational stress. The same data would indicate whether the increased absences were or were not a "blip on the screen" due to a random manifestation of behavioral health problems in a few employees that skewed attendance records. Management data would show whether the absenteeism coincided with (or closely trailed) a workplace development, such as the hiring of a manager who might now turn out to be dysfunctional. Finally, personnel files or management data would be used to disqualify extrinsic variables, such as a large number of no-shows on a couple of workdays due to inclement weather.

Generally at least 30 percent of managers and supervisors and at least 15 percent of nonmanagement employees should participate in any survey and interview process if the organization is to obtain a statistically significant sample. Of course, participation is dependent on work schedules, management priorities, and policies with regard to internal data collection activities, so employers should plan carefully in order to make the necessary accommodations. The objective indicators are also dependent on the availability of data. In organizations that retain little data or have poor record-keeping systems, plans may need to be made first for improving data collection. Then auditing activities can begin perhaps six months or a year later.

The survey and interview portions of the behavioral risk audit process should be completed at least once a year in order to establish longitudinal trends. Personnel and healthcare data, if they are maintained on computerized data systems that allow for convenient aggregation of data, should be compiled quarterly or even monthly. A company may also wish to analyze its Pareto-group— that 10 to 20 percent of employees who incur the greatest behavioral risk exposures—to characterize its high-risk high-cost work population and to determine the interventions that would be most effective to reduce that population's impact. This can be done on a less-frequent basis, perhaps annually.

The detailed audit process that is described in the rest of this chapter and in Chapter Four revisits the employee behavioral risks and organizational behavioral risks introduced in Chapter Two. Each of the risks to be audited has an average of six indicators, and companies may find they need to add or delete indicators for any single risk. The goal in performing the audit should be to select indicators that most accurately reflect a specific risk, and these may vary from one organization to the next. Selecting the indicators carefully will also hold the audit process to manageable proportions.

Employee Behavioral Risks

The behavioral indicators that follow are grouped according to the behavioral risks with which they are associated. Nonsurvey objective data can indicate the behavioral risk exposures for which actual dollar figures can be assigned (such as healthcare costs) or estimated dollar figures can be assigned (such as absenteeism or turnover costs). (The Appendix contains sample behavioral risk audits for managers and employees.)

Problems Associated with Excessive Work Demands or High Job Stress

Stress is a lot like pain: we all know that it exists, but we cannot strap a gauge around it and take a reading. The best we can do is measure the indicators that suggest the degree to which it exists. In this case, the indicators are a sampling of the problems most likely to result from high job stress, whether it is the result of excessive work demands or other factors in the organization. Employers should recognize first that stress is a natural biochemical reaction to change and is not always bad. In fact, *eustress*, or good stress, can be a safety valve to relieve *distress*, or bad stress. What is important is whether stress manifests itself in undesirable behaviors that lead to risk exposures.

Employers should also recognize that stress arises in part out of a person's unique reaction to work and personal life events. Stress is something that individuals can regulate and modify. Therefore, the following objective and subjective indicators measure not only the risk exposures associated with personal stress but also employees' overall coping skills in stressful situations.

- *Existence of excessive work demands that negatively impair employee's concentration at work and diminish their ability to meet established performance standards* (based on an employee survey). This subjective indicator, considered in relationship with objective measures of productivity and output, provides evidence of the extent to which excessive work demands cause defects in the manufacture of products or delivery of services. This indicator should be considered with other nonbehavior-related workplace developments that might impact manufacture and delivery, such as the introduction of new equipment, new software programs, or multiple work shifts.
- *Excessive utilization of healthcare benefits associated with high stress* (based on healthcare utilization data). While the buildup of stress can manifest as any number of medical problems, five that correlate highly with work stress are

Panic disorder

Tension and migraine headaches

Posttraumatic stress disorder (among people who have previously
suffered severe traumas)

Depression

Somatic illnesses

- *The number of job-site accidents* (based on management
reports).
- *High attribution of employee departures to excessive work pressure*
(based on employee exit interviews). The most easily measured
cost indicator for this risk is the expense of recruiting and training
new employees. While loss of the departing employees' talent and
expertise may actually be the most enduring long-term cost, that
degree of that loss would have to be based more on conjecture
than established fact.
- *Reports of "high stress" and "increasing stress" at work* (based on
employee and management surveys). Not only does this indicator
provide a subjective measure of stress, it also reveals any discrepancy between management's acknowledgment of workplace stressors and employees' experience with stress. Moreover, stress among
the various levels of management can be subjectively measured.
For example, one company implementing a Total Quality Management initiative was generating middle-management stress by
creating a horizontal organization that squeezed out that middle
layer of management.
- *Reports of life stress,* as distinct from work stress (revealed by
a variety of measurement tools). Measurement tools may be stand-
alone tests or parts of health risk appraisals and quality-of-life surveys. Typically, they measure such factors as emotional adjustment,
family stress, self-esteem, and ability to cope with problems and
control anger.

Job-Related Problems Resulting from a Lack of Balance Between Work Life and Family Life

Most adults spend the vast majority of their time tending to two
sets of responsibilities: earning a living and meeting family respon-

sibilities. In recent years, both workplace and social factors—such as increased workloads, more difficult commutes, and dual-career families—have made a balance between work and family life harder to achieve. The high divorce rate in the United States has increased work organizations' vulnerability to this risk.

Boston University's Job and Homelife Study, which was first performed in 1985 and updated in 1992, shed light on the extent of the problem. The first study found that 36 percent of male workers and 37 percent of female workers in one major American corporation experienced "a lot of stress" in balancing work and home life. An additional 11 percent of females experienced "extreme stress." Overall, eight out of twelve items on the study's Job/Family Management Scale—including avoiding rush hour, making healthcare appointments, and going on errands—were made easier than for a sample of "normal families," perhaps due to the availability of work-and-family benefits. Nevertheless, other data showed that employees endured certain hardships regardless of whether the benefits were available. For example, between 1985 and 1992, time spent on child care and home chore responsibilities increased 17.5 percent for men and 32.0 percent for women. Also, in 1992, 10 percent of respondents reported presently caring for an adult dependent, and 52 percent anticipated becoming caregivers within the next five to ten years.

Employers should measure these objective and subjective indicators:

- *Reports of excessive difficulty in balancing work and family life responsibilities* (based on employee and management surveys). These surveys will indicate how much stress employees actually *feel* in this area. Then the following indicators will provide data on underlying factors and how this difficulty is presently affecting the organization.

- *Prevalence of employees who are caregivers for children and/or elderly parents* (based on employee surveys). These objective findings should be supplemented by the data described in the previous indicator and, in conjunction with the following indicators, may suggest a need for supportive programs and services.

- *Absenteeism, tardiness, and early-departure data over each of the last three years* (based on personnel files). These data provide supportive evidence of work-and-family conflict if they are skewed from the norms and historical precedents at the company. Their significance can be also determined by examining data on employees who are at greatest risk of work-and-family conflict, including both married and single employees with children. These groups can be broken down by males and females to identify any additional discrepancies. These high-risk populations can be compared with the population at lower risk, particularly married and single employees without children and the employee population as a whole. The data can then be compared with industry and geographic averages. Corroborating information can also be sought by supervisor survey.

• *Incidence of divorce among employees with five or more years of service* (based on employee surveys). This is an indicator of excessive conflict between work and family. The five-year threshold helps make this indicator more reliable. When marriages deteriorate, they do so usually over an extended period of time. The newness of a job change can help sustain a marriage for several years while the employee is becoming indoctrinated to the work organization. It may then take several more years for an employee's marital relations to reach a critical stage of deterioration under the pressure of work.

Employee Negligence, Indifference, or Premeditation That Poses a Safety Risk

That branch of science known as human factors engineering has shown that 85 to 95 percent of all accidents can be attributed to behavioral factors. Behavioral risk management is concerned about those safety risks that exist because of underlying attitudinal or psychological problems. These can be the isolated problems of an individual or the systemic pattern of dysfunctional behaviors in an organization or work unit.

For example, after two fires occurred in the same operating unit of an oil refinery, the plant manager ordered an investigation because the fires, which could have resulted in devastating plant explosions, occurred only a few months apart. An accident team composed of two psychologists investigated the causes of the fires, each of which occurred because multiple safety precautions existed simultaneously. The psychologists did not find malicious intent. Instead, they unearthed a much more alarming workplace occurrence, which they felt would lead to even more fires if left unabated. As a result of working in dangerous situations on a daily basis with few safety precautions and procedures, the operating group had suffered a "social split." The split—a systemic stress reaction to high risk of physical injury—took the form of two cliques that habitually scapegoated each other. By projecting their insecurities about the work environment onto the people in the other group, members of each group were able to contain their feelings of anxiety. Unfortunately, by diverting their conscious thoughts away from the source of their anxiety, they actually increased the potential for accidents.

Employers should measure these objective and subjective indicators:

• *Proportion of workplace accidents thought to be caused by horseplay, malicious intent, lack of alertness, or personal problems of employees* (based on accident investigation reports). Behavior-based accidents that appear to reflect an underlying attitudinal problem—that is, in which an employee is culpable—fall under the purview of behavioral risk management. So do accidents that occur because of lifestyle factors, such as an active night life or poor nutrition, that dull alertness. Other accidents, such as those that may occur as a result of employee actions but that can be corrected by job and equipment training, are not considered behavior-based accidents.

• *Utilization of workers' compensation medical, rehabilitation, and wage replacement benefits* (based on insurance data). This indicator determines the employer's exposure to work-related accidents.

• *Incidents of equipment and property loss due to employee accidents* (based on management records). This indicator also determines the employer's exposure to work-related accidents.

• *Heightened potential for accidents among employees in hazardous occupations due to (1) lack of adequate safety precautions and (2) unsafe work practices of co-workers* (based on employee surveys). Employers must first determine which jobs pose a continuous risk of serious accident or injury, such as those jobs specified by the Occupational Safety and Health Administration. Although the criteria for this indicator are nonbehavioral, they are relevant because, as the plant fire example showed, people's psychological response to the threat of accident is to "externalize" their anxieties.

• *Reports of co-workers being under the influence of drugs or alcohol while on the job* (based on surveys of employees in hazardous occupations). Up to 40 percent of industrial fatalities and 47 percent of industrial injuries can be linked to alcohol abuse and alcoholism. Behavioral risks due to substance abuse will be discussed in more detail later, but the risk is more acute in a dangerous work environment, especially since self-medicating with alcohol is one way that people cope with elevated work stress.

Violence Perpetrated by or on Employees in the Work Setting

Workplace violence is a hydra-headed beast that casts many shadows. It may take the form of homicides, nonfatal physical assaults, overt threats, and harassment (sexual harassment, which will be covered later, is excluded here). The U.S. Postal Service, where (based on self-reports) an estimated 2,000 violent incidents occurred in 1992, has recently become a national symbol of the increasing violence in U.S. workplaces. There were an estimated 333,000 violent incidents in U.S. work organizations for the same period. While one study reports that 2.2 million workers were victims of physical attack during a twelve-month period ending July 1993, 6.3 million workers—nearly three times as many—were physically threatened, and 16.1 million were harassed. Altogether, one in four U.S. workers was on the receiving end of another worker's aggressive, fear-inducing behavior.

The biographical profile of a violent person is usually that of a male who has had previous episodes of cruel and inhumane behavior. Consider the twenty-eight-year-old Caucasian man I will call "Wayne." Wayne was the youngest sibling in a family of three brothers. When Wayne was eight, he was caught shoplifting, and two years later, he was caught killing a cat. Family members remember that he seemed very calm at the time of these incidents. He attended school, earned excellent grades, and had an astonishingly high IQ. When he started dating, Wayne exhibited either of two personalities with girls: one that was calm and considerate and another that was gloomier, not as conversant, and aggressive. In high school, he began picking fights with other boys and once showed great pleasure in tying another boy to a tree and lighting kindling under him. He began using drugs as a teenager, too, preferring beer and crack cocaine. Fellow users said he got paranoid on cocaine. He became known as a loner but was also seen hanging out with "headbangers" who liked rowdy music. He developed a fascination with guns. After high school, Wayne went on to military training but was discharged from the Marines during boot camp for being unruly and not following orders. He moved back home but showed no interest in working or finding a job. One day Wayne's father shoved him into a wall and demanded that he "either find a job or get out."

The characteristic behaviors of people who, like Wayne, pose a risk of workplace violence include an appearance of being stressed or angry, drug or alcohol abuse, poor health and hygiene habits, unpredictability, inconsistent work patterns, attendance problems, and poor work-based relationships. A person exhibiting several behaviors that suggest an elevated potential for violence might be cause for concern, but the appearance of only one or perhaps two of the behaviors is not a red flag for violent behavior. Therefore, an employer should carefully weigh the evidence. Many workplace violence experts agree that the track record of employers in guessing which employees are likely to be violent is dismally low.

Organizational change activities, in particular, have employers worried about the potential for workplace violence. Today's corporate restructuring activities, such as reengineering, are dramatically changing the way work is done and, in the process, rendering many work skills and areas of knowledge obsolete. There appears to be a correlation between the prevalence of organizational change activities (Pitney Bowes Management Services found that 83 percent of the largest industrial employers were engaged in reengineering by 1994)—which disrupt the organization's status quo and usually diminish job security—and a separate finding that workplace violence had increased to its highest level in five years.

Three factors need to be considered in order to assess the risk of workplace violence with a behavioral risk management audit: above-the-surface, at-the-surface, and below-the-surface incidents. Employers should measure these objective and subjective indicators:

- *Incidence of violent acts* (based on management and supervisory reports). Data on violent acts can be recorded to include the severity of the violent act and its location and department. These data identify trends in above-the-surface violence.
- *Number of threats of violence* (based on management and supervisory reports). This indicator, which shows at-the-surface problems with violence, should also document any disciplinary actions taken against employees.
- *Current threat of workplace violence* (based on employee and management surveys). This subjective indicator, reporting perceived harassment and other forms of intimidation, can reveal problems brewing below the surface. It should measure whether the threat of violence is (1) imminent, (2) moderate but increasing, (3) moderate but declining, or (4) remote. These data should also be broken down by location and department, as appropriate.
- *Incidence of supervisor-employee conflict and of customer-employee or contractor-employee conflict* (based on management and supervisory reports). Workplace violence may involve more people than employees and managers. It can also be perpetrated by or on nonemployees, including consultants, contractors, and service providers. Any employer that comes into frequent contact with the public—a retail company, for example—should be on guard. Conflict data are used to identify the precipitants to violence at the work site.

Lawsuits Filed by Disgruntled Employees

Groups such as the National Federation of Independent Business were actively lobbying for tort reform in 1995 because of the ease with which frivolous lawsuits can be filed in our litigious society. This political movement reflects, in part, employer concern about the glut of prosecuting attorneys who are advertising their services and actively soliciting cases.

Many lawsuits filed by employees against their employers are based on legitimate grievances, and many others have arguments on both sides that merit jurisprudence. However, the fact that many lawyers do not get paid unless they win the case is incentive for them to seek an award regardless of the case's merits. The increasingly frequent filing of negligent-hiring and negligent-retention lawsuits, which are based on employee contentions that a company failed to take proper action against another employee or a job candidate, is evidence of today's "victim mentality," which finds it normal to file a suit first and seek a workable solution afterward.

Whether a case is frivolous or legitimate, it imposes a cost on the employer, even if it never gets far in a court of law. Like workplace violence, behavior-based legal issues can be thought of as above-the-surface, at-the-surface, and below-the-surface risks. Employers, then, need to consider the potential for lawsuits based not just on legitimate claims of individuals but also on claims that result from poor employee relations, a below-the-surface risk. Employers should measure these objective and subjective indicators:

• *Court cases associated with defending against (1) employee lawsuits and other legal actions against the organization taken by employees (such as grievance proceedings) over each of the last three years and (2) lawsuits filed by outside sources due to the actions of employees* (based on legal department data). This above-the-surface indicator outlines the scope of legal risks associated with employee behavior.

• *Proportion of lawsuits and other legal actions that resulted in a favorable finding for the employee* (based on legal department data). This indicator determines the risk exposure.

• *Number of threats that lawsuits or other legal action will be taken against the organization by employees* (based on management or personnel reports). This is an at-the-surface indicator that suggests the likelihood of future lawsuits.

Sabotage and Theft

According to a 1994 survey conducted by KPMG Peat Marwick of 501 Dun and Bradstreet companies, 77 percent of them experienced fraud in the past year, and 52 percent believed fraud would become more of a problem in the future. Moreover, fraud experts estimate that less than 10 percent of the cases are ever discovered. In small work organizations, this behavioral risk exposure is often noticed when supplies disappear following a recent hiring. A significant risk exposure to fraud can take a small organization right out of business. In larger companies, the problems can be harder to detect, because of the larger employee base and, often, less direct supervision. Indeed, the losses due to sabotage and theft are usually underestimated because of the low proportion of cases that are actually caught. For that reason, in addition to objective and subjective indicators, another set of data is delineated—security risks that may constitute an open invitation to an employee with a predilection for theft.

Employers should measure these objective and subjective indicators:

- *Documented number of cases of sabotage and theft by employees* (based on management or personnel reports).
- *Estimated cost of documented cases of sabotage and theft* (based on management estimates).
- *Belief that the organization faces "a high risk" or "an increasing risk" of sabotage or fraud by employees* (based on employee and management surveys). These findings can also project the occurrence of undocumented cases, based on trends in longitudinal surveys. As increased risks are noted, estimated costs may be said to increase. Additionally, findings indicating "a high risk" that are not matched by a high number of documented cases suggest that the organization may be especially vulnerable to fraud.
- *Employer takes adequate precautions against sabotage and fraud* (based on employee and management surveys). Do employers attract these problems by negligence, which a saboteur or thief, using twisted logic, might interpret as an open invitation? This indicator will elicit perceptions about security.

Contributing factors include

- *Frequent replacement of compact high-technology equipment* (based on management commentary).
- *A heavy amount of off-premises work by nonsales staff* (based on management commentary).
- *Lack of visible security on premises* (based on management commentary).
- *Heavy proportion of employees not under direct supervision* (based on management commentary).

Conflicts Due to Racial or Gender Disharmony

These conflicts are grouped together because they all are forms of oppression based on a demographic variable and all have a strong likelihood of inciting confrontations and other problems. What numbers do not show, however, is that even a single racial or gender slur in the workplace can sour an employee's attitude, not just toward the perpetrator but also toward the company and its other employees for years to come. The likelihood of that reaction and accompanying increased risk for the company reflects the victim mentality and ready availability of legal remedies in society at large.

However, a work organization can also serve as, in effect, a safe harbor that insulates employees from harassment through steps such as proactive management. Additionally, for employees who have experienced harassment elsewhere and bring that emotional baggage into the organization, a safe harbor environment can soften their jaundiced attitudes and suspicion of others.

Employers should measure these objective and subjective indicators:

- *Lawsuits and other legal actions taken by employees against the organization alleging (1) racial discrimination, (2) gender discrimination, and (3) sexual harassment over each of the last three years* (based on management reports, affirmative action/equal employment opportunity [AA/EEO] or diversity officer reports, or personnel data). Financial costs associated with this risk exposure should also be examined. Reports from sales representatives and public relations staff can indicate whether any business losses occurred as a result of negative publicity.

- *Number of threats that employees will file lawsuits or take other action against the organization due to hostilities arising from racial, cultural, or gender differences over each of the last three years* (based on management reports, AA/EEO or diversity officer reports, or personnel data). To maintain these data, of course, managers and supervisors must be willing to report problems rather than trying to bury them.

- *Number and durations of work stoppages or other productivity disruptions attributed to employee-on-employee confrontations over racial, cultural, or gender differences* (based on management reports, AA/EEO or diversity officer reports, or personnel data).

• *Number of incidents of supervisor-employee confrontations over racial, cultural, or gender differences* (based on management reports, AA/EEO or diversity officer reports, or personnel data). When bias is exhibited by people in positions of authority, the resulting problem is infused throughout the organizational culture. Even when a particular confrontation is due to employee bias, management has to be concerned about the perception that is created.

• *Prevalence of racial diversity in (1) management ranks and (2) the rank-and-file, compared with prevalence in the community at large* (based on personnel data). If the proportion of managers from racial minorities is significantly lower than the proportion of rank-and-file members from racial minorities, or if either proportion is significantly lower than in the community at large, that difference could be an indicator of racial bias. Further data analysis could shed light on decision making—particularly about recruitment, raises, and promotions—that disfavors a particular group of people.

• *Prevalence of gender diversity in management ranks compared with the rank-and-file* (based on personnel data). Like the previous indicator, this one can offer insights into instances of bias, such as the existence of a glass ceiling. Because some studies have shown that men tend to hire men and women tend to hire women, bias is not necessarily premeditated. The sooner it is recognized, though, the sooner it can be remedied, before it leads to a risk exposure.

• *Perceived management hostility toward employees in a racial minority* (based on a survey of employees from a variety of racial backgrounds).

Problems Arising from Employee Alcohol and Drug Abuse

One transportation company had earned a reputation for safe, reliable service after seventeen years of accident-free driving with a 90 percent on-time record. The vast majority of its sales volume was from repeat customers, mostly organizations with busing needs and VIPs wanting limousine services. The company's good name and airtight book of business changed in a heartbeat, however, when one of its buses rammed into a car waiting at a traffic light. Several passengers were rushed to the hospital with critical injuries, and the other fifty passengers were shaken up. To make matters worse, the driver had a blood alcohol level of .12, making him legally drunk.

With so much public pressure to make driving safer, evidenced by such recent innovations as dual air bags and integrated child safety seats, intolerance for accidents caused by driver impairment is rife. Scrutiny is even greater when accidents are caused by professional drivers. Consequently, this accident was a business and public relations debacle for the company. It was reported throughout the local metropolitan media market, from which the company had drawn the majority of its business. Current customers fled, and sales volume over the next year dropped 45 percent, which led to a proportionate number of layoffs. It took several more years before the company recaptured most of its lost business, but it never was able to equal the rate of growth it enjoyed prior to the accident.

There is ongoing spirited debate in the addictions field and the public at large about whether alcohol and drug abuse are "diseases" or acts of "willful conduct." The disease concept serves a constructive purpose in the process of rehabilitating addicts, but is no alibi when chemical dependency dramatically disrupts the rights of others. No business can afford to ignore the consequences of alcohol and drug problems, because all businesses rely on employees to protect their investments, maintain good relations with customers, and perform high-quality, mistake-free work. This reliance is a part of the social contract between employers and employees.

Employers should measure these objective and subjective indicators:

- *Number and proportion of employees referred for treatment of alcohol and drug abuse over each of the past three years* (based on data from an employee assistance program or other behavioral health benefit gatekeeper used by the work organization).
- *Number of disciplinary actions taken by management for on-the-job alcohol use or impairment and for drug use* (based on management reports). This statistic is subject to interpretation: it can show the extent of these problems at the work site, and it can provide evi-

dence of the effectiveness of management's efforts to identify substance abuse.

- *Number of warnings and of penalties from a government agency for failure to comply with federal drug-testing requirements.* In most work organizations, these requirements are not an issue. However, all employers need to be aware of the potential for debarment from federal contracts or financial penalty.

- *Management awareness of employee alcohol and drug use* (based on employee surveys) and *management reluctance to act on cases of employee alcohol and drug use* (also based on employee surveys). Employees almost always know when their co-workers are drinking or using drugs in ways that affect on-the-job alertness and productivity. These indicators are important because they show the extent to which management recognizes job-related problems and is willing to act. A lack of action by management can invite more severe risk exposures later.

Malingering by Employees on Disability Health Insurance or Workers' Compensation

Employers have become alarmed at how much money workers' compensation drains from their coffers. However, closer inspection suggests reasons why. Consider the case of an office employee who experiences a work-related back injury and draws 500 *tax-free* dollars per week while out on workers' compensation. There is strong temptation to ride that gravy train as long as possible, perhaps even prolonging what was originally claimed as a short-term disability into a permanent one.

One librarian who worked at a college sprained her wrist while filing books. She was awarded one month off the job to recover, with full workers' compensation benefits. After the month was over, her lawyer contacted the college's insurer to inform them that she would not be able to return to work for another five months because of the psychological stress that she would be under, fearing that her wrist would be reinjured. At last check, she was halfway through her third month of disability payments, and the case was not yet resolved. The college, however, felt that the damage *to it* had already been done.

According to Edward M. Welch, director of the Michigan

Bureau of Workers' Disability Compensation, "In my experience, most men and women want to return to work during the first few weeks after their injury. . . . If, however, these people are allowed to sit idle for six months or a year, everything changes. Their attitude toward work, their attitude toward themselves, their relationship with their employers and even their families, all deteriorate."

Welch's statement is one explanation why disability costs for employers are now estimated at 8 to 10 percent of payroll, up from 2 to 4 percent in the early 1980s. What is more, when an employer uses a workers' compensation carrier, it typically pays back $3 to $4 in premium adjustments (by modification of an employer's loss conversion factor) for every dollar of the actual claim. The loss conversion factor is like a motor vehicle point system that does not "forgive" the traffic violation (or the work-related accident) for a specified number of years. Until then, it is factored into the premium. Therefore, a work-related accident has a protracted financial impact, suggesting that employers should think in the long term about their accident risks and solutions to prevent or minimize them.

Employers should measure these objective and subjective indicators:

• *Employees' average length of time spent receiving disability health insurance or workers' compensation benefits prior to return to work* (based on claims data from the disability and workers' compensation carrier or third-party administrator [TPA]). This information should be compared with state and industry averages. Additionally, the average length of time should be computed for the highest-risk cases—those 10 to 20 percent of cases that comprise the longest disability periods. These data will identify the discrepancy between low-cost and high-cost cases, which will be helpful in determining the need for psychological interventions.

• *Changes in employees' average length of time spent on disability or workers' compensation* (based on claims data from the disability and workers' compensation carriers or TPAs). This indicator tracks trends in disability, but should take into account severe cases that might skew the averages.

• *Prevalence of stress-related workers' compensation claims* (based on data from the company's insurer or TPA). As in healthcare utilization, an increasing prevalence of stress-related compensation claims can indicate organizational stress (which is discussed in the next chapter).

- *Percentage of disabled workers filing for additional time off* (based on data from the company, health insurer, or TPA). Also, the 10 to 20 percent of longest-duration workers' compensation cases should be analyzed for evidence of exploitation.

- *Percentage of surveyed employees who know of workers who presently or previously exploited the disability or workers' compensation system to increase benefits or prolong the period during which benefits are drawn* (based on employee surveys). This indicator suggests the degree to which employees are exploiting the system to maximize unearned income.

Behavioral Healthcare Utilization

Health insurance companies typically report that only about 8 percent of all healthcare claims costs are for behavioral health treatment. This is in marked contrast to research data showing that approximately 20 percent of the adult population has a current behavioral health disorder and that these health conditions are among the most expensive to treat. However, in a work environment where fitness for duty—determined by level of alertness, ability to concentrate, and freedom from chemical impairment—is paramount, the need to rehabilitate people from behavioral disorders speaks for itself.

Data on mental health and substance abuse benefits utilization are subject to interpretation. For example, the presence of healthy or unhealthy environmental factors (including workplace conditions) and the effectiveness of workplace and healthcare resources in identifying the disorders can either increase or decrease the utilization rate.

Employers should measure these objective and subjective indicators:

- *Percentage of (1) employees and (2) dependents treated for behavioral health problems* (based on data from the healthcare provider, TPA, managed behavioral healthcare provider, or benefits department). This indicator identifies trends over time; it also illustrates the effectiveness of specific interventions (such as those identified in Chapter Five). These data can be compared with industry and geographic averages.

- *Inpatient days per 1,000 employees and dependents, broken down by mental health and substance abuse episodes, for each of the last five years* (based on data from the healthcare provider, TPA, managed behavioral healthcare provider, or benefits department). When compared with industry and geographic averages, this indicator suggests both the severity of problems and the incidence of overtreatment or undertreatment.

- *Outpatient days per 1,000 employees and dependents, broken down by mental health and substance abuse episodes, for each of the last three years* (based on data from the healthcare provider, TPA, managed behavioral healthcare providers, or benefits department). These statistics should be compared with industry and geographic averages, if available. Employee data and dependent data should be handled as separate subsets, since the workplace is an environmental factor directly impacting employees but not dependents.

- *Behavioral healthcare claims* (based on data from the healthcare provider, TPA, managed behavioral healthcare provider, or benefits department). Data should be compiled for diagnoses found in the American Psychological Association's *Diagnostic and Statistical Manual* (4th ed.) (DSM-IV), including substance abuse and mental disorders, affective disorders (depression, mania, bipolar disorder), psychotic disorders (schizophrenia), anxiety disorders, posttraumatic stress syndrome, and others. In some systems, coding is based on unit of service (such as one hour of family therapy) instead of on condition. In those cases, the data are less likely to be as specific to the behavioral health condition but may be more useful for determining behavioral healthcare expenditures. The data can also be broken down by enrollee for Pareto-group analysis.

- *Claims and cost data for medical healthcare conditions that correlate highly with an undiagnosed behavioral healthcare problem* (based on data from the healthcare provider, TPA, managed care provider, or benefits department). Substance abusers are among the greatest consumers of healthcare benefits, especially if the primary condition goes undiagnosed. In fact, studies have found that as many as 93 percent of alcoholics have had major medical conditions before being treated for the primary alcoholism problem. Although there are literally hundreds of secondary medical diagnoses of alcoholism, ones that correlate highly with alcoholism are hypertension, ulcer disease, and chronic obstructive lung disease (15 to 25 percent of cases), also gastritis, epilepsy, and peripheral neuropathy (10 percent of cases). This indicator is significant because it helps to identify cost risk exposures. As long as alcoholism and alcohol dependence are underdiagnosed, employers are overpaying for medical healthcare.

Preventable Physical Illnesses Among Employees and Dependents

It is astounding to think that healthcare costs alone can bring down a business. Yet that is exactly what happened to some employers during the late 1980s and early 1990s, partially fueling the debate on national healthcare reform. Through managed care providers, health maintenance organizations, and other alternatives to indemnity care, medical cost escalation has been partially staunched.

However, no one should assume that cost and patient-flow management is the entire solution to the healthcare crisis. The fact that more than half of all healthcare costs are preventable or modifiable suggests that the pattern of high health insurance utilization and escalating costs is reversible. Even a single medical condition such as obesity can trigger explosive healthcare costs because of the myriad medical treatments for it. Obesity and its complications commonly manifest as elevated blood pressure, arthritis, diabetes, gall bladder disease, obstructive sleep apnea, and depression.

As the primary payers of private healthcare, employers need to know their employees' costs and to intervene when these costs appear to be excessive or escalating rapidly. What is perhaps even more important is that preventable physical health problems can splinter into other behavioral risks, such as increased potential for accidents due to a person's physical limitation or preoccupation with a medical condition, increased absenteeism due to ongoing medical treatment, job turnover when employees locate a better medical plan elsewhere, and diminished quality of work, arising from physical restriction.

Employers should measure these objective indicators:

- *Excessive healthcare claims by employees and dependents for lifestyle-related diagnoses* (based on data from the healthcare provider, TPA, managed healthcare provider, or benefits department). Analysis of these data can quickly escalate into a major research project, so some parameters are helpful. There are seventeen major diagnostic categories (MDCs) and virtually all of them include medical conditions that can be attributed to life-style factors. The practice of preventive medicine is dedicated to the in-depth study of these conditions. However, since wellness and health promotion interventions have a cascading positive effect on virtually all areas of bodily functioning, it is more practical for employers to limit analysis of healthcare claims data to a few key areas. Three MDCs that are particularly useful because the illnesses and diseases associated with them have both early-stage and late-stage warning signs are

Diseases of the circulatory system (including arteriosclerosis and other conditions partially controllable through diet and exercise)

Diseases of the respiratory system (including emphysema and other often smoking-related conditions)

Diseases of the digestive system (including ulcer and other conditions that in some cases are controllable through stress management, diet, and exercise)

Depending on the composition of the workforce, some additional indicators may be helpful. In a work environment that requires a lot of heavy lifting, employers should examine data on musculoskeletal conditions. If the workforce includes a high number of women of childbearing age (eighteen to forty years old), data on complications of pregnancy can also be reviewed.

Employers should keep in mind that they do not have responsibility for the health of their employees. But any employer that sponsors an employee health plan and is concerned about the lost work time that medical conditions cause does assume risk in relation to employee health.

- *Medical claims for treatment for AIDS and HIV infection* (based on healthcare utilization data). Many employers have been reluctant to address AIDS and HIV (human immunodeficiency virus) issues in their organizations, partly out of the stigma still associated with these diseases and partly for fear of catastrophic costs. The former concern is born primarily out of ignorance. And in regard to costs, the second concern, a recent survey shows the expected maximum cost to an employer of an HIV-infected employee in medical, disability, life insurance, and pension coverages is $32,000 over five years, far less than the $85,000 to $100,000 frequently cited.

Employers can seek to minimize the occurrence of behavioral HIV transmission among members of their benefit plans. Behavioral methods of transmission include homosexual contact, heterosexual contact, and intravenous drug use. Among Americans, these methods of transmission accounted for 82 percent of all new AIDS exposures from 1993 to 1995, according to the Centers for Disease Control. However, employers are cautioned that because the probable number of employees who are HIV-positive is low, confidentiality concerns may arise from analysis of diagnosis-specific information.

The Financial Cost of Behavioral Risk Exposures

The objective indicators described so far in this chapter document losses in terms of various incidents, medical claims, court cases, missing or damaged equipment, work stoppages, and other factors. Since the solutions to behavioral risk exposures are based in part on cost-benefit considerations, it is desirable to express behavioral losses in monetary terms, also, as direct and indirect costs.

The direct costs include

- *Healthcare costs for behavioral healthcare and medical healthcare that are related to life-style or to stress.* Ideally, these costs will be identified by individual claim and thus can easily be retrieved and aggregated by computer. If the data are presented as units of treatment service, the costs can be based on the cost to the organization per unit of service, deducting costs for copayments made by the beneficiary. These expenses should include claims costs for AIDS and HIV cases when the virus was contracted through personal behavior.

- *Workers' compensation costs.* These expenses will include costs incurred when short-term disability cases become long-term cases and when accidents are deemed to be the result of employee culpability.
- *Employee lost work time costs.* These costs will include excessive lost work time due to absenteeism, tardiness, and early departures. Absenteeism should include exploitation of personal and medical leave. *Excessive use* can be defined as that which is above industry or geographic norms.
- *Court awards and related legal costs.* If the legal exposures associated with behavioral risk can be determined as a proportion of the legal staff's total workload, organizations can factor in those compensation and related costs.
- *Recruitment and replacement costs for turnover associated with behavioral problems.* Since employers often do not document the reasons for employee departures, they may wish instead to determine an acceptable level of turnover, perhaps the industry average. Then, taking into consideration fluctuations such as relocations and downsizing activities that skew the rate, employers can base their cost exposure for behavioral problem turnover on any excessive turnover.
- *Cost of supervisory time spent handling employee behavioral problems.* This includes the cost of excessive time spent resolving such employee problems as disputes with co-workers, plus the cost of work time lost due to these problems (when supervisors need to participate in grievance proceedings, for example). Because part of a supervisor's job is to address employee problems, the organization may wish to determine an acceptable level of time spent on them (perhaps three hours per week), then determine its cost exposure based on time spent beyond that level, assigning a monetary value to the supervisor's time.
- *Equipment or property damage costs.* This is the cost of repair or replacement of equipment or property that has been stolen or damaged as a result of employee action. This calculation should include losses of items of substantial value but not of

supply-closet items like paper or pencils, which may or may not have been used on work-related business.

The indirect costs are

- *Costs of lost sales and suspected lost sales resulting from unfavorable publicity about behavioral risk exposures.* This information can be derived from reports of sales representatives, senior managers, and others involved in generating revenue.
- *Costs of work defects.* There can be many reasons for defects (faulty work design, for example) besides employee behaviors, but companies can observe whether these costs rise or fall as direct risk exposure data do.

Tailoring the Employee Audit Process to an Organization

Employers have some options in how the audit process is constructed and what it measures. Much depends on the amount of money an employer wants to invest in the audit. The organization may choose to analyze only objective healthcare and personnel data, foregoing the costs of administering management and employee surveys and interviews to obtain subjective data and the costs of the time needed to integrate and analyze the results. The objective data will still provide accurate information about the behavioral risk exposures. However, use of objective data alone will restrict insights about risk factors and the likelihood of future risk exposures, since it is the subjective indicators that primarily measure organizational behavioral risks (discussed in Chapter Four). When subjective data are ignored, organizational behaviors that contribute to the risk exposures are ignored.

The audit can measure risks across an entire organization or be limited to certain business divisions or wholly owned subsidiaries. In the latter case, the behavioral risk audit can be location specific or gradually phased in, with the limited audit acting as a pilot project. A limited audit makes sense, too, when an organizational unit has its own distinct work culture, a canopy inside of which work is performed. Important insights might be lost if behavioral risks for, say, a semiconductor manufacturing unit were integrated with those from a heavy industrial operating unit.

A behavioral risk audit process can also integrate special indicators with generic ones. One U.S.–based international metal fabrication company, for instance, has large numbers of American expatriate families. The company incurs an average cost of $1.3 million for each family's three-year overseas stint, so aborted assignments are not kindly looked upon. Surprisingly, the greatest determinant of a failed assignment is not employee job failure or inability to cope with the foreign culture. It is the *spouse's* inability to cope. In this situation, then, an audit might include a survey or interview question about spouses' overseas experience.

In a nuclear facility, a special indicator might be the number of times the Nuclear Regulatory Commission has caught an employee asleep at the control panel or noted other infractions. In a hair styling salon, it might be the number of times a stylist nicks a customer's ear. In a police department, it might be the proportion of public complaints about police conduct to the number of calls responded to. Behavioral issues are pervasive in work organizations, so the risk indicators selected for auditing should be those deemed to have the greatest impact on the organization.

Indicators can also be created to respond to special social and geographic factors that can affect individual or team productivity, such as cult or gang activity, the life-styles of ethnic and cultural groups, gambling addictions (when job sites are within 200 miles of a casino), and work requiring extensive employee-customer contact (such as on-site work at clients' facilities).

The behavioral risk audit should compile data based on such organizational variables as job classification, location, and department. It can also gather data on such demographic variables as family status, gender, and race. However, the greatest insight will be gained from Pareto-group analysis, which fragments data to identify the occupational and demographic characteristics of the highest-risk and highest-cost employees and to identify any patterns of risk exposure.

Necessary Precautions When Auditing High-Risk Employees

Advances in computer technology are making data integration more feasible for employers. Additionally, since more companies today are self-insured, employee healthcare data are now more likely be handled internally. Therefore, employers may think to use data integration to identify the highest-cost employees for the purpose of discharging them. For example, data integration might show that in addition to consistently using all of her vacation, personal, and sick-leave days year after year, an employee also had healthcare use that was excessive from the company's point of view and that substantially increased the company's costs.

However, in part because of the potential for employer abuse, the Americans with Disabilities Act (ADA) has outlawed the integration of personnel and healthcare utilization data. The ADA is also intended to ensure the confidentiality of medical information and protect the job rights of disabled employees, including alcoholics and those with severe mental health problems.

For this reason, Pareto-group analysis is best performed by an independent external consultant, as much to protect a company from legal action as to restrict what it does. Employer attempts to intervene in the analysis can have devastating legal and employee-relations consequences. Furthermore, they may jeopardize a company's ability to discipline an employee for legitimate reasons because that employee can claim that discriminatory action was taken as a result of findings derived from the integrated data. The independent consultant, then, must also take precautions not to provide data to the employer in a form that can easily compromise employee confidentiality. Providing such data opens the consultant to potential liability, also.

Problems in Measuring Behavioral Risk

It takes time to develop the internal record keeping and controls to accurately measure behavioral risk. Various healthcare and employee data and management and supervisory records may not presently be available. Personnel records may be incomplete. Certain healthcare data, such as the diagnostic categories used by the healthcare provider, insurer, or third-party administrator, may be too general for meaningful analysis. Personnel and healthcare data may be difficult for the external consultant to integrate because they are encoded differently; one data set according to social security number, the other according to an encrypting system, and so forth.

If employers do not presently have the data they need for a behavioral risk audit or if an insurer does not presently provide them, employers should condition future insurer contracts on data availability. Also, certain behavioral risk information derived from management, such as supervisory reports on accidents that almost occurred (near misses), may need to have criteria defined in order to ensure more accurate record keeping by managers.

∞

What is most important for employers to gain from the employee behavioral risk audit is an awareness of the full range of behavioral costs to the organization. Many employers brush off suggestions of implementing programs and services to address behavioral risks, on the grounds of cost. When the full cost of exposures is considered, however, the cost of prevention may be a pittance in comparison. While behavioral risk management may actually increase up-front expenditures, including the cost of auditing activities, its goal is to reduce an employer's total liability for behavioral risk exposures by reducing the far greater terminal costs associated with those exposures. In short, the holistic focus of behavioral risk management makes financial sense.

This chapter has examined the auditing of employees' (and dependents') risks and risk exposures. Chapter Four describes the auditing of organizational behaviors that can create undesirable employee behaviors.

Notes

P. 43, *Boston University's Job and Homelife Study:* Googins, B. K., Griffin, M. L., and Casey, J. C. *Balancing Job and Homelife: Changes over Time in a Corporation.* Boston: Boston University Center on Work and Family, 1994.

P. 44, *85 to 95 percent of all accidents:* Lenkus, D. "Safety Awareness Alone Not Enough to Sow the Seeds for Fewer Injuries." *Business Insurance,* Oct. 17, 1994, p. 3.

P. 44, *two fires occurred in the same operating unit:* Hirschhorn, L., and Young, D. R. "The Psychodynamics of Safety: A Case Study of Oil Refinery." In M.F.R. Kets de Vries and Associates (eds.), *Organizations on the Couch: Clinical Perspectives on Organizational Behavior and Change.* San Francisco: Jossey-Bass Publishers, 1991.

P. 46, *Up to 40 percent of industrial fatalities:* Bureau of National Affairs. *Alcohol & Drugs in the Workplace: Costs, Controls, and Controversies.* Washington, D.C.: Bureau of National Affairs, 1986, p. 7.

P. 46, *an estimated 2,000 violent incidents:* Thompson, J. D. "Employers

Should Take Measures to Minimize Potential for Workplace Violence." *Ideas and Trends in Personnel,* 1993, *317,* p. 1.

P. 46, *one study reports that 2.2 million workers:* Northwestern National Life. *Fear and Violence in the Workplace.* Minneapolis: Northwestern National Life, 1993, p. 4.

P. 46, *twenty-eight-year-old Caucasian man I will call "Wayne":* Adapted from Meloy, J. R. "Violence Risk Assessment Case Study." Paper presented at "Assessment of Violence Potential" seminar, Philadelphia, November 7, 1994.

P. 47 *Pitney Bowes Management Services found:* "Another Word for . . ." *Business Week,* November 7, 1994, p. 6.

P. 47, *separate finding that workplace violence had increased:* Society for Human Resource Management. "SHRM Survey Reveals Extent of Workplace Violence." *EAP Digest,* 1994, *14*(3), 25.

P. 49, *survey conducted . . . of 501 Dun and Bradstreet companies:* KPMG Peat Marwick. *1994 Fraud Survey.* New York: KPMG Peat Marwick, 1994, p. 2.

P. 49, *fraud experts estimate that less than 10 percent:* Levi, P. "Employee Fraud Can Be Difficult to Uncover and Halt." *The Montreal Gazette,* June 22, 1992, p. C-6.

P. 55, *"most men and women want to return to work":* Welch, E. M. "New Strategies for the 1990s." In R. A. Victor (ed.), *Challenges for the 1990s.* Cambridge, Mass.: Workers Compensation Research Institute, 1990, p. 43.

P. 55, *disability costs for employers are now estimated:* Northwestern National Life. *Back to Work.* Minneapolis: Northwestern National Life, 1994, p. 4.

P. 56, *among the most expensive to treat:* Robins, L. N., and Regier, D. A. *Psychiatric Disorders in America.* New York: The Free Press, 1991, p. 329.

P. 58, *medical diagnoses . . . that correlate highly with alcoholism:* Ashley, J. M. "The Physical Disease Characteristics of Inpatient Alcoholics." *Journal of Studies on Alcohol,* 1981, *42,* 1–11.

P. 60, *expected maximum cost . . . of an HIV-infected employee:* Farnham, P. G., and Gorsky, R. D. "Costs to Business for an HIV-Infected Worker." *Inquiry,* 1994, *31,* p. 76.

P. 60, *82 percent of all new AIDS exposures:* U.S. Department of Health and Human Services. Public Health Service. Centers for Disease Control and Prevention. "First 500,000 AIDS Cases—United States, 1995." *Morbidity and Mortality Report,* 1995, *44*(6), 1.

P. 63, *One U.S.–based international metal fabrication company:* Yandrick, R. M. "EAPs Help Expatriates Adjust and Thrive." *HR News,* Jan. 1995, p. B7.

Chapter Four

Assessing Organizational Factors That Contribute to Behavioral Risks

The employee behavioral portion of the behavioral risk management audit process identifies and measures behavioral risk exposures, but the data it produces do little to assess whether organizational factors are contributing to employee problems, and if so, just how those factors affect employees. The purpose of the organizational behavioral audit, then, is to garner evidence of organizational problems that underlie behavioral risk exposures.

Employee risk exposures can be precipitated by an isolated and basic organizational problem such as a single ineffective manager; a broader but still limited problem such as an "overheating" division or work unit, or a problem suffused throughout the organization such as a pathological difficulty that results in a distinct pattern of disharmony among all the participants in a work system. Consequently, the information in an organizational behavioral audit can be used to implement solutions that will set the organization on the road to becoming more efficient, self-regulating, and healthy.

Codependency, for example, one major form of dysfunction that can afflict an organization, is more familiar to millions of Americans as a family problem. The hallmarks of codependency include a highly dysfunctional often chemically dependent individual, a cast of other members of the individual's group who adapt coping behaviors that "enable" the dysfunctional individual, a resulting homeostasis that preserves the status quo instead of confronting the problem, and denial that the problem exists. Persons who are codependent meet at least one of these four criteria:

They are in subjective distress and are unable to stop impulsive, self-defeating behaviors.

They experience role impairment in which the distress is so severe that they are unable to function in a normal environment.

They deny the problem.

They function in a chaotic environment.

One organizational development consultant is fond of explaining how, upon being hired by a company's board of directors to resolve interpersonal conflict throughout the organization, she sent the entire board to treatment for codependency. Some of the directors had taken dysfunctional behaviors from their family lives and reproduced them in the work setting. Some were borderline chemically dependent, brusque with subordinates, relied on the management hierarchy to maintain control, and instilled fear through threats and punitive actions. The consultant held that once the directors completed the treatment—during which they were educated about the ways codependent systems originate and are perpetuated and given guidance on how to deal with the problems the systems create—the board members were better prepared to resolve the everyday operational problems faced by line managers and employees. Without the treatment, she asserts, the company would never have been able to repair itself, since the problems started at the top and percolated down throughout the organization.

Some of the behaviors exhibited by the members of a codependent system are secretiveness, crisis management, overcompensating, perfectionism, dualism, and scapegoating. In the workplace, workaholism, too, can be a coping mechanism. These are all defensive tactics, born out of fear of the dysfunctional individual, who usually has significant or decisive economic power over others. Not surprisingly, family-owned businesses in particular are a seedbed for codependent work relationships.

This theory of dysfunctional organizational behavior was explained by Anne Wilson Schaef and Diane Fassel in their book

The Addictive Organization. The system cultivates roots throughout an organization and may perpetuate itself through hiring and promotion practices. Intervention often occurs only at a late stage in the form of leadership changeover, which runs the risk of replacing one bad leadership team with another. Or a senior decision maker may have an epiphany, realizing that internal changes are necessary for the organization's long-term survival. Without intervention, though, the company will likely experience decline and atrophy, finally collapsing under internal and external pressure, or if it is in a healthy industry, it may struggle along in long-term mediocrity.

The Organization as an Organism

Many experts in organizational behavior recognize that work organizations take on distinctive personalities, replete with egos, defense mechanisms, inhibitions, and so forth. These personality traits may have originally belonged to a charismatic leader who carried the company to success in earlier days; after which they became "institutionalized" through succession, the adoption of decision-making paradigms, and policies that endured past the active participation of the original leader. These corporate personalities—marked by some of the same behavioral traits ascribed to humans—may establish organizations as leaders or plodders, mavericks or traditionalists, strategists or bumblers. It comes as no coincidence, then, that the term *organization* has the same etymological root as *organism* and carries the suggestion that a company (or its operating units) functions in a unitary, often reflexive, way.

One of the basic assumptions of behavioral risk management is that the institutionalized behaviors of work organizations shape the functioning of their component parts—right down to individual employees and, by extension, employees' family members. By examining the internal parts of the company through assessment of behavioral risk exposures, dysfunctions in the whole company or in any part of it can be identified.

Many business owners and senior decision makers are reluctant to look at their organizations' behaviors as the underlying cause of internal problems. There are two primary reasons for this: first, organizational behavior and culture are ambient concepts, dealing to some extent with perceived environments, and many businesspeople are more comfortable with more palpable issues; second, an examination of organizational behavior exposes management's own actions to scrutiny. That is why blame for internal problems, particularly personal disputes and animosities, tends to be laid at the feet of the individuals directly involved rather than linked to some systemic problem emanating from the top.

Opportunity for Change

Today, our state of awareness about dysfunctional organizational behavior is about where employers were thirty to forty years ago in their thinking about individual workers who abused alcohol. At that time, there was substantial institutional denial of problems caused by alcohol, but a handful of progressive organizations— Kodak, DuPont, and Kennecott Copper among them—implemented occupational alcoholism programs to deal with these problems forthrightly. Since that time, thousands of work organizations have directly addressed their employees' substance abuse problems.

Today, Total Quality Management, reengineering, and other restructuring initiatives—which have dislodged much of the sediment that blocked the avenues of creative business thought—have opened a window of opportunity for us to devise new solutions for correcting organizational problems. Indeed, we might ask, Why shouldn't companies have an efficient, integrated process for managing loss due to behavior-related workplace problems, just as they have processes for improving production, maintaining machinery, and researching and developing new products?

Proactive business leaders will conclude that if their companies do *not* deal with behavioral problems, internal losses will diminish their profitability and competitiveness. This makes more sense now than ever because, in today's marketplace, competitors are no longer familiar and just across town or the state; instead they may be on the Pacific Rim or Western Europe or Australia. Business leaders need to be more proactive in developing techniques to eliminate inefficiency, putting their focus on achieving full potential rather than on just trying to keep up with the Joneses. The organizational behavioral audit is a first step in achieving that potential.

The Organizational Behavioral Audit

The employee behavioral audit described in the previous chapter relies heavily on indicators derived from objective healthcare and personnel data. In contrast, data necessary for an organization's behavioral audit include

- Patterns of employee behavioral risk indicators that suggest systemic dysfunction in the organization
- Organizational behavioral risk data—primarily subjective indicators derived from management and employee surveys
- Operational data and other organizational indicators, such as productivity levels, rates of manufacturing defects, and business transactions, that establish relationships between behavioral risk factors and the company's business performance

The first set, the patterns of employee behavioral risk, is derived from performing the audit process described in the previous chapter. The last two sets of data are derived from the audit of organizational behavioral risks. As in the discussion of the employee audit, the indicators to be measured in the organizational audit are grouped according to the behavioral risks outlined in Chapter Two.

Poor Internal Communications

Individuals' poor communication or inability to communicate is the root of many of society's ills. It is the death knell of organizational dysfunction. It can create fissures, not just between individuals, generations, races, and genders but also between workers, teams, units, and affiliated organizations. Conversely, good communication can heal emotional wounds, create new alliances and, by enhancing understanding and teamwork, help an organization achieve its potential.

Communication in an organization occurs on several different levels, and the larger and more diversified the organization, the more complicated the communication channels are likely to be. Communication may be in the form of missives from executive management to all employees, annual reports, dictates from higher to lower levels of management, daily face-to-face communication among managers and between supervisors and rank-and-file employees, and feedback from the rank-and-file to supervisors and back up through the management ranks. All this communication can be direct or indirect, clear or ambiguous, complete or fragmented.

The most critical communication occurs between supervisors and rank-and-file employees, the people who actually make the products and provide the services. In a recent study of supervisors and employees who were asked to rank in order ten specific items people might be thought to want from their work lives, there was a startling disparity in the ranking of the sole item addressing communication, "feeling of being in on things." While this item rated dead last with supervisors, it was third among employees, behind "interesting work" and "full appreciation of work well done," but, significantly, ahead of "job security" and "good wages." This finding not only underscores the value of having good internal communications with employees but also suggests that supervisors may give short shrift to the importance of communicating well with their subordinates.

Employers should measure these objective and subjective indicators:

• *Rate at which formal communications are issued from management to employees during periods of organizational change, compared with the rate during periods of relative calm* (based on management reports). Diligent efforts to communicate forthrightly with employees at critical times can defuse unfortunate news. Failure to do so can breed distrust and disloyalty and have lingering consequences once the dust settles.

• *Employees' sense that communications from management are "misleading" or "dishonest"* (based on employee surveys). This perception can arise when information is not fully disclosed or when it is sanitized to the point that the recipient might consider it biased. When employees feel there is a story behind the story, it breeds anxiety.

• *Frequent dictates from senior management to line management, and from line management to employees, that are contradictory or ambiguous* (based on employee and management surveys). Panicky, confused communication is a reliable indicator of an organization nearing or in a state of turmoil. Usually a sudden change in policy or plan can be accomplished without a lot of fanfare, but if the organization repeatedly shunts back and forth between an original and revised plan or if its decisions about daily operations lack consistency, there is potential for mass confusion. In organizations with two or more work sites, the potential for problems increases in multiples. All these difficulties may be compounded further if decisions are communicated only by word of mouth.

One consumer electronics company, for example, through an aggressive marketing plan, obtained four major contracts in one month to manufacture stereo systems. The systems had customized components that required set-up time and orders for special parts. On three occasions, senior management changed the work schedule in order to maximize its business opportunities. This disrupted employees' vacation plans, made weekend trips difficult for employees' families since overtime was announced as late in the week as Friday afternoon, and caused confusion during assembly of the systems. At one point, partially assembled systems had to be set aside for completion at a later date. Eventually, worker frustration reached a fever pitch, evidenced by manager-employee confrontations and a higher than usual number of work defects.

• *Feelings that rumors are a "common occurrence" or that they are destructive to employee relations* (based on employee and management surveys). This indicator assesses the presence of an "underground" communications network, which can be thought of as a disease whose strength is inversely proportional to the effective use of the organization's formal communications channels.

• *Prevalence of "unwritten rules" regarding workplace do's and don'ts* (based on employee and management surveys). When a new employee hired to do policy rating at an insurance company found that he was being avoided by co-workers within a month after starting, he knew that he had inadvertently broken a rule of propriety. Could it have been his casual conversation with a litigation specialist, the memo he wrote to his boss, or the cologne he wore? In many organizations, the unwritten rules are more powerful codes of workplace conduct than the provisions in the personnel manual. The presence of many unwritten rules is indicative of an organization that controls information beyond what is necessary to safeguard sensitive information.

• *Reports of amount and quality of feedback received by management from employees* (based on employee and management surveys). This measures the reverse flow of information. If employee feedback is deficient, it may signal that employees believe management asks for their input only as a matter of form and does not act on it or that employees are simply not aware of the channels.

• *Belief that management provides "adequate" lead time when announcing major organizational changes to employees* (based on employee and management surveys). Are employees given fair warning about matters that could affect their employment status or livelihoods? Employees' responses to this indicator will clue in senior management to the importance of timeliness.

The preceding indicators, evaluated for both employees and management, will highlight disparities in employee and management perceptions about the quality of internal communications. A high degree of disparity could precipitate undesirable employee behaviors, as employees may sense a systemic problem that management does not see. Because management structures are seldom monolithic in midsized or large organizations, disparities in perception between layers of management can signal discord as well. Further, these disparities will reveal whether line managers identify more closely with upper management or with rank-and-file employees, or whether they strike a healthy balance.

Lack of Management-Employee Trust and Cooperation

Without trust and cooperation, relations between management and employees are, as though by definition, contentious. This contentiousness is written between the lines of two industrial-age concepts diametrically opposed in intent and application: *employment-at-will,* a de facto "doctrine" that holds that the employer has the right to discipline (or terminate) an employee in any way and for whatever reason the employer sees fit, and *collective bargaining,* a concept that says workers can collectively strike and that, outside of right-to-work states, requires workers to join labor unions in unionized work settings.

One can conclude, then, that the presence of conditions that typical precede the formation of labor unions can be a good measure of the failure of management to provide adequate employee supports. In the 1970s, Charles L. Hughes did much of the pioneering work in attitude surveys that revealed reasons why labor unions form. He found that if employee survey scores were consistently below 50 percent favorable in six specific areas of inquiry, the likelihood of a union movement was very high. Those areas, which also correspond highly with labor-management trust factors, were fair management, job security, open communication with superiors, company pride and loyalty, fair compensation, and equitable treatment. Questions in each of these areas can be accompanied by the following objective and subjective indicators:

• *Disparity in compensation between employees and line management and between layers of management* (based on management reports). This disparity is usually measured in multiples of compensation. For example, the income differential between a chief executive officer and a typical rank-and-file employee in a large U.S. corporation is commonly more than 500:1. By contrast, some companies—typically small employers—put a cap on the income of the highest-paid employee of five to ten times higher than the lowest-paid full-time employee. Corporate America is littered with anecdotes about senior managers who, in the midst of austerity budget cuts, award themselves bonuses for "making the hard decisions," and other mangers who, after failing to manage effectively, are sent into retirement with golden parachutes. Understandably, such behavior can breed contempt among employees.

• *Degree of cooperation between management and rank-and-file* (based on employee and management surveys). A large disparity between employee and management responses signals that employee behavioral risk exposures may be on the horizon.

• *Belief that management does not follow through on what it promises* (based on employee surveys).

• *Existence of a policy prohibiting nepotism in the ranks of management* (based on management report). In larger organizations that ostensibly hire based on merit, one sure-fire way of infusing resentment is nepotism. It communicates to employees that management jobs for family members are sinecures. It may also lead other managers as well as rank-and-file employees to believe that they are being exploited by having to labor to enrich one key person's family. The exception is the small, family-owned business, which is often formed to further the family's efforts to work together. As family-owned businesses grow and outsiders are hired, though, eventually nonfamily members may exert pressure to discontinue the practice of nepotism.

Lack of a Supportive Organizational Culture

Organizational culture comprises workplace attributes that determine what it feels like for employees to work in the company. Those attributes include values, conflicts, dilemmas, myths and stories, taboos and violations, ceremonies and rituals, metaphors, paradigms for handling employees and customers, and images presented by the organization. In his book *Creating Corporate Culture*, Charles Hampden-Turner refers to organizational culture as a "cybernetic system" that "steers itself and perseveres in the direction it has set for itself despite obstacles and interruptions. An automatic compass, for example, indicates which direction a ship must be steered in order to compensate for being blown off course or to avoid an obstacle." The indicators used in a behavioral audit, then, should elicit data about organizational factors that set the organization's automatic compass.

Employers should measure these subjective and objective indicators:

• *Presence and promotion of people-oriented organizational folklore* (based on management commentaries and employee surveys). Organizational folklore is an allegorical representation of the organization's values and beliefs. It is often created around how crises were admirably or abysmally handled. At its best, the folklore is success stories that confer on the organization a sublime quality. At its worst, the folklore is horror stories about management's unfair treatment of employees, customers, and the public. Consider one now-depressed Illinois town, where five years ago a distribution center for a major computer manufacturer laid off 40 percent of its workforce, which it deemed "surplus." In coffee shops, former employees still talk about how one person, upon being given his pink slip, calmly went out to his car, donned an outfit with a cape and an "S" on the chest, ran back into the facility, clambered up a fifty-foot storage rack, and from the top pronounced himself "Surplus Man."

- *Existence of and active use of an employee recognition program* (based on management commentaries). Cheering on the efforts of rank-and-file employees is another indicator of a supportive culture, if that encouragement is perceived as a genuine effort to honor hard workers. If, however, it is seen as a platform to reward employees who "brownnose" management, the recognition will be detested.

- *Existence of employee career paths within the work organization* (based on management and employee commentaries). This indicator, which shows organizational commitment to establishing long-term work relationships, may include educational and training opportunities necessary for advancement. It reflects fundamental human resource management.

- *Involvement of the company in community affairs* (based on management commentaries and employee surveys). This indicator demonstrates the organization's commitment to the communities from which it draws its labor supply as well as to the personal lives of current and future employees. Employees will notice, however, whether the involvement is magnanimous or self-advancing. One retail store chain in the Midwest, as a matter of unwritten policy, considered all interactions with its publics—the community and local business and trade groups—first and foremost as "business ops." Consequently, it spawned cynicism with the public, including its own employees. On several occasions when the company became embroiled in unfortunate situations such as lease disputes with building-management companies and run-ins with customers that reached local newspapers, it nearly always ended up with egg on its face. This caused periods of business drop-off that resulted in periods of internal flux.

- *Existence of an "absenteeism culture," denoted by rates of absenteeism* (based on personnel data). Some would argue that all time off—whether for vacation days, medical leave, or personal leave—is deserved if it is not in excess of that allowed under the employer's benefit plan, regardless of the reason. This kind of entitlement mentality can prompt employees to skew the system, using medical leave for personal leave purposes, for example. Behavioral risk management looks at the amount of lost work time that is above the norm for the industry and geographic area in order to determine if this mentality exists.

Lack of Supportive Programs, Services, and Benefits

This indicator relates to the paradigm for handling employees, one of the elements of organizational culture cited earlier in this chapter. Supportive programs and services and the benefits that complement them are all helping resources and cultural enhancements. Therefore, even though the purpose of programs and services is to reduce behavioral risks and costs, by their very existence they also serve to create a worker-friendly organizational culture. Typical areas for these programs and services are employee assistance, wellness and health promotion, balancing work life and family life, diversity training, and managed behavioral healthcare. While it is possible for these programs to be operated so that they become liabilities to cultural development—especially when they are perceived to be clandestine activities to pry into the lives of employees—overwhelmingly they are considered to be assets.

Benefits should be structured as pathways and financial payment mechanisms that help employees (and often family members) to access the programs and services and, when necessary, outside resources. Benefits should not be considered giveaways but rather tools that advance organizational objectives.

Employers should measure these objective and subjective indicators:

- *Solicitation of employee feedback to ascertain the need for and interest in supportive programs, services, and benefits* (based on management reports). This indicator shows whether management is demonstrating attentiveness to the needs of its workforce.
- *Belief among employees that management fulfills employee needs for supportive programs and services* (based on employee surveys).
- *Perceived problem with confidentiality of helping resources* (based on employee surveys and corroborating management information).
- *Documented cases of confidentiality breaches by helping resources* (based on management records, court records, or other sources). Such breaches are likely to be well known by employees, and initial information on this indicator could be elicited in employee focus groups.

A Sustained High Level of Organizational Stress

Some companies operate in chronic high-pressure situations. One stock and bond company trading in the highly volatile options market was concerned about a run of losses by its trading teams, comprising managers, floor traders, traders, and brokers. Trading review sessions revealed that information was often ignored that would have exposed certain trades as bad risks. Because a single trader on average handled eighty orders per day for trades valued at about $1.5 million, the company knew its greatest risk was impaired judgment. The greatest contributing factors to impaired judgment, it reasoned, were near-catatonic stupor arising from despair or exhaustion, or frenzied behavior resulting from panic or excessive optimism.

Through stress management training, the company sought to help its team members to interpret some workplace events differently so these situations would invoke less distress, and to seek balance between their work and private lives so as to offset the distress they did experience. The company also taught its personnel to take in stride minor investment losses, since they are easily recouped, even as it sought to prevent major losses. This strategy helped employees maintain their composure when in the eye of a trading storm; this in turn helped the company to improve its financial performance relative to its competitors. Continual stress management training for new employees and refresher courses for current ones have enabled the company to sustain its advantage. In evaluation surveys, employees self-reported that overall, they felt a 25 percent reduction in stress.

Chronic stress can occur in lower-pressure slower-paced work environments, too. It can happen where employees work in fear of job loss, discipline, failure of assignment, and castigation by managers or co-workers. Stress can spread throughout an organization and then go into remission, just as a disease may. Most often, stress escalates during periods of organizational change, such as job consolidation, downsizing, and employee empowerment. Stress is a normal response to these events, but it can be partially offset by the manner in which organizational changes are communicated and instituted, and by the coping skills employees are given to deal with change.

A more enduring risk to the organization occurs when, after a major change that brings "system shock," the level of stress does not abate because the organization never reestablishes a status quo.

Employers should measure these objective and subjective indicators:

• *Changes in productivity requirements for employees* (based on management reports). Generally the Total Quality Management and reengineering movements are about getting more productivity from each person in the work system. Because of the diverse nature of jobs in many companies, though, measures of productivity vary. Some outputs are verifiable on a daily or even hourly basis, as they are in many mechanistic work systems. In an organic work system, where output is partially a derivation of intellect and creative thought, productivity may be measurable only by customer satisfaction following completion of a project. Longitudinal reviews of productivity expectations show whether increased demands placed on employees are time-limited or indefinite. If they are indefinite, without corresponding improvements in equipment or technology that make work easier, employee behavioral risks are likely to increase. This indicator can use any or all of the following three measurements: units of output per unit of time (to measure the pace of work), average number of weekly hours (to measure the time spent working), and number of discrete management decisions to increase productivity per employee (which provides a rationale for taking the two previous measurements).

• *Improvements in training or technological improvements* (based on management reports and employee surveys). These improvements should have an offsetting effect on any increased stress generated by new productivity requirements. However, the rapid infusion of high technology into work without accompanying workforce training can increase stress as well. Another important consideration is that technology that automates job tasks—enabling one employee to juggle more balls—increases job complexity and mental strain.

• *Employees feel unable to cope with the pace of work* (based on employee surveys). This subjective indicator reveals the creeping in of despair and morale problems, which can splinter into various employee behavioral risk exposures.

• *Supervisors feel unable to cope with the pace of work and the dictates from higher levels of management* (based on management surveys). An organization's "management" is not monolithic; it is more like sedimentary rock with its varying layers. In fact, in most organizations, it is middle managers who are the endangered species. Therefore, depending on the configuration of work units in the organization, it may be appropriate to consider responses to this indicator by layer of management.

• *High level of conflict between (1) employees and line managers and (2) line managers and senior management* (based on employee and management surveys). Organizational stress results in strains in interpersonal working relationships.

Lack of Controls in Hiring and Promotion

Hiring and promotion controls are an employer's best defense against behavioral risks brought in from outside the organization. In essence, these controls safeguard the organization against the behavioral risks of society at large. The behavioral traits tested for could include an individual's propensity for theft, violence, emotional instability, unsafe work behavior, bad work habits, confrontations with supervision, causing customer relations problems, and quitting the job. Although it is an ethical question whether the scope of job-candidate testing should go beyond the stated requirements of the job and the candidate's past work experience, many employers would argue that, in order to protect their investments, the categories mentioned here are legitimate avenues of inquiry.

In hiring, employers should measure these objective and subjective indicators:

• *Use of preemployment testing to measure characterological traits (this does not include drug or alcohol testing, which is covered elsewhere)* (based on management commentaries).

• *Use of interview techniques that provide evidence of a candidate's characterological traits, such as his or her ability to communicate with other employees* (based on management commentaries). Employers want to build cooperative relationships among employees, especially in empowerment-based work teams. Interview techniques to support this behavior might be introduced by having a candidate interact with employees, then asking the employees whether they think the candidate should be hired. This indicator arises from good basic human resource management.

In promoting, employers should measure these objective and subjective indicators:

- *Use of testing to measure leadership qualities* (based on management commentaries). This indicator applies both when considering candidates for line management, especially when they are promoted from the rank-and-file, and for "fast track" promotions to senior management posts from line management. Often, managers are promoted based on their ability to balance budgets, meet production deadlines, and the like, without equivalent consideration given to their abilities in interpersonal communication, example setting, and empathy for others. In fact, many managers strong in the former qualities are often deficient in the latter because they were never necessary for advancement. But when managers reach senior levels and have a defining role in the organizational culture and establishment of work relationships, they need to exercise "people skills" such as tact, diplomacy, and ability to motivate.
- *Use of interview techniques that provide evidence of a candidate's characterological traits* (based on management commentaries).

Tolerance of Confrontive or Avoidance Behaviors

Tolerance of behaviors that are confrontive and tolerance of avoidance behaviors are flip sides of the same coin, both are inappropriate responses to workplace dilemmas. Confrontations between employees fuel the fires of animosity and discontent, while avoidance of addressing employee conduct and work-performance problems allows them to fester. Both are forms of anarchy, one overt and the other covert, that occur when a supervisor lacks or ineffectively uses problem-resolution skills.

In the shipping department of one manufacturer, two employees who were assigned to construct large skids continually butted heads. Their personality clash was fomented by a confined work space and having to share a hydraulic nail gun. The supervisor knew that problems existed between them, but preferring to focus his energy on paperwork, his only intervention was to give an occasional admonishment to the employees to "work the problem out between yourselves." By abdicating his responsibility, the supervisor had effectively imposed playground rules, and as commonly happens on playgrounds, one day the workers got into a fistfight. One was hospitalized and received workers' compensation for several months. Management's knee-jerk reaction to the situation was to suspend the other employee for a week, then transfer him to another department, as well as to impose the workplace equivalent of temporary martial law, which left the other employees with the impression that *they* were being punished for the situation.

Supervisory avoidance protects and compensates for the "weak links" in the production process. When much time and energy are expended to compensate for one or a few individuals, it is likely that the everyday work considerations of other employees will be ignored. When either avoidance or confrontation is tolerated, most employees are likely to conclude that management "doesn't have its act together," which results in a perception of lawlessness or skewed justice in the workplace.

Employers should measure these objective and subjective indicators:

- *Belief that supervisors hide employees' problems* (based on employee surveys). What induces supervisors to hide employee problems? It may be misguided empathy or an effort to protect the dysfunctional employee, based on friendship. The risk of this behavior reflects the promotion of individuals to management from the rank-and-file and a lack of good training.

- *Belief that management does not intervene effectively in disputes between employees* (based on employee surveys). When workplace lawlessness prevails, it shows that organizational norms are inadequate for addressing workplace disputes in a sane, civil way.

- *Belief among supervisors that senior management puts excessive demands on their time* (based on management surveys). This may be an underlying factor that distracts supervisors from addressing emerging workplace problems that have not yet resulted in confrontation. If supervisors feel too much pressure to meet paperwork demands, engage in troubleshooting, and so forth, they may be more inclined to let festering employee problems slide.

- *Belief among supervisors that supervisors in adjacent work units have a problem with vocal or physical confrontations* (based on management surveys). Perhaps it is not seeing the trees for the forest, but it seems to be a characteristic of human nature that problems in someone else's neighborhood are usually more apparent than those in one's own. For example, one survey of human resource managers showed that they perceive on-the-job substance abuse as more serious in other organizations than in their own (48 percent versus 40 percent for companies with over 2,000 employees). Therefore, this indicator should supplement self-reporting.

- *Amount of supervisory training per year in interpersonal skill building and employee problem resolution* (based on management reports). This indicator provides evidence of sensitivity (or lack of it) by senior management to the need to address and resolve "people problems" in the organization.

- *Perceived quality of supervisory training* (based on management surveys).

- *Availability of (1) a dispute-resolution process for problems between employees and (2) a helping resource for troubled employees* (based on management reports). These are support services as much for supervisors as they are for employees. Supervisors are less likely to tolerate confrontive behaviors or harbor an enabling environment if they know they have back-up help to get this "monkey" off their backs.

Dysfunctional Work Relationships Among Managers and Employees

Problems in work relationships can radiate upward to higher management, laterally to managers in other departments, and downward to the rank-and-file. Dysfunctional work relationships may be a systemic or a localized problem.

Employers should measure these objective and subjective indicators:

- *A high incidence of we-they thinking* (based on employee and management surveys). "We-they" dualistic thinking is characterized by backbiting, scapegoating, and the formation of cliques. Such dichotomies are prevalent in the restaurant business, where most employees are involved either in preparing meals or in waiting on and serving customers. This was the case at most of the stores of a Southeastern U.S. restaurant chain, where managers were recruited from the ranks of food preparers. As a result, customer service was noticeably deficient. In one restaurant, the head manager tended to stay in the kitchen, was generally unavailable to respond to the problems of servers, and chastised servers when they attempted to tell her the complaints of the customers, with whom she had virtually no interaction. The dining area was often disorganized, and as a result, servers fended for themselves instead of helping each other by restocking supplies and preparing seating areas. Customers often had to wait two hours to be seated, despite being able to see empty tables from the bar and waiting area, and another hour and a half for their meals after ordering them. Most of the best servers quit inside of three months out of frustration. The restaurant deservedly earned a bad reputation, and business was halved within a year of the opening owing to a lack of repeat customers.

• *High prevalence of confrontations between line managers and employees* (based on employee surveys). Businesses, as pointed out earlier, can be similar to dysfunctional families. Managers are often parental or authority figures, and employees are ready to take on managers when their problems with authority are unresolved. This indicator may also suggest the existence of an environment that tolerates confrontive behavior.

• *Shared value placed on product or service quality* (based on employee surveys). This indicator suggests the degree of esprit de corps among members of the work units.

Encouragement of Pathological Workplace Behaviors

Dysfunctional organizations have variously been described as "addictive," "neurotic," and "toxic." In their book *The Neurotic Organization,* Manfred Kets de Vries and Danny Miller describe five neurotic styles of organizational behavior: paranoid, compulsive, dramatic, depressive, and schizoid. The common threads that run through each type of dysfunction are mayhem inside the organization, behaviors that perpetuate the mayhem, delusionary thought that precipitates and rationalizes those behaviors, and resistance to individual efforts to correct the dysfunctional system. These patterns disrupt employees' work lives and bleed over to the lives of employees' families, too. In a behavioral risk management paradigm, these dysfunctions show up as measurable employee behavioral risks.

Another frame of reference for pathological workplace behavior is addiction, since at one time or another most of us have had to cope with the abnormal behaviors of a person addicted to alcohol, drugs, food, gambling, or other substance or activity. In a survey of 168 people in addictions recovery, Barbara Yoder asked respondents about the psychological or physical dependencies they have experienced. Interspersed throughout the twenty-item list of mood-altering and other ingestible substances were some surprises. "Codependency" was the second highest ranked dependency, behind alcohol. "Relationship dependency" was fifth, and "stress" and "worry" made honorable mentions. These four dependencies are easily transferred from home life to work life, especially in work environments that reward overachievers.

Another dependency endemic to work life, "workaholism," was ranked eleventh. Workaholism is an especially good avenue of inquiry when seeking information about addiction in work life. However, because denial is a hallmark of any addictive illness and because humans often see traits in others that they do not see in themselves, questions intended to measure this workplace behavior should be indirect. Therefore, managers could be questioned about workaholism by asking them for a subjective opinion about the workaholism they see in *other* managers. They can also be asked for objective information about how many hours in a week that they themselves work. It is likely that the findings will show a rate of workaholism far above the prevalence found in chemically dependent respondents in the Yoder study (32 percent), although somewhat less for nonmanagement employees.

All addictions have consequences, including workaholism. These consequences may take the form of stress-related and behavioral illnesses that manifest over time, confrontive workplace behavior, excessive absenteeism, failed marriages, and harmful effects on family life.

Employers should measure these objective and subjective indicators:

• *Prevalence of workaholism among employees* (based on employee and management surveys). This is the most straightforward measurement of organizational addiction but, owing to the element of denial, the problem is likely to be underacknowledged, so the following indicators are also useful.

• *The work organization encourages or rewards workaholism* (based on employee and management surveys). This is a way of making the same inquiry without directing it specifically at the respondent. For example, a survey question might ask, "Is working longer and taking on more job tasks the best way to 'get ahead' in your company?" or, "Do managers here routinely sacrifice personal and family interests to serve the company?"

• *A high proportion of employees who commonly work into the evening hours and weekends* (based on employee surveys). Some situations dictate that extended hours be worked over a time-limited period, but when extended work occurs indefinitely, the potential for behavioral risks is elevated.

• *A high proportion of managers who work ten or more hours a day in their efforts to "get ahead"* (based on management surveys). Working to excess often occurs during periods of organizational flux. This flux can lead to a systemic form of amnesia—forgetfulness or dim recollection about prior workplace practices—after which the practices that usurped the old practices during the period of flux become the new status quo.

• *Belief that the organization has a clear, achievable corporate mission and strategic plan* (based on employee and management surveys). Are the mission and strategic plan really achievable? Are they used to induce an unsustainable level of performance and commitment? One southern California company with 150 employees in the electronic components manufacturing industry set a defect-rate goal of .0003 percent, despite the fact that its current defect rate was 1 percent. This .0003 percent goal was impossible, given the company's current means of production. The fear that set in led to scuttlebutt throughout the company that downsizing and replacing employees with robots was planned, since that was the only way such a goal could be achieved. Both line managers and employees feared for their jobs. What followed was excessive brownnosing by both employees and line managers with their superiors in hopes of enhancing their own security, and cases of badly jangled nerves alleviated only by periodic emotional breakdowns.

In some cases, dysfunctional managers create crises and then coddle employees who can't cope with the new pressures. In this way, the senior managers who were responsible for creating the pressurized environment are the same ones to later come to the emotional rescue of those least able to survive in it. In so doing, the senior managers alternate playing good-cop/bad-cop roles. This is one way in which some managers seek to control subordinates and fulfill their unmet need for caring or dependency from others.

This indicator can also show whether there is poor internal communication, based on employee awareness of what the corporate mission and strategic plan are.

Dysfunctional Work Teams

Management gurus create the templates by which organizations periodically renew themselves. Renewal is the organizational equivalent of a generational change in a family, and the templates the modus operandi by which transition is made. Each template is temporized, cut differently than the one before it in order to suit the times. In this way, reengineering in the 1990s has replaced management by objectives in the 1970s.

The new templates provide guidance in two key areas: first, structure and operation and, second, people's interaction and behavior. Organizational development and quality improvement consultants, often the pied pipers of organizational renewal, typically devote at least 75 percent of their efforts to the first area. They often assume that whatever flag management decides to run up the pole, employees will enthusiastically salute.

The focus on behavior may occur, not out of design, but out of necessity, when interpersonal conflicts among the participants of the newly formed work teams occur and resistance to further change sets in. This often happens because the superior-subordinate dependency relationships that have long been a part of work units have been dismantled and replaced with more collegial coach-participant relationships, leading to confusion and perhaps even a sense of loss by employees. The work teams may also lack a model for solving problems.

Besides receiving training in the structural components of work teams, employees need to learn skills in intergroup and intragroup confrontation and to undertake individual and group sensitivity training. They need to dip their toes in the waters of work team operation, not just be thrown in. Team development consultant John Meyer says that behavioral training should be implemented *before* structural and operational changes begin, rather than after, which is the standard. Failure to do so significantly increases the probability of breakdowns after about a year and a half of teamwork.

> A traditional strategy to change focuses on the organizational structure only. The new manager or new CEO will automatically introduce new policies and practices that influence the way things are done at a particular plant or organization. New communication systems are established along with new reporting charts. New task performance appraisals are designed. The new manager brings on a flurry of changes that suggests movement and improvement. This is often referred to as the "honeymoon period" where all activities are perceptually quite interesting and satisfying. This period is also short-lived.

> As time passes, it is clear that the activities become more behaviorally oriented. It appears most changes become sabotaged at this critical point. It appears that there is a strong organizational resistance at the group behavioral level that impedes good-intentioned managers and executives in most organizations. Often, the manager is not prepared to deal with the strong resistance of the group dynamics in force at this point.

The following indicators assess whether work teams—self-directed, directly supervised by a manager, or otherwise managed—are failing to work.

- *Explanation of work team implementation* (based on management reports). A history of the implementation of the work team process, particularly with regard to implementing the structural components vis-à-vis the behavioral components, is essential background information.

- *Reports of interruptions in the implementation of the work team process* (based on employee surveys).
- *Amount of resistance to the work team process* (based on employee surveys). This finding should be compared with the previous indicator.
- *Emphasis on employee accountability* (based on employee surveys). The counterbalance to employee empowerment—which is part and parcel of work team concepts—is accountability. Without it, the potential for exploitation by employees increases.
- *Belief that the company has fair and democratic work team rules that are equitably applied* (based on employee surveys). Where there is no fairness, dissention will follow.
- *Work teams are able to resolve team disputes without interrupting production* (based on employee and management surveys). Problems can and do occur on work teams. The question is, Can they be effectively resolved without bringing production grinding to a halt?

Inattention to Workplace Safety

In many industrial workplaces, large yellow conspicuously placed placards keep tally of the number of accident-free days or hours and the number of mishaps. What lies behind the numbers? Safety engineers no doubt credit them to efforts in two areas: first, the enforced use of safety equipment such as goggles and respirators and the introduction of ergonomics to the workplace and, second, employees' increased job skills and safety awareness. The engineers are correct on both counts, but that is not the complete story behind the success of any truly accident-resistant organization.

As Figure 4.1 illustrates, a necessary third area of effort is *behavioral* safety, which in most companies is only starting to broach management awareness.

The objective and subjective indicators of behavioral safety include these:

- *OSHA or other rating of company or production-unit safety* (based on management reports). This and the following two indicators

Figure 4.1 Factors Responsible for Occupational Health and Safety.

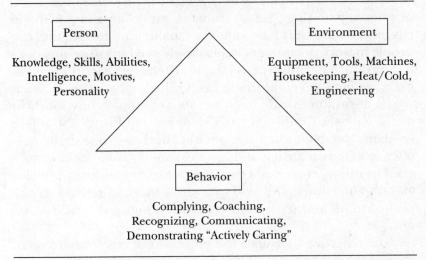

Person

Knowledge, Skills, Abilities,
Intelligence, Motives,
Personality

Environment

Equipment, Tools, Machines,
Housekeeping, Heat/Cold,
Engineering

Behavior

Complying, Coaching,
Recognizing, Communicating,
Demonstrating "Actively Caring"

Source: Geller, E. S. "Ten Principles for Achieving a Total Safety Culture." *Professional Safety,* 1994, *39*(9), p. 19. Reprinted by permission.

must be measured due to the prevailing attitude in many work organizations that safety precautions are a nuisance. The implication is that employees may be passive about safety risks. Objective data on actual safety experience are a counterbalance to that passivity.

• *Number and severity of accidents attributed to human error and number of near misses* (based on management reports).

• *Prevalence of employees exposed to hazardous substances* (based on OSHA or management reports).

• *Effectiveness of safety practices in adjacent departments* (based on management surveys). Here, as in the indicator of confrontive work behaviors, supervisors may be more forthcoming about problems in work units other than their own.

• *Employees' belief that they work at moderate or high physical risk* (based on employee surveys). Does the safety reality of a work environment live up to the safety perception? Perceptions about safety are as important as reality, especially with regard to the likelihood of future accidents and hazardous workplace exposures.

Continual Crisis Management

Continual crisis management suggests the presence of an organizational pathology. Just as humans, especially those living in city environments, can become "adrenalin junkies," so, too, can people in work organizations collectively need to create situations that produce excitement. As the biochemical reaction to crisis becomes familiar, comfortable, and relied upon to bring about spurts of productivity, it becomes sought after—consciously or unconsciously. Continual crisis management brings about that reaction. Notably, though, it does not affect everyone similarly. It often manifests as anxiety and even fear among non–decision makers. Over time, continual crises can deplete organisms (humans and organizations) and lead to confusion, productivity accomplished in fits and starts instead of continuously, and ineffectiveness.

The objective and subjective indicators of crisis management include these:

- *Prevalence of knee-jerk decision making by senior management* (based on manager and employee surveys). It is one thing to make efficient business decisions, another to make rushed ones that do not adequately anticipate problems and consider alternatives.
- *Belief that the organization routinely manages by crisis* (based on employee and manager surveys). In fairness to younger companies that are not yet financially established, I would point out that managing by crisis can be a necessary part of their growing pains, since new business—and its attendant work deadlines—must be taken wherever it can be found. However, companies whose short-term financial solvency is not in question should be able to avoid continual crises.
- *Routine habit of rushing through projects or other work tasks only to repeat them later* (based on employee and supervisor surveys). This is a ground-level manifestation of crisis management.
- *Lack of long-range organizational planning* (based on management surveys). An established company should have a long-range or strategic plan, just as it has an organizational mission, and should articulate it to the entire workforce.
- *High prevalence of on-the-job anxiety* (based on employee surveys).

Organizational Factors and Operational Data

Some additional business-related variables should be considered in the audit process. They are not *behavioral* per se but can alter the likelihood of behavioral risk exposures.

• *Ineffective job and work design.* This organizational factor is just as important as any single behavioral risk. If work is not designed effectively, if it does not add value to the work lives of employees, it is likely to lead to increased turnover, increased work defects, and other risk exposures. The following are examples of job and work design indicators that can be built into the employee survey:

Degree to which employees feel they have control over their work lives. A lack of control contributes to job stress that workers feel.

Degree to which job tasks are ergonomically sound. If a person's body does not conform to the job tasks required, there are accident, injury, and perhaps psychological risks.

Degree to which a balance is perceived between technological and human capabilities. Do employees feel that management has, first, seriously attempted to avoid displacing employees with technology and, second, done a good job in integrating technology and employees? This indicator will provide insights.

• *Top five major workplace developments within the last five years individually identified as favorable or unfavorable by employees, managers, and supervisors.* This indicator reveals any discrepancy between management and nonmanagement employees in their perceptions about the favorable or unfavorable impact of major organizational developments on the workforce. Developments such as the appointment of a new chief executive officer, the introduction of a new product line, or a merger or acquisition often have a seismic impact on operations throughout an organization.

• *Rate of work defects.* This indicator hinges on a variety of workplace factors, such as lack of job training, equipment glitches, and the implementation of new work processes, but it may also corroborate other data suggesting elevated behavioral risk.

• *Turnover.* This is a behavioral risk exposure for which there are myriad possible factors, many of which are unrelated to behavioral risk factors. For purposes of the audit, employers should segregate the following factors that precipitate turnover: downsizing, voluntary departure, involuntary departure (termination), and mutually agreed upon departure. The last two factors are more likely to be influenced by behavioral risks than the other factors. Employers need to determine an acceptable rate of turnover, then investigate to determine whether behavioral factors might be contributing to any excess.

• *Changes in corporate structure and turnover in senior management.* These are the most significant developments that occur in a company, and their consequences influence activities on all levels.

• *Use of preferred stock options and other compensation rewards to attract and retain employees.* Non-healthcare-related employee benefits have obvious positive benefits for a company. Often unrecognized, however, is the fact that they can lock a person into an organization when he or she cannot get the same generous level of benefits elsewhere. Consequently, benefits packages may inadvertently create a situation where *less* turnover occurs than is healthy. In those cases, behavioral risk exposures may be elevated.

Tailoring the Audit to Fit the Organization

The indicators just described are not necessarily the only ones available to an organization. Additional or replacement indicators may be used, depending on the organization and its internal processes. For example, income comparisons might be limited to income derived from salary or wages in one organization, while in another company it might be appropriate to include income from bonuses, deferred compensation, and profit-sharing payments. Workplace safety indicators should be based on the safety risks of a particular company. A laboratory, for example, might include the number of instances of mishandling flammable, explosive, or toxic materials. Work defects indicators will have different definitions of defects. In mechanical work, defects are usually easily concretely measured (in defective parts per thousand, for example). In companies where each new project is substantially different from the prior one, the definition of defect might be a missed deadline, revision, or low level of client satisfaction.

Organizational auditing instruments are available that measure organizational culture, assess workplace safety, look for organizational "hot spots," and so forth. They have similarities to the behavioral risk audit process but may have differing underlying premises.

How to Analyze Behavioral Risk Data

Once the information gathering for the behavioral risk audit is complete, it can be analyzed in myriad ways. In addition to determining behavioral risk cost exposures, as described in Chapter Three, the analysis can be structured for four particular purposes in the following ways:

• Determine numerical equivalents for subjective risk factors (derived from survey), each of which can be plotted longitudinally to detect emerging risks over time. For example, responses to the employee survey question about the level of stress at work can be assigned an overall rating. If there are five possible responses—"high," "increasing," "moderate," "decreasing," "low"—with high registering 1.0 and increasing .50 and the rest being discarded, the numerical values could be added together, then divided by the total number of respondents. If this overall score increases from one audit period to the next, the company should consider the wisdom of organizational changes that may have affected the finding.

• Use the same numerical equivalents to compare specific risk *factors* with actual behavioral risk *exposures* and thus to search for cause-and-effect relationships. The stress numerical equivalent can be compared with behavioral risk exposures for substance abuse treatment, supervisor-employee confrontations, and so on. For example, an employer could correlate

Perceptions of organizational rewards for workaholism with perceptions of stress arising out of a poor balance of work and family life—to reveal the degree to which work demands are affecting employees' family life

Claims data for substance abuse with claims data for medical healthcare conditions that relate highly with undiagnosed substance abuse problems—to determine whether many substance abuse problems are undiagnosed

Managers' perceptions about the quality of supervisory training with the number of supervisor-employee and employee-employee confrontations

Management reports about the utilization of preemployment testing with the occurrence of various employee behavioral risk exposures

Employee comments about recent negative workplace changes with the manifestation of various employee behavioral risks—to determine the impact of the changes

• Determine whether risks and risk exposures are confined to a particular part of the organization or are organizationwide. Localized problems are likely to be associated with one or a few people in authority positions, while organizationwide problems are likely to be systemic. This determination gives some contour to the problem, as though it had been plotted on a computer-generated topographic map.

• Aggregate findings for each behavioral risk. One way to make the analysis more efficient is to consolidate the findings. For example, findings from each of the six indicators for dysfunctional work teams can be added together for an overall score. This score can then be analyzed vis-à-vis data on behavioral risk exposures to identify any apparent cause-and-effect relationships.

Using Study Data to Index Behavioral Risks

Employee and organizational behavioral audits provide management with powerful information on which to make business decisions. The data can be used to construct an index of behavioral risk indicators, that is, a selection of audit findings that collectively serve as a barometer of behavioral risks and exposures in the company. Put into chart form, the indicators can be placed side-by-side with selected business factors. When business decisions are contemplated by senior management, behavioral risks and exposures can then be weighed vis-à-vis other business factors, such as the company's marketplace position, production capacity, return on investment, shareholder profits, public image, productivity disruptions, and so on.

Realistically, most business decisions are not clean and neat; they arise from political agendas. Some decisions are made with the knowledge that an advantage gained in one sphere of interest will have repercussions in others. Oftentimes, though, business decisions are made primarily on shareholder and management interests, not on employee factors. The behavioral risk audit rectifies that imbalance by putting the internal well-being of the organization into clearer focus.

Phrasing Survey Questions Without Antimanagement Bias

Surveys of employees and managers should not have an antimanagement bias. However, because the behavioral risk management audit process is tailored toward the identification and measurement of problems—including systemic problems that originate or are exacerbated by upper management—it may appear to have an antimanagement bias. To neutralize the potential for bias and to avoid inciting employee problems by the simple act of administering the survey, questions should be phrased in a balanced, nonpartisan way.

For example, if a question is intended to identify any perceived management "hostility toward" or "bias against" a racial minority, asking the question point-blank might invoke a skewed response that does not accurately reflect the person's attitude or belief. However, asking employees about management's "fairness" toward racial minorities, and offering a possible range of responses from "always" to "never," will diminish the potential for unintended consequences.

The real value of the behavioral risk outcomes data lies in the workplace solutions they generate. Just as the audit process analyzes the full spectrum of behavioral risks, the solutions—which include organizational culture development; programs and services; supportive benefits; policies and procedures; and management, work team, and employee training—should be holistically conceived.

For example, the audit process may reveal that the company should revise its policies (or address its lack of them) regarding employee mental health and consistently support the improved policies through organizational culture development, programs and services, benefits, and training. These solutions are interconnected in that innovations in one area boost the effectiveness of the other areas, just as a lack of attention to one area can partially offset the contribution of the others.

In Chapter Five, we move on to a discussion of these behavioral risk solutions, which make a workforce more competitive and productive.

Notes

P. 68, *Persons who are codependent:* Rigaud, J. Interview with author. "Is Codependency Treatment a Worthwhile Health Benefit Expense?" *Open Minds,* Apr. 1990.

P. 68, *dysfunctional organizational behavior was explained:* Wilson Schaef, A., and Fassel, D. *The Addictive Organization.* New York: HarperCollins, 1988.

P. 72, *ranking of the sole item addressing communication:* Kovach, K. A. "What Motivates Employees? Workers and Supervisors Give Different Answers." *Business Horizons,* 1987, *30*(5), 58–65.

P. 75, *surveys that revealed reasons why labor unions form:* Hughes, C. L. "Why Employees Stay Is More Critical Than Why They Leave." In *Making Unions Unnecessary* (2nd ed.). New York: Executive Enterprises, 1990.

P. 76, *"cybernetic system" that "steers itself":* Hampden-Turner, C. *Creating Corporate Culture: From Discord to Harmony.* Reading, Mass.: Addison-Wesley, 1990.

P. 84, *they perceive on-the-job substance abuse:* Schreier, J. W., and Pugliese, B. J. *Substance Abuse in Organizations 1971–1993: Changes, Management Issues and Policies.* Brookfield, Wis.: Far Cliffs Consulting, 1993, p. 84.

P. 85, *five neurotic styles of organizational behavior:* Kets de Vries, M.F.R., and Miller, D. *The Neurotic Organization: Diagnosing and Changing Counterproductive Styles of Management.* San Francisco: Jossey-Bass, 1984, pp. 24–25.

P. 86, *survey of 168 people in addictions recovery:* Yoder, B. *The Recovery Resource Book.* New York: Simon & Schuster, 1990, p. 6.

P. 89, *Team development consultant John Meyer says:* Meyer, J. "The Future Is Now, Disguised as Chaos." Unpublished paper, 1994.

Chapter Five

Determining the Right Strategy for Your Organization

Following completion of the behavioral risk audit process, a work organization has the information necessary to implement solutions. Behavioral interventions are geared toward three primary issues: behavior-related health problems, conduct, and work performance. (I use the term *work performance* rather than the more common *job performance* because changing employment relationships are antiquating the concept of the job in some situations, while work—the purpose for which jobs exist—will endure.)

Designing a behavioral risk management strategy requires an understanding of how and why behavioral problems manifest themselves in work organizations. Effective solutions to diminish risk exposures are ones that conform to the contours of the organization. There is no such thing as a "typical" company when it comes to diminishing behavioral risk, since even companies in the same industry can vary greatly in their methods of production or service delivery, reward systems, marketplace positioning, culture, and other organizational characteristics that can be risk factors. Therefore, behavioral risk management is not a template process.

Suppose a northern California timber harvesting company were to undergo a behavioral risk auditing process. This company of 750 employees is made up primarily of crews of loggers, each headed by a supervisor, who are dispatched to engage in clear-cutting operations. The crews typically work twelve-hour days for six or seven days a week over several weeks at a time, then they are off duty for a week. Two years ago, fearing price undercutting from lumber imported from Canada, the company started to demand 25 percent more productivity from each team. There were no changes in clear-cutting techniques, technology, or equipment to help ease the burden placed on the loggers. Pursuant to this edict, the company became concerned about increases in its workers' compensation liability, so it decided to audit its behavioral risks.

The audit, taken ten months following the modified productivity requirement, revealed that deep rifts had developed between managers and employees and among employees. Large discrepancies were found between management and employee responses to the surveys, especially with regard to the pace of work, stress level, resolution of team disputes, and management by crisis. Employees admitting to marital problems doubled from 6 to 12 percent. Absenteeism increased from 4 percent daily to 7 percent. Four turnovers more than might have been expected occurred the first year after the move to increase productivity and nine the second. Healthcare claims increased. Employee alcohol consumption and on-the-job drug use did, too. So did the occurrence of practical jokes, long a tension outlet for the crews, over which management had fought long and hard to gain control. Finally, after three consecutive years of freedom from serious worker injuries, four accidents occurred in a six-month period, primarily from falling trees and branches. Almost every objective and subjective indicator suggested internal strife.

Because adverse external business conditions precipitated this company's decision to increase productivity demands, at first employees were relieved that they were not laid off, but as they felt increasingly overburdened with work, they experienced anger and, later, despair. That physical and mental duress resulted in the elevated behavioral risk exposures. Had senior management taken some relatively inexpensive steps to prepare the organization and its employees for the new "get-tough" business strategy, however, it could have softened the decisions it made as a result of the external business conditions.

As a result of the audit, the company took steps to diminish its behavioral risk exposures and risk factors. First, it changed some of the behavioral norms in the work culture. Since in this macho work culture there was an unwritten rule of "every man for himself," communication between management and employees had been poor. The company encouraged the upward flow of communication by introducing formal meetings in each crew to discuss work issues and identify concerns to raise with management. The company also introduced a conflict-resolution process so that problems between employees and between employees and management would not fester. These steps helped management keep its ear to the ground and respond faster when adverse work conditions arose.

Second, employees were encouraged to avoid inappropriate workplace behaviors, especially playing practical jokes, showing up high or drunk, and circumventing safety rules. Two volunteer employees from each work crew were trained in behavioral safety, then assigned on a rotating basis to observe crews in order to suggest safety improvements.

Third, employees were given training on how to manage stress in their lives and engage in healthier off-the-job behaviors—such as better diets—that would enhance job performance and soften the pervasive we-they attitude that had developed at the company. Fourth, a confidential counseling resource was made available for employees, providing an outlet for employees who were the most susceptible to cracking under stress. Fifth, a ten-minute preshift stretching routine was implemented to prevent physical injury.

This example illustrates how interventions can be an investment of time, energy, and caring more than of money and how they can be selectively applied for specific problems. It is likely that such interventions would also diminish the company's behavioral risk costs.

Five Types of Interventions

Some benefits managers shy away from risk management solutions to employee (and family) problems out of a belief that the solutions would necessarily involve austerity measures, such as programmatic cutbacks. On the contrary, however, the behavioral risk audit can reveal the costs to companies when they *do nothing at all* or when their interventions are ineffective, just as a favorable cost offset by the involved parties demonstrates effectiveness. Certainly, this approach is consistent with the business priorities of most companies today.

Behavioral risk interventions are based on five distinct, but interlocking elements: programs and services; supportive benefits; policies and procedures; organizational interventions; and supervisor, work team, employee, executive, and board member training.

Large employers generally make use of these elements but do so in a disjointed fashion, resulting in intervention cacophony instead of harmony. For example, professionals and managers involved in delivery of different programs and services may work in different departments, have infrequent or no communication, and have no cross-referral of employees whatsoever. Each may also claim to be singlehandedly responsible for the same outcomes that the others claim responsibility for. Benefits may not be structured in the manner that best suits program and service delivery. Organizational development specialists may have no contact with program, service, or benefits staff, even though they strive to control many of the same behavioral risks.

Further, all involved in interventions may have a myopic view of how their tasks contribute to the overall performance of the organization and, consequently, miss opportunities to collaborate with other functions. This may lead to situations where corporate policies and procedures associated with some behavioral risk activities are not consistent with those that regulate other activities. Similarly, training activities administered to managers and employees for particular programs may not be integrated with performance management and other forms of training sanctioned by top management.

As each of the five behavioral risk elements is discussed, one of my primary objectives will be to illustrate ways it can become enmeshed in the fabric of the organization. The first two of the five elements—programs and services and supportive benefits—are discussed in this chapter. Chapter Six explores organizational culture development, behaviors, and other factors. Chapter Seven describes manager, employee, work team, executive and board member training. Chapter Eight addresses staffing issues, along with the policies and procedures that bind the elements of behavioral risk management strategy together. Once this foundation is set, Chapter Nine gives examples of behavioral risk management in action.

Before beginning the description of programs and services on the one hand and supportive benefits on the other, it will help to have a clear view of the differences between these two categories. Programs and services differ from benefits in these ways:

- They are organic spheres of activity inside of or sponsored by an organization, whereas benefits are inanimate passageways to those programs and services or various outside activities.
- They are intended to resolve specific organizational problems, including behavioral risk exposures of employees' family members, that incur a cost for the employer.
- They do not involve therapeutic or other counseling or other services specifically geared toward personal (as opposed to job-related) improvement, as benefits do.
- They do not require a copayment by the employee or family member for the basic program or service.
- They are not defined as a benefit under the Employee Retirement Income and Retirement Security Act.

In the behavioral risk management paradigm, employer-sponsored benefits serve first to facilitate the use and enhance the effectiveness of programs and services. This is distinct from the traditional perception that benefits confer entitlement on employees and often family members. So we should look at this concept more closely.

Newspaper classified job advertisements often contain the redundant passage "competitive salary and attractive benefits plan." This is code language for, "We intend to pay you only the median salary, at best, for someone with your qualifications, regardless of your ability. Therefore, we want to entice you with benefits, which may be more than you want or need, because they are a cheaper form of remuneration for us." Benefits are often packaged as alternative compensation, something to attract the best job candidates and lock in current employees. They include everything from healthcare coverage to a retirement plan to preferred stock to a company car.

This is how most employees think of benefits. In the present discussion, however, benefits have the meatier purpose of diminishing future behavioral risk. Like programs and services, they can be placed on a continuum running through prevention, early-stage intervention, and late-stage intervention. These benefits can include

- Access to and delivery of behavioral healthcare counseling and treatment
- Ongoing work-and-family benefits
- Ongoing wellness and health promotion activities
- Job perks that entice employees to stay with the company in situations where they might otherwise leave

These benefits generally take the form of healthcare; life insurance; a voucher or stipend for a particular service in the community such as day care, a health-promotion, or a life-management activity; or employer contributions to wealth-accrual plans such as pensions and other retirement accounts that employees would need to pay more for if they sought the service on their own. However, employer-sponsored basic assessment services that can indicate to employees whether they ought to access certain benefits, such as healthcare, are not benefits in and of themselves, unless they additionally provide activities, such as ongoing behavioral health counseling, that meet one of the benefit criteria.

Interspersed throughout the descriptions of behavioral risk programs and services that follow are explanations of the benefits that facilitate them.

Program and Service Interventions

Employers probably already have some programs and services that manage or control behavioral risk, although they may not be promoted to management and employees that way. They may tout themselves as "helping," "advocacy," "cost-containment," or even "policing" activities, but they all contribute to the same superordinate mission of managing or controlling behavioral risk. However, staff members of these programs and services may not have considered where they fit on a risk management continuum, and without this panoramic view, they may not be coordinated or structured in a way that most effectively serves the organization.

The program and service activities discussed in this chapter are listed in Table 5.1. They are grouped by the program or service that they are commonly identified with, and each is plotted for its position(s) on the prevention, early-stage intervention and late-stage intervention behavioral risk management continuum. Many activities apply to more than one level of intervention. For example, a health risk appraisal is preventive when it identifies a person's susceptibility to a behavioral risk exposure and it is early-stage intervention when it identifies a person who already has the onset of a problem but at the time of the appraisal was not aware of it. (Table 5.1 does not list administrative and promotional tasks associated with programs and services: for example, data management and newsletter publication and distribution.)

Since behavioral risk management defines success by minimizing the amount of risk exposure to the organization, the process begins with identification of individuals who pose elevated risk of productivity or financial loss to the organization. This may include, for instance, employees with a record of multiple accidents and health plan participants who excessively use healthcare benefits. Here are the several case-finding techniques.

Consultation with Management of Problem Employees

This is a coaching process in which a work-based problem assessment professional aids a supervisor in confronting an employee who is experiencing on-the-job problems. The consultation should instruct the supervisor how to present objective conduct and work performance evidence, avoid diagnosis of the problem, and resist efforts by the employee to divert the discussion.

Confrontive Techniques

Once high behavioral risk individuals have been identified, they may need to be persuaded to obtain help. This persuasion may be gentle or forceful. Following are two interventions, one for hierarchical and the other for team-based work environments.

Table 5.1 Behavioral Risk Management Activities for Individuals.

	Prevention	Early-Stage Intervention	Late-Stage Intervention
Case-finding interventions			
Consultation with management on problem employees		•	
Confrontive techniques			
Constructive confrontation		•	
Peer or team member confrontation		•	
Substance abuse testing activities			
Periodic	•	•	
Random	•	•	
Suspicion-of-use		•	•
Self-identification of problems		•	
Individual problem-related behavioral interventions			
Confidential problem assessments			
Work-focused employee problem assessments		•	
Clinical assessment of behavioral health problems		•	
Problem resolution		•	
Referral to treatment for a behavioral health problem		•	•
Preauthorization for behavioral healthcare		•	•
Utilization review and case management		•	•
Employee reintegration following treatment[a]	•	•	
Work-based follow up[a]	•	•	

[a]These activities are intended to prevent problem reoccurrence following an employee's return from behavioral healthcare and to allow early identification of adjustment problems that could jeopardize future behavioral health.

	Prevention	Early-Stage Intervention	Late-Stage Intervention
Behavioral health fitness-for-duty evaluation[b]	•	•	
Critical incident debriefing		•	
Conflict interventions			
Ombudsman		•	
Mediation		•	
Conflict resolution		•	
Binding arbitration		•	•
Stress reduction activities	•		
Life-style behavioral interventions			
Health risk appraisal	•	•	
Light-duty physical conditioning	•		
Self-help groups		•	•
Interventions to achieve balance between work and family			
Flexible work practices	•	•	
Dependent care information and referral	•	•	
Diversity interventions			
Awareness education	•		
Diversity-based mediation		•	•
Workers' compensation case management			
Routine checks on injured employee by work organization		•	
Psychiatric case management of injured workers		•	
Reintegration of employee to the workplace[c]	•	•	

[b]This activity is intended to prevent the reoccurrence of behavioral health problems that render an employee unfit for duty and to allow early identification of personal problems that could jeopardize the employee's future fitness for duty.

[c]These activities are intended to prevent problem reoccurrence following an employee's return from workers' compensation medical care and to allow early identification of adjustment problems that could jeopardize future behavioral health.

Constructive Confrontation

Managers are often ambivalent when it comes to intervening in the problems of employees. Consider, first, that people are usually promoted to line management because of long tenure and knowledge of production or service delivery. They are not usually trained in principles of human behavior and relationship building in a work setting. Second, most people are not confrontive by nature; they prefer to be supportive or to lead by example. Third, they may have personal relationships with subordinates in need of intervention. Therefore, most supervisors prefer a soft-sell approach to addressing employees and their problems.

Nevertheless, sooner or later almost all managers are faced with the unpleasant prospect of having to confront a subordinate about his or her subpar conduct or work performance. Sometimes the manager puts it off until the situation affects the manager's relationship with his or her superior. Managers should take solace, however, in the fact that they need only address workplace and job performance issues; they are not employees' personal problem solvers. In fact, misdiagnosing an employee's personal problem can expose the company to legal problems. This has happened many times when employees on doctor-prescribed medication were thought to be drinking, using illegal drugs, or carousing until late on weeknights, leading to a lack of alertness and inattentiveness at work.

The technique used to address the employee is constructive confrontation, which should be taught in supervisor training and reinforced during consultation with the work-based problem assessment professional. The goals of constructive confrontation are to confront the employee with objective evidence of the conduct or work performance problem, break through the employee's denial of the problem, and offer opportunities for assistance. (If there is an underlying behavioral health problem, it is the assessment professional's task to break through that second layer of denial.) Employees in denial are usually escape artists in the way they scapegoat co-workers, deflect attention to some other workplace issue, and try to turn the problem back on the supervisor. Constructive confrontation calls upon the supervisor to be even-tempered and deliberate and to repeatedly return to the facts of the situation when the employee uses evasive tactics.

The prospect of discipline may need to be raised with the problem employee, along with a recommendation that the employee use the assessment resource, but disciplinary action should not be conditioned on whether the employee actually uses the resource.

Peer or Team Member Confrontation

Peer pressure is often a more effective motivator than threat of job loss to induce a problem employee to accept help, and some labor unions apply it very effectively. Peer pressure and threat of job loss combined, though, constitute a particularly powerful tool. Think of the added impact it has when your union members or work peers tell you, "We have noticed that you haven't been pulling your load around here. You've been absent and late a lot, and when you are here, your head seems to be somewhere else. That puts an added burden on the rest of us. Additionally, you have been argumentative and hard to get along with. Besides, you've been disciplined a couple of times by management in the past, and you know we can only 'go to the mat' so many times before they will fire you anyway. Why don't you accept some help?" The same type of peer intervention can be employed on work teams because the message of "don't let down the team" can be just as powerful a motivator as "don't let down your union."

An added advantage of intervention by peers is that, once a person accepts help, confrontation quickly turns to social support. This is vital to the help-seeking process and, in the case of behavioral health problems, the recovery process.

Peers and team members can be trained to conduct these interventions. Constructive confrontation could be a part of job training for team leaders. Work-related confrontations with an individual need to be orchestrated if they are not to degenerate into shouting and finger-pointing sessions. A trained leader can focus on keeping the discussions on track.

Substance Abuse Testing

Employee drug testing hit the workplace during the late 1980s with nothing less than the force of a tidal wave. According to a study by the American Management Association (AMA) of its member companies, testing for drugs has increased from 21.5 percent of survey respondents in 1987 to 77.7 percent in 1995. At the same time, positive test rates have fallen from 8.1 percent in 1989 to 1.9 percent in 1994. The positive test rate is not a pure comparison, though, owing to the growth in surveillance types of testing—including periodic and random testing—relative to suspicion-of-use testing. The latter would yield a higher positive test rate. Therefore, the AMA says the lower rate cannot confirm an actual decline in drug-taking behavior, although the percentages are certainly suggestive.

As of January 1995, alcohol testing is now piggybacked on drug testing in the transportation industry, and that technique almost certainly will have a ripple effect through other industries. There is a fundamental difference between the two types of testing, though. Drug testing detects the simple presence or absence of an illegal substance. Some drugs are water-soluble while others are fat-soluble. A person testing positive for a fat-soluble drug such as marijuana—the most commonly used illegal drug—could test positive days or even weeks after the effect of the drug has worn off. Alcohol testing designates a threshold above which the person is assumed to be *intoxicated at the time a test is given.* From the employer's perspective, the alcohol-test standard is a truer measure of the likelihood that the ingested substance will have an effect on an employee's work conduct or performance.

There is also an inherent conflict in substance-abuse testing. In the work setting, a positive test result might be interpreted by management to mean that the individual is impaired, has a lower standard of conduct or work performance or poses a higher safety risk than other test takers, or needs rehabilitation. None of these may necessarily be true. Employers have to determine what adverse action needs to be taken against an employee testing positive. Only 22 percent of respondents dismiss positive test takers immediately, according to the AMA, which advises that actions regarding employee discipline be performance based. The subtext seems to be that a dismissal is warranted only if the employee has already had other disciplinary action taken against him or her. But if drug-taking behavior itself does not have a serious employment consequence, how can it be effectively deterred? Fully 64 percent of positive test takers are referred for counseling and treatment, according to the AMA study. But a positive drug test is not a measure of drug dependency or addiction. In fact, recreational users might consider rehabilitation to be frivolous once they enter treatment and see how hard-core addicts' problems are much greater than their own. (The hard-core users, incidentally, are usually craftier at evading getting caught during drug tests.) For all these reasons, an employer needs to define the company's purpose in drug testing, what the consequences of drug taking will be, whether disciplinary actions will take employee work history into account, and what legal risks there are to the disciplinary actions being considered.

Finally, employers should understand that substance use testing carries with it some extra paid helpers besides test administrators and lab analysts. Drug testing begun in 1989 in the transportation industry created the medical review officer (MRO) function, whose job is to analyze test results and investigate other circumstances that might lead to false-positive readings. Basically, the MRO is an employee safeguard against damaging reports due to such factors as inaccurate results or mishandling of samples. The breath alcohol technician (BAT) and substance abuse professional (SAP) are functions created by the transportation industry's new alcohol testing law. BAT-designated people are certified by the U.S. Department of Health and Human Services to administer breath alcohol tests, and SAP-designated people are certified to provide evaluations and referrals of positive test takers.

Self-Identification of Problems

Employees and family members who believe they may be experiencing personal problems should be encouraged to seek help. This can be done, first, by promoting awareness about how to contact assessment resources. Media include poster displays and paycheck inserts. Second, self-administered paper-and-pencil surveys can address such personal issues as emotional stability, self-esteem, work stress and personal-life stress. When an employee is having problems in multiple areas, the suggestion should be made that he or she seek an assessment resource.

Telling employees through several different media about self-identification of problems and help seeking reinforces early identification of problems. Additionally, promotional messages should include ones that destigmatize help seeking. One such poster says simply, "At one time or another, everybody needs help." Employees also need to know that the help-seeking process can identify not only personal behavioral problems but also work conflicts that may not be of an employee's making.

Behavioral Interventions for Individual Problems

Behavioral interventions for individual problems often are associated with employee assistance and managed behavioral healthcare. They include the following programs and services.

Confidential Problem Assessments

This service is one of the linchpins of behavioral risk management. Most work organizations are familiar with the programmatic term for the assessment process: *employee assistance.* However, employee assistance typically encompasses a wide variety of other tasks, including the development of provider networks, organizational consultation, and behavioral health benefits management. For this reason, I am using the term *assessment resource* (or *assessment professional*) in lieu of *employee assistance,* when the assessment task specifically is what I am discussing. (Interestingly, under the terms of a service contract with IBM that went into effect in 1995, Medco Behavioral Care Corporation—a large national service delivery firm—is providing in-person assessment services and brief counseling under the name "assessment, counseling and referral" [ACR] instead of "employee assistance.")

Problem assessments have two foci: workplace issues and personal or clinical issues. Accordingly, this intervention is split into two subtasks.

Work-Focused Employee Problem Assessment

This subtask is oriented toward keeping employees fit for duty, whether the workplace issues are the primary problem or only a contributing factor. Referrals to the professional performing the problem assessment may take the form of a supervisor's referral, an employee's self-referral, or if the issue was first addressed as a personal or clinical problem, a cross-referral from the professional doing a clinical assessment. Supervisory referrals may be used in conjunction with the disciplinary process for employees who are exhibiting conduct problems or not performing at an acceptable level.

There are several pivotal issues to consider in work-focused assessments. In order to ensure effectiveness, it is essential that the assessment professional be knowledgeable about the industry, company operation and quality of employee relations, and other factors that could impact on behavioral risks. This function is typically performed by employee assistance programs (EAPs). However, EAPs are increasingly outsourced, and when they are not present at the work site, the likelihood of management referrals is diminished. This is born of the fact that in our social relationships, we are more likely to initiate contact with someone we have met before, face to face, than with someone we have never met. An external work-based problem assessment resource has to overcome this hurdle and that can only be accomplished through ambitious program promotion. This hurdle is an even greater obstacle when a case involves sensitive work issues that must be handled discretely. In these cases, managers usually like to be very familiar with the person upon whom they are relying.

The work-focused assessment process also monitors patterns of problem occurrence and severity. These patterns provide evidence of organizational dysfunction and indicate whether the dysfunction is highly localized, confined to a particular site, or organizationwide. You will recall that the employee behavioral risk audit process can detect the same problems. Unlike the audit process, though, which takes a "snapshot" at the time of the audit, continual problem assessment can detect problems as they occur.

Employees should be encouraged to self-refer for both work-based and personal problems, since there may be an interrelationship between the two that can be detected by a comprehensive assessment. For example, one female employee was simultaneously coping with three problems: failure to complete work assignments in a timely fashion, for which she received a warning from her supervisor; disputes with her husband, which were becoming more frequent; and legal and financial problems due to an auto accident that was deemed to be her fault. At the time of her problem assessment, she was very confused and felt that the "walls were closing in" around her. At her interview, though, the disputes with her husband were found to predate the other problems. Therefore, she was referred out for marital counseling, which set her back on the road to stability. As often as not, a precipitating problem is work related, but the psychological burden that a troubled person shoulders makes it difficult for him or her to trace multiple problems back to the initial problem.

Confidentiality is a critical element for building trust in the assessment resource. Therefore, if information derived from assessments is used to inform management about elevated behavioral risk in a particular part of the organization—such as multiple self-referrals from a particular department in a brief period of time—the information must be passed along in a way that does not jeopardize the confidentiality of individuals. Breaches of confidentiality can lead to emotionally charged reprisals and legal problems.

Clinical Assessment of Behavioral Health Problems

This subtask assesses the personal problems of employees and family members. Assessment professionals seek to identify mental health, family, substance abuse, and other severe life problems for employees and family members, problems that may require ongoing counseling or outside referral. This assessment does not particularly address workplace issues and therefore does not require extensive knowledge about the work organization. However any assessment of a person's functioning should inquire about his or her work life.

It is often the case that behavioral health counseling or treatment is indicated by the assessment. Increasingly, EAP and managed behavioral healthcare service providers are asked to provide ongoing counseling, too. Employers' most common rationale for this is that they do not want employees and family members to be inconvenienced by having to explain their personal problems to multiple professionals. Nevertheless, this practice crosses the demarcation between a workplace service and a benefit.

The commonly accepted standard for distinguishing between problem assessment and mental health counseling is that one to three sessions constitutes the former; four or more sessions, the latter. Another standard has been established by the Employee Income Security and Retirement Act (ERISA), which is enforced by the U.S. Department of Labor. ERISA, which specifies the components of a "defined health benefit plan" for self-insured employers, emphasizes the assessment or counseling professional's qualifications for delivering EAP services. Companies whose assistance or counseling services qualify as benefits plans are subject to taxation and compliance with federal regulations (see Chapter Twelve, on legal issues).

Employers need to consider whether to perform both personal and workplace problem assessments in person or on the telephone. Employers have been leaning toward the latter method, but working by telephone creates a problem for any assessor who has a client in a state of denial or feeling ashamed of a problem. As John Barthes has said, "What I hide by language, my body utters." This insight is supported by abundant research demonstrating that at least 60 percent of meaning in a social context is communicated nonverbally. For this reason, the potential for a faulty or incomplete assessment increases dramatically when the assessment occurs via telephone. The driving issue behind telephone assessments, though, is simple: they cost less, at least initially. When primary behavioral health problems go undiagnosed, though, the potential for secondary behavioral risks increases dramatically and results in higher costs later.

Problem Resolution

If an employee has a basic workplace or personal problem that has a straightforward solution and shows no pattern of recurrence or pathology, it is usually handled by the assessment professional without outside referral. The professional summons the resources of the workplace (including other work-based programs and services, for which a cross-referral would be made, with the employee's approval), free or self-help resources, and his or her own problem-solving skills.

Referral to Behavioral Health Treatment

When an employee's mental health or substance abuse problem is beyond the ability of the individual to control without the aid of counseling or treatment, the assessment professional will make a referral based on the most cost-effective resources in the community. Included in the cost-effectiveness equation is the appropriateness of care for the individual based on psychological and social factors. For example, a drug-addicted individual who has a physically abusive parent should be rehabilitated in a safe environment away from home.

Preauthorization for Behavioral Healthcare

Referral to counseling or treatment typically requires access to the employer's benefit plan. Because many employers have been alarmed at the cost escalation of behavioral healthcare (which in recent years has been greater than the cost escalation of medical healthcare, which in turn has been greater than the general inflation rate), most managed health plans have implemented a preauthorization requirement so that the plan can verify the individual's qualification for benefits and assign an appropriate level of care.

These preauthorizations for care are usually handled by telephone, a method that can invite abuse by utilization review or managed care firms that are under pressure to contain costs or that have cost-containment incentives in their contracts. There have been reported instances of denial of care in spite of clinical indicators of its necessity. For example, one teenager who was covered under her father's health benefit plan from work was dually diagnosed with chemical dependency and depression. She was also thought to be suicidal. The managed behavioral healthcare provider, a subcontractor to a health maintenance organization, authorized seven days of residential chemical dependency treatment. When she was not stable enough for discharge after that time, the treatment provider requested that she be approved or transferred for acute psychiatric treatment. The managed care provider declined. While it appealed that decision, the treatment provider awarded her a "scholarship," which for all intents and purposes is free treatment. During the several-day wait for the appeal decision, she attempted suicide, trying to slash her wrists with a paper clip and other objects in her room, but was unsuccessful because none were sharp enough. When the treatment provider's psychiatrist consulted with the managed care psychiatrist, the latter continued to deny treatment, deeming her behavior a "weak" suicide attempt. The case then went to a second appeals level where, after more contentious argument before a review panel and the threat of a lawsuit by the treatment provider and the patient's family, payment for a continuing stay was finally approved. By that point, however, her mental health has deteriorated to the point where she required a total of sixty days of inpatient care at a cost of $42,000, instead of what might have been only thirty days at a cost of $15,000.

Most employers do not want their workers hassled in this way. Therefore, they should ensure that any service provider with whom they contract to perform preauthorization is reputable and has not been cited for violations of public policy—such as state utilization review laws—or involved in lawsuits alleging inappropriate denial of care.

It should be understood, though, that the current niggardly preauthorization and continuing-stay practices arose out of the total lack of benefits management when healthcare costs escalated during the 1970s and early 1980s. At that time, the lack of checks and balances almost *invited* exploitation by both employees and behavioral health treatment facilities. Before one major U.S. aerospace company implemented EAP-driven preauthorization several years ago, its audit of benefits records found numerous cases of employees who received between five and fifteen episodes of inpatient substance abuse treatment. Each episode provided twenty-eight days of treatment at mostly company expense, during which time the employee was also off the job. The EAP staff felt that employees conveniently relapsed every time they wanted some time off work.

Utilization Review and Case Management

Utilization review and case management are tasks in the authorization process for continuing care once an employee or family member has entered the behavioral healthcare system. Utilization review is a system that keeps tabs on what the patient's position and progress are in the treatment delivery system. Case management is ongoing clinical monitoring, and as the case example just given shows, it can also affect the availability of treatment.

Employee Reintegration Following Treatment

This is a highly personalized task traditionally performed by EAPs. Reintegration usually consists of one or more meetings between a supervisor, an employee, and an EAP staff member following the employee's treatment for a behavioral illness. This often under-performed, underappreciated task helps the employee reacclima-tize to the work environment, establishes expectations about the employee's return to productivity, and starts to rebuild damaged work relationships.

One female employee, for example, returned to her place of employment, a software-development firm, while recovering from manic-depression. Before treatment, she had foiled several work assignments by unexcused absences and disruptive behaviors that included intermittent bouts of exhilaration and crying, resulting in missed deadlines and defective products. Despite seven previ-ous years of service to the company, her immediate supervisor had begun to question whether she was ever that productive in the first place. Meanwhile, her co-workers agreed that she was "damaged goods" and feared that she would try to reopen old psychological wounds with them. The reintegration process was extremely help-ful to her because it established concrete expectations and opened up communication with her supervisor. As a result, she found the courage to be more forthcoming with co-workers about the prob-lems she experienced and to invite them to help her in her process of recovery.

Reintegration is simple; yet it is also tedious because it involves getting the supervisor and employee to agree upon an agenda, time, and location for a meeting. However, it does minimize the probability of relapse. Therefore, employers should establish a pol-icy that at least one reintegration meeting be held for any treat-ment episode involving at least one week of lost time.

Work-Based Follow-Up

A recovering employee reentering the workplace simultaneously fights two uphill battles: to make a successful return to full pro-ductivity and reclamation among his work colleagues and to con-tinue to improve in behavioral health. Rates of relapse can be high for recovering alcoholics and substance abusers. Typical rates are

35 percent in the first twelve months for adults and 45 percent for adolescents. Given the negative influences in the lives of many people with behavioral health problems, follow-up is necessary to prevent the loss of an expensive employer investment, which for one inpatient episode averages 19.9 days and costs $7,676. Follow-up goes hand in hand with aftercare, a therapeutic intervention usually performed by a treatment provider to help the former patient return to normal living. (Aftercare is described in the benefits section later in this chapter).

One specific kind of valuable follow-up is critical incident debriefing. Most people cannot shake the lingering aftereffects of a traumatic event by simply deciding to "get over it." This is true for Vietnam veterans, sexual abuse survivors, people who survive devastating earthquakes, retail businesspeople whose stores are looted during a riot, witnesses to a homicide at work, and others. Companies cannot afford to ignore these occurrences and their repercussions because the natural human reaction to them is to harbor anger about having been exposed to them, anger that can later be misdirected at others, including employers and co-workers.

Following the October 17, 1989, earthquake in the San Francisco Bay Area, for example, employer responses ranged from attempting to restore business as usual to providing inexpensive critical incident debriefing sessions for groups of employees. Such debriefings enable people to "ventilate" their feelings to a mental health professional and to co-workers while the professional assesses whether any of the group members experienced serious psychological disturbance, for which a further therapeutic intervention might be necessary. Therapists have noted that months after the San Francisco earthquake had occurred and the jitteriness immediately following the event had subsided, many employees were being very disagreeable to each other, missing work more often than before the event, and suffering more physical health and stress-related problems than would ordinarily have been the case. Normalcy was still not restored. Companies should assess their risk of exposure to critical incidents and plan accordingly.

Behavioral Health Benefits

In order for individuals to be referred outside of the work system for behavioral healthcare, benefits are needed. Among employees, this is necessary not only for the resolution of personal problems but for restoration of work performance as well. Companies should consider a health plan that is comprehensive, requires copayments, and has managed care features, including preauthorization. It should not have excessively low annual and lifetime payment caps, as that could cut off necessary care in extreme cases despite the presence of medical necessity. Copayments help to ensure that benefits are not exploited because the beneficiary gets a little "pinch" each time he or she accesses the healthcare system. Deductibles help to depress unnecessary utilization, but high deductibles or ones that are applied to each family member instead of the family as a whole may discourage them from receiving healthcare even when it is highly advisable.

It has become a common practice for workplace functions that perform behavioral interventions to manage the behavioral health benefits also. As described above, employers need to be sure that managed behavioral healthcare and EAPs balance quality service delivery with cost containment. Cost control is the overriding objective of many programs but, when they are stingy in granting approvals for care, they act more as an antibenefit than benefit, by restricting access, type of care, duration of care, and choice of medical professionals. As in choosing assessment services, a company should not necessarily assign management of the benefit to the lowest bidder. It should choose the one that is willing to have its performance evaluated based on beneficiary satisfaction surveys as well as utilization rates and other performance measures.

Behavioral health benefits—or as they are still often called, mental health benefits—sometimes are given short shrift in benefits packages, with a separate set of deductibles and expenditure caps that result in less generous benefits than for medical care. In a risk management paradigm, though, these benefits are vital. The emergence of multiple models of treatment for mental health and substance abuse treatment has flattened the cost for an average treatment episode over the last ten years. Now, instead of one-size-fits-all models of care (like the now-obsolete twenty-eight-day inpatient, substance abuse model that was the standard for years), variegated levels of care include residential, intensive outpatient, short-term outpatient, and structured outpatient programs; day treatment, foster care, and group therapy. Some benefit plans, instead of relying only on conventional treatments, also include "alternative" care, such as wilderness programs and gestalt treatment that combines empowerment with self-defense for sexual- and domestic-abuse victims. Employers should provide coverage for addiction in its various forms, including eating disorders, sexual addiction, and, if the work site is located within driving distance of casinos, gambling addiction.

Although primary treatment of a behavioral disorder is the largest investment in the treatment of a plan participant, any benefit plan should make provision for a strong aftercare program. Aftercare is essential to ensure that the patient does not suffer a relapse, decline in social functioning (which can then lead to relapse or other behavioral health problems), or other loss. Here is an example that illustrates the importance of aftercare. An adolescent female receives treatment for a chemical dependency problem. According to data from Caron Foundation, a treatment provider, there is a 30 percent probability that she has also been a victim of sexual abuse, a 64 percent probability of physical abuse, a 15 percent probability of a learning disability, a 27 percent probability of an eating disorder, and a 27 percent probability of a psychiatric disorder. Also, about one-quarter of female adolescent addiction patients have suicide ideation. Once she returns from chemical dependency treatment, it is against long odds that she will remain chemical free.

There are now a variety of benefits schema for delivering behavioral healthcare.

• Health maintenance organizations, or HMOs, are closed systems of care that control both supply and demand of healthcare. Patients and employers receive a specified range of benefits for a set charge. In an HMO, the treatment professionals may be employees of (and the facilities may be owned by) the HMO, or else have exclusive treatment-delivery agreements in which they agree with the HMO to provide specified services for a flat charge, regardless of the volume of patients or the severity of their illnesses. A gatekeeper, typically a primary care physician, is used by the HMO to direct patients to other HMO medical staff or to outside providers who contract with the HMO.

This model of care is oriented toward preventive health and, consequently, often imposes greater restrictions on behavioral health benefits than other types of coverages. An abundance of anecdotal evidence suggests that many HMOs are inadequate in dealing with serious behavioral health problems. For this reason, some companies offer employees indemnity plans as well, or even have a "slush fund" available that an EAP may use when the HMO will not approve intensive levels of behavioral healthcare.

• Preferred provider organizations, or PPOs, are integrated intermediary healthcare delivery systems comprising selected providers who have agreed to a set of care-delivery and financial preconditions in exchange for patient referrals. They often specialize in a certain type of care, such as behavioral health. PPOs contract with employers, insurance carriers, or third-party administrators.

• Point-of-service plans, or POSs, are like PPOs except that they utilize a gatekeeper, who may refer patients inside or out of the healthcare delivery system. Typically, referrals outside of the network for specialized care are permitted but at a reasonable financial penalty, such as a separate deductible and increased copayments.

• Indemnity plans are traditional insurance plans in which providers give patient care on a fee-for-service basis. In such a system, there may be no controls over the plan participant's access to care nor over provider's delivery of care. Unmanaged indemnity plans are considered by most to be a vestige of the insurance and healthcare delivery system that led to runaway healthcare inflation in the 1970s and 1980s.

• Integrated behavioral healthcare delivery systems integrate behavioral healthcare delivery and managed care components. This emerging model is the result of extensive consolidation in the marketplace during the early 1990s.

• Employer-provided behavioral health treatment is offered in some large companies. They may administer behavioral health treatment or provide counseling up to a certain number of sessions—typically eight to twelve—before referring the person to outside resources. The counseling may be provided by internal behavioral health professionals or an external service provider that also provides such workplace-based services as employee assistance. This model is subject to compliance with U.S. Department of

Labor rules as a "defined benefit plan," however, which has financial and reporting implications that are discussed later.

Many employers find the distinctions between the various plans and their alternatives confusing. Sometimes, they do not understand what they are getting until they are actually in business with the healthcare delivery system and subject to its machinations. Regardless of the type of plan selected, however, employers need to be sure about certain conditions before they sign on the dotted line of any behavioral healthcare delivery contract. From the standpoint of diminishing behavioral risk among employees, employers should seek assurances that

- Plan participants will receive personalized care that takes into account socioeconomic variables such as ethnicity, age, and gender.
- The patient invests in the treatment, too, through deductibles and copayments, for example, and has a financial stake in his or her own recovery.
- The treatment plan takes into account the patient's work circumstances.
- Specialized care outside of the established provider network is available.
- Aftercare is provided where appropriate.

Conflict Interventions

Interpersonal and conduct problems at work are an everyday occurrence in work organizations and can be the source of disruptions in productivity. This is little wonder, when one considers that many employees spend almost as much time with co-workers as with their spouses. The difference is that marriage partners choose each other while employees who work side by side have been grouped together by the employer, an arranged marriage, of sorts. Additionally, co-workers must comply with a code of behavior that often tightly regulates their actions, while couples in a household setting are freer to roam and "be themselves."

Consider Carol and Bill, two meat packers. Carol and Bill had differing religious beliefs, she was usually quiet and reserved while he was loud and outgoing, she was serious while he was jovial, and she was meticulous about her packing techniques while he liked to cram the boxes and "make things fit." When they had conversations, they often ended with her either becoming reticent or nitpicking while he made insulting references about her to other workers. Their co-workers said that if Carol saw black, Bill saw white. Their work relationship was difficult from the start and then deteriorated further over several months. Finally, on one day when tensions between them were high, Carol commented to Bill that he should "stop packing boxes like he was laying bricks," to which he responded that she should stop acting like an "ice queen." She walked off the job, which disrupted production for the rest of the day and put the entire plant in a somber mood. Carol was terminated, while management gave Bill a written warning and placed it in his personnel file. About half the employees, especially the females, thought that Carol had been dealt with unfairly, which created divisiveness throughout the plant for several weeks. In fact, Carol felt that management, which usually took a hands-off approach to employee problems on the plant floor with the expectation that they would work themselves out, was unresponsive and had no recourse.

Companies that give employees a lot of latitude to make decisions and solve problems need to be aware of the increased potential for disagreements such as this. An authority figure in a traditional work environment might impose a form of final and decisive "management justice" without regard to whether the outcome was right or wrong, or a union steward might be the means of resolving the problem. However, now that managements are becoming less autocratic and union representation in work organizations has significantly dropped, employers need to make accommodations for swift, fair, and effective resolution of problems that occur between people, teams, and management.

There are five primary ways of resolving workplace conflicts: through an ombudsman, mediation, dispute resolution, arbitration, and litigation. The first four give the decision-making authority to the disputants, the work organization, or perhaps a labor union, while litigation removes the authority from the work environment and puts it in the hands of the judicial system. Litigation is the "risk exposure" that employers struggle to prevent.

Ombudsman

Management must be continually sensitive to employee problems and concerns so that working conditions do not become intolerable. Organized labor has traditionally accomplished this through shop stewards, who took the roles of complaint handler and grievance officer. In the latter role, the shop steward heard, through "due process," claims of violation of a worker's rights by the employer, and the matter was settled by binding arbitration. Since the 1950s, though, as unionization of employees has dropped from 35 percent of the U.S. workforce to about 15 percent today, the use of grievance procedures has diminished.

The role of an ombudsman is to bring problems and concerns to the attention of management in order to settle them informally. In this respect, an ombudsman is usually an employee advocate. For example, an employee in a large research firm felt that an inordinate amount of work fell on his shoulders, forcing him to work consecutive weekends to complete projects, spend long hours in front of a CPT computer terminal that emits radiation, miss family events, and so forth. At times, other employees worked under the same conditions, but in his view, they jeopardized their physical and emotional health. He approached the division manager, who was sympathetic about the situation but offered no recourse. Without an ombudsman or other resource designated to buffer employees against potentially dangerous working conditions, he had no true options to prevent more serious problems. Many organizational behavior experts believe that the absence of a grievance officer to buffer employees from exploitive management dictates has left a void that has contributed to the escalating violence in U.S. workplaces.

One note of caution, though. On the one hand, the ombudsman's role should be kept separate and distinct from the problem-assessment process. A problem assessment professional must take a position of neutrality and must be free to make objective judgments about an employee's behavioral issues without being drawn into complaint or grievance issues. On the other hand, the two functions complement each other. Referrals can be made from the assessment resource to the ombudsman when employees have complaints about the company, and the ombudsman can refer employees to the assessment resource when there is evidence of a behavioral health problem.

Mediation

Mediation is the first of three neutrality-based nonadversarial methods of resolving workplace conflicts among employees, work teams, and managers. These three—mediation, conflict resolution, and arbitration—are sometimes called "alternative dispute resolution," being an alternative to litigation, where the disputants are adversaries with the option of negotiated settlement no longer available.

Mediation is the least invasive process and least likely to leave in its wake anger, tarnished relationships, and thoughts of retaliation that could result in renewed conflicts later. This nonconfrontive informal means of resolving disagreements between people has a successful track record in settling marital and family disputes, such as child custody and support and joint property distribution. Businesses are discovering it as an early-stage intervention for resolving such legally charged matters as employee accommodation under the Americans with Disabilities Act and management actions that culminate in a wrongful-retention or -discharge lawsuit. Businesses also use mediation as a means of heading off nonlegal behavioral risk exposures: for example, when interpersonal conflicts and inequitable decision making on work teams result in poor morale, sabotage, excessive absenteeism, and other problems.

Organizational and business mediator Edward P. Hanna cites these advantages of mediation over litigation:

It is a creative process that assists both parties in reaching a fair and workable agreement. What is "fair" is decided by both parties equally.

Cooperatively reached agreements have significantly higher rates of compliance and allow for continuation of relationships.

The process of mediation teaches both parties effective and positive goal-based communication skills for future negotiations.

Mediation is confidential and protects parties from public exposure.

Mediation is inexpensive and cost effective compared to litigation.

If the mediation process does not produce a final agreement, all other dispute resolution alternatives remain available to both parties.

The mediating entity can take several forms. In 97 percent of all cases, it is a single, or "solo," mediator. This person may be a designated internal or external mediator who has the expressed trust and support of both management and employees. Another mediating entity is the team with an odd number of appointees from within the organization, outside it, or both, chosen to resolve work conflicts. In the tier, or escalating, approach, the first step uses one mediator. Failing a resolution, another mediator joins the process. Failing resolution, a third mediator joins the group. According to mediation expert Walter A. Maggiolo, the tier approach has been found effective because of the infusion of a "new face and perhaps new suggested alternatives." For most work situations, a solo mediator is sufficient.

Mediation in work environments enables the parties in dispute—managers, employees, and work teams—to use a person trained in effective listening and impartiality to help them reach a *mutually agreeable solution* to a problem. In other words, the mediator provides an opportunity for the disputants to air their views, recites back to them his or her understanding of the facts, shares additional information germane to the problem at hand, and suggests possible courses of action.

In work teams, the team leader, as part of his or her training, can learn cursory mediation skills and then capably and impartially lead team decision-making meetings. The leader would not be practicing mediation, *per se,* but would be borrowing from that skill set in order to maximize the number of daily work situations that are routinely settled.

Conflict Resolution

Conflict resolution is similar to mediation but differs in a couple of key ways. First, it removes the decision-making process from the disagreeing parties and gives it to an impartial third-party listener.

However, the decision of the conflict-resolution specialist (in most cases, a mediator) is not necessarily binding; he or she renders an opinion and explains that opinion.

Often, a process that starts as mediation *becomes* conflict resolution. For example, if a mediation results in a stalemate, but the disputants have become comfortable with the mediator, they may ask him or her to make a decision for them. However, the mediator's "call" will not necessarily be accepted by both parties as a binding decision, since a strong possibility exists that one of the disputants will be dissatisfied with the decision. If the dispute is of a work-related nature, however, a speedy resolution is of utmost importance when production or service delivery slows or ceases pending a decision. Senior management may wish to establish a policy that makes the conflict-resolution activity binding, in order to get on with the press of business.

Second, in the work setting, conflict resolution's primary goal is not so much to settle the immediate dispute as to teach people how to solve problems creatively, which also involves teaching them how to communicate their views clearly. This ability is paramount because issues needing resolution occur day in and day out at work. When problems are resolved but the disputants are not given problem-resolution skills, old disagreements recycle. It is common knowledge among conflict-resolution specialists, for instance, that 70 to 80 percent of all equal employment opportunity filings are by repeat complainants.

Conflict-resolution activities may involve an entire work unit or even multiple units. Conflicts this large typically come to the attention of top management or the human resource department, either of which may initiate the intervention. The problem may involve a team, for example, that is angry with the department manager and an adjacent work team and whose members are squabbling among themselves about who is responsible for what problems and what the solutions are. The more chaotic the situation, the less likely a result that pleases everyone. The objective is to resolve the problem in a manner that leaves some sense of satisfaction among the participants *that the process worked* even if the solution was not favorable to some of them. A favorable view of the process lessens the chance that residual animosity will create other problems later.

Employers are advised to keep in mind that all conflicts cannot be prevented. As one team-training company has found, "One thing is for sure—where there is a team there is bound to be conflict. It cannot be avoided." Problems can take the form of conflict between individual team members, one person's conflict with the rest of the team, the team's conflict with one team member, conflict between several members, conflict between teams, and team conflict with someone outside of the team.

Furthermore, some conflict enhances people's productivity. In organic work environments such as academic and research circles it is often the norm that one person can challenge another person's ideas. This challenge can elicit high levels of creativity and push people to new heights. So while people must accept times when they "agree to disagree," those disagreements should be about thoughts and ideas, not individuals. Where an exchange of different ideas turns to personal attacks, insensitivity, injudicious language, or the blackballing of certain individuals, breakdown is sure to follow. In these cases, of course, provision should be made to call in a third party to settle the conflicts.

A variation of this conflict-resolution model can be applied in companies that contract professional, technical, and support services from a temporary services firm. In this case, the individual(s) deciding disputes should be mutually appointed by the company and the temporary services firm.

Binding Arbitration

This technique is usually spelled out in the language of collective-bargaining contracts since arbitration is most prominently used in unionized work settings. Binding arbitration is likely to be a more formal process than mediation and conflict resolution, with arguments and cross-questioning, and depending on the terms of the arbitration, the arbitrator may have to make an up-or-down decision with no room for compromise. If that is the case, however, there should still be an opportunity to use mediation to resolve the dispute as long as a binding decision is yet to be made.

While mediation may be desirable for resolving issues with strong legal overtones, in order to prevent the filing of lawsuits, employers are likely to consider protracted mediations too inefficient to resolve everyday problems between employees. Therefore, a swifter conflict-resolution process whose terms are binding—after nonbinding approaches have not worked—is preferable for most work situations.

Stress Reduction Interventions

Although the two sets of behavioral risk management strategies just described—interventions for individual problems and conflict interventions—are very effective early-stage interventions and can prevent much more costly risk exposures, they do not constitute primary prevention of behavioral problems.

The culprit behind so much that goes wrong with work organizations is elevated stress. Stress in the human ecological system is like heat in the natural environment; it leads people to feel uncomfortable, have shorter tempers, and dwell on insignificant issues that otherwise would roll right off their backs. It can cause workplace conflict as well as emotional and physical illness.

There are three primary ways for employers to combat stress: first, help employees to handle workplace stressors with equanimity (discussed in this section); second, reduce stress (discussed elsewhere in this chapter); and, third, abate stress in the work organization (discussed in Chapter Six).

With regard to the first approach, consider the aphoristic statement "To have a stress-free day, take a night job." The underlying thought is that stress always exists at work, and the best way to handle it is to learn to cope with it instead of trying to avoid it. Stress is a *reaction* to environmental factors, so a portion of stress can be eliminated by helping people to react differently to situations that provoke the stress response. For example, employees can be taught to avoid "replaying the same tapes," as a clinician might say, when they encounter a situation that produces their reflexive stress response. This is primarily an educational issue. Employees might be taught, for instance, about the biomechanics of the stress response, given suggestions about how to behave and think differently when familiar stress-producing situations arise, and shown how to simplify their lives while setting realistic career goals. (Stress management education for employees often takes the brown-bag lunch format. This is an effective design because it easily conforms to the employee's workday and does not cut into his or her free time, all of which he or she may need to fulfill home-life obligations.

One particular way that employees as a group can relieve stress is to form a stress management support group. A variety of books feature structured exercises that do not require the instruction of a therapist or paid facilitator. For example, *Structured Exercises in Stress Management* preaches that everybody should consider himself or herself a stress manager and offers dozens of structured exercises to this end. Among the simple techniques it advocates are controlled breathing, a "five-minute vacation" in which a relaxing spot is visualized, and use of a job stress grid that helps employees isolate the sources of stress and develop solutions accordingly. Many people find that stress management is like an amalgam of self-help and spiritual renewal and, for that reason, has benefits that go well beyond the workplace.

Many behavioral risk interventions produce reduced stress as a secondary benefit. Clinical and work-problem assessments, work-and-family services and benefits, conflict resolution, life-style management, and following the onset of stress-related illness, referral to behavioral healthcare all provide a measure of comfort to employees, who feel their needs are being tended to. Because some people may need to learn stress management in a therapeutic environment, the problem assessment professional should be able to make a referral to community resources.

Behavioral Safety Interventions

Just because a company has made ergonomic improvements and added state-of-the-art safety devices to its equipment does not mean it is accident-free. In fact, a company that *assumes* it is safer may be increasing its risk by letting down its guard.

Consider what happened to a small plastics manufacturer after it completed a safety campaign. The company accrued $450,000 in workers' compensation claims over the next two years even though it carefully administered traditional safety programs and ergonomic improvements. That total included $120,000 for benefits paid arising from filings for extended leave time, despite aggressive interventions by the workers' compensation case management firm used by the company's insurer. The company's state workers' compensation rating increased from a commendable .73 to 1.02, which was slightly above average, resulting in an almost one-third increase in annual premiums. What could account for the poor outcomes? Perhaps part of it could be attributed to bad luck, but the company also had no system for monitoring safety behaviors. For example, it did not audit whether employees were properly wearing protective equipment, had received behavioral education, were using tools and equipment safely, and were adhering to lockout/tagout and other procedures—the actual risks that preceded the accidents.

Behavior-related safety interventions include the following tasks.

Behavioral Safety Coaching

E. Scott Geller, of Virginia Polytechnic Institute and State University, advocates a five-step coaching process that has the mnemonic name "COACH," shorthand for care, observe, analyze, communicate, and help.

First, by *actively caring* and by addressing safety issues with individuals in a manner that is not critical or humiliating and that at the same time expresses appreciation for the work they are doing, team leaders and managers are likely to cause employees to reciprocate with safer work behavior. Actively caring also means not letting the unsafe behaviors of co-workers slide by; it takes the view that safety is a shared responsibility.

Second, *observation* can be augmented by developing a "critical behavior checklist" that is tailored to a specific workplace and job classifications. The checklist can include, for example, body positioning, visual focusing, communicating, pacing of work, moving objects, and complying with permits.

Third, *analysis* of a safety situation should take into account such extenuating circumstances as comfort, long hours, and lack of work breaks. This makes analysis a fact-finding rather than a fault-finding exercise.

Fourth, *communication* involving role-play exercises provides corrective feedback without singling out particular individuals. This also can include education on effective communication.

Fifth, *help*, another mnemonic device, stands for humor, esteem, listening, and praise.

Behavioral coaching need not be performed only by a supervisor. It can also be done by trained peers, who may be perceived by employees as less autocratic. In this way, employees can be given the tools to do their own behavioral interventions and empowered to self-regulate themselves, with the supervisor playing a limited coaching role.

More safety professionals are also becoming aware of the advantages of such behavioral interventions as case finding, work-focused problems assessments, conflict intervention, and stress management. They are finding that although these interventions are not primary safety management activities, they can be effective in accident prevention.

Behavioral Safety Inspections

Unannounced inspections are within the purview of site and district managers at many companies. However, they promote the we-they thinking common in adversarial work environments. In a transport and delivery company, think of the package loader laboring in the belly of a truck, where it often soars over 100 degrees on summer days. Suddenly glancing over his shoulder, he sees two white-shirted managers scrutinizing his every move. They write down a few remarks and, without saying a word, walk away. At the end of the shift, the employee is criticized by his supervisor for posing a safety risk because he let a couple of boxes sit on the trailer deck while he loaded.

As a replacement for or in addition to safety inspections, trained co-workers can observe individual peers with the peers' full awareness, then offer suggestions to them for safer behaviors.

Behavior-Based Accident Investigations

This after-the-fact task looks for signs of actions that underlie the occurrence of accidents. Rather than simply recording obvious causal factors, such as ergonomic deficiencies, for example, a safety investigation should also explore behaviors found on the safety checklist. This task requires more than cursory investigation, though.

For example, a pressman working in a printing operation lost his hand after he caught it between rollers while trying to adjust a sheet of paper. An investigation found that the light curtain, an electronic beam that would automatically stop the press if the light was broken, failed to operate. The inquiry concluded that the light curtain, which had not been inspected for two years, had malfunctioned.

In a behavior-based accident investigation, however, behavioral ramifications would be explored, too. In this case, by interviewing fellow pressmen and the foreman, the investigation would have revealed that the light boxes that carried the beam had been altered because it resulted in pauses in press operation and employees considered it onerous. This investigation would have also found that the worker was fatigued when the accident occurred because he was concluding a double shift.

Behavioral Interventions Related to Life-Style

Interventions related to life-style are often associated with wellness and health promotion programs. These interventions may be provided by health maintenance organizations, health insurance carriers, vendors specializing in wellness and health promotion, or company personnel such as occupational nurses. They may involve heavy investment in such things as fitness facilities or be as simple and inexpensive as lunchtime walking clubs. Wellness and health promotion—alternately called prevention and health risk management—is primarily remedial intervention for what many employers perceive as the single greatest threat to their ability to turn a profit: employee overuse of medical healthcare benefits.

One large Midwest food-processing company studied its health benefit utilization and cost data over thirty years. The collected findings showed that use and costs were stable and predictable for employees and family members through early adulthood and middle age. When they reached about age fifty, though, their healthcare use and expenditures "exploded." Additional research suggested that many of the older beneficiaries had neglected their health for many years. The data showed that minor health problems in employees' late twenties and early thirties developed into serious and irreversible diseases like arteriosclerosis and emphysema. What really worried the company was that its baby-boomer bubble was creeping forward in age and that inside of twenty years, its population of employees over age fifty would double.

You may be inclined to shrug off sponsorship of wellness programs, services, and benefits because they strike you as a "soft" business issue compared with quality control, product development cycles, global network development, and the like. But the profits that these latter activities generate can be consumed, first, by billowing costs to care for employees' and their family members' preventable healthcare conditions and, second, by the productivity losses—measured in lost work days, loss of talent, and new recruitment and training costs—that can easily exceed even high-risk employees' health benefit costs and far outpace the cost of programs and services that could have prevented the conditions with early-stage interventions.

Wellness activities can be implemented very inexpensively and favorably affect the company in surprising ways. If employees engage in an exercise routine together, it builds esprit de corps. Many small business owners have found that introducing employee fitness and diet programs and cheering on employees' efforts are the first step toward a people-centered organizational culture. The benefit is derived from the fact that light and moderate exercise helps employees feel healthier right away, reducing sick time and resulting in fewer trips to the doctor's office.

The list of possible wellness and health promotion activities is extensive. Here are just some of the activities available to employers at reasonable cost.

Health Risk Appraisal

Health risk appraisal takes a snapshot of an employee's health. It informs the employee of nascent physical ailments and ones that he or she may be vulnerable to later in life. Appraisals typically screen for such behavioral factors as smoking, diet, exercise, well baby care, and alcohol and drug use.

Light-Duty Physical Conditioning

The most beneficial life-style interventions for most people are not high-impact physical fitness regimens. The type of physical fitness portrayed in the Nike commercials appeals most to fitness-minded people, who may also be the most compulsive or addiction-prone. In other words, fitness junkies who test their physical and perhaps even psychological limits in order to attain the "runner's high" derive a therapeutic psychological benefit or add meaning to their daily existence. This has little relevance to the lives of the vast majority of adults, though, and companies would derive no benefit from encouraging employees to engage in such strenuous physical fitness. In reality, it could increase health risks.

Instead, light-duty physical conditioning is a better option. This consists of moderate but regular physical activity such as walking, biking, and stair climbing, which can positively affect a variety of health-related variables and are less likely to result in injury than more strenuous sports.

The best plan of attack to attain employee long-term wellness, therefore, is to encourage exercise moderation. Employees who receive a strong self-responsibility message from the culture of the organization may rely more on themselves than on peer pressure for the motivation to adhere to their exercise. Nevertheless, attracting the most physically fit to a new wellness program can be effective in generating excitement in the company for that program. The ultimate goal should be to reach the broad band in the middle of the employee group, comprising about 60 percent of all employees, in order to make favorable life-style and behavioral change meaningful to the organization.

Self-Help Groups

Three particular problems that have negative impact on health-care use are substance abuse, smoking, and poor diet. People with difficult-to-break habits in these areas have found that they often have better success with peer support. The self-help movement, which started in 1935 when alcoholics found that they could support themselves in recovery, has expanded to include self-help groups for practically every problem-in-living a person can have. Where interest is expressed by employees, group meetings can be sponsored by work organizations and held on company grounds. However, many groups have individuals who participate only on the condition of anonymity, and employers must be careful not to breach this trust.

Wellness and Health Promotion Benefits

Wellness and health promotion activities are generally considered benefits because they provide ongoing assistance beyond assessment, pay for assistance that would otherwise come out of employees' own pockets, and are not directly tied to productivity and other workplace issues on a person-to-person basis (even though productivity improvement may be part of the mission of the activity). Many healthcare organizations now offer employer wellness services that include an almost endless litany of activities. These, too, are benefits if they are employer-paid or subsidized, because they provide ongoing assistance. Among them are classes, along with individual and group counseling, for smoking cessation and caffeine reduction, instruction in CPR and first aid, programs in cholesterol reduction, aerobic classes, weight control programs, health fairs, health education courses, and personalized nutritional analysis. Employers considering providing employees with access to these services should do so with the desire to reduce the incidence and cost of late-stage healthcare episodes.

Some companies have used creative benefit schemes to prod employees into taking better care of themselves. One major self-insured company encourages employees to participate in wellness and health promotion activities by granting them "allowances" to be expended on flexible health benefits. The rationale for this plan was a finding that 35 percent of the company's healthcare costs were life-style related. Under the flexible plan, employees are tested for tobacco use, blood pressure, aerobic fitness, weight and body-fat content, and cholesterol level. A penalty-based system, the allowance is adjusted downward for each category in which they fail (for example, having blood pressure higher than 140/90 and not being under a physician's care).

Employers frequently make a mortality-based argument against wellness and health promotion benefits and activities. Some argue that wellness and health promotion will enable retired employees to live and thereby draw retirement benefits longer, which the company will have to pay for. The future liability for this, they argue, far outweighs the present and near-future liability for employees' healthcare costs. This argument is valid if the company's retirement plan is a defined *benefit* plan, such as a pension in which employees become vested after a specified number of years. In a defined *contribution* plan, like a 401(k), however, employees earn a specified amount of money for retirement, which may begin to accrue immediately upon their being hired. Typically, both the employer and employee make contributions to these plans. Therefore, the employee has a lump sum of money to dispense as he or she chooses in retirement, rather than a guaranteed lifetime pension benefit paid by the company that begins on the day an employee retires.

Defined contribution plans enable employers to control their cash flow better, and employees are freer in their retirement planning since they do not have to follow provisions set forth by the company's pension trust. Moreover, defined contribution plans are often considered preferable to defined benefit plans because the latter require long-term tenure with the company before the employee qualifies for payment following retirement.

Furthermore, pension plans—which generally disburse retirement benefits in greater allotments when employees work with the company until retirement—can lock in poor-performing employees. Research has shown that various job and personal factors can create inertia that prevents employee turnover that would be good for both the company and the individual.

Interventions to Achieve Work Life and Family Life Balance

A Midwestern household was grappling with the problem of lack of affordable child care. The father was employed at a food-processing company, working twelve-hour night shifts over five days each week. The mother worked a standard nine-to-five shift as an administrative assistant at a health insurance company. Day care costs for their two- and five-year-olds were prohibitive, and the maze of state and federal regulations had caused extensive delays in the day care subsidies for which they were eligible. One weekday morning, while the mother worked and the five-year-old was in kindergarten, the father fell into a deep sleep following his shift, and the two-year-old decided to take an unsupervised morning stroll. The father, awaking with the door open and the child gone, believed he had been kidnapped. Eventually, the child was found several blocks away, but not before the police were called to the scene and had conducted a house-to-house search. When this story appeared in the newspapers, the day care problem that had become rife in the community really hit home. It forced employers in the community to recognize and help provide solutions to the problems employees were having in balancing work-and-family responsibilities.

Employers have several options for helping workers cope in this uphill battle.

Family Development Education

Family development education informs employees about work and family programs, services, and benefits that are available to them through the company and that have information about basic family development. This information focuses on such areas as how a balance between work and family can be achieved, immunizations for children, and so forth.

Flexible Work Practices

Despite the label of "benefit" sometimes given to flexible work practices, they are no giveaway. Employees may be allowed to modify their work schedules, cut back their hours (with an equivalent cutback in pay), share jobs, work at home, and try other options that enable them to meet their dual obligations while inconveniencing the company in only modest ways. Parents with children at home often feel very vulnerable because of all the demands placed on them, and making flexible work available goes a long way toward enhancing employee loyalty.

Dependent Care Information and Referral

Dependent care information and referral is an employer-sponsored service that provides working parents with a specialist's advice about places to turn in obtaining care for children and elderly parents. Small companies are prone to contract out for this service, while larger companies may offer either on-site services or service location assistance from a staff member or external information-and-referral specialist who can assist in locating a provider.

Unpaid Leave

The Family and Medical Leave Act of 1993 (FMLA) requires that employers of over fifty employees provide twelve weeks of unpaid job-protected family and medical leave for the birth or adoption of a child, the serious illness of a family member, and certain other reasons. This public policy remedy provides the same kind of buffer between management and employees that a labor union might have offered thirty years ago. Had FMLA been in effect in 1992, one employee at a textile company would have used family leave when her son spent two weeks in the hospital following surgery to remove a potentially fatal bone cyst from his neck. She had requested that she be allowed to work the second shift so that she and her husband could alternate spending time with her son during his recovery. Her immediate supervisor refused, and she appealed to her shift supervisor, who ultimately approved the request. However, the process of approval intensified an already difficult family situation. If another occasion arises, she vows, she will take unpaid leave under FMLA and forget about accommodating her employer's needs.

Additional work-and-family options are contained in the benefits section of this chapter. Many companies have found such activities produce surprisingly impressive results. One division of Johnson & Johnson that paid attention to work-and-family needs had an absenteeism rate 50 percent lower than the rest of the company, and AT&T found that giving new parents unpaid parental leave cost only 32 percent of the employee's salary versus 150 percent in replacement costs if the employee left the company. A survey by the Society for Human Resource Management also showed that nearly three times as many employers (30 percent of 1,004 respondents) offered child care services in 1992 as in 1988 (10 percent).

Before implementing this type of assistance, however, employers should be fully aware of employee demographics and needs, which can be derived from the behavioral risk audit.

Work-and-Family Benefits

Work-and-family benefits have become popular with employees due to an increasing prevalence of dual-career parents and single parents, the aging of the baby-boom generation, and work commutes made more time consuming and stressful due to heavier traffic. One survey found that among salaried employees of 1,035 major U.S. employers, the most common work-and-family benefits available through their employers were

Child care assistance (offered by 84 percent of participating employers), in the form of dependent care spending accounts, employer-sponsored child care centers, and sick child or emergency care programs

Elder care programs (offered by 24 percent), in the form of counseling, long-term care insurance, financial support of outside facilities, and so forth

Family and medical leave (offered by 66 percent) for the birth or adoption of a child or for the care of a seriously ill family member

Adoption benefits (offered by 21 percent), in the form of some type of reimbursement assistance

Diversity Interventions

The diversity movement in the workplace is sometimes regarded as a by-product of affirmative action and equal employment opportunity laws in the United States, but its mission is nonpolitical and productivity focused. Diversity interventions beat a retreat from protected classes, sinecures, and forced integration, the political constructs that sometimes polarize the U.S. public. When a work group shares information on a project, a manager gives directions to a subordinate, or an apprentice learns from a journeyman, the primary concern should be productivity, not on how or why a person was chosen for a particular position. Sometimes, though, the emotionally charged issues of people's skin color, ethnicity, religion, gender, age, and the other variables that make them different in some ways from one another do interfere with productivity. Casual conversations among diverse people can, in a wink, elicit biased opinions that leave feelings hurt and tempers flaring. Sometimes this can happen without a person's even realizing he or she is insulting others.

In these cases, it may be advantageous to raise diversity issues in order to promote understanding, sensitivity, and tolerance among people toward each other and to establish work expectations. On the one hand, diversity initiatives should raise everyone's comfort level in working together with others. On the other hand, diversity interventions are not intended to improve self-esteem, make reparations for past social injustices, or even eliminate bias in people's private thoughts. They are to ensure that diversity issues do not impair the communications and interactions necessary to accomplish work.

Awareness Education

When a female worker of Southeast Asian extraction is faced with a disagreement, her cultural mores dictate that she avoid confrontation and not make direct eye contact. Without an understanding of her cultural mores, though, non-Asian employees may interpret her behavior as regressive and counterproductive. Prevention-based education about cultural differences is advantageous to employees in workplaces that are rapidly becoming diverse. Such education should inform people of cultural differences, encourage tolerance, and reinforce performance expectations. It should not be apologetic in tone or become caught up in some of the more extreme dogmas of the political correctness movement. Examples of inappropriate diversity awareness education occurred during a Federal Aviation Administration workshop on gender differences and sexual harassment, which was held in the wake of the U.S. Navy's Tailhook scandal. The workshop included "sensitivity" training given to male air traffic controllers that included subjection to sexual innuendos and grabbing of crotches and fannies by female controllers as the males "walked the gauntlet" (according to one published report). Situations such as these are more likely to be somebody's idea of "getting even" than training that promotes workplace harmony. In response to both there was a strong public backlash and retaliatory lawsuits.

They are in marked contrast to an educational forum in which subtleties of workplace behavior interpreted as discriminatory, thoughts about people who feel shortchanged by "preferential" treatment of others, and stereotypes are raised in a setting controlled by a neutral facilitator. An employer can also use such a forum to explain hiring and promotion practices, efforts to comply with federal law, and use of other criteria besides diversity in personnel decisions. It bears repeating, though, that the superseding issue in awareness education is to promote nondiscriminatory work behavior by both employees and managers.

Mediation

Diversity-based mediation may be handled as a subset of the conflict-resolution process cited earlier or, in larger companies, be used in special-case situations. The cultural problems at issue may originate as social phenomena external to the company, such as the well-documented backlash from Canadian nationals that occurred in Vancouver several years ago when large numbers of Japanese were emigrating to Canada. Once a person of diverse background is hired in a work organization, though, it is the organization that must make efforts to ensure that this hiring does not disrupt productivity and work harmony.

When disputes with diversity overtones do occur, however, they need to be resolved in a manner that takes into account the individuals' cultural differences. Therefore, mediation in these cases may need to be more inductive and less formulaic than for other disputes. The standard mediation process may need to be altered, for example, so that an alternative to nose-to-nose communication is available. Such a deviation might feature the mediator as a nexus between the two parties, who do not meet in person, or it might require a written correspondence to resolve the problems. In these cases, the mediator brokers a solution over the course of multiple passes of communication.

Workers' Compensation Case Management

Workers' compensation was created in 1911 because workers injured on the job lacked legal recourse for recovery of lost wages, costs of medical care, and long-term disability benefits. The system prevented workers and their families from becoming destitute while awaiting legal response to injury claims. This no-fault system was intended to prevent heated disputes between injured workers and employers. Instead, the problems have become aggravated, due in large part to the awarding of benefits for cumulative injuries like repetitive motion injuries and, in some states, mental stress injuries.

Behavioral ramifications often follow the onset of worker injury or illness. One administrator with an employee assistance firm describes how psychological malaise can turn to retaliation against the company: "There is a dynamic where disabled workers recovering at home get scared, wondering what will happen to them on their return to the company. This can be followed by anger. They start talking with friends and end up hiring an ambulance-chasing attorney. The next thing you know, a lawsuit has been filed and they milk the system. Personal-injury attorneys are noted for instilling an air of entitlement with injured workers."

In addition to vocational-rehabilitation remedies for physical injury, employers have the following two interventions available to diminish the size of this behavioral risk exposure.

Routine Work Organization Checks

The process of actively caring does not apply just to accident prevention or the reduction of bogus claims. Employers can influence whether an employee *wants* to return to work by routinely checking on the injured worker, beginning shortly after the accident occurs. This should be done by a representative of the company, such as the work-based problem assessment professional or risk manager. The concept of actively caring also suggests why checking by an internal resource is preferable to checking by external service provider, such as the workers' compensation insurer. At the same time, this strategy can backfire if relations between employees and management are contentious. The injured worker may believe that the company—which may be assigned blame for the injury by the employee, perhaps with help from a personal-injury lawyer—is meddling in his recovery.

Psychological Case Management for Physical Injuries

Employers and workers' compensation carriers alike are beginning to see that significant cash savings can be realized by recognizing and responding to the psychological trauma that can accompany

any personal injury. For that reason, psychiatrists are more frequently being included on the team of medical professionals helping to speed along recovery. Likewise, an employer resource should be available to case manage the psychological component of injuries. This strategy applies doubly to stress-related cases, in which the psychological component of the injury is, by definition, central to the case.

Workplace Reintegration

Like the employee recovering from behavioral health problems, the physically injured employee who is ready to reenter the workplace should have a reintegration meeting with a representative of the company—perhaps the work-related problem assessment professional—and the employee's manager. This meeting should establish expectations for the employee's reentry and head off the potential for attitude and morale problems that could surface later.

What Programs and Services Do Employers *Really* Need?

There is almost no end to the range and possible combinations of services that can help employers control behavioral risk. Most employers are prudent businesspeople who want to invest up to the point of diminishing returns, but not beyond it. Therefore, they are not interested in paying for the services that are far afield of their most pressing behavior-related issues.

Two models of controlling behavioral risk will be presented in Chapter Eight. The first model puts the primary focus on controlling behavioral health risk exposures, making clinical assessment of behavioral health, case management, and benefits management central to controlling behavioral risk. The second model emphasizes controlling risks related to work conduct and performance, putting the focus on work-based problem assessments and conflict resolution. These models will help employers prioritize the programs and services that they can use to control behavioral risk.

This chapter has discussed a wide range of programs, services and benefits that diminish behavioral risk in work organizations. The stage is now set to study the interventions that promote a healthy ecological system wherein employees work, that is, a healthy organization. As we shall see in Chapter Six, organizational behaviors and other workplace factors have as much influence on a person's health and well-being as do the other biological, psychological, and sociological factors in his life.

Notes

P. 109, *disciplinary action should not be conditioned:* Trice, H., Roman, P. M. *Spirits and Demons at Work.* Ithaca, N.Y.: Cornell University Press, 1972, pp. 170–196.

P. 109, *confrontation quickly turns to social support:* Feuer, B. "An Innovative Behavioral Healthcare Model." *EAPA Exchange,* Oct. 1992, pp. 28–33.

P. 109, *According to a study by the American Management Association:* American Management Association. *1995 AMA Survey: Workplace Drug Testing and Drug Abuse Policies: Summary of Key Findings.* New York: American Management Association, 1995, p. 1.

P. 110, *Only 22 percent of respondents dismiss positive test takers:* American Management Association. *1995 AMA Survey,* p. 3.

P. 112, *under the name "assessment, counseling":* "Medco Wins IBM Account: New EAP Design." *Open Minds,* 1994, *8*(8), p. 1.

P. 119, *expensive employer investment . . . averages 19.9 days and costs $7,676:* National Association of Addiction Treatment Providers. *Treatment Is the Answer: The White Paper on the Cost-Effectiveness of Alcoholism and Drug Dependency Treatment* (based on a study performed by MEDSTAT). Washington, D.C.: Author, 1991, p. 3.

P. 120, *variegated levels of care include:* Yandrick, R. M. "Conoco's Behavioral-Health-Benefits Plan." *HR Magazine,* 1994, *39*(1), 50.

P. 120, *Some benefit plans . . . include "alternative" care:* Yandrick, R. M. "Multiple Choices." *EAPA Exchange,* 1990, *20*(8), 34–36.

P. 121, *data from Caron Foundation:* Caron Foundation. Unpublished study performed by New Standards, Inc. Wernersville, Pa.: Caron Foundation, 1994.

P. 122, *imposes greater restrictions on behavioral health benefits:* Glazer, W. M., and Bell, N. N. *Mental Health Benefits: A Purchaser's Guide.* Brookfield, Wis.: International Foundation of Employee Benefit Plans, 1993, p. 23.

P. 125, *shop stewards: AFL-CIO Manual for Shop Stewards* (Publication No. 75). Washington, D.C.: AFL-CIO, n.d.

P. 126, *Organizational and business mediator Edward P. Hanna cites:* Hanna, E. P. Notes provided to R. M. Yandrick, August 1995.

P. 127, *"new face and perhaps new suggested alternatives":* Maggiolo, W. A. *Techniques in Mediation.* New York: Oceana, 1985, pp. 85–90.

P. 129, *"One thing is for sure—where there is a team":* Fisher, K., Rayner, S., and Belgard, W. "Resource 15: Managing Team Conflict." In *Tips for Teams: A Ready Reference for Solving Common Team Problems.* New York: McGraw-Hill, 1995, p. 210.

P. 131, *Among the simple techniques it advocates:* Tubesing, N. L., and Tubesing, D. A. (eds.), *Structured Exercises in Stress Management,* Vol. 4. Duluth, Minn.: Whole Person Press, 1988.

P. 132, *a five-step coaching process:* Geller, E. S. "Safety Coaching: Key to Achieving a Total Safety Culture." *Professional Safety,* 1994, *40*(7), 18–24. Also, Geller, E. S. "The Psychology of Occupational Safety." Paper presented at the 25th Annual Institute on Mining Health, Safety and Research, Blacksburg, Va., Aug. 29–31, 1994.

P. 137, *One major self-insured company encourages . . . wellness and health promotion activities:* Lewis, D. "Risk Rating at Hershey." *Journal of Healthcare Benefits,* July/Aug. 1994, p. 48.

P. 138, *various job and personal factors can create inertia:* Hughes, C. L. "Why Employees Stay Is More Critical Than Why They Leave." In *Making Unions Unnecessary* (2nd ed.). New York: Executive Enterprises, 1990.

P. 140, *such activities produce surprisingly impressive results:* Galen, M., Palmer, A. T., Cuneo, A., and Maremont, M. "Work and Family: Companies Are Starting to Respond to Workers' Needs—And Gain from It." *Business Week,* June 28, 1993, pp. 80–84, 86, 88.

P. 140, *three times as many employers . . . offered child care services:* Woolsey, C. "Employers Profit with Family Benefits Expert." *Business Insurance,* Jan. 20, 1992, p. 3.

P. 141, *most common work-and-family benefits:* Hewitt Associates. *Work and Family Benefits Provided by Major U.S. Employers in 1994.* Scottsdale, Ariz.: Hewitt Associates LLC Management Compensation Services, 1994. This study also includes findings for employers' use of resources and referrals, employee assistance programs, and work and family managerial initiatives.

P. 142, *during a Federal Aviation Administration workshop:* Gordon, J. "Different from What? Diversity as a Performance Issue." *Training,* 1995, *32*(5), 26.

P. 143, *disputes with diversity overtones:* Duryea, M. L. "Training Intervenors to Work Cross-Culturally." In *Cultural Diversity at Work.* Seattle, Wash.: The GilDeane Group, 1993, p. 3.

P. 144, *"There is a dynamic where disabled workers":* Yandrick, R. M. "Workers' Compensation: Beating the Blame Game" (comments of Andrea Velasquez, vice president of administration and business development for Psych-Care EAP). *EAPA Exchange,* 1993, *23*(10), 6–9.

Chapter Six

Organizational Interventions

In Chapter Five, I profiled a broad cross-section of the programs, services, and supportive benefits involved in controlling employee behavioral risk. In this chapter, I will continue to discuss organizational interventions that can influence behavioral risk. Whereas early interventions for employees (and family members) are provided in case-by-case fashion, organizational interventions seek to prevent behavioral risk exposures in a wholesale manner.

Organizational interventions affect the work culture and environment of the company, factors that influence whether behavioral risk exposures across the workforce are likely to increase or decrease. To understand why culture and environment are central to behavioral risk management and its holistic approach, consider this: many companies spend substantial sums of money for employee-intervention specialists such as mediators, employee assistance professionals, and industrial psychologists to provide the programs and services described in the last chapter. But these specialists' work is often frustrated because they are unable to change the systemwide dysfunctions that are producing sick or underperforming employees.

Predominant Cultural and Environmental Factors

Before exploring the various organizational interventions that diminish behavioral risk exposures, I will discuss the ingredients of a work culture and environment, looking at those that contribute to a healthy culture and environment and those that do not. This information will support the ideas in the second half of this chapter, where interventions are explored.

The predominant cultural and environmental factors in an organization include

- Organizational culture development
- Leadership style
- Leadership development and renewal
- Organizational structure
- Adjustment to the marketplace and government
- Organizational change management
- Internal communication processes
- Employer-worker partnerships

These categories are not all-inclusive, but they have perhaps the greatest impact on behavioral risk. Others, such as the physical appearance of the work environment, are excluded here because their impact on behavioral risk is probably minimal unless other risk factors are elevated. The reason is that as an employee increases his or her length of service with a company, factors such as physical surroundings usually diminish in importance in the employee's psychological orientation to the organization and her work while the importance he or she attaches to the quality of work relationships increases.

It also bears repeating that the organizational behavioral risks described in Chapter Four arise primarily from the behaviors and other factors which follow. For example, a sustained high level of organizational stress is often a consequence of cultural and structural factors, marketplace conditions, and change management activities. Therefore, the focus in this discussion is on the *precipitants* to organizational behavioral risks and the organizational interventions that affect them. Corporate culture and internal communications, presented in Chapter Four as organizational behavioral risks, are discussed here as well because they also can be precipitants to other risks.

Organizational Culture Development

Organizational culture, literally and figuratively, is tough to grasp. Culture is not a palpable "thing" that can be seen, felt, or empirically measured. One business cartoon shows the gruff elderly head of a company, having just read a document about workplace culture, barking at his secretary through his intercom to "find out if my corporation has any culture." One feels that if the secretary replied the corporation didn't have any, he would have ordered five crates.

A frame of reference often used by executives to describe their organization is "family," which can be either a thoughtful or a bogus reference to the way the organization operates and the regard that its members have for one another. Family is actually a neutral term because, like companies, families can operate in health or dysfunction. What family should represent in the employment setting if it is present is interdependence and shared experience among people working in the same system.

Healthy families are usually those in which the parents, as chief decision makers, have made a conscious decision to take the best care of their children and others in their custody. Often they are willing to sacrifice accumulation of wealth, career advancement, and time spent pursuing special interests in order to maintain or improve the health and well-being of their dependents. Their focus is typically on behaving responsibly and making sacrifices in order to raise their children well, helping them to follow the Golden Rule rather than seeking rapid material gains or compromising their integrity or ethics. When someone says, "I had a good [or bad] childhood," he or she is really saying, "I was raised in a good [or bad] family culture."

Like family culture, organizational culture has a strong influence on the behavior and mental health of the people in the system and can significantly diminish behavioral risk exposures. Through a combination of positive reinforcement of favored employee actions, promotion of institutional fairness, and the holding of employees to high standards of accountability, for example, a work organization can have a positive influence on the actions of employees in a noncontrolling way. Such a culture might render selfish and counterproductive employee behavior, such as dishonesty and theft, all but unthinkable. In this respect, organizational culture development is as much a loss management as a productivity enhancement tool.

Three cultural phenomena raised by Hampden-Turner deserve a closer look: values, myths and stories, and paradigms for handling employees and customers.

Organizational Values and the Values Statement

Organizational values are those that are *shared* by the members of the organization and that influence the organization's behavior. Not all company actions put employee interests at the head of the values list. For instance, decisions to relocate, discontinue projects, modify compensation plans, and outsource highly technical functions that can no longer be done efficiently inside the company may be made for a variety of competitive, legal, and financial reasons. The changes may be unavoidable. When considering organizational culture development, however, what is important is the manner in which the changes are implemented.

One way of reassuring employees and their dependents that their interests are being tended to is a value statement. This document is a set of guiding principles observed by division leaders and professionals involved in managing behavioral risks throughout the organization. It reflects the interests of both management and employees, and it serves as a standard against which a company can measure its behavior and, ideally, establish and reinforce a positive work culture built on trust. The value statement is likely to have the strongest impact as a written agreement between the employer and employees.

As an expression of mutual respect, the value statement should be balanced between the interested parties and reflect both employees' concerns and the organization's concerns about the external world and marketplace and its position in that marketplace. Following is a model behavioral risk value statement, drafted by organizational effectiveness consultant James M. Oher. (The Allied Priorities Company is fictitious.)

The Aligned Priorities Unlimited Company is committed to:

- According the same value to the needs and general welfare of our employees as it does to the business and financial goals of shareholders, executives and customers.
- The prevention, early identification, intervention and resolution of personal and organizational problems which potentially compromise our employees' morale or effectiveness.
- The provision of assistance to helping employees resolve personal problems following onset. However, this effort is not a substitute for disciplinary action that may have already been initiated.

- The implementation of programs, services and benefits which are effective in reducing the costs employees incur through excessive absenteeism, tardiness, preventable healthcare conditions and illnesses, and productivity losses. This will be accomplished through reporting and continuous quality improvement as defined by our quality leadership team. Individual employees will not be forced into these programs, services and benefits, although Aligned Priorities may target segments of the company for promotion of them.
- The integration and redesign of these programs, services and benefits by the most efficient means possible without compromising their integrity.
- The provision of assistance to our employees with balancing the alternating demands of work and family life.
- The accordance of respect for the ethnic, cultural, and gender differences of our employees, and to the equitable and sensitive addressing of interpersonal problems arising from diversity issues.
- Raising the awareness of programs, services and benefits—through customized promotion and employee education—which help manage behavioral risks.
- Respectfully observing the confidentiality and privacy of our employees and dependents who use programs, services and benefits. These records are protected by privacy and confidentiality laws. Aligned Priorities will also abide by the highest ethical standard provided by selected healthcare and legal professional boards.
- Avoidance or minimizing of organizational activities that may be disruptive to employees' lives, without first considering every alternative. These activities include downsizing, relocating, and office and plant closings.

Myths and Stories

The second organizational culture phenomenon, myths and stories, speaks to the heart and soul of the organization. At their best, myths and stories are company folklore that casts on the organization a sublime quality, provides workers with a sense of shared heritage, and is a psychic connection with predecessors in the company. Additionally, this folklore often communicates the sense that spirituality should be central to people's lives. One company that has had a people-centered philosophy for seventy years is Herman

Miller Corporation, a Zeeland, Michigan, furniture manufacturer. The company's 800 employees are periodically reminded of the organization's folklore, which includes the following story: "In the 1920s the millwright was the individual on whom the entire activity of machine maintenance and power operations depended. One day the millwright died. The company's founder, D. J. DePree, went to visit the family. After some awkward conversation, the millwright's widow asked if it would be all right if she read some poetry. After she finished, D. J. asked who wrote it, to which she replied her husband, the millwright. On his way home, as the story goes, D. J. DePree felt the Lord working in his heart. 'I will never know whether millwright was a part-time poet or a poet working as a part-time millwright,' he thought to himself."

This experience began Herman Miller's journey of working to understand the diversity of people's gifts and talents and skills. This story and others have been remembered through three historical phases of corporate renewal, the most recent in the early 1990s, when the company converted to work team processes. Thus, folklore enshrines a company's most venerated leaders and transposes their values onto future generations.

In a figurative sense, folklore is an organization's "eternal flame." However, when companies become caught up in organizational transformation—reshuffling staff, dealing with crises that come fast and furiously—sometimes institutional amnesia sets in. When that happens, the organization's legacy is lost, the folklore no longer seems relevant, and the organization may become spiritually debased.

Employee and Customer Paradigms

A third important feature of organizational culture phenomenon is its paradigms for handling employees and customers. One paradigm that is characteristic of the so-called quality companies is supplier-customer integration, enabling employees and customers to interface. One leather products company allows employees who cut and stitch leather into pants, vests, and other consumer products to talk directly with purchasing agents of retail stores. In the same way, employees at the company who prepare hides and tan them into leather communicate directly with agents of the garment company that stitches the garments and whose name goes on the label. These nexuses provide a medium for more than just the issuing of complaints; they help employees to better understand their customers' expectations and their own roles in the production process.

Another paradigm is made up of the programs and services that perform individual behavioral interventions. Some employers seem to regard these programs and services as their primary cultural development tool, whereas the real value of the programs and services is to augment the culture. However, they may also be exploited to give the *appearance* of a strong culture or to manipulatively apply quick-fix interventions instead of to deliver a holistic employee behavioral risk management strategy that is valued by both management and employees. One company with a work-and-family program and benefits, for example, discourages their utilization by not publicizing their availability, but it extols them to current and prospective customers.

Leadership Style

Leadership style is distinct from organizational culture, but its impact on culture—and resultant increase or decrease in behavioral risk exposure—can be profound. Effective leadership can set the groundwork for the development of a positive, people-oriented culture while ineffective leadership can uproot or atrophy the existing culture. There are four generic types of leadership style.

- *Entrepreneurial,* which relies on the charisma and business acumen of the leader or founder. This is an effective leadership style for small and young organizations needing to be swift afoot, but to be successful in the long run, most organizations must grow beyond it.
- *Strategic,* which is rooted in organizational traditions, plural leadership, external marketplace conditions, and long-range planning. This is a healthier model of leadership for a large organization because it is more circumspect, aware of the world around it, and long-term focused. At some point in every strategic organization's past, it has made a successful transition from entrepreneurial to strategic leadership style.
- *Chauvinistic,* which is internally focused, has a we-they orienta-

tion to the outside world, and overemphasizes its institutional superiority. It may be stereotyped as an "elitist" style, used by leaders who are primarily navel gazers.
- *Exclusive,* which has a traditional clublike orientation. It is common among the knowledge industries, in brokerage firms and Ivy League schools, for example.

The escapades of John Z. DeLorean at General Motors and his subsequent formation of his own company was a cause célèbre among many cultural theorists. DeLorean assailed the basic assumptions of GM's culture during the 1970s, which included power relationships with subordinates, suppliers, dealers, and sub-contractors; management rewards and punishments tied to short-term profits; deprioritization of things that could not be easily counted and monitored by the finance departments, such as safety and quality; and the subordination of people (who, once they are promoted, have the right to inflict similar humiliations on *their* subordinates).

The work environment that DeLorean encountered at GM probably fit the chauvinistic model most closely. What he created, though, was worse: an entrepreneurial culture that outlived its practicality. As Hampden-Turner explains: "DeLorean's subsequent adventures in Northern Ireland and the catastrophe of his gull-wing sports car also suggest that his chief talents were theatrical. His self-celebratory protests were not more viable and effective than the culture he attacked."

An authoritative voice in decision making could help to prevent some of the follies like those just described that beset senior management. This individual could explain how an inappropriate leadership style is destroying the organizational culture and increasing behavioral risk and how leadership style can be tweaked to produce positive behavioral risk indicators. For example, a company's senior leadership may want to aggressively enter new markets. Meanwhile, the workforce may still be struggling to cope with job demands created by the last flurry of marketplace-oriented activity, a struggle evidenced by increases in behavioral risk indicators. The voice calling this to senior management's attention would be that of the behavioral risk manager (an occupational function that will be described further later). This manager might suggest delaying any market expansion a half year or so, "until we know the production systems and employees are ready to handle more change," or exploring another option that would "soften the shock to employees of knowing that more changes are on the way."

Leadership Development and Renewal

Organizational leadership occurs on three levels: among the board of directors, the executive leadership, and the line management. In a healthy organization, board and executive leadership acts as part of a system of checks and balances, much like that found in the legislative and executive branches of government. When effective checks and balances are lacking, the result can be unethical, inept, or abrogated leadership.

One candy-bar manufacturer received a surprise inspection from the U.S. Department of Agriculture after the agency received an anonymous tip that the company was using spoiled peanut butter. The agency seized the drums of the tainted ingredient, bought from multiple suppliers, from the company's warehouse. As reported on the television news, employees, speaking on the condition of anonymity, had said the company had also used other spoiled ingredients, including chocolate, coconut, and almonds. Both the president and vice president of operations disavowed any wrongdoing. Despite their protestations, the company was last reported under Chapter 11 of federal bankruptcy law. One of the telling outcomes of this situation was that employees were happy to tell of other bad products the company could have used. One can surmise that this company had a lack of effective checks and balances and that, as a result, many unsettling issues were occurring at the factory-floor level as well as at the upper levels.

Businesses can be set up so that the counterweight to an unbridled executive is an active, involved board of directors. Too often, though, the oversight of many boards is limited to minding personal stock portfolios, providing general business direction, and ensuring that fiduciary responsibilities are met.

This board behavior is based in part on the fact that company shareholders are often short-term investors of one to two years who may be less concerned about the long-term health and welfare of the organization than about their immediate profits. During a televised 1995 discussion of organizational culture and leadership behavior, Henry Schacht, executive committee chairman for Cummings Engine Company, suggested that major investors be encouraged to invest long term.

> When [a prospective major investor] comes to us, I'd say, "Why don't you buy a large block of stock, agree not to trade for five years, but come sit on the board. If your ideas are better than ours, and you can convince the rest of our directors, terrific. . . . But to buy shares just to sort of give us a 'poke' and go away, I don't think that's as effective as really putting your investment dollars there and [coming to] sit on the board and accept some of that responsibility. Stay long enough so that you really make the money that you feel your changes will bring."

According to management consultant William R. Montgomery, the *in*appropriate behaviors of board members often include

- Election or appointment of new members based on prominence in the community, representation of a particular group (based on ethnic or gender considerations), and familiarity to other board members
- Individual subservience to the will of the group, without raising vital questions about protocols and involvement in the affairs of the company
- Lack of recognition of social responsibility
- Behavior that is distant, removed, insensitive, and aloof
- Attempts to micromanage the affairs of the organization

Part of the social responsibility of the board is to ensure that the company has a safe, supportive work environment. This requirement should be put in writing, assigned to the chief executive officer (CEO) to enforce, and considered during the CEO's performance evaluation.

One on-again-off-again office romance at an insurance brokerage ended with the man attacking the woman at work, which was reported in the next day's metropolitan newspaper. The company's board did not consider the attack to be any of its business but was irate about the press report. Had the board sought to ensure a safe, supportive work environment, it would have asked the CEO:

What policies do you have to address employee conduct problems?

What programs or services are available for employees experiencing personal problems? Are those services actively promoted to management and employees? If so, how? What physical presence do professional staff members of these programs and services have at the job site(s)?

In what ways are managers trained to identify and intervene in emerging conduct problems?

With regard to this particular case, were there behavioral signs that the attack might happen? Was anything done about it by the employees' immediate supervisors?

What measures do you plan to take to prevent this type of incident in the future?

Many corporate directors are not even aware of the mechanics, rules, procedures, and internal governance endemic to effective board membership. If they are, they know they have the tools to diminish behavioral risk; they can exercise their authority to hold the CEO accountable for daily occurrences inside the organization. Similarly, if members of senior management know that the board will hold their toes to the fire when behavioral problems arise, they will probably be more proactive.

Organizational Structure

The structure of an organization can be a bridge or a roadblock to efforts to manage behavioral risk holistically. Traditional work organizations have discrete, largely autonomous infrastructures. Examples of these functions are development, production, accounting, finance, human resources, legal, marketing, strategic planning, and so forth. These infrastructures often operate in almost mutually exclusive fashion.

One model of the future work organization proposes five interconnected organizational entities: a knowledge/learning center, a recovery/development center, a world service/spiritual center, a world-class operations center, and a leadership institute. This model embodies Aquarian-like ideals—that is, its resources are harnessed to develop a healthier society and world. It takes a panoramic view of the company and its place in the world. Activities to manage behavioral risk would be augmented by this model's expressed purposes, one of which is "to break down barriers between functions and foster and accelerate systemic thinking." Efforts to manage behavioral risk would probably emanate from the recovery/development center, whose purpose in part would be to prevent or alleviate "institutionalized 'sickness.'" Far from being a pipe dream, elements of this model are being implemented in numerous private companies and government agencies.

Other visions of future organizational structures are quite different. Among them is the virtual corporation, in which a core group of decision makers handles strategic planning responsibilities and oversees the execution of work tasks. The tasks are then carried out by teams of individuals who might contract with the organization for anywhere from two weeks to ten years. Temporary and personnel agencies can be expected to provide employers with service teams in the near future through employee leasing and other types of work relationships in lieu of permanent full-time employment. In these situations, behavioral risk management activities may be partitioned between the two employment entities or jointly administered.

Some labor unions already function as quasi-personnel agencies in this respect. An example is the National Maritime Union (NMU), which provides the maritime companies with whom it contracts able-bodied seamen, stewards to work in ships' food service departments, pumpmen, electricians, engine mechanics, and other classifications of workers. They serve on ocean-crossing assignments that typically run four months in duration. The NMU offers its members health and welfare benefits, member assistance services for behavioral health problems, and upgrading and retraining. Some of the activities that control behavioral risk include constant rotation of supervisors by the maritime companies, union meetings aboard ships to identify common problems that seamen are having and to enable any frustrated workers to ventilate, and oversight of log books by the U.S. Coast Guard. These interventions diminish the potential for insubordination and other forms of retaliation. They also illustrate how the union is as much responsible as the company for setting the "organizational" climate aboard the ships.

A union is different from a personnel service, however, in that, under the union contract, a company cannot refuse to employ the workers it is given. The NMU has three levels of qualification, based on sailing time, while the U.S. Coast Guard certifies workers' skills. Workers in the same category of tenure, "full book member," for example, are assumed to be coequals in ability and qualification, as are those with the same Coast Guard certifications. Therefore, when an opening is announced at an NMU union hall, it is automatically given to the qualified member who has not had a work assignment for the longest period of time. In a nonunion environment, the employer is more likely to reserve the right of refusal over personnel.

Alternative employment mechanisms can create some unintended behavioral risks, however. For example, one metal fabricating company decided, after several years of rumored major organizational changes, to outsource some of its departments. The employees in these departments—including maintenance, storage and supply, and as a pilot project, one operating unit—were hired by a service company that was given the contract to perform the functions. However, the employees were paid 20 percent less than they previously made, and benefits were eliminated. To the employees, the one tangible difference besides the compensation and benefits changes was that they now wore a different identification badge in the facility and were on one-year contracts.

That brief contract brought about a "short-timer" attitude on the part of both the permanent and the temporary employees; the latter felt as though people with whom they were colleagues a few months back were now treating them like "union scabs." This fomented several confrontations, increases in absenteeism, and incidents of sabotage and theft, all of which received the tacit sanction of managers. The managers, having grown "battle weary" during the several years of uncertainty that had been hanging over them like a storm cloud, passively condoned the disruptive behavior.

Adjustment to the Marketplace and Government

Companies are always struggling to catch up with or keep a leg up on the competition, a fundamental part of doing business in the free-enterprise system. One of the risks companies face is developing "blinders" as a result of an exclusive focus on anticipating or reacting to external factors. For example, a decision to relocate a facility may be based primarily on proximity to suppliers and customers, more favorable business tax codes in another state, or location of a technical institute that produces people with certain skills. Employers need to be continually mindful, however, of how the organization's behavior in the external environment affects its internal functioning. If behavioral risk exposures proliferate, they will affect the financial earnings and reserves of the company and thus diminish its future capacity to respond effectively to external influences.

Similarly, a company needs to stay apprised of developments in the public policy arena, such as tax-code changes, mandates, judicial precedents, and other public policy matters, not to mention the raft of new legislation that is introduced in each state and federal legislative session. When employers are continually reacting to current and proposed government mandates, their energy and resources are likely to be diverted toward defensive strategies for staying within legal boundaries. This may come at the expense of proactive initiatives related to doing what is best for the organization and its employees, including managing behavioral risk.

Organizational Change Management

Every organization goes through transitions. They may be endogenous in that growth is controlled and in accordance with the company's strategic plan or, as we just saw, exogenous and linked to the economic climate and market conditions. If the need exists for the company's product or service, change based on endogenous factors is a stronger likelihood. This kind of change is preferable because it enables the company to control the change process instead of primarily responding to external influences.

Organizational change occurs on many levels: the development of new business units, leadership turnover, a decision to make a public stock offering, the need to enter new markets, and so forth.

Consider one company's succession of major organizational changes, which took it from a mom-and-pop glass-making operation to a large bottling company over a forty-eight-year period. The succession of changes included the owner's relinquishment of daily management and supervision in order to concentrate on marketing and sales, addition of new managers and employees when the company won its first major contract, departmentalization when the organization reached about forty employees, introduction of formalized personnel policies and procedures, procedures for communication channels, introduction of a professionalized human resource department, relocation to a larger facility, changeover to computerized equipment, development of a long-range and strategic plan, implementation of Total Quality Management, merger with another organization, establishment of a board of directors, opening of other facilities outside of the immediate locality and subsequent relocation of employees, offering of private stock, establishment of franchises, offering of public stock, relinquishment of divisions, and change of senior executive leadership. Prior to making each of these decisions, the company considered the pluses and minuses, consequences and trade-offs of each move. However, another key question in all these changes should be, What proportional value is behavioral risk being given when juxtaposed with business opportunity and short-term financial gain?

Internal Communication Processes

Internal communication shapes how organizational activities are comprehended by employees. Because it affects whether and how employees react to those activities, internal communication is vital to behavioral risk management as well. Internal communication determines whether employees stay on an even keel psychologically and emotionally or whether they develop pathological attitudes toward management and its intentions. For example, in situations in which downsizing following a planned merger appears inevitable, there is a strong probability that employees will assume either of two attitudes. In the more positive of the two attitudes the employee thinks, "I know where my group and I stand with the proposed merger, so I'll continue to do what I am doing until there's a change." Consequently, any negative impact on productivity is likely to be low. The more negative attitude among employees may be expressed as, "We're waiting for the second shoe to drop. As soon as our senior managers get the best deal for themselves, we'll be let go." Here, the productivity consequences are likely to be greater and negative.

In other situations, communication may be a part of the pathology of the organization. One pediatric hospital was experiencing sharply reduced reimbursements for deliveries in its neonatal intensive care unit (NICU). This led to a variety of management proposals to reduce the wages of NICU nurses. One proposal was to institute an across-the-board wage freeze. Another was to reduce the shift differentials (the additional pay for working evening, night, weekend, and holiday shifts), and annual percentage raises would not be cut.

The nurses knew from an information "leak"—in which information traveled from a manager to one of the doctors to a nurse with whom he was romantically involved—that a change was coming. The senior nurses, who recalled a similar belt-tightening situation eight years ago, felt that the freeze was the fairest option, but senior management instead chose to reduce shift differentials, which cut some nurses' incomes by as much as $120 a week. Rumors rampaged through the units of the hospital that management's decision was based on efforts to induce some of the nurses who worked mostly second and third shifts to quit; then the hospital would move some of the first-shift nurses into the empty slots. That way, management would save money by reducing staff as well as cutting pay differentials. In reality, management had no intention of cutting back on staff, and the differentials were cut back to a level only slightly less than healthcare industry standards. This information was never communicated to employees, though. To floor nurses, the situation was one more straw bowing the camel's back. To patients, it manifested as neglect and a lack of caring by hospital employees.

There were multiple problems at the hospital, but this situation illustrates how problems can be aggravated and perpetuated by lack of direct, concise, two-way communication. Contrast this case with companies that bring people in as associates or partners and conscientiously promote information sharing. These companies have implemented such communication media as employee breakfast sessions with the boss, computerized hotlines, associate response centers, interactive video meetings, and other types of instant or brief-delay feedback loops. These strategies are much more effective for time-sensitive decision making than newsletters, whose "news" is usually stale by the time it appears, and suggestion boxes.

It is hard to overestimate the power of good communication. On the one hand, it can call upon a person to bare a part of his or her soul and tell others just how he or she thinks about things, often before getting any information in return. This may leave some people feeling vulnerable. On the other hand, good communication helps a company earn a valuable commodity—employee trust, which is doubly valuable during periods of transition. Additionally, good communication can induce the more defensive employees to be more open and forthcoming.

Employer-Worker Partnerships

Organizational change occurs on many levels, but the most important to people's work lives is perhaps what is often called the workplace social contract. If employers want to manage behavior, they should consider the explicit and implicit assumptions under which employees work. Many companies have been making a sea change in the expectations and conditions of work under the traditional contract. The following list describes some of the changes.

More and more, the employment relationship is negotiated between employers and workers, both industrywide and case by case. The current change process—sometimes called the de facto social contract—is a pell-mell interim period arising out of the lack of a clear corporate vision and renewed workplace social contract. The result has often been worker alienation, an atmosphere of risk aversion, job insecurity, and employees motivated more by self-interest than loyalty to the organization. One can read in almost any issue of the *Wall Street Journal* or *Business Week* about careers unceremoniously cut short, employees subjected to significant pay cuts, and jobs declared antiquated. In fairness to employers, though, these developments have taken shape largely due to external factors, including the emergence of the global economy, the continuing transition to an information society, and other factors that are rendering obsolete the traditional social standards of the workplace.

Indeed, organizational-effectiveness expert James Francek says

Condition	Traditional	New
Employment relationship	Long term	Time limited
Reward for performance	Promotion	Acknowledgment
Management style	Paternalistic	Empowering
What loyalty is	Remaining with the company	Responsibility and good work
Nature of employment	Lifetime career	Job contracting
Compensation	Linear (for example, pay scales)	Nonhierarchical
Employee relationships	Mutually dependent	Bonded by quality of work
Career development	Career paths sanctioned by company	Individual choice; nontraditional career paths

that the concept of the "job"—with its inherent ties to the traditional employment contract—is becoming obsolete. "Work," which has fewer strings attached to it and is more inclusive of alternative work arrangements, is a better descriptor in that it more accurately reflects what employers are interested in paying for. However, this de facto period of management-employee relations has produced much angst for employees while usually not resulting in a coinciding level of pain for senior leaders. Indeed, as mentioned earlier, "making the tough decisions" that lead to layoffs and pay cuts is often financially rewarding for the person willing to take the heat.

In this change process, employer-paid healthcare, retirement, and other benefits are likely to become rarer, leaving many workers in free fall, without the peace of mind of a safety net under them. Overall, this will lower the self-esteem of workers that comes from self-sufficiency, reduce the number of fit workers (because there will be more untreated health ailments), and diminish the overall health and welfare of the workforce.

Much as severe increases in workload cannot be sustained

indefinitely without negative consequences, neither can an unbalanced or exploitive work relationship. The eventual outcome will be worker backlash such as a reemergence of unionism or the appearance of another structure to serve as a buffer between employers and workers or to buoy certain employee groups at the expense of others.

Everyone agrees that many of the fundamental rules of business life are changing. In fact, the simple advertising slogan of one major automaker, "The rules have changed," is a bellwether. No matter how much the workplace changes, though—even if jobs and employees eventually are replaced by work and contract personnel and other short-term providers of talent and labor—employers will still have to contend with behavioral risk. Work stress, poor work attitudes, behavioral health problems, retaliatory actions, and other facets of human psychology and behavior will continue to manifest themselves. The risks cannot simply be transferred out of the organization. Thus, short of inventing a pill whose psychoactive properties endow everyone with happiness, motivation, a strong work ethic, and immunity from behavioral illness, employers must continue striving to create a positive organizational climate for workers in order to diminish behavioral risk.

In modern work environments, three interdependent elements are necessary to diminish behavioral risk—empowerment, self-responsibility, and employer commitment (see Figure 6.1).

The first leg is employee or worker empowerment. Much has

Figure 6.1 Interdependent Elements That Diminish Behavioral Risk.

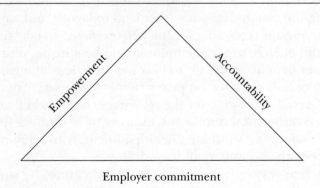

Employer commitment

been written about empowerment, but it generally is understood to be a transfer of decision-making authority from management to workers. These transferred privileges include allowing workers to raise objections to company decisions and decision-making processes, seek out opportunities to learn, introduce their own ideas about how to make products and deliver services, and make choices as to the best use of benefits and other work-related privileges. Not everyone is initially comfortable with empowerment such as that endemic to self-directed work teams. This discomfort is especially the case among those who are docile or who would exploit a power structure or hierarchies for personal gain. However, empowerment is a paradigm within which most employees eventually grow comfortable. Empowered employees understand that they have the capacity to effect positive change in their lives, are capable of self-improvement, can alter their stress reactions to environmental circumstances, and can overcome self-reinforcing cycles of destructive behavior.

These precepts should be supported by a long-term commitment from the employer that the empowerment initiative will not be abandoned. The commitment may be expressly written as a value statement, mission statement, or statement of intentions. Whatever its form, it must be periodically reaffirmed and supported by the everyday actions of managers, who must "walk the talk." Sometimes this may mean allowing employees to make mistakes in order to learn from them.

Employers cannot simply hand over the keys to the business, of course. Accountability is the counterweight to empowerment. The tenets of accountability include engaging in mature work behavior, being responsible for personal actions, accepting the consequences of those actions without alibis, and taking on risk in a manner that is not likely to jeopardize oneself or others. The essential readiness to accept responsibility can be reinforced to employees in various ways. For example, in a benefits program, a medical savings account, under which employees are provided with funds to purchase their own healthcare coverage, puts the onus on beneficiaries to make cost-conscious decisions about their care. Defined contribution retirement plans require employees to make decisions regarding participation, contribution rates, and asset allocation in order to ensure adequate retirement income. Profit-sharing plans link overall company performance with personal income and generate peer pressure against behaviors harmful to the company. Credit systems in which employees receive a financial incentive to participate in wellness and health promotion activities gently but forcefully nudge employees toward self-initiated self-care activities. One survey found that 11 percent of current employers currently offer credits and another 18 percent plan to add them in the next three years. Similarly, alternative work arrangements, such as flextime, prompt employees to structure their work and personal time in ways that allow them to achieve better life balance. These efforts should be accompanied by both education and literature that reinforce the accountability and self-responsibility themes.

The company can transpose these themes onto the performance of work by enforcing policies intended to promote cooperative work behavior; giving opportunities for employees in work units to establish their own rules whenever possible; and emphasizing communication by management, not only on policies and practices but also on the management rationale for implementing them. Finally, expectations about employees' work behavior—that is, working cooperatively, settling disagreements peaceably, entertaining varying points of view in work teams without unduly delaying decisions—should be communicated. Also, conferring privileges on employees such as attending outside training events expresses management commitment to employees, but these privileges must be balanced with the message that management expects existing work to be completed properly and on time. In work team situations, empowerment supplies employees with the latitude to decide how and when they are going to complete their work. The group then self-regulates itself using peer pressure.

Effective Organizational Interventions

Now that the organizational behaviors and factors that have a powerful impact on the corporate climate have been described, what interventions can be used to diminish the likelihood that they will affect behavioral risk? Organizational interventions fall primarily into six areas:

- Organizational culture change
- Internal consultation on business practices that elevate behavioral risk
- Situation-specific interventions with management
- Team building and work team problem intervention
- Specialized interventions
- Training activities (discussed in Chapter Seven)

These general categories of interventions are common to the organizational development, organizational-effectiveness, quality improvement, and other types of consultants who whisk in and out of the workplace to help companies design everything from marketing plans to severance packages to strategies for sidestepping governmental regulation and competitors. The behavioral dynamics inside the work organization are often neglected, though, perhaps because behavioral interventions are not thought to be as likely to produce immediate results as other measures, such as introducing a new product, would be.

For companies that are maintaining data and whose human resource professionals are keeping accurate records, however, there is ample evidence to demonstrate the viability of behavioral risk as a legitimate business issue. Four sources of information are relevant to assessing organizational behaviors and other factors: the audit process, the confidential work-based assessment resource, an ombudsman or dispute-resolution person, and the human resource manager or other high-level manager to whom appeals for help with management or organizational problems may be made by workers.

The audit process, of course, already has been described. The other information sources are occupational managers and professionals through whom line managers and employees can impart information suggesting organizational behavior problems or other factors. The problem may be that a male supervisor is harassing women in his department, that a management decision several months ago to accelerate production has alienated employees and is leading to instances of sabotage, or that a group of engineers is squabbling over product specifications. The rule of thumb about complaints is that for every person registering a concern or complaint, there are twenty-five others with the same issue who are silent. Therefore, when the same concern is expressed by multiple people, or when information from one information source is corroborated by another, it is a signal that an organizational "undertow" may already be gathering strength. Then an organizational intervention should be considered.

Organizational Culture Change

Organizational culture is the sum total of events—some large, but many small—that shape people's perception of work life inside the organization. A major event can have such significance to the members of the organization that it becomes a *symbol* of how employees feel about the organization. The symbol remains valid, though, only when it is reinforced by the hundreds of everyday interactions inside the organization. When this is the case, the symbol is retained in the collective memory of the organization and passed along to new members. Because an organizational culture is shaped by *events,* it can be nurtured—although culture development events that become enduring symbols are not necessarily premeditated, highly choreographed, or dramatized. They may be simple and unexpected, like the story of the millwright at Herman Miller, yet profound.

Many organizations today are instituting rapid cultural change—treating that change as a priority in today's business environment—which can be revitalizing to employees or a painful shock treatment. One of the more interesting documents on this subject is *High-Velocity Culture Change: A Handbook for Managers,* by Price Pritchett and Ron Pound. It contains some of the best and worst thought about contemporary culture change in the workplace. Two of its better ideas are to break old work habits by offering employees a better alternative and to unleash creative talent. Some of the worst ideas are contained in the advice to managers to accept that employees will become traumatized, think nothing of high turnover, and simply allow trust to evaporate. "Leave skid marks," the handbook says. Some companies are doing just that by undertaking cataclysmic steps in the name of employee empowerment. The practice of empowerment is deceitful, though, when management uses it for such purposes as pumping employees for information and knowledge without providing anything except empty promises in return. Unfortunately, some of the more radical management literature helps such managers to rationalize such below-board behavior.

Regardless of what specific initiatives are used to develop or change the culture, preparing employees for them is essential. As a 500-person company ponders ways to implement organizational change, imagine what a positive step it would be to hold a "summit" at a local high school auditorium, in which senior management openly discusses with an audience of employees the operational changes being contemplated. Such an event, if it is a sincere effort to apprise employees that changes are on the way and to obtain employee input, and not a manipulative effort to create a false sense of calm before the storm, could be a defining moment in the formation of the new culture.

The summit would not be an attempt to sugarcoat the truth. Instead, for example, it could be used to tell employees that they will have to develop computer skills or even that some of them will be laid off. It would inform employees how the company will help them acquire necessary knowledge. Further, it would give employees the chance to ask why the changes are being made. The summit would set new expectations and tell employees how their work behaviors will have to change and technical competence will have to increase. It would give employees some time for mental preparation.

Internal Consultation on Business Practices That Elevate Behavioral Risk

Organizational behaviors may take the form of individual management decisions, reinforcement of organizational traditions, and patterns of risk taking that give an organization a culture consistent with conservatism, aggression, or another quality. These behaviors can create and reinforce harmony among participants in a work system, or they can lead to tensions and retaliation.

Internal consultation to senior management on behavioral risk issues may be focused on prevention or early-stage intervention. It is preventive when behavioral risk issues are considered prior to making a business decision, minimizing the probability that deleterious consequences to a decision will be overlooked. In the same way, internal consultation on behavioral risk can yield corrective strategies. Following are two examples that retrospectively consider how serious risk exposures could have been controlled better through prevention or early-stage intervention. In each case study, an organization that experienced high behavioral risk exposure is compared with one in a similar situation that did not.

Two Approaches to Reengineering

In one metropolitan area of 500,000 people, reengineering activity in the healthcare industry led four major hospitals to consolidate, forming two healthcare "systems." As one of the hospitals was transitioning into one of the systems, it made severe staff cutbacks and simultaneously implemented work teams. The thrust of the work team initiative was cross-functional training, so that respiratory therapists could do the work of electrocardiograph technicians and the like. However, the board and executive leadership of the healthcare system had not taken into consideration the additional stress to which staff would be subjected. They also failed to recognize that the employees were coping with the "death" of one organization and the "birth" of another. As a result, overwhelmed employees went into a sort of group shock—many of them quit and one angry employee planted a debilitating virus in the computerized management information system.

In contrast, the management of another one of the merging hospitals took a variety of preventive steps. It consistently provided notices to employees about its plans, explained the market forces that necessitated the merger, met with groups of employees to obtain feedback on realigning the new system in a way that would minimize the number of furloughs, heavily promoted stress management activities, considered problems of pattern behavior evidenced by its assessment resource, surveyed employees to assess their workload, and phased in cross-functional training over a longer period to contain the accumulated stress that employees were experiencing. The second system engendered a balanced, longer-term commitment to change, avoidance of employee alienation, and commitment to retaining talent. While the transition was

an unhappy time for many employees in both systems, the second
suffered fewer of the deleterious side effects that beset the first.

Two Approaches to Collective Bargaining

Now consider the diametrically opposite state of labor relations in
two well-established companies whose rank-and-file employees were
represented by the same labor union. The first, an Eastern U.S.
heavy equipment parts manufacturer, was engaged with its labor
union in collective bargaining for almost two years. The polemics
were so extreme that the two sides could not even agree on
whether the company had locked out the union or the union had
gone on strike. Shortly after the strike began, replacement workers were brought in. The hostile environment at the plant was
marked by fatalities, including the death of a union member who
tried to blockade the front door and was hit by a delivery truck.
Two middle-aged managers had heart attacks requiring open-heart
surgery, several employees who were Vietnam veterans were treated
for posttraumatic stress disorder, marriage relations of numerous
employees became strained, employees choosing not to strike were
harassed, and heated supervisor-employee confrontations ensued.

Even under the best of circumstances, relations between
employees and management would have been strained in this
declining industry, where well-paid employees had few skills trans-
ferable to other industries or work settings. The adversarial relationship between management and employees, however, had been
slow-cooked over four generations. Resentments were deeply
entrenched, and as a result, the intransigence on both sides was
often based on tradition instead of logic. The organizational culture and its attendant values, metaphors, images, and paradigms
were imbued with adversity. Clearly, the advantages the company
might have gained by nurturing a positive organizational culture
held in joint custody by the company and union had been ignored
for years.

Contrast that environment with the unionized work setting
of a Western truck parts manufacturer. There had always been
contentious issues during collective bargaining at this company,
especially during the early 1980s when sales dipped and an
administration widely viewed as antiunion occupied the White
House. However, mutual respect always presided over negotiations,

and contracts were renewed without strikes. Third-generation management and labor personnel were able to arrive at agreements together, and this was set up by the "We're all in this together" mind-set that was prevalent on the shop floors. Grievances were settled without lingering aftereffects, and the feeling on both sides was that justice usually prevailed. Consequently, labor-management cooperation was an established, time-honored tradition in the company. The progeny of this cooperation included joint educational programs, generous benefits, and an information clearinghouse. The cultural attributes that contributed to a hostile work setting at the farm equipment parts manufacturer were assets in this case. And in the final analysis, few of the behavioral risk exposures that occurred in excess at the first company were problems in the second company.

An organizational intervention in the first labor situation would be late stage, at best. However, it could start with an examination of the build-up of employee behavioral risk exposures in the company. These would be examined across different departments, demographic groups, job classifications, and other categories. Relevant data from programs and services that control behavioral risk would be examined, too, including utilization rates, behavioral problem types, and patterns of referral. If the financial costs to the company and the amount of pain to the workforce were to be established, it would be easier to begin melting down the resistance to cooperation.

The second scenario illustrates a company and union that have propagated a positive organizational culture, incorporated change processes without causing organizational stoppages, and established management-employee partnerships that are reflected in the joint structure. These behaviors create the foundation upon which both the company and union can exercise a lot of give and take with each other.

The Need for Transformational Activity

Behavioral risk is by no means the only criterion on which organizational development strategies are implemented, whether in a union or nonunion work setting. The mainstay business economic considerations of finance, market-share, legal, and other factors that interest short-term shareholders usually take precedent. Introducing behavioral risk issues to the discussion, however, provides some balance to the decision-making process, because they account for the well-being of the workforce, which by its very nature is a long-term business interest.

Organizational behavior interventions require a commitment from management when the change needing to be made affects organizational culture, because this is nothing less than a transformational activity. Blumenthal and Haspeslagh say organizational transformation occurs at the time when "a majority of individuals in an organization must change their behavior." (It is different from restructuring, which might entail organizational delayering and downsizing without necessitating behavioral change.)

Consider the hurdles to be surmounted in implementing a work culture based on wellness and health promotion in order to drive down employees' healthcare problems. Research has shown that if ten people start an exercise program, on average five of them will quit within six months. Further, 70 percent of the U.S. adult population does not participate in regular physical activity. There are three reasons for this: most adults live highly structured lives; once life-style patterns are established, especially ones marked by sedentariness, inertia is hard to break; and most people will not sustain healthy exercise unless it is very convenient for them to do so. Among the tools for enforcing exercise adherence are peer support and participation, self-monitoring, competitions and rewards, and education on behavior modification, including the normalcy of relapse in the change process. When behavioral strategies such as these are used simultaneously (in a "package") adherence increases to as high as 97 percent after six months. Knowing this, a multifaceted organizational intervention can be planned and executed accordingly.

Fitness and healthy living habits can become building blocks for other cultural shifts, such as desirable work-related behavioral changes. These may include active participation in work teams, safer workplace behavior, commitment to quality, less use of sick leave, and diminished tolerance of the inappropriate work behaviors of others. When changes can build on one another, a synergistic approach to organizational change takes root.

Situation-Specific Interventions with Management

One of the most prescient diagnoses ever of a pathological organizational behavior was made in the highest of reaches of U.S. government by a nondiagnostician. White House aide John Dean told
Richard Nixon, "We have a cancer within—close to the Presi-
dency—that's growing."

We can all agree that some behavioral risks are going to occur
no matter what preventive measures are taken. The objective
should be to minimize the amount of financial risk exposure and
other negative consequences to the organization. In the Nixon
White House, numerous top staff members were indicted in the
Watergate conspiracy, and the president resigned under the
specter of impeachment. This brought about the dismantling of
the highest echelon of the executive branch; it signaled an unmitigated failure to control behavioral issues.

Situation-specific interventions are called for when there are
elevated risks in a segment of an organization (identified through
the behavioral audit process or through patterns of referral
detected by employee behavioral risk resources). Here, I consider
two types of interventions for inappropriate management behavior, the first is a departmental intervention and the second deals
with an individual manager or executive. (Note that patterns of
behavioral risk can run horizontally, through a large department,
for example, as well as vertically, by lineage, from one abusive manager to successive ones.)

Departmental Intervention

The accounting department of one dairy products company experienced both patterns of behavioral risks. An intervention team of
two psychologists was called in to work with a manager who had
twenty-three productive years with the company. Her record over
the last five years, however, was stained with employee complaints
to human resources that had become more frequent over the past
year. Additionally, as employee stress increased on her watch,
phones were broken, the company faced an employee lawsuit, customers and suppliers were mistreated, and employees exhausted
every benefit available to them. Upon being interviewed by the psychologists, though, she said that her employees treated her with

the same disrespect she gave them. "You want me to treat them nicer? Look at *them!*" she retorted.

On further inquiry, the psychologists found that she was only the latest in three generations of what employees called "marine corps management." When the psychologists looked elsewhere in the department, they found other abusive managers and employees, though to a lesser degree. This situation struck the psychologists as being similar to the intergenerational conflict in many abusive families, which spans from parent to sibling ("You're going to pay the consequences, just like I had to"), and can induce similarly abusive behavior among extended family members. They also noted that the work system had a pathological selection system— it attracted emotionally unstable employees who would lash out against it yet subjugate themselves to it by staying. Employees who seemed to be more independent and who exhibited better emotional and mental health would simply leave.

The company implemented a two-part intervention. First, two managers in the department (including the one with whom the intervention started) were assigned to attend intensive management development training that included instruction on behavioral change. They were encouraged to receive psychological help using their benefits plan. Work team sensitivity training was instituted for all managers and employees in the department, also. Second, if the interventions failed to produce better harmony and fewer problems, senior management would replace personnel.

Individual Executive Intervention

An eight-year executive in a midsized company with an excellent performance record was thought by co-executives to have a problem, although they had difficulty describing it in terms of behaviors. Often, important behavioral indicators in executives are very subtle, even when they are significant, and are not corroborated by changes in job performance in the early stages of a problem. For example, this executive was usually the first at operations review meetings to raise objections and had been highly assertive and also imaginative and inventive in projects and searching for solutions. Then his level of enthusiasm seemed to drop, he was less outspoken, and his output reflected past ideas instead of new ones. "He's not the person he used to be," was the reaction of co-executives. As a result of this perception, his name no longer appeared on promotion lists. Trust, which is central to the team relationships in executive suites, also eroded.

His immediate supervisor called an executive-intervention consultant, who spoke with the executive. Executive-intervention specialist Paul A. Sherman says the statement, "I'm concerned about the effect that any problems you may be having will have on your career" is an effective lead-in. This stark, light-of-day fact, delivered in a private and intimate business setting, is a powerful motivator, since an executive's self-image and esteem are commonly entwined with career more than any other aspect of his or her life. Once the executive opens up, life and career information can then be pored over in search of the primary problem(s).

In this case, after two extensive intervention sessions of three to four hours each, the specialist determined that the executive had been promoted to a position for which he lacked some needed technical knowledge. Even though the executive had received four promotions in two years and had an income of over $200,000—more than three times what he received before the promotions—he felt unable to call attention to his technical deficiencies for fear of being terminated. Additionally, the executive had some complications in his personal life, namely, that his teenage son and daughter were experiencing adolescent growing pains. Regarding himself as an expert problem solver, the executive had tried to take those issues on as well. The specialist eventually referred the executive and his children for family counseling. His more lasting intervention was on the organizational level, however. He gave the company recommendations for specific technical training for the executive. In the end, the executive retained his post, functioned much more effectively at work, and received help on how to counsel his children.

Sherman says that if a company waits for overt signs of chemical or emotional impairment in an executive before intervening, any mental health or substance abuse disorder may be so far along in the disease process that the person's career is irretrievable. He feels that in initiating the helping process for a colleague, executives need to trust their intuition, as they often do when making business decisions. If they feel a colleague needs help, they are probably detecting subtle behavior changes subconsciously even though they have not yet consciously interpreted them as a problem.

Specialized Interventions

Not all possible organizational interventions can be neatly pigeon-holed by category. Some are narrowly targeted and may be of short or long duration. Consider these.

Therapeutic Humor

But seriously, folks! Humor is the pressure release valve of life. Consider one state children's services agency whose employees coped for two years with a battery of legislative proposals that would have cut funding by one-third and consolidated the agency with the welfare department. Parents were increasingly angry with the case-workers as more families were applying for services, due to high unemployment. Employees at the main administrative office were becoming testy with each other, behavior one employee described as "picking at each other's scabs." Even though there were no overt problems between supervisors and employees, most workers felt it was only a matter of time before a major dispute would erupt.

Then management sent in the clowns. Workplace therapeutic humor specialists use songs, stories, and group exercises to release pent-up frustration. They are often highly talented people with training in psychology or human behavior modification. They come with a bag full of tricks and jokes and always involve the audience as participants. When participants have relaxed and let down their guard—that is, after the specialist has pried a psychological opening in their minds—he or she inserts messages about mutual respect and workplace cooperation and ways to break up everyday work tension that will be recalled later during tension-filled work situations. Humor interventions can have a tremendous therapeutic effect. Employees often pick up on the humorist's message to use laughter to bring people together and poke fun at a common dilemma.

Mentoring

This activity has far more utility than just grooming the next generation of executives or providing guidance before dispatching new envoys. It is from mentoring that upwardly mobile managers and professionals learn the behavioral norms of the organization, avoid the pratfalls of internal politics, and "keep their noses clean."

Mentoring, a kind of sponsorship without actual responsibility for the welfare of the other, may be both a formal and informal process. It occurs informally when one occupational professional hires another as his or her underling and schools the new person on ways to conduct himself or herself in the corporate setting. It occurs formally when an experienced hand in the company is paired with a newcomer of an identical demographic variable who helps him or her to survive and achieve career progression (this method is used particularly for women and minorities). The pairing may occur at the time of hiring or only after a person missteps in the organization.

Special interventions such as humor and mentoring should be judiciously used, however. It is inappropriate, for example, to bring a therapeutic humor specialist into a downsizing company or to implement mentoring just when traditional pathways of career advancement are being eliminated.

Team Building and Work Team Problem Intervention

Dysfunctional work teams can be both cause or victim of organizational problems. To illustrate, at a paper production company distribution site with 105 employees, a psychological wall existed between office and warehouse personnel. A perpetually unstable working environment was mired in mistrust and anxiety. Salespeople and managers vied with each other for power. Salespeople, for example, were authorized to make promises on quantities of orders and deadlines for deliveries irrespective of the workload or materials that would have to be transported from other distribution sites. Managers fluctuated between digging in their heels in a "no-can-do" position and reinforcing the time crunch that salespeople sought to impose. This semi–crisis management mode only grew worse when the facility's general manager retired. Corporate headquarters hired seven successive replacement general managers, who came and went over the next two years. One finally agreed to stay, but he had a hands-off policy toward his division managers, some of whom were on "ego trips." These power trips occurred, in part, because none of them had received professional management training—which instills basic management skills such as impartial decision making—and their inabilities were perpetuated by the general manager.

Problems such as high defect rates, absenteeism, and frequent accidents persisted. After a year, the company hired a national quality improvement (QI) consulting firm to implement quality teams at the facility. All employees went through the eight-month QI program, followed by a "graduation." The teams were supposedly empowered to make production decisions, and employees were enthusiastic during the initial stages. Productivity was high, defects were low, and employees seemed contented. Communication opened up between office and warehouse personnel. After ten months, however, the quality program "seemed to disappear into the cracks," according to one employee. The general manager was seldom seen at the facility anymore, managers were anxious to reclaim their power, and they began holding their own private QI meetings. Salespeople once again became autocratic. In other words, the company reverted back to its old habits. Later, a new paper distributor came to town and one of the managers departed for the new company with five of his employees. Then another manager inadvertently mentioned that the company was considering consolidating the distribution location with another one, opening a new site about halfway between the two centers, which were 110 miles apart. Employees deduced that this would mean moving or having hour-long commutes. At last check, a number of the employees were looking for other work.

Several things had gone wrong in this organization. First, senior management failed to correct the problems between salespeople and line managers. Although the power issue with line managers would have been resolved if the work team movement had been successful, the power issue with salespeople would eventually have resurfaced. Second, employee empowerment was treated as a quick fix and had no genuine commitment from senior management. Thus, empowerment evaporated, leaving managers to recoup their decision-making authority. The company also had an unrealistic time frame for implementing the work teams. Consider all of the subtle but important behavioral changes that employees must make in order to transition successfully to quality-based work teams. These behaviors include listening to understand, giving feedback to help others, taking on new assignments, requesting help, getting a point across to others, participating in group meetings, keeping the boss informed, resolving issues with others, making positive responses to negative situations, dealing with changes, working smarter, and being team players. Each of these behaviors requires a series of behavioral steps. For example, requesting help entails asking for it as soon as it is needed, articulating the total situation or problem, describing all the solutions tried so far, and then working with the helper to solve the problem and decide on an action plan. Further, in addition to learning to take all these behavioral steps—which cannot be permanently instituted without fundamental attitude changes—employees must learn how to engage in group problem-solving activities, use flowcharts, comply with exact manufacturing specifications, and deal competently with all the other issues native to quality-based work teams.

The Right Mix of People

Positive group interaction gives work teams their electrical juice, and negative interaction poisons the team process. Work teams engender the development of interdependent, often intimate relationships between people, but sometimes, personalities do not mix well. Think of the potential for conflict when your team throws into the same pot extreme externalizers—people who under stressful conditions become loud, unruly, and action-oriented—and extreme internalizers—people who bottle up problems. Or the potential for flat productivity when there is no take-charge person, when there is no cutup to bring some levity to the group, or when there are too many members who are long on creativity but short on follow-through. To optimize productivity and diminish behavioral risk, employers can promote good behavioral dynamics.

Consider, for example, two companies that transitioned to work teams. Both were assembly companies of between 50 and 100 people. Both had presidents who considered themselves to be visionaries and believed that their workforces could manage themselves better than supervisors could. Both replaced the plant manager with a certified quality auditor to facilitate the transition. Both condensed many narrow job categories into a couple of broad categories; both changed from supervisory to group decision making; both changed the reward system from recognizing individual performance to recognizing team performance and individual breadth of skills; both cross-trained on technical skills to allow team members to move from job to job; and both trained on administrative procedures. However, only one of the companies trained team members on resolving interpersonal conflicts, sensitizing them to diversity issues and effective communication.

The consultants at both companies handpicked a steering team to implement the work teams, which numbered seven at each company. Each steering team helped select team leaders to serve for one year in that rotating position. The leaders were the key links to the internal organization and to external customers and suppliers, had the highest degree of accountability for the team, had at least one year of tenure with the company, were eligible for a year-end bonus based on team success, and were to serve as mentors following their year as team leader. Finally, both consultants had checklists of qualifications on which candidates for team leadership were be evaluated, and these checklists, shown below, were where the difference lay.

First Consultant	Second Consultant	Qualifications
✓	✓	Physical health
✓	✓	Judgment
✓	✓	Analytical ability
✓	✓	Job fit
✓	✓	Attention to detail
✓	✓	Initiative
✓	✓	Influence among team members
✓	✓	Ability to plan and organize
	✓	Ability to learn
	✓	Ability to communicate orally
	✓	Self-motivated
	✓	Cooperative
	✓	Tolerant of stress
	✓	Possessing self-esteem

The first consultant tended to focus exclusively on a candidate's technical skills, knowledge, and physical characteristics. The additional areas covered by the second consultant were those attitudinal and personal qualities most likely to influence team members' behavior. Consequently, the first company nominated team leaders who were proven in their jobs but not necessarily proficient at preventing or resolving disputes, appearing objective, being open-minded and, most importantly, maintaining group unity and motivation. (Companies that promote from within to the management ranks, in particular, have this tendency to name employees with good work habits but without effective leadership qualities.)

Team Conflicts

Behavior-related team conflicts can arise from a wide spectrum of causes: an avoidance or "smooth" conflict style in the team leader; a lack of trust, leading to a communication vacuum and inadequate delivery of information; comfort with a particular task, leading to a disinterest in learning other team members' tasks; technical proficiency combined with interpersonal deficiency, resulting in a nasty or curt way of addressing teammates; and horseplay or laziness.

For example, in one public relations and advertising firm where individual accounts were assigned to teams of employees, defensiveness among the creative staff became a recurring problem. One team member recognized that a proposed advertising campaign was inappropriate for the firm's conservative community-minded customer. He reasoned that the campaign would have too much éclat for a customer that historically had used mostly radio spots with no music, sound effects, or other fanfare, so he proposed to a second team member that they raise the issue with the senior vice president. His colleague took exception, feeling that the proposal was fine and that the team was too far along to change direction. The two had a standoff that eventually required the senior vice president's intervention, and they were never able to work together on the same account again.

Another example illustrates the chaos that can ensue when interdependency is introduced to employees who previously worked very independently. The research and development lab of a chemical company attempted to foster an "intrapreneurial" work environment in which the technicians were encouraged to challenge each other's hypotheses and findings. As the laboratory was physically separate from manufacturing activities, the work environment was insulated from the rest of the company as well. In a short period of time, hostilities between chemists led to a bunker mentality in which psychological defenses were raised and cliques formed. So much time and energy was diverted from experimentation, validation tests, and other product development activities that output declined. The technicians eventually retrenched to the status quo ante and their individualized work habits. In this case, no ground rules for appropriate work team behavior had been established. The failure to help the technicians exercise good interpersonal skills—empathy, tolerance, and positive reinforcement—doomed the effort to failure. The appropriate intervention would have established appropriate behavioral boundaries.

Chapters Five and Six have considered a variety of interventions. Presented as separate and distinct solutions, some interventions have focused on individuals, others on the organization. To be a truly holistic concept, however, behavioral risk management must bridge the two. The intervention that builds this bridge is training. For example, training should be the primary medium through which messages about empowerment and its counterbalance of self-responsibility are conveyed to employees. Training should also establish the behavioral expectations for everyone in a work system and provide education on the psychological processes through which behavioral change (or modification) occurs.

Managerial, work team, and employee training are part and parcel of behavioral risk management. Moreover, to accomplish its objectives, training that diminishes behavioral risk must be integrated with other types of workplace training and not relegated to last place in the training lineup. It must also be more than a nonmandatory exercise done in an off week. Chapter Seven discusses in more detail how behavioral risk training will improve the performance and effectiveness of your organization.

Notes

P. 150, *Three cultural phenomena raised by Hampden-Turner:* Hampden-Turner, C. *Creating Corporate Culture: From Discord to Harmony.* Reading, Mass.: Addison-Wesley, 1990.

P. 151, *model behavioral risk value statement:* Oher, J. M. "Values: Making a Statement of Mutual Respect." *EAP Digest* (Behavior Risk Management supplement), 1994, *14*(6), 35–36.

P. 153, *"In the 1920s the millwright,"* Miller, H. Unpublished source, n.d.

P. 154, *four generic types of leadership style:* Reimann B. C., and Wiener, Y. "Corporate Culture: Avoiding the Elitist Trap." *Business Horizons,* 1988, *31*(2), 36–44.

P. 155, *"DeLorean's subsequent adventures":* Hampden-Turner, C. *Creating Corporate Culture: From Discord to Harmony.* Reading, Mass.: Addison-Wesley, 1990, p. 187.

P. 156, *One candy-bar manufacturer:* Associated Press. "Spoiled Peanut Butter Seized from Candy Firm." *Harrisburg Patriot-News,* May 28, 1995, p. A-7.

P. 157, *When [a prospective major investor] comes to us:* Schacht, H. (panelist on the television program). "Profits and Promises: Reinventing the Corporation," produced by Seminars, Inc., in association with the Columbia University Graduate School of Journalism and Channel Thirteen/WNET, distributed by the Public Broadcasting Service, March 1995.

P. 157, in*appropriate behaviors of board members:* Montgomery, W. R. "Board Members' Responsibilities and Legal Liabilities." *Transit Journal,* Summer 1979, pp. 43–50.

P. 158, *model of the future work organization:* Mitroff, I., Mason, R., and Pearson, C. "Radical Surgery: What Will Tomorrow's Organizations Look Like?" *Academy of Management Executive,* 1994, *8*(2), 11–21.

P. 164, *employment relationship is negotiated:* Kinyon, R. "The Changing Social Contract: The Employer-Employee Dance." Paper presented at the 1995 Annual Conference of Employee Assistance Professionals Association, Boston, Nov. 1995.

P. 165, *concept of the "job" . . . is becoming obsolete:* Francek, J. "EA and the Death of the Job." *Employee Assistance,* 1995, *7*(9), 14–17.

P. 168, *11 percent of current employers currently offer credits:* Hewitt Associates. *Hot Topics in Benefit Flexibility.* Lincolnshire, Ill.: Hewitt Associates LLC, 1995.

P. 170, *"Leave skid marks":* Pritchett, P., and Pound, R. *High-Velocity Culture Change: A Handbook for Managers.* Dallas: Pritchett, 1993, p. 44.

P. 175, *"a majority of individuals":* Blumenthal, B., and Haspeslagh, P.

"Toward a Definition of Corporate Transformation." *Sloan Management Review,* Spring 1994, pp. 102.

P. 175, *adherence increases to as high as 97 percent:* Robison, J. I., and Rogers, M. A. "Impact of Behavior Management Programs on Exercise Adherence." *American Journal of Health Promotion,* 1995, *9*(5), pp. 379–382.

P. 176, *"We have a cancer within":* Dean, J. W., III. *Blind Ambition: The White House Years.* New York: Simon & Schuster, 1976, p. 201.

P. 178, *"I'm concerned about the effect":* Sherman, P. Interview with author. July 1995.

P. 179, *Humor interventions:* "Laughing Matters: Taking Your Job Seriously and Yourself Lightly." *JAMA: The Journal of the American Medical Association,* Apr. 1, 1992.

P. 181, *subtle but important behavioral changes:* Zenger-Miller, Inc. *Quest: Quality Enhancement Through Skills Training.* San Jose, Calif.: Zenger-Miller, 1995.

Chapter Seven

Behavioral Risk Training

Suppose the behavioral risk interventions for workers and organizations described in the prior two chapters have been implemented in a company. What assurances are there that a work system's executive leadership, managers, employees, and all their family members will actually use the available interventions?

The intervention that makes the behavioral risk management strategy engaging for people is training. For the behavioral risk management strategy to accomplish its objectives, training must

- Educate internal customers about human and organizational behavior, how it manifests itself, and how it can be changed.
- Explain how to access and use programs, services, and benefits.
- Show how managing behavioral risk is relevant to the making of products and the delivery of services.

Historically, getting "prime time" for training on any topic other than how a product is made or service is delivered (that is, revenue-generating activities) has been difficult, especially when that training lacks the explicit endorsement of senior management. Consequently, when the training finally occurs, the occupational professionals delivering it may not be taken seriously, or they may give instructions that conflict with training given by others. If

---

The sample training script in this chapter is adapted from Milbauer, R. (Producer). *The Dryden File II*. Hartsdale, N.Y.: Motivision, MCMLXXXVIII. Videotape. It is reprinted here by permission.

senior managers and training planners understand the pervasiveness of behavioral risk in an organization, however, scheduling and perceived importance should be less of a problem.

Consider the training presented by one employee assistance firm, brought in by a business organization to talk with supervisors about identifying substance abusers and referring them for help. The problem identification process presented conflicted with information the company's in-house training department had given the supervisors about the same problem. The message supervisors received from the in-house trainers had been "we want to deal with this problem in-house and eradicate it." The message they received from the EA firm was "send us the employees who are giving you problems, and we will deal with them." Given the choice, the vast majority of supervisors chose to abide by the in-house trainers' instructions. The EA firm ended up looking like a highly specialized off-to-the-side "do-gooder" function that only helps the least fortunate. Further, the EA firm acted as its own worst enemy when it sent in a twenty-six-year-old fresh face just a few years out of social work school to tell fifty-year-old supervisors how they should deal with workplace tensions that had existed in the company for years. The trainer did not know the supervisors' work lexicon or the specific problems management was having with employees. Following her training session, the supervisors returned to the jobs they did by rote, the handouts were filed away and the instruction was forgotten. After the training, the EA program was even more underutilized by supervisors than before.

The EA training communicated the correct message, but without the express endorsement of top management and in conflict with the training of authority figures in the organization, it became a sideshow. Training in how to control behavioral risk must be made relevant to everyday tasks in the organization, integrated with other training, and reinforced by the availability (and preferably the visible on-site presence) of staff involved in service delivery for further consultation.

Exhibit 7.1 lists the considerations that trainers whose topics include behavioral risk should take into account when constructing a curriculum, and the following sections describe them in more detail. The chapter concludes with examples of training curriculums in action.

Exhibit 7.1 Designing a Behavioral Risk Training Curriculum.

Training topics:

- Behavioral change
- Stress management
- Coping with organizational changes
- Access to and use of programs and services
- Workplace conflict resolution
- Government-mandated drug and alcohol awareness education
- Dynamics of organizational behavior

Audiences:

- Managers
- Employees
- Executive leaders and boards of directors

Types of training *(or the curriculum within which the behavioral risk training is offered):*

- Performance management
- Quality management
- Work team
- Safety
- Employee orientation
- Executive and board of directors orientation

Logistical considerations:

- Focus on individual or organizational behavioral issues, depending on the audience
- Position of behavioral risk training in the curriculum
- Length of training
- Refresher training
- Continual training

Training Topics

What behavioral risk topics should be taught to people in a work organization? Traditionally, a trainer who is a program staff member will instruct the audience—usually managers, sometimes employees—about access to and use of one or more programs. Behavioral risk training, however, with its heavy preventive focus will also educate people about actual individual and organizational behavioral issues. In other words, the holistic focus of behavioral risk management is reflected in the training. Here are seven topics that should be included in the training curriculum.

Behavioral Change

Employers find time and again that making permanent behavioral change can be their prickliest issue when they are attempting organizational transformation. The problem of retrenchment to old behavioral patterns is like a resistant virus. It may reemerge long after the time when it is thought to be under control and therefore has been neglected. Management needs to accept that at points along the way employees will become despondent, and employees must recognize that this feeling is a normal part of the change process. Both managers and employees need an appropriate frame of reference for understanding behavioral change. For example, did you know that former smokers relapse, on average, four times before quitting for good? Managers and employees need to recognize the psychological stages of change—precontemplation, contemplation, action, and maintenance (discussed in more detail later)—and express them in the context of their jobs.

The behaviors that are most important to controlling workplace behavioral risk are communication and interaction with others. These behaviors are often exhibited through informal networks, which constitute the central nervous system of a work organization. These strands of communication and interaction become increasingly complex and important as an organization becomes less hierarchical, according to David Krackhardt, who specializes in organizations and public policy.

Computer-generated "sociograms" graphically depict these communications and interactions. Two models, shown in Figure 7.1, illustrate the difference between hierarchical and team-based work systems. The classic bow tie configuration illustrates how information in a hierarchical system has a semi-orderly flow that reaches a centralized point. The circular, or web, configuration is more characteristic of work teams, in which communication and interaction are considerably more complicated. These sociograms illustrate why interpersonal problems continually arise on some work teams. Their communication pattern is in stark contrast to the way solutions were previously dictated by management quickly and efficiently. (Ironically, those dictates often led to employee alienation and probably expedited the work team movement.) Because the locus of control for implementing solutions, problem solving, and other team activities has changed, moving from the manager (a central point), to team members (diffuse points), the need for promoting appropriate individual behaviors among employees speaks for itself.

To stress the importance that senior management places on good team behavior practices, training sessions should be introduced by a senior manager who can endorse the process and communicate its importance; conducted by a QI or other professional who is willing to educate workers on more than just quality standards, such as those in ISO 9000; and reinforced by a worker who has good rapport with his or her peers. Acceptable and unacceptable team behaviors must be specified. Here are some examples:

Acceptable Team Behavior	*Unacceptable Team Behavior*
Actively listening to promote two-way communication	Being unwilling to set aside personal needs
Making "I" statements (instead of "you" statements that infer blame)	Aggressively using words like "always" and "never"
Respecting others' rights, needs, and feelings	Exhibiting a negative attitude toward change, other people, and team building in general
Encouraging others to participate in discussions that involve the team	Showing a need or preference to be a "star" rather than a team member

Figure 7.1 Hierarchical and Team-Based Work Systems.

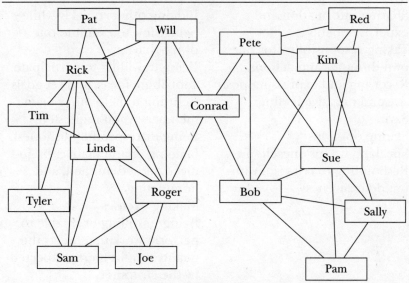

The classic bow tie configuration

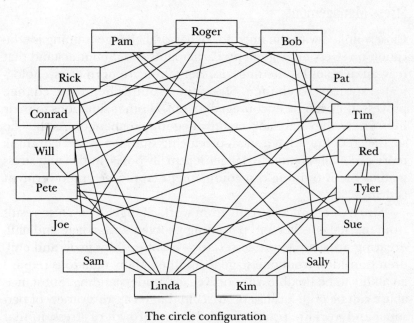

The circle configuration

Source: Adapted from drawings by David Krackhardt using Krackplot software, 1994. Reprinted by permission.

Acceptable Team Behavior	Unacceptable Team Behavior
Sharing information and expertise openly	Judging others quickly while being slow to examine one's own behavior
Taking responsibility for one's own thoughts and actions	Being unwilling to participate, contribute ideas, and set goals
Receiving and expressing positive and negative feelings	Refusing to help other team members when requested
Saying no	Being disrespectful, dishonest, blaming, manipulative, preju-
Stating opinions	diced, closed minded, and
Speaking up for oneself	dominating
Responding to criticism without defensiveness	Making excuses
	Being unwilling or unable to perform work that meets the quality requirements expected by the customer

Stress Management

Closely linked with the need for behavioral change training is education on stress management. Participants should understand that fear, anxiety, and sometimes disorientation are normal psychological responses to change. Once they comprehend the change process, they can be encouraged to look at other situations in their lives where they have successfully negotiated changes. As they do so, they redefine what a stress-producing situation is and can think more rationally about the danger it actually poses. In this way, stress management training can complement employee empowerment activities.

Stress does not arise only from work change. It can also result from marital conflict and parenting problems. Marriage and childrearing are change processes, too—relationships grow and children transition from one stage to another. Many situations require an ability to be flexible, supportive, and understanding. Substance abuse can be both a cause of stress, in that it causes a variety of personal and worklife problems, and an outgrowth of stress, in that the substance can be a form of self-medication, to compensate for the lack of other coping mechanisms. Stress can also accumulate from trying to balance too many activities. Since people usually go through several major metabolic changes during adulthood, a late-twenties "Type-A" individual experiencing the first such change may need to reduce the number of things he or she tries to accomplish in a day. People who do not adjust may suffer the consequence of elevated blood pressure, chronic fatigue, or some other symptom.

Stress management training, then, should be based on helping people to be better problem solvers. Since stress has solutions, managing stress means taking steps to reduce the distress-producing aspects in one's life or to replace them or balance them with activities that produce eustress. Lacking this ability, people may develop emotional problems that plague them throughout adulthood.

Coping with Organizational Changes

Among the most feared changes in the work environment are empowerment, team building, downsizing, transformation, relocation, reorganization, and merging. They often induce the greatest stress response because a failure to fit into the changed organization has an inherent economic impact and may stigmatize an individual, causing feelings of shame. Often during change, employees "bottom out," then rebound, as shown in Figure 7.2. Employers should temper any thought that helping employees acquire new coping skills is the complete solution to maintaining workforce equilibrium, however. Without an effective corporate communication program to help employees understand the direction of the organization and to brace for changes, training is disingenuous. The communication should also have an efficient feedback mechanism that facilitates discussion beyond formal announcements. Otherwise, the emotional roller-coaster ride of fear and relief may still result in a variety of emotional and physical health problems.

Access to and Use of Programs and Services

Once training participants understand the behavioral problems and issues in the work environment that contribute to behavioral health, employee conduct, and job performance problems, the

Figure 7.2 The Process of Change.

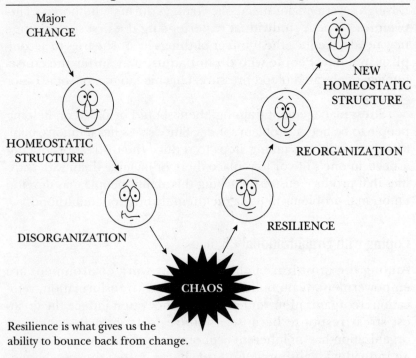

Major
CHANGE

NEW
HOMEOSTATIC
STRUCTURE

HOMEOSTATIC
STRUCTURE

REORGANIZATION

RESILIENCE

DISORGANIZATION

CHAOS

Resilience is what gives us the
ability to bounce back from change.

Source: Titcomb, T. J. "Resilience! Positive Strategies for Managing Change"
(Training module). Family Service, Lancaster, Pa., 1994. Adapted from the
work of nineteenth century biologist Claude Bernard. Reprinted by permission.

training should describe how to access and use the programs, services, and benefits that help people deal with the problems. This
part of training includes information on the full scope of program
activities. Often, there is more at an employee's or manager's dis-
posal than meets the eye. Many of us belong to membership organizations, for example, that provide everything from credit cards
to travel discounts to conventions and educational programs. In
the same way, a wellness and health promotion program might
include such secondary benefits as prostate exams, blood testing,
and life-style assessments that will be underutilized unless they
are promoted. The same caveat applies to problem assessment
resources, drug-testing and medical review services, work-and-

family programs and services, behavioral health benefits utilization, conflict resolution, and the ombudsman.

Workplace Conflict Resolution

When the people involved in a workplace conflict begin to lose control of themselves, when there is an impasse between employees or between a manager and employees, for example, the conflict resolution process should come into play. Usually a progression of incidents precedes any major blowup having considerable job or career consequences for the parties involved, and any such preliminary incident is an opportunity to apply a formal conflict resolution process.

For example, an editor and a writer on a magazine staff may have a communication problem, resulting in article submissions from the writer that are different in format, content, or writing style from what the editor had in mind. The editor may, in fact, be the writer's "boss" but may also want to continue the working relationship. Conflict resolution would provide a peaceable solution. This training should explain how people can access this process and what they can expect from it.

Government-Mandated Drug and Alcohol Awareness Education

Drug and alcohol awareness education is required under various federal, state, and local statutes and regulations. These include the Drug-Free Workplace Act, which applies to many federal government contractors; the drug- and alcohol-testing regulations of the U.S. Department of Transportation; and the drug-testing regulations that apply to companies serving the defense, nuclear, and energy industries. (The legally required education is discussed in Chapter Twelve.)

Dynamics of Organizational Behavior

The dynamics of organizational behavior are an important topic for the people responsible for the direction of the organization: setting its culture, changing its structure, responding to the marketplace, and so forth. Consequently, they should be trained, first, on warning signs of dysfunctional organizational behavior—what causes them, and how they lead to elevated employee behavioral risk—and, second, how dysfunctional organizational behavior manifests itself as behavioral risk exposure.

Audiences

There are three primary audiences for behavioral risk training. *Managers* make up the most important audience, since they are the ones who deal with behavioral health, conduct, and work performance problems at the operational level of business. *Employees,* especially those in settings that use empowerment-based work team concepts, should also be trained, since they are now assuming many of the responsibilities once associated with traditional supervision. The third audience, which has been most neglected with regard to behavioral risk issues, is *executive leaders and boards of directors.* They set the tone for the organization and can have a profound effect on organizational behaviors and factors that influence employee behavioral risk exposures.

Types of Training

Any training program that is not spliced into the company's primary training initiative and is not delivered in a manner consistent with the company's strategic objectives runs the risk of being ineffective or irrelevant. Following are examples of primary training initiatives that are common to U.S. companies and that can include behavioral risk training.

Performance Management

Even though the name of this training program may vary somewhat, performance management is the most commonly accepted term in the 1990s for human resource–driven management training. Performance management is the process by which

- Business objectives are translated into operational guidelines.
- Financial and operational performance measures are set for managers.

- Employees' performance expectations are established.
- Performance reviews are carried out for both managers and employees.
- Coaching and feedback is provided.
- Rewards are given for individual and team accomplishment.

Performance management also specifies the behavior expected from employees and managers, and help-seeking venues for behavioral problems.

Training is the primary medium through which managers are informed and educated about performance management priorities. In larger companies, this training is typically a highly formalized, professional presentation, for which an employer may have invested $1,000 or more for each manager who participates.

Quality Management

There are three universal processes for managing quality:

Quality planning, which entails identifying customers, developing product features to their needs, transferring plans to the operating forces, and other preimplementation activities

Quality control, which evaluates product performance, compares performance to market goals, and acts on the difference

Quality improvement, which establishes the infrastructure and projects teams, identifies improvement projects, and provides teams with resources, training, and motivation

In order to lay the groundwork for and then upgrade quality management, the content of training for managers is learning operational flowcharts, process control features, feedback loops, record-keeping standards, and other technical and procedural matters.

There is also a behavioral component, however, in the prerequisites that must be met in order for workforce participation in quality programs to be implemented and sustained. For example, Juran wrote that upper management needs to undergo training to understand participative management, the process by which all employees have a role to play in planning and decision making. Midlevel and line managers must learn to accept that they will be delegating management prerogatives and, in so doing, will have to deal with employee apprehension about receiving them.

Work Team

Work team training is related to quality management training in that work teams are usually the scions of quality initiatives. In addition to giving instruction on the actual performance of tasks, the essential mission of work team training is to maximize the benefit derived by the organization from each individual's capabilities. This training is based on the populist belief that everyone has the essential tools—critical-thinking, analytical, and mechanical inclinations—that can be used to further the objectives of the team and organization.

A paradox of work teams is that while employees are collaborating they must simultaneously resist the temptation to engage in groupthink and prematurely agree with the other group members. The basic research performed on human relations between 1945 and 1950 by the Office of Naval Research (ONR) is relevant here. In an effort to measure whether the "majority effect" of peer pressure modified and distorted judgments, ONR devised a procedure for placing an individual in a position of radical conflict with all other members of a group. The situation was simple enough: all the subjects (male college students) had to do was match the length of a given line with one of three very noticeably unequal lines. Each subject was put in a group of eight and instructed to individually match the lines. The subjects would find themselves suddenly contradicted by the seven others, who were instructed to select an unequal line in order to create the conflict. After twelve trials per individual, 74 percent of subjects had made at least one error, and 28 percent had made more than six. By contrast, only 5 percent of a control group made any errors at all. The ONR researchers drew two conclusions that are significant to work team environments: first, social support is a source of power and stability for people, and second, having once committed himself to yielding to a group, the individual finds it difficult and painful to change his direction, which is tantamount to a public admission of having acted improperly.

Empowerment-based work team training, then, should seek to

enable members to move toward *independence* of thought rather than *distortion* of perception, judgment, or action. In this way, teams will harness the most creative and passionate work from the individual, the alternative to which could be a bad decision by a few group leaders that has been rubber-stamped by a substantial majority of followers.

Behavioral risk training in a work team setting can be supplemented with periodic trainings for one or several work teams at a time on a specific aspect of behavioral risk. In this way, they are introduced to a behavioral risk function, such as managed behavioral healthcare, while learning about the related behavioral risks and how they develop, requiring intervention. Raising the level of awareness in this way is a preventive measure that also facilitates intervention that occurs earlier than it otherwise might have.

Work team training must also have a heavy emphasis on interteam and intrateam communication, cooperation, and problem resolution.

Safety

Preparing employees in dangerous environments to work safely involves three levels of training. The first level is traditional accident prevention procedures, including first aid and medical services, fire protection, method of walking on work surfaces, handling and storage of hazardous materials, personal protection, equipment, and control of dangerous environments. The second level is behavior-based safety processes that are intended to interrupt a causal chain in which several unsafe acts or conditions must precede each accident. This training might be aimed at preventing, for example, a leak or explosion where several valves are simultaneously left unsealed, the malfunctioning of a meter that detects ambient gases, and the failure to perform routine inspections. The third level seeks to curtail underlying attitudinal problems that fall into the categories of negligence, indifference, or premeditation. (These problems may be a part of the causal chain in the second level.)

Behavioral safety training is concerned with the second and third levels, which promote "actively caring" behaviors among employees, which form the linchpin of any safety culture. Behavioral safety expert E. Scott Geller says this is best implemented and reinforced in an empowered work environment.

Employee Orientation

Employee orientation is a "welcome aboard" gathering in which employees are introduced to everything from personnel policies to work rules to the benefits plan. It is also an opportunity to introduce employees to resources that are available to them for personal problems, interpersonal conflicts at work, and health improvement. The behavioral risk training curriculum can be brought to their attention.

Executive and Board of Directors Orientation

Board members are a company's trustees. That is, they are the ones to whom the health and welfare of the organization are entrusted. This solemn responsibility entails moral and legal obligations. The executive staff members may be trustees as well if they are ex officio (or nonvoting) members of the board. In this respect, their role more resembles that of a board member than manager or employee in the company. However, the manner in which board members are appointed, oriented, and trained can spell the difference between whether board meetings and independent interactions of members more resemble a cadre of overseers of a sacred trust or a clubhouse.

Orientation for board members should cover the mission and objectives of the organization, its history, structure, relationship with the community, role of the chairman, composition of the board, and its bylaws. Training should review fiduciary responsibilities, meeting rules, limitations of power, budgeting, profit and loss statements, balance sheets, audit reports, legal issues of boards, role of committees, and the keeping of minutes.

The board should also be trained on appropriate and inappropriate behaviors of both boards and organizations. They can be educated on the causes and manifestations of behavioral risk, how organizational behaviors contribute to them, the kinds of policies and practices that are likely to increase behavioral risk exposures, and the role of a board in interceding against behavioral risk. This information will be valuable to the board in maintaining the checks and balances it has with the executive leadership. Balancing this education should be a clear delineation of board boundaries to prevent micromanagement of the company and subsequent board-executive leadership conflicts.

Logistical Considerations

An effective training regimen presents information in a way that is appealing. Presentations should hold the interest of participants as they stimulate thought, dispense handy rules of thumb (such as mnemonic devices) for dealing with everyday work situations, and make their points using realistic work-related situations as examples. To the extent practical and affordable, training can be facilitated with multimedia formats. As long as no confidentiality protections or cultural mores in the company are violated, the training can include past examples of behavioral situations that people in the organization are aware of. Behavioral risk training should include examples of appropriate as well as inappropriate behavior. The training should leave people wanting more.

While behavioral risk training may be viewed by senior management only as adjunctive to other training, it can be vastly more interesting and capable of captivating an audience than other training. Human behavior has intrinsically dramatic elements. Consider these keywords and phrases, borrowed from the case studies in Chapter One, that evoke strong images or hit emotional chords: psychiatric, compensatory awards, pathological, discipline, termination, intoxication, boot camp culture, codependency, supervisor's dog house, and dysfunctional family. Such terms can effectively be interspersed in the trainer's dialogue with participants.

Behavioral risk training is enlivened by good delivery, and a variety of logistical considerations help to make it effective as well. They include the following.

Focus on Individual or Organizational Behavioral Issues

Behavioral risk training can be divided into two subcurricula: individual behavioral issues only (for employees) and integrated individual-organizational behavioral issues (for managers, executives, and board members).

Individual behaviors should be emphasized during employee training, because employee work constitutes the microscopic affairs of the organization, which are characterized by individual actions and interactions. Training for managers also should be weighted toward individual behaviors, but it should include some discussion of organizational behaviors, because managers are a bridge between the microscopic and the macroscopic affairs of the organization. The intent is not to make managers experts on organizational behavior, but to raise their consciousness about dysfunctional work systems. Senior managers and board members should have equally weighted training on individual and organizational behavioral risks. They need to understand the cause-and-effect relationships between the two, how their actions in minding the organization affect these risks, and how behavioral risk management is integral to their responsibility for providing a safe and healthy workplace.

Position of Behavioral Risk Training in the Curriculum

Every day newspapers break large and small stories. What makes a story about new research findings in the treatment of Alzheimer's disease or the latest White House scandal a major event or an afterthought? In large part, it is the prominence and position of the article. Does the article appear in Section A or one of the succeeding departmentalized sections? Is it on the front page or an inside page? Does it run above the fold? What type size and degree of boldness is the heading?

Similarly, the prominence and position given to behavioral risk training matters. First, as we have seen, behavioral risk training should be integrated with a major training initiative—placed in the first section of the newspaper, so to speak. This gives it legitimacy and credibility. Second, it should be positioned where it fits sequentially.

For a moment, let's distinguish between work-related and non-work-related behavioral risks. The work-related ones include behavioral health and other personal problems that directly affect work performance. The non-work-related ones address primarily physical healthcare and life-style issues, especially those of dependents, that do not directly affect work performance.

For the curricula described earlier, the first priority is the work-related behavioral risks. For that reason, they should be positioned near discussions of related issues, such as the disciplinary process (during performance management training), preventing work team conflict (during work team training), and responsibility for a safe and healthy workplace (during executive and board training). Managers should be taught, for example, that the work-based problem assessment resource is an *empowering* tool for them because it removes from their shoulders the onus of assessing and resolving employee problems that interfere with the work unit's productivity, even as they begin to take disciplinary measures against the individual. (In addition, managerial attempts to resolve behavioral problems can put the company on legally slippery ground.)

The non-work-related behavioral risks do not have a direct connection with productivity issues but should be mentioned to raise awareness of the availability of related programs, benefits, and services. Executives and board members should understand the role of wellness and health promotion and of work and family benefits as prevention-based behavioral risk activities. Managers should be aware of them so that they can be suggested to employees, as appropriate. Employees should know the range of services and benefits provided and understand how to access them.

Length of Training

Returning to the news story analogy, another factor that determines the impact of a late-breaking feature is the number of column inches it occupies. Reporters do not determine this length, however; editors do. So it is with training. The training planner (as editor) should grant an optimal length of time for behavioral risk training. For example, during employee orientation, the discussion of behavioral risk programs, services, and benefits may last only fifteen minutes or so. More detailed discussions may follow later in periodic brown-bag lunches on life-style issues and during continual work team training. In management, executive, and board of directors trainings, initial training should run four to eight hours.

Refresher Training

Human nature being such as it is, the key to optimizing behavioral risk management is to keep it in front of—and in the minds of—the various audiences. At least two hours of refresher training for managers, executives, and board members should be provided annually. However, the Achilles' heel of any such training is that, if participants feel that it is, in fact, retreaded information, they are likely to tune out. Therefore, it should not be presented as review. Rather, the packaging and lead-in to the training should cover a specific facet of human behavior (focusing on "optimizing employee work performance in teams" instead of "behavioral risk," for instance) and be billed as "advanced training." Weaving in recent developments in the company is a whetstone that will sharpen interest. Giving varied case examples will keep people interested, too.

Continual Training

The training regimens just described are not necessarily the be-all and end-all of behavioral risk training. Continual training keeps the programs, services, and benefits out in front of employees. It does this by offering training to managers and employees in the form of brown-bag lunches, breakfast meetings, or perhaps paid work time training. By having the staff of a single program or service sponsor each continual-training session, the organization can create learning situations in which the intended audiences can learn about a particular behavioral risk in a less formal setting, the resource(s) responsible for addressing it, and a face to associate with it.

Training Curricula in Action

There is no one-size-fits-all model of behavioral risk training, because organizations vary so greatly in training practices, operations, and other factors. Therefore, the following sections describe four different examples of training curricula that incorporate behavioral risk information and that can be adapted for use in different work organizations.

Management Training for Employee Problem Resolution in the Context of Performance Management

Human resource management is human potential development, labor force maintenance, and management of loss arising from employee problems. According to trainer Donald A. Phillips, performance management training typically focuses only on the first two areas, however, while development of skills for handling employees who present persistent stubborn problems for managers may sadly be neglected. Managers are not often schooled, for example, on how problems progress from minor skirmishes—the time when problems can still be easily addressed and effectively rectified—to major conflagrations.

Here are two examples. A single mother with two children worked as a receptionist in a legal firm. Over her first two years with the firm, she had a spotless record. However, about six months after being divorced and being awarded primary custody of her children, she begin showing up for work ten to fifteen minutes late once or twice a week. A few weeks later, she started calling in sick, and her tardiness continued to increase. Additionally, she seemed frazzled and less able to focus. Her supervisor, frustrated by the demise of what had been a highly reliable employee, finally said, "Straighten up or pack your bags." From there on, their relations soured, and she left the company. If the supervisor had been trained to handle employee behavioral problems, he could have raised his concerns after the first couple of times she was tardy. Had he done so, she would have explained the difficulty she was having with, first, finding a reliable and competent day care provider and, second, preparing the children for day care, transporting them, and getting to work on time. Then the supervisor could have helped her to accommodate her competing priorities by referring her to a work-and-family specialist (on staff or working under a contract) to make other day care arrangements. In this way, a potentially serious behavioral risk exposure could have been routinely handled while it was still a minor problem.

The second example took place at a steel company, where an employee who worked an open hearth had a reputation for being uncompromising, irritable, and difficult with co-workers. However, he always showed up for work and was productive. His behavior seemed to be cyclical—he would be in good spirits and cooperative with co-workers for a couple of weeks, then easily aggravated and argumentative for a couple more. Over time, his disposition worsened. In this unionized shop, he was protected against disciplinary action, so he often told his supervisor to "take a hike." Eventually, though, he became so unbearable that he wound up involved in three grievance proceedings because management was trying to get rid of him. This situation became a burden for the union, also, which found it increasingly difficult to defend his behavior to the company and other union members. Finally, he was forced by management (with the tacit support of the union) to seek psychiatric counseling in order to keep his job and was diagnosed with clinical depression, an illness that sometimes underlies the behavior of "difficult" or angry employees. Had his supervisor carefully documented his conduct problems when they first appeared several years earlier and tried then to refer the employee to assistance, it could have saved everyone involved a great deal of time and aggravation, as well as money spent in grievance proceedings, treatment costs, and lost work time.

Management training on addressing employee problems should include procedures for responding to performance and conduct and to critical incidents. Both responses are based on the availability of a work-based problem assessment resource when the problem is beyond the scope of the supervisor.

Performance and Conduct Problems

Problem resolution comprises four steps:

1. Corrective feedback
2. Problem solving
3. Consultation
4. Corrective interviews

Let's look at each step. When issues and concerns such as tardiness begin to show a pattern, managers should be taught to approach the employee in a nonconfrontive but straightforward way and point out how his or her performance or conduct is disruptive to the organization. This corrective feedback is a counseling step, not a disciplinary or confrontive intervention activity. The manager should be tough on the problem, not the employee.

The employee should be asked if there is a problem he or she would like to discuss and informed of the assessment resource. Managers should listen carefully so the problem is fully aired. As authority figures, managers sometimes try to structure a solution for an individual without first getting all the facts. They should be taught only to nod their heads when they comprehend each point the employee is making. When the employee is done explaining, then the manager can begin to work *with the employee* to structure a solution, if this is necessary or desired by the employee. (Donald A. Phillips's "Performance and Conduct Checklist" in the Appendix can help managers decide whether to contact the assessment resource about the problem employee.)

The problem-solving and counseling stages follow if the problem persists. The supervisor might begin the discussion with this direct but still nonconfrontive statement: "We've got a problem." Saying "you" points the finger at the employee; saying "we" diffuses potential defensive or angry employee responses. The problem-solving stage, too, should focus on the problem, not the individual.

Role-play exercises are a valuable training aid for managers as they learn these stages. The following is a sample training script (adapted from the training videotape *The Dryden File II*) for the problem-solving stage, involving an employee, Tom, and a supervisor, Matt.

Tom: What's up, boss?

Matt: Let's sit down and talk for a few minutes. We've got a problem that I think you and I can resolve together.

Tom: Okay, I'm with you so far.

Matt: Do you realize how many mornings you've been late getting in?

Tom: Look, I apologized for this morning—

Matt: I'm not talking about this morning; not specifically, anyway. It's just that this morning is like so many others.

Tom: I guess it kind of sneaks up on you.

Matt: And this morning isn't the first deadline you've missed, either. It's not like you, Tom.

Tom: No, it isn't, is it? Look, Matt, you know better than anybody else what kind of siege I've been going through at home lately. I guess it made me slip a little more than I thought. But the worst is over now; I'm sure of it.

Matt: There's nothing else?

Tom: I've just been . . . You know, a couple of weeks ago, I threw my back out, and the doctor gave me some painkillers. They've been making me a little fuzzy in the mornings. Maybe I should stop taking them.

Matt: Tom! If your doctor says to take them, take them! I'm not being unreasonable. I just want to know if there's anything the matter that I can help you with.

Tom: Look, Matt, what you're telling me in the nicest possible way is that I'd better shape up. I've got to show up on time and get my work done. Right?

Matt: Well, yeah. But I'm serious about wanting to know if there's anything the matter I can help with. The company has a confidential problem assessment resource that can help you for any personal reasons. You don't have to tell me about it, but they're there to help when you need it. Please keep it in mind.

If a problem persists, particularly after two or more problem-solving sessions, it is time for the supervisor to consult with an expert resource. Depending upon the company, that expert resource might be the supervisor's boss, a human resource professional, or a work-based problem assessment specialist.

Consulting with an expert resource (usually the assessment professional) should not be viewed as an inadequacy on the part of the supervisor. Rather, it is an acknowledgment that it is unreasonable to expect a supervisor to resolve all problems presented by employees. Some organizations provide human resource management training to supervisors that usually includes

- Setting expectations for each employee and communicating them

- Providing feedback and problem solving
- Motivating the employee to accept help, when appropriate

This training acknowledges, however, that in some complex conduct or work performance problems, a supervisor may need expert advice. Therefore, all performance management systems must provide high-quality consultation to supervisors upon demand. The consultation resource helps the supervisor better understand the situation and consider the alternatives available for dealing with it. It is *not* for the purpose of telling the supervisor what to do. The consultation process may involve several sessions over a period of months and ends when the supervisor has resolved the persistent problem by one means or another. A consultation session might focus on the need for the supervisor and employee to have a corrective interview, for example, and might prepare the supervisor for it.

The following sample corrective interview with an employee, picks up on employee Tom after his problems have become progressively worse.

Matt: Please shut the door and sit down, Tom.

Tom: Look, Matt, I really feel bad about missing the report deadline yesterday. I have had—

Matt: Tom, sit down!

Tom: Sure, Matt. [*He sits.*] What I was saying was that I was on my way in when—

Matt: [*Gestures to quiet Tom.*] Okay, okay.

Tom: Well, if you don't believe me—

Matt: Whether I believe you or not isn't all that important, Tom. What *is* important is that you weren't here yesterday, and you didn't bother to call in. That is part of the pattern that has developed.

Tom: Hey, that's not fair, Matt!

Matt: You've been consistently late, muffed assignments, missed schedules, and have been in arguments with people.

Tom: Whoa, hang on! It hasn't been nearly as bad as you're making it sound.

Matt: I'm just reading from the record. You want to take a look? [*Tom doesn't bother.*] Your performance has become a problem, a serious one. I'm prepared to take action, and it's not going to be pleasant.

Tom: Just because I missed a day? Come on, Matt!

Matt: I want you to get it through your head that we're talking about whether or not you end up keeping your job. You and I are going to review your performance on [*examines his desk calendar*] the 30th, to see whether you've brought your work up to par before I take formal disciplinary action. I also recommend that you see the company's problem assessment resource which I mentioned to you before—if you haven't already. Here's the phone number. [*Pushes a card across the desk.*]

Tom: Is that an ultimatum?

Matt: About your work? Yes, it is!

Matt's threat of action links the corrective interview process with the steps of a progressive discipline policy. (Typically, progressive discipline includes oral warning, written warning, suspension, and termination.) If the problem at hand and the nature of the work relationship had been different, this conversation might have focused on whether Tom should visit the corporate ombudsman or initiated a conflict resolution process (both described in Chapter Five), rather than focusing on his seeking help for personal issues.

Critical Incidents

When people think of a critical incident, they usually envision an earthquake, an assault with a deadly weapon, or another potentially deadly premeditated form of aggression or violent act of nature. Critical-incident responses apply beyond terror-evoking events, however.

The definition of critical incident should include early indicators of potentially serious workplace events or problems that might arise later from untreated trauma. These indicators and events include

- Physical violence or threat of physical violence
- Injury or accident while on duty

- Physical or mental impairment, from mild to gross
- Bizarre conversation or behavior
- Threats of suicide
- Sudden death of a co-worker
- Intimidating, threatening, or abusive language or behavior

Any of these events may be followed by mandatory referral to the work-based problem assessment resource in order to protect the people involved, safeguard company property, and defuse a potentially volatile situation before it becomes a large-scale risk exposure. Additionally, any delivery of very disturbing information to an employee should be documented, although it may be accompanied only by the suggestion of a referral rather than a mandatory referral.

Peer Training in Work Team Settings

Peer training on problem identification and referral is the counterpart of the employee problem resolution training model and appears in the unionized work team setting that does not have a strong management presence. Peer training also may apply in a professional environment, such as a legal or medical practice group. Unions have historically used peer intervention training very effectively. The fear of being ostracized by one's peers is often at least as powerful a motivating influence on behavior as disciplinary action by management. Similarly, the threat of censure by one's professional accreditation or certification body may weigh more with an employer than other actions.

Peer training in a union or team environment involves educating interested employees to be peer counselors who assume one or both of two roles: promoting awareness about the availability of the problem assessment resource, thereby performing an outreach function, or providing assessment, referral, and follow-up services. The former role requires only cursory training about behavioral health problems and preventive activities and using the assessment resource. The latter requires a much more intensive level of training. One such peer counselor training program involves nearly 100 hours of learning about addictive illnesses, personal problems, health problems such as AIDS and chronic stress, the provision of assistance following critical incidents, and the performance of interventions. These peer counselors do not provide therapeutic services, however, as that would require a master's degree in mental health.

The peer counselor may lead an intervention with an employee. These peer-based interventions are likely to be less confrontational than management-driven interventions. However, the peer counselor may contact the assessment professional for advice on how to approach the individual (just as a supervisor would), and the assessment professional may even be present during the intervention. Also, the potential of adverse job action may still lurk in the background as additional leverage to get the employee to seek help.

Stress Management and Behavioral Change Training

I have mentioned the issue of employee empowerment several times. Workplace empowerment is not a scepter that grants to its owner mystical powers, as some people infer from its name. It is a tool that can liberate talent and know-how but that can also be misused, underused, or rejected without employees ever becoming formally oriented to it.

One way to indoctrinate empowerment among employees is work team training that encourages employee involvement. Another is stress management and behavioral change training, particularly when its intent is to help employees cope with organizational change and uncertainty. Eugene V. Martin addresses all three issues—involvement, change, and uncertainty—in his empowerment model of stress training, describing two separate stress interventions: organizational, which involves staunching the "cascading events" in the work environment that produce the "involuntary" stress response, and individual, which is increasing a person's capacity to arrest the stress situation rather than just respond to it.

The environmental cascading events can be addressed at the executive and board levels, where many macro decisions and activities addressing business and operational issues are initiated and then flow down to the microlevel as personal stress. This cascade will seem even worse when employees and managers are already having difficulty balancing work-and-family responsibilities, engaging in unhealthy life-styles, and coping with other stress-inducing factors. This causal chain can be brought to executives' and board members' attention during their training, to show them the importance of shaping their decisions in ways that reduce behavioral risk.

An employee's ability to arrest personal stress is limited in a traditional hierarchical work structure. A supervisor may simply ignore an employee's request for amelioration of a difficult situation, be it related to work hours, harassment by co-workers, or problems with the supervisor. In a team environment, though, the stressful situation can be brought to the attention of the group, and group members can act upon it as a unit.

Behavior modification components can easily be integrated into stress management and other training. The purpose of behavior modification training is to increase employees' awareness of their behaviors and make them more knowledgeable about psychologies underlying general behaviors in order to help them change their work behaviors. For example, they need to understand the process by which simple habits, such as prescription drug use, can over time form an addictive pattern involving psychological dependency that is hard to break. They need to learn how inflexible thinking develops over time and is reinforced through the mental process of rationalization. Conversely, employees should also be taught how behaviors are broken. They need to be educated on the four distinct stages of behavior modification: precontemplation, contemplation, action, and maintenance.

The precontemplation stage is characterized by a lack of awareness of the need for change.

The contemplation stage involves conscious thought about the need for change and initial efforts such as research on sources of assistance. The latter part of this stage involves mental preparation for change.

The action stage requires making concrete behavioral changes and sustaining the changes over an indefinite period.

The maintenance stage is the process of inculcating the new behavior.

It is inflexible thinking at the precontemplation stage that underlies the axiom, "You can't teach an old dog new tricks." This belief is pervasive among managers and workers who are waiting it out for retirement or who cannot seem to muster the willpower to modify their behaviors even though societal or workplace standards may dictate it. One fifty-year-old manager of the maintenance department at a ship parts manufacturing facility used to rebut the suggestions of subordinates who wanted to update the manner in which they performed their jobs with the expression, "The way we've always done it works fine, thank you." He was not prone to commending employees on their daily work, and habitually complained about new, computerized machinery that was being installed. This manager also liked to impress upon employees his views about societal problems, without being challenged because he was, after all, the boss. To those around him, he bore a distinct resemblance to the television show character Archie Bunker. He assailed, for example, "joggers whose sinks are full of dirty dishes," women who had hold full-time jobs, and young people who don't want to get dirt under their fingernails. With each lesson he had for an underling, this tall man of large paunch would accentuate his main point by taking a pinch of snuff and placing it inside his lower front lip. This habit felt essential to the leadership persona he had created for his male subordinates. Many of them detested the deliberate behaviors that constituted his leadership persona and considered his ideas outdated. People over whom he had limited influence he simply ignored. This manager might subconsciously have feared that progress would pass him by and he would become irrelevant. Perhaps that was why he was on blood pressure medication and ran up a six-digit medical benefit tab during the ten years before he died of a massive heart attack at age fifty-five.

In any change process, there will always be some who resist. However, if an education or training agenda is used to help employees understand the psychological and behavioral change processes that must accompany the environmental changes, they will be more prepared to accept the results or, at the very least, to understand their own thoughts and feelings.

The Organizational Hardiness Training Model at Dell Computer

Let's look further at how employers are diminishing risk by helping employees cope with change. Some companies now openly talk about the "permanence of change." They also recognize that a company that neither instills in employees a mind-set that prepares them for continual revolution nor equips them with the skills to bounce back from organizational chaos is at risk of never achieving its potential.

Consider what Dell Computer did. Dell, which throughout the 1990s has been growing despite cutthroat competition in a turbulent industry, was looking for a way to minimize the organizational chaos and workaholism rampant in the industry. Realizing that it could not control the external factors that daily tested the organization and its employees, Dell designed its Organizational Hardiness Project in 1993 to help employees, work teams, managers, and the organization as a whole withstand sometimes adverse working conditions resulting from a fluctuating marketplace. Under the guidance of an organizational psychologist and an internal human resource director with social work training, it seeks to support the mental health of employees as it creates an empowered organization.

The project has five "dimensions" of organizational effectiveness, areas on which the teams and their members seek to improve: leadership, quality management, organizational communication, team culture, and job satisfaction. The project, implemented in 1995, is being pilot-tested in six departments—among them accounts payable, research and development, technical support, and field service. The eighteen-month interventions are taking place in twelve-person teams of co-workers, each containing people of equal rank—vice presidents, managers, or employees. Participants are tested, primarily through pencil-and-paper surveys, for emotional centeredness, wellness, optimism, social centeredness, intellectual stimulation, and spiritual life purpose.

From the survey findings, the "Team Well-Being Profile" is being constructed which, in turn, is being used to design a customized "prescription." The prescription has six elements:

Interviews with leaders, to assess their need for training

A presentation to the team about the project

Team assessment of the leader

Assessment of the team by the project leaders

Training, done in conjunction with the Center for Creative Leadership, based in Greensboro, North Carolina, which teaches lifestyle management, capitalizing on stress, team processes, managing change, and achieving peak performance for leaders

Assessment of the team's and of individuals' new level of functioning

Preliminary reports from participants have been favorable. Objective measures of team functions in the areas of team purpose, role, strategy, processes, people, feedback, and interfaces are currently being applied.

Change Management Programs at Family Service of Lancaster

A model similar to the Dell Computer model has been developed and implemented for its business clients by Family Service of Lancaster (Pennsylvania). It has two parts: the Resilience! Positive Strategies for Managing Change program for employees, and the Leaders' Forum for senior management. The resilience program is based on bouncing back from chaos to a homeostatic environment. This brief employee training course places heavy focus on both instruction and the sharing of experiences about acting assertively, maintaining flexibility, having supportive friends, honing a keen sense of humor, thinking creatively, building strong self-esteem, and keeping a clear focus on life. Currently, the training occupies five half-day group sessions, with about two weeks in between each one so that participants can apply what they learned. The session topics include, in this order, changes in society and their impact on human beings, organizational resilience, team resilience, individual resilience, and overcoming barriers. Along the way, employees and supervisors are taught the organizational change process (see Figure 7.2) and signposts of personal stress. During the sessions, which are highly interactive with minimal structure, participants are also instructed about how to set clear goals, ask for and accept participation, and share information.

The Leaders' Forum is a two-year curriculum for business leaders that is based on community building in the company setting. The first year begins with resilience training for business leaders, featuring biweekly off-site meetings for groups of about six. The community focus begins following the resilience training and adheres to a pyramid-shaped training module. Establishing a shared vision and mission are at the base; mutual respect, mutual support, and assertive communication are in the middle; and collaborative problem solving is at the top.

Family Service of Lancaster has found that "collaborative problem solving," an executive behavior and leadership skill that is the ultimate objective, usually does not fully develop if the preceding steps are waived. During the problem-solving exercises, actual situations inside the organizations of participating leaders are used as case examples. Each situation is dissected, contributing factors are explored, barriers are identified, and plans of action are developed in these brainstorming sessions. During the second year, the leaders help others at their companies develop collaborative problem-solving skills. This part of the Leaders' Forum is much less structured than the resilience training during the first year, and Family Service staff consult with the leaders as needed.

Behavioral Safety Training at Santa Fe Railway

The railroads are leaders among the safety conscious and blue-collar industries in using the behavioral risk management paradigm. The main impetus has been safety improvement, because railway accidents and injuries are usually severe, the disability costs can financially cripple a railway, and the impact on productivity and morale is devastating.

The former Santa Fe Railway (which merged with Burlington Northern in late 1995) has integrated disability management, vocational rehabilitation, employee assistance, critical incident response, and behavioral health management activities to control behavioral risk exposures. It is cementing these activities in the work culture through education and training. Santa Fe relies on five training regimens: safety training and certification of employees, supervisory training, safety committee training, critical incident response training, and audit and consultation teams.

The certification training is given by supervisors to employees and covers conforming to safety rules and using safe work behaviors with specific machinery. Santa Fe actively seeks to empower employees by authorizing them to intervene when they see safety problems, by taking a subperforming locomotive out of service, for example, or red-tagging a faulty track switch. Supervisory training provides instruction to managers on constructive confrontation, a method that has been proven effective in interceding with behavioral health problems. Because the railways traditionally have had a male-dominated, macho culture, alcohol abuse has been a long-standing concern and, more recently, drug use has become an issue. Constructive confrontation, as described in Chapter Five, helps supervisors to cut through the denial, alibi making, and scapegoating that can obscure a primary problem of addiction or dependency.

The safety committees are five groups of about twenty union employees or managers each. Group members receive training on a specific safety concern then return to their work sites throughout the Santa Fe system to transmit the same training to other employees. The five areas of concern are slips, trips, and falls; material handling; power tools; upper extremities injuries; and back injuries. The committee members periodically observe others' work and give advice, and they conduct small-group safety discussions. They also meet once a year to update their knowledge base. Critical incident response training is provided to 150 peer trauma responders in a one-day training course held once a year at four sites throughout the railway system. Because these responders are volunteers, not trained mental health professionals, they do not provide critical incident stress debriefing or other clinical interventions. Rather, they are a frontline supportive resource, offering compassion and camaraderie, helping co-workers involved in accidents to understand when contributing factors to an accident were beyond their control, apprising them of critical incident counseling services, and letting them know that the counseling and any lost time are paid for by the company.

Pulling together the behavioral risk management initiative are four audit and consultation teams, also known as central safety committees. Each comprises eight occupational professionals, who are experts in engineering, logistics, maintenance, signal communications, telecommunications, occupational medicine, or behavioral safety. Each team, headed by a corporate vice president, is periodically dispatched from headquarters to visit Santa Fe work sites and to conduct observations of employee safety behavior.

When a team arrives at a work site, it splits into two groups, each conducting a morning safety audit over half of the grounds. Team members look for particular unsafe practices related to their specialties. For example, signs of unsafe work attitudes, noncompliance with work rules, poor housekeeping practices, uninspected fire extinguishers, and so forth. At lunchtime, the teams switch places. The training comes at the end of the day, when the team holds an impromptu safety consultation with the "work gangs," which range in size from three to fifty employees. Team members point out that their activities are not a formal inspection nor are they linked with any disciplinary process. Rather, their goal is to prevent the pain and suffering that accidents and injuries cause employees and their families and to reduce financial loss to the company. The employees often reciprocate by showing that they appreciate such nonpunitive feedback.

In all cases in this five-tier approach, training is conducted in a manner that is neither denigrating, intimidating, nor likely to arouse resentment. The training does, however, consistently keep the message of accident prevention before employees, and that is key to building a safety culture.

Having examined the theory behind behavioral risk management and the interventions associated with it, we have covered the what and why of this loss management concept. We still need to consider the who and how. Specifically, who executes these activities? Who leads the charge? And how are the pieces brought together?

These questions address the need for a manager of behavioral risk, an experienced multidisciplinary professional who can interpret audit findings; in smaller companies, deliver behavioral risk services; and be a trusted consultant to management while protecting the privacy of employees. This person would participate in senior staff meetings and influence myriad organizational decisions—from whether to relocate a company's operation to phasing in new computerized equipment to adopting work team concepts—developing new communications policies, calling attention to pathological organizational behaviors, and recommending solutions. This role calls for both situational leadership and long-range strategic interventions. The behavioral risk manager's focus on loss management would be, in most cases, a voice of caution and of responsibility to employees, something that is often missing from senior staff and board of directors decisions. This role is discussed in depth in the next chapter.

Notes

P. 191, *behaviors are often exhibited through informal networks:* Krackhardt, D., and Hanson, J. R., "Informal Networks: The Company Behind the Chart." *Harvard Business Review,* July–Aug. 1993, pp. 104–111.

P. 199, *three universal processes for managing quality:* Juran, J. M. *Juran on Leadership for Quality: An Executive Handbook.* New York: Free Press, 1989, p. 23.

P. 199, *Juran wrote that upper management:* Juran, *Juran on Leadership for Quality,* p. 295.

P. 200, *ONR researchers drew two conclusions:* Asch, S. E. "Effects of Group Pressure upon the Modification and Distortion of Judgments," *Groups, Leadership and Men: Research in Human Relations.* New York: Russell & Russell. 1951.

P. 207, *According to trainer Donald A. Phillips, performance management training:* Phillips, D. A. Personal communication, July 1995.

P. 209, *sample training script . . . for the problem-solving stage:* Adapted from Milbauer, R. *The Dryden File II.* Hartsdale, N.Y.: Motivision, MCMLXXXVIII. Videotape.

P. 211, *sample corrective interview with an employee:* Adapted from *The Dryden File II,* MCMLXXXVIII.

P. 212, *definition of critical incident:* Phillips, D. A. "Management Training: When Problems Persist" (Training program). Washington, D.C.: COPE, 1994.

P. 214, *empowerment model of stress training:* Martin, E. V. "Designing Stress Training." In Quick, J. C., and others (eds.), *Stress and Well-Being at Work: Assessments and Interventions for Occupational Mental Health.* Washington, D.C.: American Psychological Association, 1992, pp. 207–224.

P. 215, *four distinct stages of behavior modification:* Jacob, B. "Birth of a Healthy Habit: Strategies to Guide Behavior Change," Part 1. *Workplace Health,* 1994, *3*(3), p. 1.

Staffing the Behavioral Risk Management Function

In this and the following chapters, the rubber meets the road. Chapters Two, Three, and Four developed the theory of behavioral risk management. Chapters Five, Six, and Seven identified a variety of interventions and training activities. Now, in Chapter Eight, I will describe behavioral risk management as an integrated process, looking at the role of the behavioral risk manager and staff and at behavioral risk management models, policies, and activities. In Chapter Nine, I will present some examples of how behavioral risk management is currently being practiced.

The key to putting any workplace concept into operation is first to design and implement an appropriate model for service delivery. The resulting structure may be internal or external or both, and inter- or intradepartmental. The linchpin of the whole behavioral risk management structure is a leader or, to use a Total Quality Management term, *process owner.* Various staff members, whether internal and on the company payroll or external and under contract, are the *task owners.* Steering *committees* of volunteer workplace personnel encourage others to use the process, thus helping behavioral risk management to achieve the objective of diminishing behavioral risk. *Policies and procedures,* aided by process maps, meld the operation to the contours of the work organization. The remainder of this chapter considers each of these factors in greater detail.

The Behavioral Risk Manager (or Process Owner)

Behavioral risk management is an organic function, able to shape itself to fit the work organization, based on management's objectives and the company's behavioral risks.

The one constant in behavioral risk management is the occupational professional or manager who serves as the process owner. This person is the nucleus, trainer, interlocutor with senior management, and maybe even provider of direct services to employees. He or she must be able to navigate a management information system, since controlling behavioral risk is a data-driven exercise. The behavioral risk manager (or BR manager) is equal parts technician, clinician, creative genius, and experienced company hand. Because the BR manager has access to sensitive or confidential employee information, he or she has to maintain the highest ethical standards of mental health professionals. The BR manager also has to know the company's business and be able to tell senior management where its grand schemes run risks in regard to the company's internal health and well-being. Because behavioral risk management is an interdisciplinary concept and integrates both individual and organizational aspects of behavioral risk, the BR manager must be able to think in spatial and not just linear fashion. In small and midsized organizations, the manager of behavioral risk may concurrently be the behavioral health benefits manager, conduct organizational development interventions, and perhaps fulfill other roles as well.

Companies are sometimes tempted to try to coerce private information on problem employees from occupational professionals, if not by persuasion then by subpoena in cases where an employee has a claim against the company. To avoid this unfortunate situation, the behavioral risk manager should have academic training as a psychologist or in another mental health discipline, perhaps along with professional certification, so that he or she is bound to a code of ethics and professional conduct that protects him or her against compromising situations.

Because behavioral risk is omnipresent in work organizations, companies with at least 500 employees, associates, or contract employees (or the full-time equivalent) should consider assigning a full-time behavioral risk manager. Behavioral risk management may be a centralized operation or splintered among different functions. The person may manage a hierarchy with a discrete base of operation or be more of a free-floater who receives information from various functions that control one or more aspects of behavioral risk, then acts as an internal consultant to the functions and to senior management. In larger, multisite companies, BR managers should be regionally located and accessible. In areas where they cannot always be conveniently on site, interactive video technology is a desirable alternative because it retains the advantage of face-to-face contact with staff, managers, employees, and service providers.

The management of behavioral risks should be an *internal* company activity. This cannot be stated too strongly. The presence of an internal BR manager signals that the employer assumes ownership of its risks and is not trying to transfer them out of the company.

Competency and Working Knowledge

The people who are qualified to become process owners are likely to have a training and experiential background in human resources, family counseling, organizational development, internal employee assistance, or perhaps wellness and health promotion. Typically, the person chosen should have been employed by or associated with the organization (or at a minimum, with another organization in the same industry) for ten or more years. This will ensure that he or she is familiar with the company's work and its traditions, management styles, and aspects of operation.

The BR manager needs to be fluent in all aspects of behavioral risk management because he will communicate with staff members and external service providers about their specialized areas of competency and knowledge, with all levels of management about management concepts and operations and about the handling of specific problem situations, and with employees about ways the system is designed to serve them. The necessary areas of competence and working knowledge are briefly described here.

Chemical dependency and other addictions. Many behavioral risks are associated with drug and alcohol abuse. Substance abuse is most dangerous to a work organization when it becomes accepted in the culture. Therefore, knowledge of the issues surrounding drugs and alcohol is essential and knowledge about other addictions and their behavioral symptoms is also helpful.

Drug testing and medical review. A general understanding of the types of drug testing (such as preemployment, random, and probable cause), testing technology, and review procedures for detecting problems with testing results (especially false positives) is helpful.

Mental health. Depression and other mental health disorders need to be understood, because people affected with these disorders can often still work.

Behavioral safety. Knowledge of the action steps associated with modifying behavior in dangerous environments is key to preventing accidents.

Behavior modification. Knowing the psychological antecedents to behavioral change is helpful when performing behavioral risk interventions and breaking through self-reinforcing behavioral cycles.

Family systems counseling. As we have seen, organizational pathology is often akin to family dysfunction, so knowledge of family systems counseling is useful.

Organizational behavior and systems behavior. Organizational psychology training helps the BR manager trace patterns of employee behavioral risks back to organizational behaviors or other factors.

Confronting problem employees. An ability to handle employees exhibiting conduct or job performance problems fairly and appropriately is key to organizational effectiveness.

Conflict resolution practices. Besides needing to understand the dynamics whereby seemingly minor conflicts among employees and managers escalate into acts of aggression and retaliation, BR managers need to know the processes for defusing these dynamics.

Critical incident stress debriefing. The ability to conduct these debriefings entails an understanding of the immediate and delayed human responses to critical incidents and an ability to pick out the individuals participating in group debriefing who need personalized counseling.

Benefits management. This area requires knowledge about which benefits best serve the workforce and workers' families, what the dollar caps and exclusions are, how plans are administered in a manner consistent with defined benefit plans, and so forth. Knowing the availability and accessibility of benefits is helpful when referring employees to behavioral healthcare and lifestyle-oriented healthcare benefits.

Life-style management. A knowledge of preventable physical diseases and illnesses, stress-related problems, and the effects of sedentary life-styles, poor diet, and unhealthy habits such as smoking, along with corrective strategies, is helpful.

Diversity issues. BR managers must understand how to keep racial, gender, and other demographic differences from creating fissures in work units, one outcome of which is affirmative action complaints.

The workers' compensation system. BR managers must know that this federally mandated, state-regulated insurance system has a set of ground rules that keeps it separate and distinct from the provision of health insurance.

Principles of Total Quality Management, reengineering, and other management theories. A basic understanding of the theories that lie behind contemporary companies' methods of production and service delivery and an ability to apply these theories to behavioral risk activities and staffing is an asset.

Psychometric testing. The theory and practice of attitude, pre-employment, and other kinds of psychological and behavioral measurement in order to detect high-risk individuals has become increasingly valuable to companies and knowledge of these tests should be part of the BR manager's competency.

Computerized information management. Being able to navigate in different databases, integrate information, and do basic troubleshooting is a valuable commodity when combined with the other knowledges and competencies listed here, since behavioral risk management, as already mentioned, is data driven.

Research and evaluation techniques. Understanding the basics of research design, performance, and validation is important in the analysis of data.

Public policy issues. The Americans with Disabilities Act, Family and Medical Leave Act, regulations of the Occupational Safety and Health Administration, and other laws and regulations, are among the public policy issues on which the BR manager can establish him- or herself as an indispensable internal consultant.

Training. The BR manager's ability to be an effective trainer is central to the promotion and utilization of programs, services, and benefits by managers, employees, executives, and board members.

Knowledge of ancillary occupational issues and functions. BR managers should have some knowledge of the areas of compensation, corporate communications, labor-management relations, and others that impinge on employee behavior.

Management and administration. As in any "system," management and administration are necessary to develop policies and procedures, make flowcharts, establish staff expectations, do budgeting, and so forth, and the BR manager must possess administrative abilities.

Job Tasks

Job tasks are the pieces in the BR manager's nine-to-five routine. They may be performed directly by the manager or coordinated with other behavioral risk functions.

Auditing of employee and organization behavioral risks. Auditing risks may require performing or collaborating with an external data management or research organization. Collaboration involves obtaining data sets from other sources, such as a third-party administrator and the personnel department; deciding whether to include data if they are incomplete or otherwise unreliable; and arranging for the collection of new data that are essential for the audit but not presently collected.

Benchmarking as a means of improving performance. Outcomes across different work units should be analyzed in order to identify what a unit with a low rate of behavioral risk exposures is doing that can be replicated or adapted in units with high rates.

Program evaluation. Programs and services should be evaluated based in part on their integration with other functions, effectiveness of specific tasks performed, and relevant findings from the behavioral risk audit. For example, a conflict resolution service can be evaluated on

- The overall rate at which problems of individuals and interpersonal problems of work teams occur (and perhaps recur) in the organization

- The proportion of cross-referrals to the work-related assessment resource
- The proportion of employees and managers who report favorably about the state of their relations (derived from audit data)

Overseeing of behavioral risk management functions integration. This activity begins with cross-training among the relevant functions so that each has a working knowledge of the others. It also includes cross-referrals of individuals or teams needing assistance or collaborative training. The effort can be enhanced with process maps that provide a visual frame of reference.

Intervening with impaired senior executives and managers. Depending on the circumstances and personal knowledge required, the BR manager might perform such interventions personally or use an external executive-intervention specialist. The issues related to executive intervention are both very subtle and of high impact.

Consulting with benefits department on benefit plan design and access. Health benefits that are too limited or hard to access because of stringent requirements are of little use. Conversely, benefits that are too liberal and have no access management invite exploitation.

Consulting with senior management on behavioral consequences of strategic business decisions. A crucible for the BR manager is his or her ability to stay in the management loop and contribute productively to decision making in the highest reaches of a work organization.

Troubleshooting. Case-specific situations may arise requiring a BR manager's intervention into staff or service provider activities: for example, to give guidance on how to use information from confidential client assessments discretely to make organizational development interventions.

Arranging cross-competency training of staff. Providing and coordinating cross-competency training for staff members is essential to the integration of behavioral risk programs and services, especially if they are scattered among multiple departments.

Directing of staff meetings. This task, too, is essential to integrating programs and personnel within the behavioral risk management function.

Acting as internal consultant to legal, human resources, benefits, and other managers. This consultative role also helps to integrate the behavioral risk management function throughout the organization and to establish its credibility.

Ongoing monitoring of internal and external management decisions and the onsets of employee (and dependent) behavioral problems. Behavioral risk is perhaps the most important measure of the internal health of the organization. Tracking it using audit and program evaluation data, then juxtaposing it with a time line or other log of company activity, sheds insight on cause-effect relationships.

Audit of benefits data to determine employee Pareto groups. This audit to identify the 10 to 20 percent of employees who are in high-risk groups produces highly sensitive information about individual employees that cannot be shared with others in management (although aggregated data that preserve confidentiality can be shared). The information must be protected by the ethical and professional conduct standards of the BR manager's profession. In some situations, companies may want an external researcher to perform this audit; the BR manager then is the person who arranges for allowable management access to the data.

Coordination with external service providers. In addition to contracting with external providers, the BR manager needs to coordinate their service delivery to ensure that appropriate cross-referrals are made, that information flows freely back to providers, that utilization reports are prepared, and so forth.

Direct delivery of behavioral risk management services. The two services most central to behavioral risk management are confidential workplace-based employee problem assessments and conflict resolution. A BR manager's ability to deliver these services may depend on company logistics and operating philosophy and whether there is any perceived conflict of interest in his or her serving as both provider of confidential employee services and management consultant.

Management, administration, and policy formulation. These tasks relate to the structural and procedural aspects of the behavioral risk management function.

Organizational Development Roles

The BR manager may assume any of four organizational development roles: advisory, consultative, service delivery, or evaluative.

Advisory role. In the advisory role, the behavioral risk manager advises the appropriate senior managers, site general managers, and others about the ways specific organizational behaviors are increasing behavioral risk or resulting in risk exposures. This advisory role might be based on the results of the two-part audit process described in Chapters Three and Four, the recurring organizational issues brought to the attention of the employee assistance program (EAP) or appearing in other communications channels to and from employees, and the general observations of the BR manager. In essence, the BR manager is a conduit for information sharing with management and the company's organizational development staff member or consultant (if there is one).

Consultative role. As consultant, the BR manager takes both the advisory role just described and also makes formal recommendations of courses of action to management and the organizational development person. These are solid-line reporting relationships and, in most work settings, would include ongoing meetings in addition to ad hoc communications. Consultation would be related to both daily operations and organizational change processes. For example, the BR manager would be included in discussions related to acquisitions and mergers, employee relocations, and the introduction of new technology to company operations.

Some situations warrant discretion if the BR manager is to retain a neutral role. For example, if through the assessment resource, the BR manager learns about employee efforts to unionize owing to shop floor conditions, he or she would probably not inform management about the organizing activities because of the potential for management retaliation. However, he or she would inform management about the conditions with which employees are dissatisfied.

The BR manager's consultations with management can also address how an institutional decision to impose a strategy that diminishes one type of behavioral risk exposure is likely to affect another exposure. For example, if management wants to install surveillance equipment in order to reduce employee theft, honest employees may regard this tactic as a form of oppression. If the same honest employees already feel alienated by other policies or practices affecting their working conditions, the new policy may increase such behavioral risks as turnover and use of sick and personal days. The BR manager can help the organization's leading decision makers to weigh such factors and can raise alternatives.

Service delivery role. In this role, the BR manager personally delivers the organizational behavior interventions described in Chapter Six and probably also is concerned with the external business decision making of the company and internal activities that have only indirect consequences for employee behavior, such as restructuring of the organizational chart and executive communication patterns. Taking on these latter concerns is analogous to representing a special interest group on the board of directors of a membership organization and then becoming involved in a wide range of decisions by virtue of being a board member.

Evaluative role. In this role, the BR manager provides initial, periodic, and ongoing evaluation of organizational behaviors. This role is in addition to any of the three aforementioned roles.

Role Ambiguity

Some scholarly papers on contemporary management thought discuss the "role ambiguity" that managers may experience as a result of reshuffled projects and of conflicting priorities, directions from superiors, and expectations that they will be authority figures in some cases and coaches in others. For BR managers, role ambiguity might arise from balancing individual protections and management interests, the BR manager's "two masters," so to speak. Ambiguity arises, for example, when the manager is privy to behavioral audit data about particular employees but unable to intervene with them because the data are confidential or because the action could be construed by the employee as being discriminatory, thus raising legal risk. However, as long as there are clear-cut guidelines about ethical and legal behavior, the ambiguity subsides.

Ambiguity can also arise when other managers envy the confidential information of the EAP. They may feel that as long as the EAP professional is an employee of the organization, that information is company property. A situation familiar to BR managers occurs when the EAP has confidential case files about a particular employee who is involved in a court case with the company. When the company subpoenas the information, the EAP professional has little choice but to turn it over. However, this can erode the trust that the program has established with company employees. Except when legally compelled to surrender information, though, the BR manager must maintain neutrality between the diametrically opposed positions of employee advocacy and management policing.

Employees, too, can become confused when a single function appears to have differing roles: advocate, neutral observer, and disciplinary agent. This confusion can occur, for example, when a problem assessor who is perceived to have a neutral role also performs fitness-for-duty evaluations that occasionally have negative results and can result in disciplinary action. The same potential for causing employee confusion exists for the BR manager. This potential bespeaks the need for a separate organizational reporting channel for the BR manager. For example, instead reporting to the human resource or other manager who is part of a direct reporting system up the management chain of command, the BR manager instead can report to one of the chief officers. A higher-echelon manager, in many cases, is less interested in or feels less entitled to private information about particular employees than a manager who works closer to floor operations.

As these delicate situations suggest, the more politically savvy a BR manager is and the better able to communicate his or her neutral position to other corporate managers and to line employees, the more likely he or she is to have the trust of people throughout the organization and to maintain the integrity of the behavioral risk management function.

Personal Career Advancement

One of the most frustrating aspects of being director of a workplace program involved in managing behavioral risk, such as employee assistance, wellness and health promotion, or benefits, is that unless one leaves the discipline altogether there is limited vertical career advancement.

The role of behavioral risk manager, however, provides an opportunity for contiguous career progression, keeping the professional in the same realm of activity as before but broadening his or her purview to include allied professionals who share the assignment of controlling behavioral risk. Additionally, as a BR manager becomes a more trusted and valued resource to the organization, he or she is likely to grow in her role by being given more opportunities to participate in organizational decision making. This is a measure of positive career advancement, which is likely to be reflected by better financial remuneration as well.

Operational Models of Behavioral Risk Management

Before we move on to the discussion of staffing behavioral risk management programs, services, and benefits, it will be helpful to look at two operational models of behavioral risk management that graphically depict the varying structural arrangements through which these programs, services, and benefits may be delivered.

Behavioral Health Model

The behavioral health model of program, service, and benefit delivery emphasizes, as its name indicates, behavioral health and life-style issues. Because the healthcare field usually operates externally to and independently of U.S. business and industry (even though a large part of it is *funded* by that business and industry), this model is unlikely to be highly integrated into the workplace. Also, because it is healthcare focused, it favors early-stage intervention and has limited potential to deliver prevention activities beyond assistance with life-style changes. Thus, in this arrangement of tasks, the workplace precipitants of behavioral health problems are of secondary importance. This model is quite separate and distinct from the organizational factors that lead to conduct and work performance problems and that are often not tied to healthcare issues (even though conduct and work performance problems, left unameliorated, can and often do become *behavioral* healthcare problems).

This model is commonly found among the large managed behavioral healthcare delivery systems. During the spasms of mergers and acquisitions in healthcare over the last decade, many mental health and substance abuse providers and EAPs were subsumed by the more heavily capitalized managed care industry. The concern for such a vendor's business customers should be that workplace interventions may be of secondary importance to healthcare delivery, for the following reasons.

First, managed behavioral healthcare providers tend to be interested in behavioral risks only if they have a causal link with behavioral healthcare that is direct and predictable. They are not likely, for instance, to have a strong interest in organizational behavior interventions, which they may regard as too far afield of their interests. Second, many managed behavioral healthcare firms have recently been aggressively pursuing contracts to assume management of state Medicaid programs at full financial risk. These high-revenue contracts, made possible when a waiver from federal regulation is granted to the states by the U.S. Department of Health and Human Services, are the real catches of the managed care world. Third, on a hypothetical level that illustrates the way interests are driven by financial considerations, if the U.S. were to implement a single-payer healthcare system, the interest of managed behavioral healthcare firms in workplace behavioral issues that are not directly health-related would likely recede even further because employers would no longer be direct payers of healthcare; instead, the government or some government-sponsored cash-transfer agency would become the managed care vendor's "customer."

Of course, there is nothing that precludes a managed behavioral healthcare firm from establishing a separate behavioral risk division that might see the importance of risk management in a different light (see Chapter Nine, "Service providers in transition").

Figure 8.1 shows the positions of behavioral risk management activities relative to the central focus on behavioral health problems in this first model.

Conduct and Work Performance Model

A behavioral risk management model that focuses more heavily on conduct and work performance issues is preferable from the organization's perspective, because it affects a wider range of behavioral cost centers, behavioral health being only one of them (see Figure 8.2). Managed behavioral healthcare continues to be involved but is no longer one of the core activities. In fact, it might

Figure 8.1 Behavioral Risk Management Activities in the Behavioral Health Model.

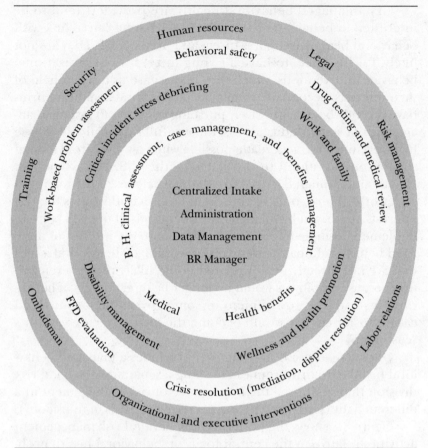

Source: Prepared by Performance Resource Press, Troy, Mich. Reprinted by permission.

even be a separate system in the work organization and administered by the benefits department, as many managed care activities are now. However, in this situation there should be a written statement of the company's understanding of how the managed behavioral healthcare function contributes to the organizational goal of diminishing or preventing behavioral risk. A comparison of Figures 8.1 and 8.2 shows how differently the functions are positioned in the two models.

Figure 8.2 Behavioral Risk Management Activities in the Conduct and Work Performance Model.

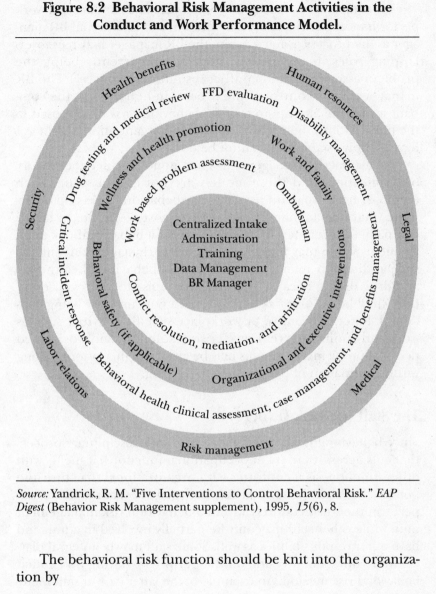

Source: Yandrick, R. M. "Five Interventions to Control Behavioral Risk." *EAP Digest* (Behavior Risk Management supplement), 1995, *15*(6), 8.

The behavioral risk function should be knit into the organization by

- Meeting organization-specific behavioral risk needs
- Having a consistent visible presence
- Promoting a high degree of interaction among the various staff members, managers, employees, and senior managers

For companies of at least 500 employees, the conduct and work performance model assumes the presence of an internal BR manager as the process owner. (Again, the BR manager may have overlapping roles in the system, such as concurrently being the problem assessment and conflict resolution resource.) The BR manager retains control of the process in-house; thus, the company avoids the attempt to transfer behavioral *risk* (as opposed to the interventions themselves) outside the organization which, as I have already established, cannot be done.

Behavioral risk management is not monolithic in either theory or application, and these models are not cast in stone. Each employer needs to audit its particular behavioral risks and determine what management activities are most desirable. In fact, a company with very few of the elements of a behavioral risk management system may initially emphasize early-stage interventions such as disability management, managed behavioral healthcare, and drug testing because it makes little sense to address prevention when behavioral risk exposures are not currently being contained. Later, preventive or workplace-specific activities such as work-and-family interventions, crisis resolution, and work-based personal problem assessments may be given a higher priority, along with the initiation of behavioral risk training.

The Staff (or Task Owners)

Since behavioral risk management is an interdisciplinary process that cuts across a variety of occupational functions, it melds with other functions as it conforms with organizational structure and politics. The some behavioral risk management staff members may perform their tasks entirely within a behavioral risk management unit, while other staff may only be partially involved in a unit and have other responsibilities as well. Some staff may be integral players while others may reside on the periphery, having no explicit behavioral risk mission. An example of the latter type of staff member is the security officer. In the execution of his or her daily responsibilities, this person patrols the premises, ensures that doors are locked in order to prevent unwarranted entry, checks name badges, protects restricted areas, and so forth. He or she is also the company's first line of defense against several behavioral risk exposures, including violent incidents, sabotage, and pilfering. Roaming the halls to seek out irregular activities, overhearing conversations wherever he or she "walks the beat," and talking frequently and candidly with managers, the security officer keeps an ear close to the organizational ground. He or she often knows which employees are high risk and can keep an eye out for them as they come and go. Identifying such peripheral but powerful allies in diminishing behavioral risk is important. These people should be in the risk management loop as internal consultants, with a dotted-line reporting relationship with the behavioral risk management team.

Task Ownership

"Task ownership" is an appropriate frame of reference for the roles that staff play. Each task owner, whether a staff member or external service provider, has a reporting relationship with the BR manager. When an external service provider is used, it is highly recommended that an *individual* employed by the service provider, such as the account representative, and not the service provider in a general sense be directly responsible to the BR manager. This priority is consistent with the highly personalized, visible, and accessible nature of behavioral risk management.

Depending on a company's size, structure, and personnel, a single well-seasoned staff member may perform a variety of tasks. A work-based problem assessment professional, for instance, might also act as mediation specialist, trainer, safety audit team member, manager of the psychological component of physical disability cases, and performer of organizational interventions. This person's educational credentials might include a Ph.D. degree in psychology and/or an M.D. degree with certification in psychiatry. The person might hold the designations of Certified Safety Professional, Certified Employee Assistance Professional, and/or Certified Addictions Counselor and have additional training in negotiating, organizational and group dynamics, and analytical studies. Of course, a person with this entire range of credentials would be a strong candidate for BR manager. In any case, the tasks performed by each staff member should always be consistent with his or her credentials.

Some programs and services are typically internal while others are external. The following is a discussion of the staff and tasks found in each of the rings in Figure 8.2.

The Center Ring

Among the center ring positions and tasks, the *BR manager* should be internal and on the company payroll, unless it is totally impractical to do so. In a small company that relies primarily on external providers, the BR manager might also be the human resource manager, the benefits director, and the safety manager or risk manager who can coordinate activities.

In larger companies, the tasks of *administration* and *data management* are likely to be internally performed, but in smaller companies it is impractical and not cost effective to bring these tasks in-house.

Training should often be internally administered, since it is a common activity among organizations of nearly all sizes. Training activities are opportunities to establish rapport with management, and this rapport is perpetuated when the trainer or person who arranges for training has an ongoing presence at the work site.

The First Ring

The work-based *problem assessment, ombudsman,* and *conflict resolution* roles should be considered central to controlling behavioral risk, as suggested by their position in the first ring. The key to ensuring that these services are accessed by managers, work teams, and employees is making them visible to their clients. They will be more visible if they are internally provided. Employees sometimes have the perception, though, that an internal program—even if it is a confidential resource—is an information-gathering arm of management. Staff members who see clients must have reputations for integrity and impartiality and must not be seen as information-gathering resources for management. These reputations help build trust, but this situation also underscores the need for a reporting structure to higher management or directly to the head of the organization that does not jeopardize the trust factor.

The Second Ring

Among the positions and tasks in the second ring, staff for *organizational and executive interventions* can be internal or external or both. In other words, a BR manager can collaborate with an external organizational development consultant on interventions. These interventions are often politically charged when they deal with sensitive management issues, and the prudent course of action here may be to contract with outside resources.

Whether staff for *behavioral safety* should be internal or external may or may not be an issue of concern, depending on the type of industry and nature of its work. This will probably be determined by whether the safety management function is internal or external. Safety is often an island unto itself in corporate work settings, and the island's focal point is the safety director. However, it should be integrated with behavioral risk management when it is present. Some companies contract this function out to a vendor that conducts safety inspections and ensures compliance with Occupational Safety and Health Administration regulations. The behavioral risk management function should seek collaboration with these vendors, although ones with a traditional environmental health and safety method of service delivery may be balky when their interest is limited to making ergonomic improvements and trying to create an "accident-proof" environment.

If *work-and-family* benefits are available, they may be administered by a specialist in child care and related issues or by the benefits department. In these cases, working jointly to promote cross-training and cross-referrals is essential. An experienced behavioral risk management staff member may be competent to preside over this function, becoming involved in the development and implementation of flextime policies and child care information and referral.

Wellness and health promotion activities and benefits vary from scaled-down versions to Rolls Royce editions with all the extras. A company wanting to promote a healthy culture should consider an in-house presence to lead programming activities and be available to employees for consultation, using either a staff specialist or a provider with an on-site presence at specified times during the work week. A company's strategy here should also reflect its workforce. For example, middle-aged employees are usually ideal candidates for inexpensive walking and perhaps aerobics programs, while younger employees are more likely to be interested in health spas and more vigorous (and expensive!) forms of exercise. If internal, wellness and health promotion is likely to be administered by the medical or benefits department. When this is the case, there should be a written statement of understanding of how the program contributes to the organization's goal of diminishing or preventing behavioral risk.

The Third Ring

The tasks of managed behavioral healthcare occupy the third ring; the primary ones are *behavioral health clinical assessment, case management,* and *benefits management.* These tasks are usually carried out externally, although some internal EAPs have integrated them as part of an expanded continuum of services. The external providers include stand-alone managed behavioral healthcare firms; so-called integrated programs that also provide EAP services; and insurance entities, such as health insurers and health maintenance organizations, that also manage and/or provide behavioral health services in addition to medical/surgical healthcare management and delivery.

Drug testing and medical review is the process by which random, probable-cause, confirmation, and other drug tests are carried out by employers wishing to establish or maintain a drug-free workplace. The drug-testing activity comprises specimen collection, results analysis, and medical review. In large companies, specimen collection sometimes is handled by medical staff under the supervision of the medical director, who may also handle medical review duties. Most employers do not perform results analysis in-house. Analysis should be carried out by a laboratory certified by the U.S. Department of Health and Human Services, since testing by noncertified facilities causes increased risk of legal action if any false positive test results lead to disciplinary action or employee character defamation. The main function of the medical review officer is to examine positive test results and converse with the employee to rule out factors that may have given a false reading.

Fitness-for-duty (FFD) evaluations are tests to ensure that an employee is mentally, emotionally, and physically prepared for the demands of the job. Usually, an FFD evaluation is a return-to-work activity performed after a person has completed a rehabilitation or educational program for a behavioral health problem. Return-to-work evaluations for persons who have tested positive for drug and alcohol use are performed by a substance abuse professional, an occupation defined by the U.S. Department of Transportation's alcohol-testing regulations. (This regulation is discussed at greater length in Chapter Twelve.)

Critical incident debriefings may be in-house or external, depending on the availability of a mental health professional *who has received additional training* in responding to critical incidents. Most companies can access these services through a mental health clinic or hospital. Companies with highly dangerous work environments should take the precautionary steps of making prior arrangements for critical incident teams to respond quickly to problems; training managers on how to respond appropriately following a critical incident; coordinating security, emergency medical, critical incident, and trauma interventions for involved employees; and making arrangements for other responses, such as handling community and media relations.

There are two levels of intervention in *disability management:* periodic subtherapeutic checks by the company to see how the injured employee is coping with recovery, offer any assistance he or she might need, let the employee know he or she has not been forgotten, assure the employee of his or her job (or a comparable one) upon return, and make psychological assessments. The periodic checks of the first four items should ideally be done by a mental health professional on the behavioral risk management staff (one who has no interest whatsoever in the work performed by the employee) or, as a second preference, by a human resource professional (who has an employment but not directly job-related, interest). In no circumstances should it be done by the employee's immediate supervisor, lest the injured worker perceive it as harassment. The decision to make this intervention and the manner of making it should be based on the state of the company's employee relations (which can be ascertained by the behavioral risk audit). The last item, the psychological assessment, is generally performed outside the organization, often in conjunction with the medical services and vocational rehabilitation activities that are a part of the person's convalescence.

The Fourth (Outer) Ring

In the fourth, or outer, ring are other occupational functions with which behavioral risk management shares common interests and to which it may have a reporting relationship. The connection with *health benefits* almost speaks for itself. Without benefits, recovery from mental health and substance abuse problems would be severely hampered. For this reason, the BR manager should be a lead player in the development of the company's behavioral health benefits plan.

Human resources may be the most logical "home" for behavioral risk management. However, the perception that employees have of the human resource function will determine whether the confidential resources of behavioral risk management really belong there. (Two decades ago, human resources was still widely called "personnel," which in some organizations was perceived to be a gestapo-like division where employees were sent to be disciplined.) If employees believe that the company uses sensitive information obtained by human resources to "get even" with employees, behavioral risk management has no place there. Progressive and enlightened companies have long since shed this image, however.

Fear of lawsuits is the preventable risk that worries many companies the most and is a primary reason why they are likely to be receptive to implementing a behavioral risk management strategy. Interestingly, *legal* may be the department that pursues the use of ombudsmen and of problem assessment, conflict resolution, and organizational development specialists, because departmental members figure these staff have the inside angle on preventing situations that would give an employee, customer, or supplier a legitimate claim against the company.

In unionized work settings, *labor relations* staff can be critical to ensuring that programs and services related to behavioral risk are executed in a manner consistent with the provisions of a labor contract. Moreover, union locals have traditionally handled conflict resolution activities (which does not produce binding decisions by a third party) by integrating them into the grievance process (which often does).

Behavioral risk management might be positioned as a subset of the *risk management* occupational function, since that keeps the focus on loss prevention and management and not on "entitlements." The distinction is significant since certain behavioral risk management functions are sometimes perceived to be employee entitlements or advocacy functions because of the way they promote themselves to employees as "helping" resources. Risk managers address serious financial liabilities incurred by a company and are likely to be receptive to the preventive strategies of behavioral risk management.

The *medical* area may be the most ideal setting for any initiative that is behavioral health focused. Senior executives and managers on all levels know that medical information is strictly hands-off, so this department more than any other is perceived as sacrosanct and protected by a cloak of confidentiality.

Finally, as we have already seen in the example of the security officer mentioned earlier, the area of *security* can make important contributions to behavioral risk management.

Using Teams in Behavioral Risk Management Interventions

Thus far, I have discussed staff assignments only as they relate to individual practitioners executing tasks. However, since behavioral risk management involves expertise from multiple disciplines, it provides many opportunities for teamwork.

First, though, a little background on work team typology will be useful. The team type usually associated with the performance of revenue-generating work is the "production or service" team. The "advice or involvement" team includes such collective endeavors as review panels, quality control circles, and employee involvement groups. The "project or development" team most closely fits the team type used by behavioral risk management functions and personnel. This team is temporary rather than permanent and is characterized by high differentiation among the expertise and responsibilities of the participants because it usually pulls occupational specialists from diverse functions.

Behavioral risk management staff members are highly differentiated because any single individual may have expertise and competency in a variety of areas, such as behavior modification, individual psychology, organizational psychology, addictions, marriage and family therapy, quality management, conflict resolution, organizational development, benefits management, work-and-family interventions, psychological trauma interventions, and life-style management. Therefore, depending on the behavioral problem being addressed, it may often be helpful to involve multiple staff on the same project. These staff members may work among themselves or with other managers and professionals involved in the situation or sharing responsibility for arriving at a solution.

For example, a behavioral risk services firm was asked to resolve a dispute between two feuding managers in a rapidly growing midsized communications company. The managers' departments shared personnel and resources and had to work cooperatively in order to get projects completed. The firm sent the account manager, who was trained in mediation, to interview the parties and their subordinates and then develop an action plan. What he found, however, was not just two conflicted managers. Beyond that, departmental employees were feeling emotionally "unhinged" from hearing ambiguous directions, the departments had a shortage of supplies because the procurement department was also in chaos due to excessive demand, the transition to a new company president was not yet complete, staff were being shuffled around to different positions for which they were not trained, and there was no plan for strategic growth. (The account manager recognized these problems as a result of behavioral risk expertise gained during cross-training.) Additionally, several key employees had become disgruntled and had left the company.

Staff members of the behavioral risk services firm jointly developed a multifaceted intervention strategy that included

Behavioral risk training for the members of the client company's board of directors and senior staff in order to promote their awareness of how their decisions might negatively affect employees

Performance management training for managers on dealing with employees more effectively

Problem assessments for several employees having trouble with internecine work relationships

Presence of on-site assessment services two days a week

Life-style management seminars and benefit plan incentives to encourage positive health behaviors

A subcontract with an organizational effectiveness consultant who specialized in communications companies to remove the structural impediments to interdepartmental collaboration

On a regular basis, the behavioral risk management firm's staff exercised teamwork by participating in cross-competency training, making cross-referrals, holding strategy meetings to decide how to handle certain group and organizational interventions, collaborating on designing benefit plans for customers, and collaborating on cases involving clients having multiple problems. Other examples of situations in which behavioral risk staff teamwork is called for are interventions in team conflicts, where employees need help with building communication skills and handling emotional problems, and clients needing exercise and diet plans as part of their addiction recovery.

Cross-competency training gives behavioral risk staff the obvious benefit of skill development. Additionally, because of the networking opportunity it provides, this training also facilitates the case-finding process and helps ensure that cases are holistically managed. As in most business endeavors, opportunity arises as much out of familiarity as need. In this way, cross-competency training among behavioral risk staff is essential spadework if staff are to achieve the comfort level with each other that is the precursor to cross-referrals.

Cross-competency training for behavioral risk management staff is especially critical in companies where the process of integration is just beginning. As today's companies consolidate and integrate functions, it is not uncommon for internal staff members who were formerly competitors—that is, working in functions such as employee assistance, wellness and health promotion, and work and family that once competed for the same pool of dollars—to find themselves working as teammates because these functions have been combined. Now the rivals of the past have to be partners, and cross-training is the medium through which partnering happens.

Committees

Among the most important assets of occupational programs and services are committees of employees and managers formed to undergird the behavioral risk management process.

Steering committees. Steering committees are very common among functions associated with behavioral risk management, such as work-and-family services and wellness and health promotion programs. Committee members are usually volunteers who advise program staff about the needs and structure of the organization during the formation of an occupational function, help create policy, promote awareness throughout the organization and, in limited cases, become involved in operations when their assistance is warranted. This operational involvement will occur rarely, but an example is a committee that routinely attempts to mediate disputes involving managers, employees, work teams, and perhaps customers and suppliers, prior to submitting the dispute to an external conflict resolution specialist. In general, though, while steering committees can be very instrumental, they should not become the tail that wags the dog in the operation of programs and services.

There are two ways to make up a behavioral risk management steering committee. The first is to staff it with department heads from related functions, such as those on the outer ring of Figure 8.2. Second, in cases where the behavioral risk management function is structured as a loose confederation of interdepartmental programs, the steering committee can comprise the committee heads of each of those functions.

Evaluation committees. Another useful committee is composed of professionals expert in a function's subject matter, who can evaluate function performance. An evaluation committee is particularly valuable for determining an external service provider's level of performance. For example, one major company that contracts with a national managed behavioral healthcare provider for assessment and case management services has a committee comprising psychologists and medical doctors who audit clients' clinical files to determine the efficacy of treatment recommendations. The same can be done for other behavioral risk management functions, even though many of their files are likely to be subclinical.

Specialized committees. In cases of particular behavioral risks, specialized committees can be formed. A threat-of-violence committee, for example, can be an effective resource both to develop strategies for preventing workplace violence and to respond to such violence early and effectively if it does happen. This committee can comprise the BR manager, a line manager, several employees, and staff representing the communication, legal, security, medical, and labor relations areas. Threat-of-violence committees have become more common as downsizing has become more frequent.

Policies and Procedures

Imagine what would happen if society did not have laws. Chaos would abound because we would have no standards against which to assess the appropriateness of our actions. Policies are guidelines that govern the operation of a function; procedures are the action steps for carrying out policies. Once a decision has been made as to how the behavioral risk management function should operate, policies and procedures cement together the necessary processes. That is why they are the last of the five strategies for implementing a behavioral risk management strategy.

Policies and procedures typically address ethical principles and administrative, operational, and legal or regulatory issues and specify prohibited activities. At their best, policies and procedures protect a function from threats from sources within the organization (when the policies contain the explicit sanction of the chief executive officer, for example), and at their worst, they are written in dense bureaucratese and reinforced by onerous procedures.

In the behavioral risk management paradigm, policies and procedures pertain to how behavioral risk management personnel comport themselves, how the behavioral risk management system interacts with the larger work system, how the organization comports itself, and how employees comport themselves. We will look at each area of concern in turn.

How Behavioral Risk Management Personnel Comport Themselves

One set of behavioral risk management policies that will appear in a policy manual deals with the actions of staff within the behavioral risk management circle. First, some of the programs and services that control behavioral risk will be governed by *confidentiality guidelines.* Foremost among these are all assessment resources, the ombudsman, the conflict resolution specialist, and any other function whose immediate purpose is to help an employee with a problem. In addition, confidentiality guidelines may be extended to include such other functions as work and family and wellness and health promotion. The interventions of an organizational development specialist may also be subject to confidentiality.

If the behavioral risk management function is decentralized and involves outside service providers, it may be necessary to restrict information so that it flows only between a particular staff member and the BR manager. Therefore, guidelines should be established to protect information obtained by a confidential program or service from being accessed by nonconfidential resources, even if those resources are also within the behavioral risk management area.

Other policies may be needed to put parameters on the *transfer of information* among behavioral risk management functions, including the administrative routing of data such as regular reports. The policy may specify that information may be transferred from staff of one function to staff of another function only via the BR manager, especially when the functions are loose knit and interdepartmental. Similarly, policies governing computerized management information system access, passwords, and data transfer may also be specified.

Committee responsibilities and activities should also be explained in the policy manual. The ground rules for *cross-training* and *jointly administered behavioral risk training* for managers, employees, executives, and board members should similarly be specified.

Professional or practitioner standards specific to each function, such as those advocated by membership associations and other governing bodies, can be useful in drafting policies and procedures. They may pertain to timeliness of response to customers and clients, boundaries of practice, conflicts of interest, and so forth. As desirable work habits are established during formation of a behavioral risk management function, the standards used for one function—say, standards for timely responses to customer or client inquiries by a managed behavioral healthcare firm—may be appropriately applied to other functions as well.

The procedures that accompany policies about personnel comportment might, for example, specify how and under what circumstances staff should access the crisis resolution and work-based problem assessment resource. In this case, there are likely to be two sets of procedures. The first will be for hearing the complaint of an individual, say, a person to whom another employee has exhibited hostile or aggressive behavior (physical or verbal). In this case, the first employee will be asserting that his or her personal rights have been violated or that his or her character has been defamed. The second set of procedures will be for addressing situations in which two or more people are not able to work together cooperatively, without any hostile or aggressive behavior. These situations might involve a manager and an employee, a manager and a work team, two managers, line management and upper management, an employee and the employee's work team, two employees, or two work teams. The same procedures could also be applied when customers and suppliers have conflicts with employees. Exhibit 8.1 contains two examples of formal procedures for resolving complaints and conflicts that fall under the behavioral risk management purview.

How the Behavioral Risk Management System Interacts with the Larger Work System

Another set of policies establishes boundaries for interactions between the behavioral risk management function (and its component parts) and other individuals, departments, work units, and occupational professionals. These policies should be consistent with the mission of the organization and further the pursuit of its goals and objectives.

Once again, *confidentiality* is a key issue. Confidentiality policies are primarily intended to prevent deleterious personal information, originally conveyed in a setting understood to be private or confidential, from being released and resulting in financial or other material damage to the individual or in defamation of his or her character. However, provisos must also be included that specify when confidentiality is not protected. For example, under "duty-to-warn" laws, information about a violation of child protection laws is not protected.

Confidentiality provisions may also address the issue of anonymity. For example, when an employee (or family member) voluntarily visits a confidential resource, anonymity is usually ensured. However, in other cases—notably when an employee tests positive for drugs or alcohol or is referred for assessment due to conduct or work performance problems by a supervisor—anonymity is no longer a factor. Usually, though, information

Exhibit 8.1 Examples of Procedures for Resolving Complaints and Conflicts.

Procedure for Resolving Allegations of Hostile or Aggressive Behavior

1. A meeting shall be held in which the complainant is apprised of options, including mediation and investigation.
2. An attempt shall be made to informally mediate the complaint. In addition to reaching a mutual understanding between the two parties, such attempts may also involve transfer of one of the parties to another part of the work organization.
3. If the complainant wishes to start an investigation, the complainant shall be informed that a written complaint will be required and that the complaint and complainant's identity will be disclosed to the person accused.
4. The complainant shall be informed of any remedies (such as restoration of pay, indemnity for other loss, and benefits) that may be available or unavailable. The complainant should also be informed of any authorizations necessary to proceed with the procedure (from the department manager, for example), consistent with company policy.
5. The formal investigation shall be performed next, which may require the appointment of an investigator acceptable to both parties.
6. Pending the results of the investigation, a response from the conflict resolution specialist shall be provided within a reasonable time frame.
7. If the complainant is not satisfied with the finding or the recommended course of action, arbitration proceedings which produce a binding settlement may be pursued.

Procedure for Resolving Interpersonal or Work Team Conflict

1. If an agreement cannot be reached between the disputants through normal managerial or work team procedures, a committee established by the organization to listen to and attempt to settle conflicts shall be brought in to meet with the dis-

putants. (The committee may want to contact the conflict resolution specialist for coaching before engaging the workers involved in the conflict.) All proceedings are considered confidential.

2. The committee shall engage the parties in order to agree on the nature of the conflict, find common ground, address the problem from different points of view, keep the discussion focused on the problem and not on individuals, and attempt to develop a solution with action steps.

3. If there is no mutually satisfactory result, the conflict resolution specialist shall be contacted in order to engage the involved parties privately and mediate a mutually agreeable solution.

4. If there is no mutually satisfactory result, the conflict resolution specialist shall issue a binding solution.

---

obtained during an assessment is confidential and may be broached only with the written consent of the individual. (The Appendix contains a sample confidentiality policy for EAP records.)

Policies governing the interaction of behavioral risk management staff with others may also apply to interactions with organized labor; reporting of program use and other data to higher management; administration of behavioral risk training; contact with managers, employees, executives, board members, and service providers; and conduct during entertainment activities. For example, a policy of no drinking by staff during company social functions might be established since drinking might be viewed as behavior unbecoming a professional who deals with individual and organizational behavioral problems.

How the Organization Comports Itself

Yet another set of policies and procedures will include those that regulate the actions of management; the organization's participation in the community and the business marketplace; and the organization's relationships with employees. Some of these policies will be prescribed by law or initiated to protect the organization and its officers against legal action—examples are policies regarding employee personal and family leave and testing for alcohol and drug abuse. These policies may affect behavioral risk management activities either indirectly or directly.

How Employees Comport Themselves

A final set of policies includes the company policies in the employee handbook that involve behavioral risk problems and issues: for example, policies on drug and alcohol abuse, sexual harassment, personal and family leave, absenteeism, work conduct, help seeking, the discipline process, and so forth. Here again, while these policies and procedures do not pertain to the behavioral risk management function, per se, they may directly affect its operations.

This chapter has delineated the tangible parts of the behavioral risk management system and identified two models of program and service delivery. But is what I have described realistic or is it one of those systems that just looks good on paper? The challenge ahead is to apply the textbook concepts of this and the previous chapters to the real world of business, where political fence lines, structural variables, changes of leadership, and other factors influence the design, implementation, and operation of subsystems in the superordinate work system. The next chapter concentrates on examples of organizations that have implemented various solutions—some holistic, others problem specific—to diminish behavioral risk.

Notes

P. 232, *scholarly papers on contemporary management thought:* Brett, J. M., Goldberg, S. B., and Ury, W. L. "Designing Systems for Resolving Disputes in Organizations." *American Psychologist,* 1990, *45*(2), 163.

P. 245, *work team typology:* Sundstrom, E., De Meuse, K. P., and Futrell, D. "Work Teams: Applications and Effectiveness." *American Psychologist,* 1990, *45*(2), 120–133.

Chapter Nine

Behavioral Risk Management in Action

Thus far, I have described ways that behavioral problems in the workplace should be defined and measured and how solutions might be implemented. This chapter turns to examples of work organizations that have successfully implemented solutions that prevent or diminish behavioral risk.

Using processes analogous to the behavioral risk audit, these companies deploy sophisticated means to determine what their behavioral risk exposures have been. The exposures are then expressed in direct costs for healthcare, behavioral healthcare, accidents, employee lawsuits, and other risks. They are also expressed in terms of productivity complications arising from the same risks. These companies have recognized, first, that controlling costs in these areas often involves changing a wide variety of undesirable individual and organizational behaviors and, second, that the most appropriate solutions are found on the prevention end of the risk management continuum.

The six organizations highlighted include conservative and progressive companies, companies that use predominantly internal programs, and companies that rely on external services. Their solutions vary greatly, in part because they have a variety of different problems and business philosophies. They are DuPont, a maintenance services company, the University of California, U.S. Oil, The World Bank, and Employee Assistance Services. In the following sections, we will examine the mechanics of these organizations as they manage and control behavioral risk.

DuPont

DuPont uses the rubric of "healthcare" to describe how it controls behavioral risk because healthcare is the number one cost the system was formed to control. As we will see, however, the interventions utilized by DuPont's Integrated Healthcare (IHC) area do not function as slash-and-burn tactics, restricting access to care or depressing healthcare professionals' fees. Rather, they take aim at the antecedents of healthcare use.

DuPont put its bread-and-butter operations through reengineering processes throughout the 1980s. Beginning in 1989 and again in 1991, it got around to reengineering the support programs, services, and benefits, a move it felt could help the company achieve its goal of offsetting $550 million in healthcare costs from 1993 to 1997. The result is a tripartite function with programs that have been renamed "competencies": EAP competency, Wellness competency, and Medical competency (see Exhibit 9.1). Their mission is to keep employee productivity high and many nonproduction losses in check.

The structural and staffing changes have been surprising. The EAP has expanded from 6 substance abuse counselors in 1988 to a multidisciplinary staff of 64 today. Occupational medicine has downsized from 165 staff in 1992 to 127 full-time and 28 part-time medical professionals. The wellness program has hired 19 site-based consultants in its program, built from scratch. The IHC management team has 14 individuals—four regional managers from each competency, an IHC director, and a vice president to whom they report. DuPont's work/life program staff of 3, like the IHC director, reports to the vice president of human resources but through a separate chain of command. The work/life staff, however, have no solid-line work relationships with the IHC competencies.

EAP Reengineering

Instead of sending in the budget militia to redesign its behavioral risk management programs and services, DuPont dispatched the equivalent of research and development teams. The EAP was the first function reengineered. Until 1989, it had been strictly a

Exhibit 9.1 Division of Labor at DuPont.

Tasks related to behavioral risk management at DuPont are performed primarily by the EAP, medical (including site physicians and nurses), and wellness programs, and the work/life program. The first three functions are housed in Integrated Healthcare (IHC), while the work/life program is separately housed in the human resources division. The tasks performed primarily by each of the three IHC competencies and the work/life program are listed here.

EAP Site Staff

- Ride circuit (employee assistance counselors serve multiple sites).
- Participate in site and regional IHC task teams.
- Plan, develop, and implement education and training programs for sites: for example, EAP orientation, supervisory training, and specialized need programs.
- Coordinate and deliver mental health and substance abuse (MH/SA) crisis intervention.
- Assess MH/SA needs of clients; motivate clients to pursue referral.
- Provide access to enhanced EAP (MH/SA) benefit.
- Coordinate MH/SA services among client, provider, third-party administrator, and supervision.
- Monitor client progress and compliance with treatment recommendations.
- Consult with supervision on MH/SA cases involving (1) management referrals, (2) threats of violence to self and others, and (3) disability.
- Provide critical incident debriefing, when appropriate.
- Develop and implement site-specific EAP plans.
- Coordinate site EAP activities with other site IHC competencies.
- Consult with work organizations (within DuPont) about the behavioral health of the organization.

Exhibit 9.1 Division of Labor at DuPont (*continued*).

Medical Staff (Selected Responsibilities)

Site Physicians and Physician Assistants

- Ride circuit (serve multiple sites).
- Provide disability management (long- and short-term).
- Diagnose and treat work-related injuries and illness.
- Administer fitness-for-duty/return-to-work exams.
- Perform medical review officer function.
- Take an active role on site safety and ergonomic teams; participate in plant walk-throughs.
- Be a resource/advisor to site management on medical, medicolegal, and safety issues.
- Individually counsel high-risk employees on ergonomics, back health, and so forth.
- Be a resource for the managed care committee.

Nursing Staff

- Perform wellness appraisals (clinical assessment, testing, screening, and referral).
- Discuss health issues in one-on-one facilitations.
- Communicate health education messages; conduct health campaigns.
- Support physicians in injury management.
- Support disability management (record keeping and case management).

Wellness Staff

- Ride circuit (serve multiple sites).
- Assess sites for past, present, and future wellness program needs.
- Develop site-by-site wellness plans, based on adaptation to site work culture.
- Coordinate and deliver the Self Care/Health Consumerism program.

- Plan, develop, and deliver training on the Preventive Care Benefit.
- Participate in ergonomic programs (work hardening and exercise recommendations).
- Facilitate wellness appraisal follow-up with behavioral change education.

Work/Life Staff

This program is separate and distinct from IHC but can still be considered a part of DuPont's behavioral risk management activities. Staff responsibilities include oversight of policies and practices related to

- Family leave
- Flexible work practices (part-time work, job sharing, job splitting, flextime, flexplace, compressed work weeks, extended work weeks, sabbaticals, and phased retirement)
- Dependent care (referral and consultation resource)
- Flying Colors (program that helps child care providers in DuPont communities attain national accreditation)
- Information dissemination and consultation to the company regarding the impact of the Americans with Disabilities Act
- Work/family committees (site activities such as summer camps, parenting classes, support groups, and others; there are over 50 such committees throughout the company)

---

substance abuse program with very limited outreach. The vice president of safety, health, and environmental affairs saw the positive results of the substance abuse program but knew it was not proficient at identifying or making appropriate referrals for psychological problems, managed behavioral healthcare activities, disability management, organizational interventions, computerized information management, and other activities that DuPont expected of a contemporary corporate program.

Consequently, DuPont assembled an interdisciplinary EAP task team, consisting of employee relations representatives, a senior manager, EAP staff, plant-based employees, and two prominent

EAP consultants. The team wrote a new EAP mission (to help employees function optimally while containing behavioral health costs) that is in accordance with the corporate mission. The reengineering process started in 1989 and led to first introduction of the rebuilt EAP in 1991. The process included these steps:

Creation of initial design by the EAP task team. The program components earmarked for review were assessment and referral, critical incident stress debriefing, management consultation, organizational consultation, crisis intervention, case management, utilization review, preferred provider network development, and maintenance (that is, an 800-number crisis line).

Review of the design by plant managers participating in geographically designated cluster groups. The plant managers next discussed the proposed design with managers and employee groups at local plant sites and then they submitted feedback to the task team.

Modifications developed and incorporated in the design by the task team.

Review of the modified design by the Plant Managers Sounding Board, made up of site managers representing a cross-section of DuPont business units. (In the DuPont culture, approval of the sounding board is commonly sought when significant proposals are floated within the company.)

Design approval by DuPont's senior management.

Budget approval and plan implementation.

Significantly, DuPont decided to keep both managerial and direct EAP services in-house so that these services could make the greatest possible contribution to the organizational culture. That feature was about the only carryover from the former program, however. Four major changes occurred in the EAP, which today is the primary manager of behavioral risk at DuPont. First, EAP benefits were enhanced and restructured to emphasize flexibility in the types of care provided. (In fact, mental health and substance abuse coverages were renamed the EAP Benefit.) Second, the EAP was designated to manage the enhanced benefit. Third, the EAP assumed the managed behavioral healthcare functions for all employees and dependents electing to use the benefit. The EAP, which uses a three-session assessment-and-referral model with its clients, also began to focus on client functionality instead of on the high-cost long-term psychotherapy that was shown to yield limited work-related improvements. To achieve this refocusing, the EAP began evaluating clients' well-being based not only on clinical indicators but also on their occupational functioning. The fourth major change was that the EAP Case Management Information System (ECMIS), which integrates all employee assistance activity throughout the corporation, was designed and implemented.

IHC Reengineering

While the EAP upgrade brought it up to speed with many other corporate programs of the day, it was still not fully integrated with line management or other employee and dependent resources on a daily basis. That changed with the second round of reengineering, which began in 1991 and resulted in the introduction of Integrated Healthcare as a function a year later.

By the end of 1990, DuPont had decided that healthcare cost escalation was a critical issue in its continued ability to turn a profit. Cost accountability, then, became the underpinning of IHC mission, which is "to provide a healthy, productive workforce through a managed healthcare approach which integrates DuPont medical expertise and programs with healthcare benefits management in a way that provides a competitive business advantage."

Considering the sheer size of staff and resources that would be committed to IHC, special focus was placed on adhering to DuPont's principles for "high performing work systems" during the reengineering process. They are (1) vision, mission, and strategic intent are to be known by all; (2) committed and dedicated leadership is to be "felt" within the organization; (3) every person is to know the paying customer and how his or her work impacts that customer; (4) teamwork and people working in teams are part of the structure; (5) everyone learns and teaches; and (6) activities are principle driven.

Built on these principles, IHC reengineering occurred in four steps:

Appointment of Health Options Task (HOT) Teams, comprising all levels of management (including plant managers); site human resource managers; and benefits, medical, EAP, and wellness staff. Two team leaders from each of DuPont's major facilities were appointed, and participants were divided into three HOT Teams—Preventative Orientation/Roles and Responsibilities, Focus on Quality, and Management of Health-Related Absences. The teams met and deliberated at headquarters five times between May and October 1992.

The HOT Teams submitted recommendations that were reviewed by the Plant Managers Sounding Board then approved by senior management. The recommendations were based on results from quantitative and qualitative questionnaires, on-site interviews with employees and management, team analyses, and preliminary reviews. The recommendations were also based on DuPont's "continuous improvement criteria," used to guide all corporate reengineering activities.

Development of a final plan by the HOT Teams.

Budget approval and plan implementation.

Even though the EAP and medical competencies have a strong managed care focus, IHC considers prevention to be a higher level of performance than early-stage intervention, since cost avoidance is preferable to cost containment. IHC is working on prevention by making a substantial investment in employee education, management education, supervisory training, and complex life-style assessments that are available to family members as well as employees. DuPont says this is essential not only to promote the prevention message but also to establish a healthy organizational culture.

Decentralized Orientation

In order to tailor its IHC services to the environments in which employees and line managers (or competency "customers") live and work, DuPont delegates as much decision-making authority from headquarters as possible, operating insofar as IHC is concerned more like four regional concerns than a Fortune 10 company. There are good reasons for a decentralized orientation to IHC service delivery. DuPont's Northeast region, for example, is concentrated along the Wilmington-Philadelphia corridor, with 22,000 of the company's 70,000 U.S. employees within a ninety-mile radius. The Mid-America region, however, includes forty-four sites in twenty-two states. The staff members of each competency are usually multisite personnel, engaging in continual road travel.

In daily operation, the IHC competencies are coordinated and integrated through numerous formal and informal points of contact between competency staff and their regional managers and between the regional managers and leadership at headquarters. For example, the Mid-America region's contacts include

Formal meetings locally for the purpose of cross-referrals among competency staff

Informal meetings locally (staff of the three competencies often share offices)

Monthly meetings of the staff of each competency, usually with interaction among the three competencies

Annual meetings of each competency at headquarters

Bimonthly meetings of the twelve regional managers and IHC director at headquarters

Meetings as needed of regional management teams

Eventually, the pinnacle of integration will be interchangeability among the managers, so that any one regional manager is able to perform the administrative duties of any other. The adhesive holding the entire IHC system in place, though, is ECMIS, the management information system that houses the software packages for each of the three competencies. ECMIS allows for data integration and provides the objective outcomes information by which IHC competencies can be held accountable and improved upon. Examples of outcomes that IHC can produce on a monthly basis include individual and aggregated data on the amount of substance abuse thought to be occurring, usage and costs, drug-testing results, safety incidents, number and cost of employees out on disability, fitness-for-duty evaluations, wellness appraisal results, and others.

A Process, Not an Event

DuPont's management expects high performance from its IHC engine, as it does from any of its significant investments.

IHC performance is being measured by (1) adherence to budget, (2) the $550 million cost-avoidance target, (3) benchmarking against frame-of-reference companies on healthcare cost increases, (4) DuPont's healthcare cost increase trend line, and (5) progress in reducing specified health risks among the covered population.

A Company Specializing in Employer Maintenance Services

Another major company, which has asked not to be named because it continues to refine its service delivery, uses a service delivery model that is the most literal example of behavioral risk management in this chapter. This company, which provides assistance such as custodial, laundry, and food preparation services to other companies, was concerned about employees' accident rate, turnover, absenteeism, healthcare utilization, and workers' compensation costs. So it adopted a behavioral risk management strategy that has integrated its behavioral risk management services as contiguous elements in its behavioral risk management program, coordinated by its risk management department. The five program components are

Preemployment screens in a variety of behavioral risk areas

A workplace stress inventory to improve on-the-job awareness and reduce accidents

Programs, training, and workshops that improve employee well-being at work

Employee incentives, motivation, and recognition to promote self-responsibility

Claims management

In cooperation with a publisher of human assessment tools, this company has developed actuarially sound preemployment screening tools that it administers to job candidates for one-third the cost of drug tests (which are also more invasive). The qualities or risks assessed include

Honesty: measures an individual's attitude toward theft and toward theft-related behavior that has previously been or that might be exhibited in the workplace

Drug avoidance: measures an individual's attitude toward drug and alcohol use as well as his or her likelihood of seeking or using illegal substances at work, especially when under stress

Violence: measures an individual's attitudes toward argumentative or violent behavior

Customer relations: measures an individual's tendency to behave courteously toward customers and fellow employees

Emotional factors: measures the likelihood of an individual to experience emotional problems that disrupt work performance

Safety: measures an individual's attitudes toward factors that can cause or prevent work-related injuries

Work values: measures an individual's attitudes toward his or her work and the presence of productive work habits

Supervision: measures an individual's attitude toward supervision and the execution of work assignments

Tenure: predicts the tendency of an individual to stay with the company once hired

Employability index: measures an individual's suitability for hiring based on the aggregated results of screening the nine issues above

The second component, the workplace stress inventory, teaches employees to handle stress in order to improve their concentration. The stress assessments are considered an awareness tool as well as a means of identifying employees at heightened risk of accidents, who are then asked to enroll in a stress-management minicourse. This process has helped the company achieve a 60 percent reduction in on-the-job accidents in a two-year period.

Employees are taught what the stress-related hazards are—such as time pressures, deadlines, excessive work hours, long commutes, conflicts with customers, and departmental conflict—then given guidance on how to deal with them. The inventory also identifies sources of eustress, or good stress, in people's lives; the intent being to help employees balance distress and eustress. The company uses a formula that measures both off-the-job and on-the-job stress, allotting each a maximum of 100 points, for a total of 200 possible distress points. The formula then measures an employee's eustress, examples of which are vacationing, traveling, meditating, taking hot baths, fishing, and hiking. The maximum here is also 200 points. When the distress points are higher than the eustress points, recommendations are given to the employee on how to balance stress.

Accompanying the stress inventory is a safety culture audit. The maintenance services company heavily promotes a safety culture among employees. Among the cultural variables measured are perceptions of leadership; safety rituals, folklore, and symbols; company heroes; and the like. Because large numbers of employees work on-site at other companies, especially hospitals and because work cultures exist at these job sites as well as in the maintenance services company, companywide—audits are commonly done of employers that contract with the maintenance services company. The cultural audit, which also helps to identify employees with attitudes unbecoming a safe work environment, has consistently shown that the poorer the audit score, the higher the rate of injury.

The third behavioral risk program component consists of the programs, training, and workshops that correct employee and organizational deficiencies identified by the prior two components. Included are stress management workshops, locus-of-control training sessions and "safeness" training, an employee assistance program, a wellness program, and cultural change workshops. While this component demonstrates the company interest in employee well-being, employees are also taught to take on ownership of these self-improvement tools and responsibility for their own safety.

The wellness program is specifically designed to help employees achieve a risk age that is 10 percent lower than their chronological age. For example, a thirty-four-year-old male employee who is fifteen pounds overweight, has a sedentary life-style, and smokes one cigar a day has a health-risk age of forty-one. According to actuarial tables, this man's average annual medical cost is $1,124. The wellness program—which includes a variety of life-style and health promotion activities, including fitness facilities and an employee newsletter—intervenes to try to bring his health-risk age down to thirty-one, for which the average annual medical cost is $478.

The company's EAP, with six internal staff members, has become an integral part of the work culture. This is reflected in the program's 80 percent annual utilization rate. Its two distinguishing features are (1) mandatory supervisor referrals for all accidents and all near misses and (2) heavy internal promotion of a video produced by the risk management department, which is popular with employees. This soft-sell program promotes self-referrals to the EAP by encouraging employees and their family members to take a self-assessment survey. The survey assesses areas of life functioning, including life stress, job stress, family stress, relationship problems, emotional adjustment, self-esteem, drug and alcohol use, wellness and fitness, referral readiness, and social support. If survey takers feel they are deficient in any of these areas, they are gently encouraged to visit the EAP.

The fourth program component—employee incentives, motivation, and recognition—promotes ownership and self-responsibility through safety management. Managers, the locus of this component, implement the company's safety program. They appoint safety teams with twenty to thirty nonmanagement workers per team. These teams are the hands-on owners of the company's safety culture. Each team member receives monthly safety training and is eligible for monthly or quarterly financial rewards (at the manager's discretion), which are conditioned on (1) an absence of lost-time injuries at the employee's job site, (2) detection of safety hazards and suggestions about how to correct them, (3) participation in accident review sessions, and (4) attendance and/or presentations at team safety sessions.

The fifth component is claims management. Since the company is a self-insured employer, it uses claims management as a financial stop-loss method for workers' compensation, medical healthcare, and behavioral healthcare claims. An unusual feature is the behavioral claims management. Risk management staff conduct an investigation of emotional and attitudinal problems of all employees responsible for on-the-job accidents, following up with an EAP referral. Because depression and other psychological problems commonly develop following physical injury, the EAP also routinely follows up with injured workers. Employees are also trained in workers' compensation procedures at time of hire, announcements are posted indicating the workers' compensation administrator who processes claims for employees in a particular location, managers are instructed to report injuries within twenty-four hours of the accident, and employees are case managed as tightly as possible.

The behavioral risk management strategy has been a critical factor in this company's profitability and customer retention. Why? Consider this: 95 percent of the company's employees' contact with customers is unsupervised. Couple that statistic with consumer research showing that when customers are happy with a service, on average they tell three others. When they are unhappy, they tell thirteen others. Employees' well-being correlates directly with customer satisfaction, providing compelling evidence that by managing its behavioral risks, the employer services company is furthering its business objectives.

The University of California

The University of California (UC) illustrates how activities to control behavioral risk can vary from one work setting to another. UC has over 280,000 faculty, staff, and other employees spread across nine campuses, five medical centers, three nuclear laboratories, and the central Office of the President. Many UC locations are the size of major universities in their own right, and each operates with substantial autonomy. For a look at two diverse approaches to behavioral risk in the same university system, I have chosen to examine the main campus in Oakland, where the Office of the President is situated, and the University of California campus at Irvine (UC-Irvine).

There are six funded service accounts against which behavioral risk-related losses are credited at the main campus in Oakland: vocational rehabilitation, industrial and group health, medical treatment, risk administration, legal services, and special programs. These funded services are not structurally linked for the most part but are well-integrated in terms of both formal and information collaboration and information sharing. The services work together as a particular need is seen.

During the 1980s, the predominant behavioral risk exposure was stress-related workers' compensation claims. The average claim had risen to $20,000 under California workers' compensation law—the most liberal in the United States—which required that injured workers had only to show that 10 percent of a stress-related disability was work related in order to receive an award. At UC, the average cost for prehearing processing, administration, and paperwork alone was $6,000. The legal standard was raised from 10 to 51 percent in 1993 through reform legislation, and claims and award payments have tumbled considerably at UC and for other California employers since then.

Currently, UC is attacking the issue of protracted disability episodes and working on meeting the compliance guidelines of the Americans with Disabilities Act. When a case involves a repetitive motion injury from keyboard use, for example, the employee's trauma about returning to data-entry work and feelings of disenfranchisement in relation to the employer can be a greater hurdle to overcome than the injury itself. Therefore, staff of the vocational rehabilitation, workers' compensation, EAP, and wellness units work in tandem on coordinating physical rehabilitation and psychological interventions for workers' compensation and health insurance disability cases. Vocational rehabilitation, of course, oversees physical recovery. The workers' compensation unit ensures that pathways are available for alternative work assignments, phase-in of responsibilities, and so forth. The EAP performs the psychological intervention. The wellness program actively instills a health-minded culture instead of a disability-oriented one, using such activities as "walks for wellness," brown-bag seminars, newsletters, and so forth. The intent is to induce employees to *want* to come back from injury. Wellness staff also help in the physical recovery by promoting proper diet and life-style management.

At the UC-Irvine campus, the focus is on conflict resolution in order to reduce the behavioral risks of workplace violence; toxic relations among administrative personnel, faculty, and staff; employee lawsuits; and sexual harassment. These risks, plus the concern of some employees that the campus confidential assessment resource might be an information-gathering tentacle of the human resource management department, led UC-Irvine to pair the ombudsman and EAP as a stand-alone unit that reports directly to the campus's chancellor and executive vice chancellors.

This match seems to be working exceptionally well. The ombudsman and EAP both handle confidential information, function as problem solvers, and address issues related to employee morale, although they do not share files without approval of the client. The ombudsman performs conflict management interventions between the client and other parties at the university. The EAP addresses client personal problems. They cross-refer about one-third of their clients, however, because, when a person feels under duress, objective reasoning about whether a problem is primarily due to the work setting or to a psychological or emotional issue can be lost. In some cases, both kinds of problems are factors, and both must be considered in a solution.

One of the areas of greatest impact has been a substantial reduction in lawsuits that have found their way to court since the two functions were joined in 1988. For example, if a female faculty member, staff member, or student (the unit serves all three) has a sexual harassment complaint, she may be more inclined to see the ombudsman instead of the affirmative action office where the case would have high visibility and possibly grave consequences. This is especially the case when the situation involves subtle rather than clearcut harassment. The ombudsman can help her to broker a solution (such as a job transfer to another part of the campus for her or the perpetrator) that ends the conflict without fanfare. Once the agreement is reached, it is filed with the ombudsman in the form of a statement signed by both parties. The EAP handles the psychological and emotional aftereffects of these cases, such as lingering anger, in addition to its usual behavioral health caseload.

U.S. Oil

At U.S. Oil, a wholesale distributor of petroleum, automotive, and lubricant products, "beer in the rear" on Friday afternoons was a longstanding part of the workplace culture. That was still true in 1988, at a time when the company was anticipating explosive business growth yet had few personnel policies or management training to regulate workplace behavior, only limited benefits, and a total absence of programs and services to diminish behavioral risk.

Concerned that the workforce of 800 employees (or associates) might not be able to stand up to the rigors of greater performance expectations, management took a risk management approach to establishing U.S. Oil as a growth-oriented company. It performed a baseline assessment of company shortcomings and needs using the St. Paul Human Factors Inventory and Audit (paper-and-pencil surveys—one taken by employees, the other by management) in order to define the areas where employee services would be needed. Repeating the process biennially, U.S. Oil has since made impressive strides toward its organizational goals. The data initially showed that the greatest disparity between U.S. Oil's rating and the national averages established by the inventory and audit was in alcohol consumption, making drinking the company's number one organizational risk. Owing to this finding, U.S. Oil eliminated drinking at its work sites and promoted alcohol awareness. (Inventory scores for employee substance use as a life-style risk have improved from 63 in 1990 to 57 in 1994, with 0 being the most favorable score.) Because U.S. Oil had a larger than average group of smokers, it also established a smoke-free environment.

U.S. Oil's programming changes have been motivated by the sense of wellness and productivity enhancement that the company wanted to promote in the workforce. The company created a wellness task force in 1989 and assigned a benefits staff person to manage program activities, including monthly fitness and wellness education meetings. Employees accrue points for attendance, and the education serves as the basis for health insurance premium reductions. Additional points are given for exercising three or more times per week and not smoking. General health screenings including blood and cholesterol screenings are regularly given. Other changes have included implementation of an EAP, which has been tailored to focus on employee education for the purpose of early behavioral problem identification, liability containment, and healthcare cost containment.

U.S. Oil learned after its 1992 inventory and audit—which occurred about six months after the issue of harassment was widely publicized in connection with the Senate hearings to approve Clarence Thomas as a member of the Supreme Court—that female associates felt somewhat intimidated by the attitudes of male co-workers, so the company publicized and reaffirmed its policy on sexual harassment. Some new wrinkles were added to the employee orientation program, which was put on videotape for outlying locations. The wellness committee also evaluates healthcare reform proposals at the federal and state levels and expresses its views to lawmakers on behalf of the company.

Finally, U.S. Oil has implemented a computerized tracking system for workers' compensation claims, and hired a person to manage claims in-house. He has mounted an aggressive accident prevention and back-to-work program for associates out on disability. Consequently, U.S. Oil's experience-modifier rating, determined by the state workers' compensation bureau, has dropped to .63, vastly better than the score of 1.0 that is considered average.

A family-owned company, U.S. Oil continues to audit its behavioral risks because it continues to change. Management is presently transitioning from one generation of leadership to the next and has been mindful of statistics showing that 85 percent of family-owned businesses fail to make this change successfully. Therefore, its risk-management activities focus as much on management as employee issues.

The World Bank

The World Bank, an international development financial institution, delivers behavioral risk management services in a manner that suits the operational and logistical landscape of the organization. The World Bank has about 7,000 permanent and fixed-term staff members and about 2,500 others who are long-term consultants and temporaries. The company is divided into two primary areas—financial and regional operations—whose work is performed throughout the world. Each region and support area (such as finance, administration) is headed by a vice president.

The World Bank had found that despite extensive performance management training provided to managers, its most persistent behavioral issue was that some employees had chronic work performance problems. This was in spite of the fact that The World Bank offered myriad employee services, including a career advisory program, ombudsman, staff association (to make recommendations to management on working issues such as space allocation), and staff counseling and consultation service for behavioral health problems. The problems that the institution particularly wanted to avert were harassment (of a sexual or threatening nature), drinking problems, and performance discrepancies.

Several years ago, The World Bank decided that it wanted its managers to be better at spotting signs of emerging employee performance problems and at intervening before the problems became severe and perhaps developed into behavioral health problems as well. To facilitate this change, the institution created the Performance Advisory Service (PAS), a five-member team comprising bank staff and consultants with expertise encompassing organizational development, human resources, management systems, intercultural learning and leadership, performance management, and strategic research and planning. PAS's roles are

Prompt resolution of all performance issues

Firm adherence to job-grade performance issues

Clear and consistent application of policies and procedures bankwide

Modification of human resource policies and procedures to facilitate fair resolution of issues

Careful design and implementation of performance improvement plans to resolve and/or prevent chronic problems

Close monitoring of performance issues (by helping managers identify employees' performance discrepancies relative to peers)

PAS fulfills these roles by, first, performing specialized interventions to help managers address their most persistent employee behavioral problems; second, running workshops for supervisors on work performance discrepancies; and, third, conducting performance management training for managers and employees. The PAS workshop for managers and supervisors, "Enhancing Individual Performance," is based on the work of the management consulting firm Aubrey Daniels, Inc., and borrows heavily from the teachings of renowned behavioral psychologist B. F. Skinner.

The PAS team uses a performance case management process that includes instructing supervisors how to analyze employee work performance and conduct problems (see Figure 9.1). The method first determines whether there is a skill or technical deficiency and, if there is not, identifies facts that suggest other causes. Among the issues managers are taught to assess for a troubled employee are work unit or co-worker attitudes that discourage performance; mismatches between the person's knowledge, skill, or ability and

Figure 9.1 Performance Case Management at the World Bank.

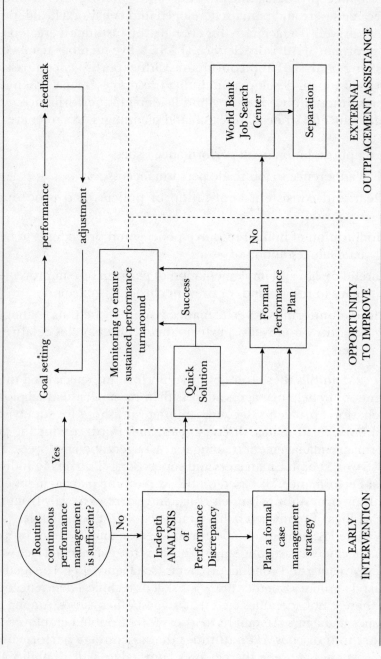

Source: The World Bank. Reprinted by permission.

the job requirements; the existence of reinforcement (attention, power, prestige, or status) for misbehaving; consequences for not performing; a known behavioral health problem; unresolved conflicts with other staff; and harassment by others.

The workshops are held institutionwide and on request by departmental management teams. Each workshop is conducted by three or four PAS advisors for a group of about fifteen managers. In essence, the workshop instructs managers that performance results are the product of antecedents, behaviors (actions), and consequences. With the aid of a case study, the participants practice pinpointing current results and behaviors (the situations); desired results and behaviors (the expectations); current antecedents and consequences (the causes); and proposed antecedents and consequences (the solutions). A key guiding principle is "you get what you reinforce." After practice with the case study, the managers apply the steps of the performance case management process to situations they are currently dealing with, working individually and in small groups with a PAS facilitator. PAS members note that this application session is where the true learning takes place.

PAS interventions occur when managers experience difficulties with specific employee performance problems. In these cases, PAS advises the manager, who in turn works with the employee on the issue. For example, two managers visited PAS to discuss a problem they had with several of their administrative assistants. They relied on the assistants to answer phones and disseminate documents by mail and facsimile as quickly as possible, since most of the information was highly time sensitive. However, the assistants chronically procrastinated, a behavior that persisted no matter how many admonishments they received from the managers. PAS learned that when the assistants procrastinated the managers did the task themselves. Therefore, the PAS recommendation was that instead of rewarding nonperformance as they presently did, the managers should meet with the assistants, specifically describe the current work performance issues and behaviors that are unacceptable, delineate the job responsibilities and performance expectations, and specify the reinforcements and consequences that would apply to performance and nonperformance. After doing this, the managers found that their theretofore nagging problem with the assistants evaporated.

PAS regularly consults with managers on specific problems that may have simple or complex solutions, and multiple resources exist for resolving individual employees' problems. The internal referral resources at The World Bank—including the staff counseling service, ombudsman, and career advisory program—commonly cross-refer employees among themselves. By using this prevention and early-stage intervention approach, The World Bank has substantially improved its ability to identify behavioral risk problems at a stage when more serious problems can still be averted.

External Service Providers

There are various types of external providers involved in delivering services that control behavioral risk to employers. These providers may specialize in employee assistance, managed behavioral healthcare, wellness and health promotion, safety and risk management, or organizational development.

Each provider supports a portion of the behavioral risk management strategy. Organizational development specialists address many of the organizational issues that concern behavioral risk management, but they do not necessarily address employee behavioral risk exposures. They tend to be concerned with matters such as organizational structure; mergers and acquisitions; executive recruitment, advancement, and replacement; and expansion into new markets. They generally work from the top down, whereas behavioral risk management uses information derived from the organizational floor to identify changes that may be necessary in the management and executive ranks.

Because of its focus on restoring dysfunctional employees to optimal functioning, an EAP is the occupational function that affects behavioral risk more directly than any other function. Managed behavioral healthcare provides many of the same functions as employee assistance (and often is responsible for tasks associated with employee assistance), but generally places workplace issues second to healthcare delivery. Managed behavioral healthcare firms specialize in large service networks and count their

BEHAVIORAL RISK MANAGEMENT IN ACTION 277

clients as "covered lives," not as "employees" or "families." Because behavioral risk services need to be tailored to the organization, highly personalized in order to focus on the multiple work- and health-related issues of employees, and physically present at the work site if they are to promote awareness and utilization, EAP service delivery is more consistent with behavioral risk management priorities than managed behavioral healthcare goals.

Many EAP providers have retained these foci even as they have expanded from local to regional to national in service delivery area and have broadened their range of services. In one 1994 survey of external EAP service providers, the twenty-six responding firms indicated that they provide a wide range of services in addition to employee assistance, as shown in the following list.

Type of Service	Percentage Responding Yes
Workplace-Related Services	
Employee assistance	100
Employee stress management	96
Critical incident stress debriefing	92
Wellness and health promotion	73
Workforce diversity consultation and services	62
Work-and-family consultation and services	38
Accident prevention	15
Healthcare-Related Services	
Managed behavioral healthcare	62
Behavioral health benefits management	42
Workers' compensation case management:	
stress-related disabilities	35
psychological component of physical disability	31
Organizational and Miscellaneous	
Organizational consultation on management of behavioral risks	58
Drug-testing results analysis	12
Drug testing	8

In the same survey, the managed behavioral healthcare providers were stronger in healthcare related services but generally weaker in services that were workplace related.

As the survey shows, in order to become better controllers of behavioral risk, EAPs need to strengthen their focus on accident prevention. (Indeed, many companies with a lot of dangerous occupations, especially those in the heavily regulated transportation industry, have internal EAPs that have adopted this ancillary focus.) However, their involvement in work-and-family services is lower than might be expected. Many EAP providers consider involvement in drug-testing issues to be a conflict of interest, because employers can use drug testing to target employees whom they consider miscreants deserving to be terminated. EAPs, however, have traditionally been a *rehabilitative* resource. Thus, drug testing presents many EAPs with an ethical dilemma.

Over the last ten years, virtually all purveyors of behavioral risk related services have expanded their focus from their original discipline. External firms that had what were perceived to be dissimilar products have broadened focus and service delivery and found that they in fact share similar interests. For example, providers that have specialized in traditional accident inspection and investigation are becoming more interested in behavioral safety issues in order to focus proactively on accident prevention. In keeping with this new focus, they are also more interested in wellness and health promotion, stress management training, organizational culture development, and employee assistance. Clearly, while many of the providers are continuing to emphasize their traditional focus, they are increasingly meeting on common ground.

How might a provider with a wide range of behavioral risk related services structure itself? It could segment operations into three distinct but interactive divisions: employee behavioral risk services, organization behavioral risk services, and management services.

Employee behavioral risk services could perform tasks associated with employee assistance, managed behavioral healthcare, wellness and health promotion, work and family, behavioral safety, diversity, critical incident stress debriefing, employee stress management, disability management, and other employee risks. This division could also handle fitness-for-duty determinations for employees in recovery from treatment who are returning to safety-sensitive jobs, for example, or for employees who were removed for reasons of conduct or observable symptoms of a behavioral disorder.

Organizational behavioral risk services could specialize in organizational interventions, including culture development, internal consultation on business practices that elevate behavioral risk, team building, and work team problem intervention. It could also handle specialized interventions, such as executive interventions. Both general and situation-specific organizational interventions could utilize information derived from the employee behavioral risk services and management services divisions. This division could also provide preemployment testing services.

Management services could handle behavioral risk audits of client organizations, all training activities (using staff from the other two divisions), drug-testing activities (probably using staff other than those in employee behavioral risk services), Pareto-group analysis, internal computerized information management, data and report generation for clients, and internal administration.

Finally, I extend a word of caution to employers who hire vendors to control behavioral risk: even if you contract with a single external firm to provide a wide spectrum of behavioral risk related services, management of the process should still be retained by you. A company does itself no favors by ceding management of its behavioral risk management process to an external provider, who will interpret the company's lack of hands-on management as lack of interest or sophistication. In such a case, when the service provider has competing priorities, it is more likely to turn its attention to the customer who is overseeing and continually evaluating the quality of the services the provider is supplying.

Employee Assistance Service

Here is a glance at one service provider that already has many elements of the behavioral risk management model in place. Founded in 1984, Employee Assistance Service has about 280 corporations and 80,000 employees under contract. It still markets itself using the "employee assistance" moniker, but its range of services today is considerably more extensive. Employee Assistance

Service (EAS) originally used a brief-therapy model of employee assistance, meaning that its service delivery included not only one to three initial assessment sessions to identify the problem and refer the person out to treatment or other assistance in the community but also as many as seven additional sessions to try to resolve the problem. Whereas about half of clients are referred out in a three-session model (with most of the referrals requiring access to the benefit plan), the brief-therapy model has cut outside referrals down to 20 to 25 percent of clients, thus reducing benefit plan use. Additionally, clients do not have to explain their problems all over again to another clinician.

Due to customer request and the results of annual feedback sessions with work organizations that cut across different demographic strata (for example, blue-collar and white-collar, urban and suburban, private and government), EAS has diversified considerably since its founding. While over most of the last twelve years, the company's growth has been in expansion of employee assistance service delivery capability, over the last three and one-half years, EAS has added a variety of services at customer request. They include managed behavioral healthcare, wellness and health promotion, case management of the psychological component of workers' compensation cases, benefits consulting, critical incident stress debriefing, elder care, management training, conflict resolution, organizational interventions, work team development, and even international relocation assistance for expatriate employees. These additional services are in keeping with behavioral risk management philosophy.

The provider's reporting structure is changing, also. President and chief executive officer Gail Gibson says that originally EAS nearly always reported to the client's human resource manager, but now it is not uncommon for it to report to the top or to a senior executive. In other cases, EAS reports to the client's risk manager, who generally has a hard bottom-line approach to service delivery.

Figure 9.2 shows the structure of EAS. It is headed by an informal board of directors made up of internal staff representing administration and operations. The president and CEO reports to this board and directs all staff affairs. The executive vice president directs a variety of services, and the vice president-EAP operations

Figure 9.2 Employee Assistance Service Organizational Chart.

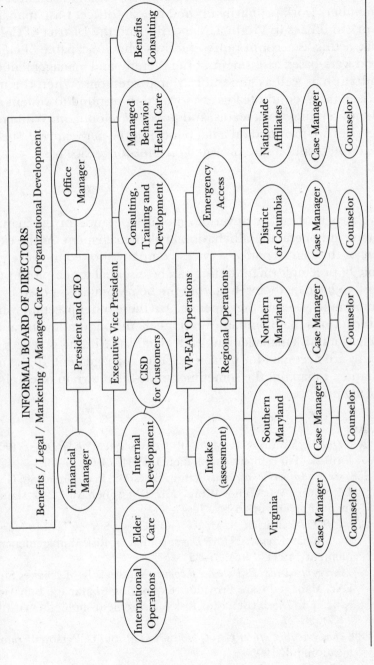

Note: CISD = Critical Incident Stress Debriefing.

Source: Employee Assistance Service, Inc. Reprinted by permission.

oversees client intake and emergency responsibilities. These staff members work primarily in the McLean office. Case managers work in offices in Virginia, Maryland, and the District of Columbia, acting as account representatives who are capable of clinical and work-based assessments, brief therapy, and management consultation as well as general case management. When the need arises, intervention teams are formed to respond to violent incidents, feuding work teams, and policy development. While most services are provided on a flat per-employee-per-year rate, specialized interventions are provided on a fee-for-service basis.

We have now looked at various modus operandi for the management and operation of behavioral risk management. As the example of the maintenance services company showed, however, the role of preemployment testing can be essential for employers who wish to insulate themselves from the behavioral risks posed by the community wherein they operate. Are there other preemployment precautions that companies can take? Although not central to a behavioral risk management strategy, effective hiring practices certainly are necessary for human resource management. In the next chapter, I map out the sometimes mine-filled terrain of employer hiring practices.

Notes

P. 262, *DuPont:* Yandrick, R. M. "Built from Scratch." *EAP Digest* (Behavior Risk Management supplement), 1994, *14*(6), 27–29.

P. 268, *six funded service accounts:* Yandrick, R. M. "Reengineering: Giving Employer's What They Want." *EAP Digest* (Behavior Risk Management supplement), 1994, *14*(4), 35.

P. 270, *U.S. Oil:* Yandrick, R. M. "U.S. Oil Uses a Survey Tool to Manage Its 'Human Factors.'" *EAP Digest* (Behavior Risk Management supplement), 1994, *14*(6), 31–32.

P. 277, *survey of external EAP service providers:* Yandrick, R. M. "Survey Shows EAP, Managed Care Providers Expanding to Manage Behavioral Risk." *EAP Digest* (Behavior Risk Management supplement), 1994, *14*(7), 26–27.

P. 280, *chief executive officer Gail Gibson says:* Gibson, G. Personal communication, July 1995.

Chapter Ten

Preemployment Screening

Catching Behavioral Problems Before They Walk Through the Door

Previous chapters have reviewed the theory, interventions, and applications of behavioral risk management. Now it is time to address three special issues relevant to the operation and success of the behavioral risk management function. This chapter looks at preemployment screening during the personnel selection process, which helps employers to prevent risk exposures by hiring the job candidates least likely to pose behavioral risk problems. Chapter Eleven discusses computerized information management, which augments a behavioral risk management function's ability to gather and use data. The commentary in Chapter Twelve on legal and other public policy issues identifies restrictions placed on employers and their risk management programs, services, and benefits.

Up to this point, our focus has been primarily on issues of behavioral risk exposures that are endogenous to the organization. We have not taken into full consideration traits that workers bring into the organization and that may reflect individual character flaws, family conflicts, and problems in society at large, all of which can affect work behavior. For example, one employee may exhibit passive-aggressive behavior reflective of a troubled childhood. Another may cope well in a staid work environment but lack the resilience necessary to cope with change. Yet another may have developed hardened attitudes about other ethnic or cultural groups, attitudes molded in conformance with the highly divisive society in which he or she lives. Such external factors can be many and varied; however, there are ways to diminish the risks they present.

Three Ways to Diminish External Behavioral Risks

Employers want to prevent social issues from becoming problems in the workplace. After all, a work organization operates more profitably if it devotes most of its energy to making products and delivering services, not to solving social ills. So employers may wish to apply any of three means to protect themselves against behavioral risks literally walking in through a company's front door.

The first means of diminishing risk is to selectively choose where facilities will be located. This decision is often based initially on the favorability of the business climate. For example, one Northeastern U.S. company, a producer of various types of high-technology equipment, traditionally operated within state borders for seventy-five years. However, most of its expansion over the last twelve years has been in the Carolinas. It made these expansion location decisions based on the presence of a more favorable business climate in the Carolinas, especially a lower business tax base. Other factors have been considered, too, such as the location of natural resources, environmental laws, availability of transportation channels, proximity to universities and technical schools, and the availability of qualified employees.

Additionally, this company conducted research to determine the degree to which social problems were likely to manifest as workplace behavioral risks. It investigated these questions: Are families in the area generally close-knit and intact? What is the prevalence of single-parent households? Is the local community steeped in religious or spiritual traditions? Does the local community have a high degree of ethnicity? Are the ethnic groups cordial or combative with each other? If there are multiple pockets of diverse peoples, does each group pose different risks in the workplace? Are people receptive to change or do they steadfastly cling to traditions? Does the populace value self-reliance or tend to be on the public dole? Is the culture of the area more cosmopolitan or more parochial? Have there been a lot of gender-related problems in the local business community? Is there a high crime rate? Have there been a lot of public health concerns (such as AIDS) in the local community? Are people generally health or sickness oriented in their life-styles?

While the company did not make the decision to relocate based primarily on behavioral risk issues, its research suggested that the overall behavioral risk in the prospective work site would not be significantly different than its current overall risk.

The second means by which companies can diminish risk is to become good "corporate citizens." The United States, to no small degree, has been built on the backs of one-industry towns, in which the company had a major hand in building the community's infrastructure. This is the quintessential example of community involvement: the corporation is involved in the establishment and development of educational institutions, healthcare facilities, social services that minimize indigence, and sometimes even employee housing. Even though "company-owned towns" are a relic of the past, many employers, working singly or cooperatively, continue to make host communities the beneficiaries of their largesse.

The benefits of community involvement are varied, but diminished behavioral risk is one of them, since it is a result of the economic stability that the company provides to the area.

The third method of diminishing behavioral risk is the only way in which it can be directly controlled on a person-by-person basis. That method is careful personnel selection. This human resource management activity is an employer's seawall against behavioral risk that can flood in from outside. A human resource manager need not be integrated with the behavioral risk management function in order to diminish behavioral risk; he or she only needs to be aware of how personnel selection serves to reduce that risk.

Job Issues Affecting Personnel Selection

Good human resource management begins with effective hiring, meaning that a human resource manager consistently finds the right person for the right job. The performance of a human resource manager is often evaluated, then, by the work performance of the people he or she hires.

The rigor with which personnel selection for each job occurs is typically predicated on several factors. The first is the overall wealth of the organization relative to its number of employees, expressed as the average amount of revenue generated per worker. The higher that average, the more important it is to make good hiring decisions. For example, in companies working in such areas as computer software and hardware development, aerospace, and specialty steel production, which generate high annual revenues relative to the number of employees, virtually every hiring decision is critical since the work behaviors of even low-level employees may have the potential to influence the generation or loss of hundreds of thousands of dollars. Furthermore, these employers generally provide among the highest-paying jobs and the most stable work environments in a community. Consequently, once employees are hired, they tend to stay with the company for a long period, perhaps the duration of their careers.

Conversely, a supermarket that employs dozens of stock persons and other workers in low-paying positions is not likely to apply the same rigor to preemployment screening. Management expects turnover to be high, more like 50 to 100 percent every year instead of the 3 to 5 percent that a high-revenue-generating company is more likely to experience. Additionally, the undesirable behaviors of a single employee (such as theft, sabotage, or accidents) are likely to have lesser economic consequences for the supermarket than for, say, an aerospace company.

A second issue in determining how rigorous hiring procedures need to be is job classification. Different positions affect company performance differently and, therefore, may be subject to varying recruitment and hiring standards. Jobs that have a significant impact on the performance of the organization—such as certain management, technical, and professional jobs—are usually also higher paying and may have hundreds of candidates for every opening. Conversely, less-significant and lower-paying jobs may have as little as a 1:1 candidate-to-job-opening ratio. In this respect, the importance of behavioral risk as a hiring consideration increases with the importance ascribed to the significance of the position.

A third issue is that safety sensitive and security-related positions require a high level of scrutiny regardless of their level of pay or position compared with other jobs in the organization. Companies engaged in technology transfer overseas, for example, risk losing millions of dollars in classified information if dishonest employees have access to the information. Also, since these industries are usually regulated by the federal government, a company with a poor performance record is more likely to be subject to financial penalty, debarment, or other penalty by an agency with regulatory oversight.

It is for all these reasons that the preemployment screening process can diminish behavioral risk.

The Scope of Preemployment Screening

Most of this chapter is devoted to one candidate selection activity, the paper-and-pencil psychological tests that employers are increasingly using to predict a job candidate's likelihood of causing behavioral risks. It is also useful, however, to recognize that there are other screening procedures that can accomplish the same objective. A review of the entire preemployment-screening process will identify these procedures and specify a test's proper place in the process.

The first step in screening is an analysis of job tasks and responsibilities, which should occur before applications and résumés are even solicited. This analysis yields the information necessary for determining the intellectual, interpersonal, and physical requirements of the position. Accurate formulation of job requirements, moreover, has become a high priority of human resource managers since implementation of the Americans with Disabilities Act (ADA) in 1992 and the increased potential for discrimination lawsuits and complaints to the Equal Employment Opportunity Commission by disabled job candidates, who may claim they met the stated requirements of the job but were disqualified from consideration because of their disability.

The analysis of job tasks and responsibilities can also specify particularly problematic behavioral risks. Depending on the position, these particular risks may run the gamut of generic behavioral risks as well as the specific risks relevant to the position and concerns of the company. For example, the potential for theft may be a particularly strong concern in filling a job that requires using a lot of high-technology equipment, poor interpersonal skills, a concern for jobs having a great deal of customer interface, and proneness to accidents in jobs in a heavy industrial environment.

Once the requirements for the position have been determined, the personnel selection process begins. The Society for Industrial and Organizational Psychology (SIOP) has identified a variety of personnel selection procedures used by work organizations. Among them are paper-and-pencil tests, performance tests, work samples, drug tests, personality inventories, interest inventories, projective techniques, integrity or honesty tests, interviews, educational requirements, experience requirements, reference checks, physical ability tests, appraisals of job performance, computer-based test interpretations, interaction with would-be co-workers, and others.

Culling résumés and applications is usually the first step in the hiring process, unless this preselection process has been done by an employment agency. Face-to-face interviews follow. These highly personal meetings, which everyone who has ever held a job is familiar with, continue to be the most important form of personnel selection, allowing the evaluator to process both verbal and non-verbal communication received from the candidate. Small, often nonverbal cues, may also reveal a person's susceptibility to behavioral risk exposure.

Candidates considered further may be subjected to another form of screening: interaction with others with whom they would be working in the organization. The ability of a candidate to converse on work-related issues with current employees is used by some human resource managers as a predictor of on-the-job conduct and work performance. In work team environments, such interactions are becoming of increasing importance in selection processes.

Paper-and-Pencil Psychological Tests

Among the other techniques cited by SIOP that can augment the selection process are paper-and-pencil "psychological," or "personality," tests. Every year, millions of paper-and-pencil screening instruments are used to assess candidates. Up to five million integrity tests alone are administered by an estimated six thousand organizations. These screening phenomena variously measure a person's qualifications for a particular job; cognitive abilities such as verbal, numerical, and reasoning skills; presentability; past work experiences; interests; and psychological and behavioral issues. The psychological factors measured might be such positive attributes as motivation to work, docility or assertiveness, and desire to learn.

Psychometric principles should be used to determine whether these tests work. In other words, an employer should ensure that the test items have been scientifically researched for effectiveness. Psychometrics measure two things with regard to paper-and-pencil tests. The first is test reliability. A test should produce similar results with each administration, somewhat as a tape measure shows the same window sill to be thirty-six inches long every time it is measured. If under similar conditions, a psychological test produces a score of 100 one time and 130 the next, there is a problem with its reliability.

The second thing psychometrics measure is test validity. A valid test measures the factor it is intended to measure, not a different (although perhaps related) one. Validity can only be proven after reliability has been established.

Of special note about psychological tests is that many of the test publishers are proprietary firms. This means, first, that they may not have exposed their instruments to independent research of their validity and reliability and, second, that they may use unconventional marketing slants and jargon to distinguish themselves from competitors. This complicates the shopping process for the employer, who has to determine whether different marketing terms have similar meanings across vendors.

Most Invasive or Unfair Forms of Personnel Evaluation

Employers need to be sensitive to applicants' reactions to various forms of personnel selection. While employers have an interest in predicting behavioral risk, they certainly do not want to do anything that could increase their risk exposure, such as creating an oppressive hiring situation. If a preponderance of applicants feel the testing is too invasive or unfair, the employer may receive complaints, alienate exceptional job candidates, generate bad public relations, and perhaps risk being sued.

Invasiveness of testing was a topic of research by researchers at the University of Iowa, who solicited the reactions of 390 current and future job seekers to thirteen selection procedures. The following is a ranking of the subjects' attitudes and beliefs about each of the selection procedures, beginning with the most favorable and ending with the least favorable.

1. Simulation-based second interview with a line recruiter
2. Reference checks with professors or previous employers
3. Business-related test
4. Written simulation exercise involving complex work issues
5. Personality inventory (reflecting the "big five" personality dimensions: conscientiousness, emotional stability, extroversion, openness to experience, and agreeableness)
6. Drug test following second interview
7. (Overt) integrity test
8. Generic first interview with a line recruiter
9. General ability test
10. Generic first interview conducted by a staff recruiter
11. Psychological assessment by a corporate staff psychologist
12. Generic second interview with a line recruiter
13. On-the-spot handwriting sample

Among the selection procedures most directly bearing on behavioral risk factors, the personality, drug, and integrity tests, as the researchers note, fall in the middle range; that is, they are likely to be more favorably received than procedures on the lower end such as psychological assessment by a corporate staff psychologist and handwriting analysis. Overall rankings were predictable, the researchers add, based on the subjects' faith in the employer's ability to interpret the procedures accurately, beliefs about the extent to which the employer actually needs the procedures, and beliefs about likely self-performance on the procedure.

Test Measurements Relevant to Behavioral Risk

In the behavioral risk management paradigm, psychological tests are intended to help employers spot psychological and behavioral factors that are not always identifiable from observation or by self-disclosure. Future behavior, of course, is impossible to predict with perfect accuracy. However, the antecedents of undesirable behavior—psychological issues that exist and can be detected in the individual at the time a test is taken or past behavior that can be uncovered by test inquiry—are facts, not events that have yet to occur. Therefore, some tests that predict on-the-job behavior have been developed and enhanced using "predictive validation" research to derive a test taker's future work performance from test responses.

Once an employer has listed and prioritized the behavioral risk exposures it most wishes to prevent, it can begin the process of researching the available tests or it can develop a customized testing instrument. The following list shows the psychological and behavioral traits that psychological tests of job candidates typically seek to detect and measure. (Employers wishing to use psychological tests may wish to obtain the services of a psychologist trained in psychometric testing to determine which traits might be most important for them to know about.)

Tendency to lie

Psychopathic deviation

Lack of self-control

Emotional instability

Impulsivity

Abasement

Aggression

Insecurity

Hypochondriasis

Depression

Conversion hysteria

Paranoia

Psychasthenia

Schizophrenia

Hypomania

Irresponsibility

Dominance

Lack of sociability

Independence

Achievement via conformance

Achievement via independence

Tension

Lack of friendliness

Excessive need for social recognition

Lack of responsibility

Lack of self-sufficiency

Lack of endurance

Some psychological tests may also say they assess desirability, "masculinity," capacity for status, and other ephemeral characteristics of dubious value. Since these traits have only an indirect bearing on the occurrence of behavioral risk exposures and are unrelated to the performance of most jobs, they are not listed above. Employers should be careful to distinguish between these imprecise traits and psychological factors relevant to a particular job, since testing for the former could expose an employer to legal risk.

Integrity Tests: A Look into Test Validity

Among the tests in greatest demand are integrity, or honesty, tests, which are a specialized form of personality test. Integrity testing is increasingly attractive to many employers because of their concern that candidates are lying more frequently on résumés, stealing on the job, and as a result of stealing, being counterproductive. A 1994 survey by AccounTemps claimed that up to one-third of all résumés may be fraudulent, 6 percent more than three years earlier. An employer may thus be tempted to use an integrity test as a quick-and-dirty method of measuring a job candidate's veracity. This characterological trait could otherwise be ascertained only through careful investigation into the candidate's employment history (which is invasive and costly) or through reference checks (which are often unreliable since many employers fear legal challenges if they give a negative reference for a former employee). However, integrity tests are not designed to evaluate whether an applicant is lying. Instead, they assess mainly how the person would respond in certain employment situations where his or her honesty would be called into question.

The American Management Association has estimated that as many as 30 percent of all business failures are attributable to employee theft. The 1988 prohibition under federal law of polygraph tests for employment screening purposes has undoubtedly contributed to the increase in the administration of integrity tests, which may seem to be an attractive alternative to a very invasive (and ultimately flawed) testing procedure.

But do integrity tests work? The American Psychological Association (APA) has reviewed nearly 300 validation studies of integrity tests, finding that "for those few tests for which validity information is available, the preponderance of the evidence is supportive of their predictive validity." Furthermore, the APA has found deficiencies in other personnel recruitment techniques intended to detect the same types of information as integrity and other paper-and-pencil tests. Those other techniques include unstructured interviews (which have a lower rate of reliability and validity than paper-and-pencil integrity tests), structured integrity interviews (which have limited validity and utility and ask questions nearly identical to the paper-and-pencil integrity tests anyway), background checks (which are costly), and on-the-job surveillance (which is costly and invasive). The authors of the APA report also noted a few drawbacks to integrity tests, however. They cited the lack of a uniform definition of "integrity"; problems with false positives and false labeling resulting from the use of "cut scores"; and employers' heavy reliance on proprietary tests, which depresses the amount of independent research performed on the tests.

More Things to Look at Before You Leap

Employers need to consider the pros and cons of testing before deciding to proceed with it. The tests should be applied evenly and fairly to candidates, and the results used to select candidates nondiscriminatorily. A company should consider its in-house expertise on psychometric testing issues, the costs of testing, and the time that would be required to administer and perhaps evaluate the tests.

The best reason for an organization to consider psychological testing is that behavioral risk exposures have been a persistent and costly problem to that organization. This is especially true when the risk exposures occur among new employees, those who have not been employed with the company long enough for organizational behavior and other workplace factors to influence the development of their behavioral problems. The worst reason is to think that because other employers down the street are doing it, it must be right for you. Here are some issues to be considered in determining whether preemployment testing is right for you.

Determine Whether You Need a Preemployment Test

Most personnel departments already use a variety of techniques to size up a job candidate during the screening and hiring process. They often begin with the résumé or employment application and proceed with one or more interviews. This is often an arduous process that leaves few stones in an individual's career unturned. Additionally, experienced job interviewers have usually developed a finely tuned sixth sense about whether a job candidate is ambiguous about wanting the job opportunity, is experiencing personal problems, and is likely to fit in well at the company. (If the recruiter works under an incentive salary plan, his or her income may even depend on this intuition.) In these cases, the competency of the interviewer and his or her techniques may be a sufficient screen, negating the need for preemployment tests. The determinants of a recruiter's effectiveness should be industry and geographic standards for length of tenure as well as the conduct and work performance records of employees after they are hired. If there seem to be a substantial number of employees exhibiting behavioral and other job problems, preemployment testing may be a viable option for improving the odds of successful personnel selection.

Since behavioral problems often result from problems with the work system, employers should be mindful of these factors as well, which might otherwise be attributed to the recruiter's lack of ability. These systemic problems can be found through behavioral risk audits. Additionally, exit interviews can be a rich source of information on organizational problems.

Research What a Test Publisher Offers You

The marketing literature of firms that sell psychometric tests to employers ranges from homemade, desktop-produced brochures to top-of-the-line full-color glossy booklets. However, the appearance and presentation of the information may not be a good indicator of test applicability and validity, so employers should question test publishers about their products. Here are some suggestions.

What kinds of tests does the publisher offer? Test subject matter—as presented in marketing materials—measures such abstract concepts as communication style, self-awareness, integrity, analytical thinking, ability to cope with stress, risk avoidance, sales aptitude, and leadership ability. Find out how the publisher has distilled these abstract concepts into discrete elements that can be measured.

What behavioral factors does a particular test measure, and why? From the standpoint of predicting behavioral risk, this question cuts to the heart of what the test seeks to do. Find out what behavioral factors its tests are specifically designed to measure, and whether the factors vary based on job classification—are they different for executive leadership rank-and-file, and work team positions?

Is the test designed specifically for workplace situations? Some tests are designed in a manner consistent with a particular job or occupational title; others are not. Be clear about what the test is intended to do. If you are interested in administering a test to job applicants that assesses a specific set of attributes, find out from a test publisher how it would construct such a test. Additionally, ascertain whether the publisher has had its tests reviewed by the Office of Federal Contract Compliance Programs (OFCCP), which monitors federal contractors. The OFCCP scrutinizes whether a preemployment test is consistent with job relatedness and business necessity.

How can the test detect whether a test taker is lying? There is always a possibility that a test taker is lying or else fudging on test items. He or she may do this in order to conceal information or to respond in a way that might put her in favor with the employer. A psychometric test should be designed so that many questions are posed to measure each trait. An effective test will typically ask anywhere from twenty-five to fifty items on the same trait (probably measuring different facets of the same trait). The large volume of items makes it less likely that lying on some of them will significantly skew the results relevant to that trait.

What criteria are used to measure behavioral risks? A test publisher should have certain rationales, or criteria, to measure each type of behavioral risk. There is a causal chain between testing criteria and the psychological factors they are intended to measure on the one hand and the psychological factors and expected behavioral outcomes on the other. Make sure the criteria are explained to you in everyday language and not in researchers' technojargon, which could be camouflaging the lack of objective criteria. Do not hesitate to ask probing questions about how the firm arrived at its criteria. Also, ask whether the test was validated in conformance with the "Uniform Guidelines on Employee Selection Procedures," as adopted by the Equal Employment Opportunity Commission.

In what ways has the reliability and validity of the testing instrument been demonstrated? Reliability and validity can be determined in several ways. First, test publishers can field test different questions intended to predict future behavior. They can give test takers a large body of test items on a particular trait, such as honesty, then correlate the results with how those test takers have performed on the job after six months, twelve months, or perhaps longer. The items that correlate most highly with future behavior are the ones most appropriate for inclusion on an actual exam. An alternative is to test current employees and compare the findings with their *prior* work performance. Second, ask if independent studies were done, by a research firm or industrial psychologist, for example. Then find out whether the research findings have been published in any reputable research journals. If so, request a reprint. Third, if the test is an off-the-shelf product, ask the publisher for evidence that the test produces consistent results through multiple administrations. Or ask what research was done during the test's development and how the test elements were validated. Be leery of testing firms that will not or cannot provide you with any information. This is a largely unstandardized industry. Given the highly specialized nature of testing, it would be worthwhile to have a technical expert, such as an employment attorney or industrial psychologist, review the instrument prior to using it as a basis for hiring decisions.

Does the test publisher use cutoff scores for the behavioral attributes on its tests? If so, what are these scores, and how did the test publisher arrive at them? Typically the distribution of test scores forms a bell curve, and test publishers commonly use cutoffs to disqualify candidates from consideration. Ascertain whether this could be discriminatory toward certain groups such as ethnic, cultural, and gender groups and whether it takes into account a margin of error that, not doing so, would substantially decrease the pool of otherwise qualified candidates.

What questions does the test ask about a person's private life? The response to this inquiry will suggest the extent to which your job candidates might perceive the test to be invasive, exploring personal issues in which an employer may have no legitimate concern. Questions about private life will also increase the likelihood of lying on tests, since a test taker may be more inclined to give the response he or she thinks you are looking for.

Is the test strictly an off-the-shelf product, or is it designed to meet the specific needs of the organization and its different job classifications? This is the first of two questions to determine the test publisher's degree of personalized service and, consequently, the cost for tests. Regardless of whether the test is customized or off-the-shelf, the results of a job analysis should confirm the behavioral aspects of the test and document that it is appropriate for use.

What technical support is provided for test administration, rating, and assessment of results? Direct assistance is likely to increase costs significantly, but it can increase the probability that the results will be correctly scored, interpreted, and applied. While some test publishers provide technical support, others may require an employer to be "credentialed" before it administers tests, meaning that the employer has demonstrated to the publisher competency in scoring and analyzing test results. However, employers should balance credentialing against any legal liabilities to which they may be exposed without technical support, the psychometric testing expertise already on staff, and the expected economic value that the candidate will have to the organization during his or her tenure.

What Public Policy Says About Psychological Testing

Most employers do not have an interest in prying into the private thoughts and lives of job applicants as a means of making hiring decisions, and they would be wise to refrain from doing so. Nevertheless, many employers feel compelled to test not only because of the productivity problems that a troublesome employee can cause but also because an organization can be sued for not exercising "due diligence" during the hiring process—a legal doctrine called "negligent hiring."

Due diligence holds that the employer took reasonable precautions to ensure that an employee would not commit an injurious act on another upon hire. A court may hold that an employer did not exercise due diligence if a plaintiff can prove that the employer should have known about the heightened potential for the injurious act to occur. Employers who test, then, usually have weighed these factors and determined that their need to exercise due diligence supersedes any legal risk they assume by testing.

If an employer decides to use a paper-and-pencil test, then, it needs to ask two questions from a legal standpoint:

- Does the test invade privacy?
- Is the test discriminatory or unfair?

Invasion of Privacy

Questions that ask whether a test taker reads the Bible for fun, has dizzy spells, is attracted to members of the same sex, is satisfied with his or her spouse, and any other highly personal questions that apparently have no connection with the tasks of a job may be at risk of a lawsuit under state invasion-of-privacy laws.

In 1989, for example, Dayton Hudson was sued because a national retail company that it owned, Target Stores, administered two psychological tests that asked questions about the religious beliefs and sexual orientation of store security officer applicants. (The tests used by Target Stores—the Minnesota Multiphasic Personality Inventory and the California Psychological Inventory—are commonly administered by psychologists and other mental health professionals in a therapeutic environment.) In the class action lawsuit alleging invasion of privacy under the California constitution, Target settled out of court in 1993 for $2 million, without admitting liability or wrongdoing. Since then, many test publishers have scrambled to revise or eliminate questions that could put them or their customers at risk.

Employers should be cautious about any preemployment tests that inquire about marital status, sexual orientation or behavior, religious beliefs, political views, or organized labor sentiments. This will help alleviate any job candidate misgivings that a test is invasive, misgivings that might lead to lawsuits.

Restrictions Under the Civil Rights Act

Another public policy pertains to testing that unfairly excludes minority-group candidates from job consideration. Interpretations of the Civil Rights Act of 1964 have put preemployment and other forms of testing for purposes of personnel selection under scrutiny. The theory of "adverse impact" holds that if members of one group are rejected at a significantly higher rate than members of another group, the test is unlawfully discriminatory unless it can be shown to be job related.

An interpretation of this principle was issued in 1978 by federal agencies charged with civil rights enforcement. Under the Uniform Guidelines on Employee Selection Procedures, a guideline commonly called the "four-fifths rule" holds that if the passing rate for any one group is less than four-fifths of the passing rate of the group with the highest rate that fact will be regarded as evidence of adverse impact. This rule would be waived, however, if the employer could demonstrate the test's job relatedness. (A test is not *required* to be job-related in private work settings, incidentally, although it must be for public sector jobs.)

One way that employers have sought to avoid adverse impact is by using "within-group norming," in which the scores for a minority group with a lower overall performance are ratcheted up to avoid discriminatory cutoffs. Norming has traditionally been used exclusively for intelligence, aptitude, and non-work-related clinical tests, however. And more recent legislation, the Civil Rights Act of 1991, prohibits within-group norming. This has since led to some complex legal discussions about how tests apply to the work setting. Because questions about behavioral risk might be substantially less likely to adversely affect a particular group than are those that measure intelligence and aptitude, they would seem to pose a lesser legal risk to employers in relation to the Civil Rights Act. However, employers may wish to ask test publishers whether there might be test bias with regard to the psychological factors that are intended to measure behavior.

State Restrictions

In addition to federal public policy, policies of the states of Rhode Island and Massachusetts restrict integrity testing. These restrictions were implemented during the late 1970s and 1980s, when a strong political movement was afoot to ban polygraph tests for employment purposes. In these two states, other types of testing, including paper-and-pencil psychological tests, were included in the restrictions. Eventually the federal Employee Polygraph Protection Act of 1988 banned polygraph use in private employment settings, but that legislation did not include written tests.

Recently, a Wisconsin appellate court held that the lie detector statute does not apply to written tests. In *Pluskato* v. *Roadrunner Freight Systems,* an amicus curiae brief, filed by the Association of Test Publishers, drew a distinction between paper-and-pencil psychological tests and physiological "devices." By concurring with the association, the court recognized a distinction between devices such as polygraphs, voice stress analyses, and psychological stress evaluators (which are prohibited), and written tests (which it says are not). This decision has helped put proponents of paper-and-pencil tests on more solid legal ground.

Buyer Beware!

Once again, before deciding on a psychological test, employers should do some investigation to ensure that the test results will produce the kinds of findings being sought, and that the results are reliable. A reference book (available in many libraries) that reviews psychological tests is the *Mental Measurements Yearbook,* published by the Buros Institute of Mental Measurements at the University of Nebraska, Lincoln. It provides annual detailed technical reviews of hundreds of commercially available tests. The reviews' high degree of detail also suggests additional issues on which test publishers may be queried, in addition to the questions proffered in this chapter. For example, a review of the Minnesota Multiphasic Personality Inventory–2 comments on such matters as controversies associated with the test, validity and clinical scales, test revisions, report categories, the test manual, and (for the on-line test version) security issues.

Additional information about integrity tests that measure specific criteria related to job performance and counterproductive behaviors is available in a *Journal of Applied Psychology* monograph that features research findings from data contributed by publishers on twenty-five tests.

Avoiding the Tendency to Typecast People

Many preemployment tests measure a job candidate's memorization ability, task knowledge, multilimb coordination, mental aptitude, and other factors that can predict ability to perform particular job tasks. By the very nature of testing and scoring, people are typecast based on the results, even when the result is a simple pass or fail. However, testing that predicts future conduct or work performance should not be assigned the same degree of validity as testing for, say, knowledge about a piece of equipment. First, the results of a psychological test are not always precise. A person's frame of mind may vary considerably from one day to the next, especially if he or she is under extreme stress, and this may affect results. Thus, these tests should be used to identify individuals with extreme psychological or behavioral traits that, in conjunction with other results of the personnel selection process, suggest that the individual is a less-than-ideal job candidate.

Second, employers should recognize that throughout history human beings have changed their behaviors in order to adapt to cultural norms, style of leadership, and other environmental factors. Most people are malleable to varying degrees, in the workplace and outside it. Fifty years ago, Dale Carnegie devised a variety of strategies to influence behavioral change as a result of positive reinforcement. In the same way, an employer can expect to influence an employee's conduct and work performance by specifying behavioral expectations and putting the onus on the employee to comply with them.

In all these respects, preemployment psychological testing is not a be-all and end-all. To restate an earlier point, it should always be done in conjunction with other personnel selection activities.

Drug Testing

Another type of preemployment test employers may wish to consider is a drug test. This activity, along with drug testing of current employees, became a tidal force trend beginning in the 1980s. Like employee testing, it became mandated throughout the transportation industry due to federal regulation, and that has had a ripple effect on other industries. A second reason that preemployment testing grabbed a foothold in U.S. business was employer fear that if every other company were to drug test, it would become the employer of last resort for drug addicts. This was particularly a concern for small employers, who often felt that after larger, wealthier companies took their cut from the labor force, smaller companies were relegated to selecting from the remaining pool, which included a disproportionate share of substance abusers.

The American Management Association's 1995 drug-testing study showed 63.2 percent of responding companies were testing all new hires in preemployment physical examinations, up from 15.5 percent in 1987. This has seemingly had an effect on job-seekers' efforts to stay clean, as test-positive rates dropped from 11.4 percent to 3.8 percent between 1989 and 1994. These data suggest that preemployment testing has had an effect on diminishing behavioral risk, although as pointed out in Chapter Five, the American Management Association notes that the groups being tested in these two years are not necessarily comparable.

Another factor that has given a green light to preemployment drug testing is that organized labor is not likely to raise objections. A union's primary interest is in representing current workers and opposing the termination of existing employees, not in representing job candidates where the most significant adverse action likely to happen is a decision not to hire an individual.

———— ∞ ————

This review of preemployment testing activity has completed the picture of how work organizations can holistically control behavioral risk. Even though personnel selection is not a formal activity in a behavioral risk management strategy, inadequacies in this process should not become the means by which behavioral risk exposures abound in companies despite the presence of programs and services that effectively handle risk. The next chapter examines the role of computers in maintaining a holistic behavioral risk management strategy.

Notes

P. 288, *identified a variety of personnel selection procedures:* Society for Industrial and Organizational Psychology. *Principles for the Validation and Use of Personnel Selection Procedures.* Arlington Heights, Ill.: Society for Industrial and Organizational Psychology, 1987, p. 1.

P. 288, *an estimated six thousand organizations:* U.S. Congress, Office of Technology Assessment. *The Use of Integrity Tests for Pre-employment Screening* (OTA-SET-442). Washington, D.C.: U.S. Government Printing Office, 1990, p. 1.

P. 290, *ranking of the subjects' attitudes and beliefs:* Rynes, S. L., and Connerley, M. L. "Applicant Reactions to Alternative Selection Procedures." *Journal of Business and Psychology,* 1993, *7*(3), 261–277.

P. 292, *A 1994 survey by AccounTemps:* Bachler, C. J. "Resume Fraud: Lies, Omissions and Exaggerations." *Personnel Journal,* 1994, *74*(6), 54.

P. 293, *attributable to employee theft:* American Management Association. *Summary Overview of the 'State of the Art' Regarding Information Gathering Techniques and Level of Knowledge in Three Areas Concerning Crimes Against Business.* Washington, D.C.: National Institute of Law Enforcement and Criminal Justice, Law Enforcement Administration, 1977.

P. 293, *"for those few tests for which validity information":* Goldberg, L. R., and others. *Questionnaires Used in the Prediction of Trustworthiness in Pre-employment Selection Decisions: An APA Task Force Report.* Washington, D.C.: American Psychological Association, 1991, p. 26.

P. 293, *deficiencies in other personnel recruitment techniques:* Wayne, J., and Schneider, D. L. "Integrity Tests: Facts and Unresolved Issues." *American Psychologist,* 1994, *49*(2), 112–118.

P. 298, *Dayton Hudson was sued:* Langley, L. "Getting Personal: Use of Psychological Tests to Screen Job Applicants Can Backfire on Employers." *Pittsburgh Post-Gazette,* Feb. 5, 1995, p. D-1.

P. 299, *prohibits within-group norming:* Sackett, P. R., and Wiik, S. L. "Within-Group Norming and Other Forms of Score Adjustment in Preemployment Testing." *American Psychologist,* 1994, *49*(11), 929–954.

P. 300, *lie detector statute does not apply:* St. Clair, M. K., Arnold, D. W., and

Thiemann, A. "ATP Plays Major Role in Reversal of Wisconsin Court Case." *Test Publisher,* Winter 1994, p. 4.

P. 301, *Additional information about integrity tests:* Ones, D. S., Viswesvaran, C., and Schmidt, F. L. "Comprehensive Meta-Analysis of Integrity Test Validities: Findings and Implications for Personnel Selection and Theories of Job Performance." *Journal of Applied Psychologies,* 1993, *78*(4), 679–703.

P. 301, *Fifty years ago, Dale Carnegie devised:* Carnegie, D. *How to Win Friends and Influence People.* New York: Pocket Books, 1936.

P. 302, *63.2 percent of responding companies were testing all new hires:* American Management Association. *1995 AMA Survey: Workplace Drug Testing and Drug Abuse Policies: Summary of Key Findings.* New York: American Management Association, 1995, p. 4.

Chapter Eleven

Computers
The Means to the End

Chapter Ten outlined the place in behavioral risk management of preemployment screening, the first of three special issues. This chapter examines a second special issue: computers. Ask occupational program managers what capital asset most greatly affects their capability to deliver services, and they are likely to answer, "Computers." Computers, or to be more precise, computerized management information systems (MIS), perform numerous tasks necessary for program operation. They facilitate data collection and maintenance, do administrative chores such as making claims payments to a healthcare provider, enhance communication among staff members, store vast amounts of information that would otherwise require multitudes of space-taking cabinets, and may be able to aggregate large volumes of data into any number of statistical breakdowns with only a few keystrokes. They can also be used as educational tools, and they make information more portable than ever before.

BR managers need an MIS to help with three essential tasks:

- Daily administration and operations
- Audits of behavioral risks
- Evaluations of programs

Administrative tasks include scheduling, file maintenance, financial management, business logs, and other office activities. Operational tasks are concerned with meeting the needs of programs, services, and staff, including handling interstaff communication, creating client files, maintaining process maps, developing and maintaining a network of external service providers, tracking cases following client referral, making cross-referrals, and so forth.

Tasks related to audits include processing survey data, importing external information on healthcare utilization and costs, accessing personnel and other management files, and organizing all these data. Program evaluations require the ability to extract the appropriate information from the audit, program, and other files and then to compile this information.

MISs are already at work in almost every phase of production, service delivery, and administration. A behavioral risk management MIS has "cousins" in the human resource, medical, and risk management departments of many companies. In fact, a behavioral risk management MIS may be required to piggyback on another MIS. If this is the case, behavioral risk management records are probably safest in the medical MIS—which also strictly limits access to information. Even there, however, confidential behavioral risk management files need to be sealed off from the rest of the database by a "firewall" that allows information in but prevents it from flowing out.

The hardest step of putting any management information system into operation is getting started. It is essential to have a game plan for designing and implementing or purchasing the system that will suit your needs. As you delve into each step along the way, complex issues having numerous decision points will absorb your attention. If you have a game plan to refer to, however, you will keep your perspective about where you are in the MIS development process.

Identify Your Needs!

Your first step will be a thorough needs assessment, to identify what you want the system to accomplish; what types of information need to be collected, maintained, and updated in the MIS; and what capabilities it should have.

If you are the BR manager who must identify these needs, a suggested strategy is, first, to keep a detailed log of your activities for one month (or anticipate your activities if you are in the process of forming a behavioral risk management function); second, encourage your staff members to do the same for their respective activities; third, hold a brainstorming session about shared needs (intercommunication and training, for example); fourth, anticipate future needs; and fifth, hold a final session to put all the information together. This perhaps laborious but very worthwhile process will reduce the likelihood that simple needs will be overlooked. For example, you will want to ensure that your MIS can accommodate "variable fields" (so that an employee's work location, type of problem, use of benefits, and so forth, can be input using only one or a few keystrokes) as well as "text fields" (where case notes and other expository information are entered).

Determine the Capabilities Required

Managers typically seek a number of capabilities in an MIS. Take into consideration such needs as the following:

- Storage capability and speed of operations
- Automatic functions, such as the stamping of date and time for all entries
- E-mail that connects staff members and service providers
- "Ticklers" that automatically remind staff to perform certain protocols, such as client follow-ups
- Translation of data sets from one operating system or database or computer language into another, using translation software
- Transmission and uploading of information from staff laptop or other computers, so all operational and administrative activities on the MIS will not have to be done in "real time"
- Maintenance of separate databases for different customers (external service providers with multiple clients have this need)
- "Multitasking" ability—such as the ability to work in several different databases at once—a time-saving convenience commonly found in the Windows format

Additional conveniences may be desired. For example, a spreadsheet program will enhance administrative activities such as budgeting and scheduling. You may also need additional storage space for professional tools such as client problem assessment instruments. Training staff may wish to have the capability to prepare training aids, such as color slides, which require special software and printing capabilities. Modems enable geographically dispersed staff to transmit information back and forth over the Internet, hold "conversations" with outside experts on a nearly infinite range of subjects, and access information on external databases.

Information Necessary for the Behavioral Risk Audit

In addition to existing data on the behavioral risk management MIS, a behavioral risk audit will probably need information from a variety of other databases, including those kept by the human resource, security, legal, medical, and benefits departments and/or those of a third-party administrator of health benefits (See Table 11.1). The behavioral risk management MIS needs to be capable of importing this data. Additionally, the MIS should exhibit ease and convenience of programming when data are entered and tabulated.

Ability to Manipulate Data

Particularly when looking for organizational dysfunction, it is vital to be able to manipulate the data by breaking it out according to demographic group, occupational category, job site, work unit, and possibly in other ways as well. Ad hoc and "what-if" analyses require an easy-to-use inquiry language that allows staff to flexibly juxtapose different categories of information; a fast processor (which might, for example, reduce the time necessary to prepare a complicated report from twelve hours to half an hour), and a database large enough to store the required information so that the processor is not overburdened as it handles the information. The MIS should also be able to plot audit and program performance results over time.

Ability to Evaluate Individual Programs

Certain data, such as reductions in accidents, utilization, and cross-referral rates, are indicators of program performance. Once evaluation criteria are established, the computer selected should be

Table 11.1 Databases in an Integrated Behavioral Risk Management MIS.

These databases constitute an integrated behavioral risk management MIS. Ideally, the information should be entered on the MIS in "real time," as programs and services are being delivered. This system is typical of an intradepartmental behavioral risk management model, with an integrated database at the center of operations. It contrasts with a system in which data are scattered on outside databases and need to be imported periodically, a situation more likely to occur in an interdepartmental model. In the latter case, data can be used for analysis and evaluation only when available from outside sources.

Data in the behavioral risk management MIS

Safety data
  Accidents
  Behavioral safety
    violations
Conflict management/mediation/ombudsman files
  Utilization data
  Activity data
  Outcomes data
Work-based problem assessment client files
  Utilization data
  Activity data
  Outcomes data
Clinical problem assessment client files
  Utilization data
  Activity data
  Outcomes data
Medical review client files
  Positive drug and alcohol
    tests
  Status of positive test
    takers

Medical health (lifestyle-related)
  Utilization data
  Claims payment data
Behavioral healthcare
  Utilization data
  Treatment data
  Claims payment data
Disability medical health
  Utilization data
  Treatment data
  Claims payment data
Workers' compensation
  Utilization data
  Treatment, rehabilitation,
    and wage-replacement
    data
  Claims payment data
Wellness and health promotion
  Utilization data
  Activity data
  Outcomes data
Critical incident debriefings
  Utilization data
  Activity data
  Outcomes data

Table 11.1 Databases in an Integrated Behavioral Risk Management MIS (*continued*).

Data in the behavioral risk management MIS

Organizational and work team consultations
  Utilization data
  Activity data
  Outcomes data
Work-and-family consultation
  Utilization data

Activity data
Outcomes data
Fitness-for-duty evaluation
  Utilization data
  Outcomes data

Data imported from other sources in the company

Personnel
  Employee data
  Dependents
  Demographics
  Absenteeism
  Disciplinary action
  Turnover
Legal actions by employees
  AA/EEO complaints
  Lawsuits (such as negligent hiring, retention, and firing)

Security
  Critical incidents
  Activity data
  Outcomes data
  Employee sabotage and theft
  Documented cases and costs
  Evidence of undocumented sabotage and theft

---

able to accommodate a software program designed to automatically extract information from multiple databases and perform needed evaluations and cost-benefit analyses. At the same time, the computer should have the flexibility to manipulate data. For example, preset formulas that measure program effectiveness may need to be modified if changes in the work environment such as restructuring or downsizing occur. Organizational change processes are likely to affect evaluation results, increasing the use of problem assessment and conflict resolution resources, for example. This is analogous to the need to make adjustments in a nation's unemployment rate based on seasonal factors and changes in international trade balances.

Data Importation Requirements

Data importation requirements will pertain mainly to the availability and format of data from different departments and external providers. Because you may be drawing information from a dozen or more databases into your MIS, it is important to be clear about whether information can be electronically transmitted on a regular basis from other sources. If tapes will be provided, your MIS system will require special equipment to read them. If a company contracts with two or more health insurers or HMOs, the data from one may not be in the same format as the data from the other, and integration may be difficult. In addition, special arrangements may need to be made for certain types of information, such as external consultants' reports on organizational interventions and legal department reports on employee lawsuits. These reports may not be available in an automated format and they and other special materials may require manual entry.

Future Needs

Purchasers most often err when they buy based only on present needs, without considering system expandability to accommodate future use. For example, they may not have the equipment necessary to back up information on the MIS hard drive, a necessary precaution in case the system fails, or "crashes," and loses all of the records, and staff thus may have the onerous daily task of copying files onto multiple cassettes or diskettes.

As you can tell from the broad range of capabilities usually sought in an MIS, even if you decide to purchase a "loaded" off-the-shelf product, the needs analysis remains critical.

Setting Up Your Own System

If management information systems are developed to meet the needs of the organizations they are serving, then no two systems will be exactly alike. However, there are some common guidelines to follow.

Determine Software Needs

Inexperienced purchasers tend to buy computer hardware first, trusting that it will support the software that they want. It is much more advisable to determine the software you want to run first, since the software is what manages the information and enables you to manipulate it. Then get the hardware that will run your software. You may wish to have this software custom designed, since very few (if any) products presently on the market have all the applications desirable in a behavioral risk management MIS.

Besides software for operation and administration, you will want to look at relational databases. A relational database enables you to cross-link information from your MIS and other MISs. Well-known examples of relational database programs are Oracle, Microsoft Access, and FoxPro.

Shop Around for Hardware

The term computer hardware describes a variety of equipment, including the computer housing and the electronic tools necessary to support the software. The main functional hardware of an MIS includes

- A disk drive (measured in megabytes or, in larger systems, gigabytes), which is the main information storage unit
- A memory chip (measured in megabytes, or RAM), on which software and files are stored
- A processor (measured in megahertz [MHz]), which provides the power and speed to access and manipulate the information
- A server, which enables multiple users to work together and share data
- A scanner, which "reads" forms and other images on paper and converts them into electronic data for storage on the hard drive
- A compact disk and random access memory (CD-ROM) player, which provides such capabilities as audio and full-motion video
- Monitors (screens), which display information
- Mice, trackballs, or similar tools, which permit rapid navigating on screens

- Back-up system, which automatically stores files at the end of each day
- Keyboards, which input information and commands
- Printers, which transfer information in the computer onto paper
- Cables and other supportive equipment, which supply power where it's needed
- Uninterrupted power supply (UPS), which prevents system crashes due to loss of electrical power
- Surge protectors, which prevent system crashes due to a surge in electrical power, as can occur during a thunderstorm
- Modems, which link users through telephone lines

Examine Types of Management Information Systems

A management information system may be as simple as a personal computer and the software loaded on it or, going up the scale in complexity, it may be a peer-to-peer network of linked personal computers, a server system, a minicomputer, or a mainframe computer.

Of these five types, the ones on either end—the personal computer and mainframe—are impractical for the behavioral risk management MIS. A personal computer accommodates only one user, and a mainframe, such as the central computer of a major corporation, is excessively large. Moreover, because a behavioral risk management MIS stores confidential information, it should be maintained on a system that is separate from the corporate mainframe for security and, perhaps, legal reasons. The middle three types are most likely to provide the necessary capabilities. In the peer-to-peer network of linked personal computers, users can share each other's resources, share a common printer, send and receive electronic mail, schedule group meetings, and so forth. However, access to individual directories can also be restricted. Each piece of information is "owned" by a user and, technically speaking, nothing is pooled.

A server system, commonly called a network, is more functional. Because information is centrally stored and accessed, a server system can accommodate multiple users and provide more shared resources than the peer-to-peer network. One popular type of server system is a local area network (LAN). A LAN makes possible communication and data transfer with people at remote sites as well as among people at the central site where the server is located. The server itself is a large hard drive to which everyone has access (whereas, on a peer-to-peer network, a user might be obstructed from accessing someone else's resources because that employee's personal computer is not operating or requires a password). Server resources could include behavioral risk management policies and procedures, report forms, benefit plan provisions, patient care criteria, work processes, system utilities, and so forth. Certain information can be walled off from unauthorized users, however. Passwords are the most common means of controlling access to particular data sets. To maximize security, multiple sets of passwords may be used.

A minicomputer is another type of system that has a shared hard drive. It uses "dummy terminals" instead of personal computers, though, meaning that information from the terminal can be saved only to the minicomputer's hard drive and not to a single user's hard drive. In this respect, a minicomputer is less versatile than a server system but, from the standpoint of daily operation, it has the advantage of not chaining each person to his or her personal computer and personal file storage because everyone's files can be accessed from anywhere there is a dummy terminal, including remote sites.

Decide How the System Will Be Maintained

We have all heard horror stories about how a system crash brought all office activity to a screeching halt. Providing for MIS maintenance is key both to preventing this sudden unfortunate occurrence and to minimizing its disruption once it does. (A good way to think of MIS maintenance is as computer risk management.) Major employers and regional and national external service providers typically can afford a computer technician on staff to provide system maintenance. The rule of thumb is to have one computer technician for every forty to fifty workstations.

Besides maintenance, the technician may also be involved in hardware and software purchasing decisions, installation, system upgrading and expansion, and troubleshooting. On a day-in, day-out basis, an MIS technician who can answer basic computer questions, solve problems with personal computers, and restore functions after system crashes is indispensable.

Small program and service providers need to make alternative arrangements for system maintenance, such as warranty coverage with the firm from which hardware and software is purchased or an agreement with a service firm or independent MIS technician. When it comes to warranties or service agreements, a BR manager should think of them much as he or she would think of extended warranties for home appliances that could incur substantial cost. The BR manager needs to determine the cost worthiness of a warranty for each piece of equipment. A monitor, for example, is probably not worth covering because monitors last only a few years and once they fail may not be repairable. Therefore, in this case, the cost of a service agreement relative to the cost of the original equipment probably makes the agreement inadvisable. The same is true for equipment such as modems, which generally do not fail and therefore are not worth covering. Still other pieces of equipment, such as processors, become obsolete within in a few years. When a service agreement does appear to be a good investment, it should ensure that the firm or technician has a guaranteed response time, has or can obtain equipment or parts needed for repairs within a specified time period, and can help staff develop a disaster recovery plan to use in the event that the network fails.

Train Your Staff

After months of researching your MIS options, making educated purchasing decisions, and getting the system operational, do not shortchange yourself on staff training needs. Usually initial staff training accounts for at least 15 percent of MIS start-up costs. There are many MIS systems in work organizations that suffer from neglect because staff know only a small amount of their system's capabilities and do not understand how the MIS could save them time and make their work lives easier. A person who has mastered a word processing program should not be assumed to "know computers."

There are two specific areas of MIS use in which staff should be trained no matter what other computer programs they may know. The first is the physical capabilities of the equipment. Staff members should be taught how to create and use spreadsheets, intake forms, business card files, e-mail, and the hundred or more other functions that will enhance their effectiveness to the organization. Once this training has been done, additional training should help staff to attack problems in new and creative ways. An MIS can enhance a person's ability to analyze and solve problems, because he or she can "slice and dice" the work. For example, a user can work on multiple projects simultaneously, meaning that information from one project can be easily cross-referenced with information from another and that information from one file can be cut or copied and then pasted into another file. Once a user becomes oriented to working from a screen instead of "hard files," the potential for increased productivity jumps significantly. Moreover, ample training early on will prevent the psychological blocks about computer use that many people experience.

What an Integrated Database Looks Like

The databases that most closely resemble the ideal behavioral risk management database are currently found in corporate medical departments and employee assistance programs. Medical department databases are likely to have much necessary behavioral risk information but will also include a variety of medical information not pertinent to conduct and work performance behavioral risks. Conversely, since medical databases are mainly *healthcare* and not *behavior* focused, they are not likely to maintain information on behavioral safety violations, ombudsman and conflict resolution files, work-and-family problems, and organizational dysfunction information. Nor are those data as likely to be subject to data analysis and reporting through a medical department's MIS. These are additional capabilities that a behavioral risk management MIS should have. An EAP database may contain these types of information, as long as the program is progressive, highly integrated in the work organization, and not focused exclusively on behavioral *healthcare* rather than behavioral risk management. In any event, data on these additional activities should definitely be part of a behavioral risk management MIS.

The data management system developed by AT&T Bell Labs, profiled below, captures the essence of what an integrated MIS can do.

AT&T Bell Labs

The Health Services Group of AT&T Bell Labs has integrated this telecommunications company's databases for the medical, EAP, benefits, and environmental health and safety functions into a single MIS. In 1993 and 1994, with the help of AT&T technicians, the Health Services Group designed and put into operation an integrated patient information system called the Quality Healthcare System (QHS). Nearly one hundred employees in the group enter and have access to QHS data, including the eight EAP staff members, who perform many of the tasks associated with behavioral risk management.

As the company developed new hardware and software applications, three principles guided the process:

The system must truly support the professional staff in their delivery of services and not just provide a sophisticated approach to bean counting. The quality healthcare system mission is to help the health services meet the medical, emotional, and occupational needs of employees in three contexts: work, home, and family. In designing QHS, the various needs of the Health Services Group were specified, then the software was developed and the hardware was purchased that would meet present requirements as well as anticipated future needs.

A prototype model will be created to determine how the system should operate. Before QHS was put into operation, a prototype was tested in which clinical data were entered into a database parallel to the existing system. After several months, computer "bugs" had been identified and eliminated.

The system needs to be able to collect more than just "concrete" data (such as demographics, problem types, and visit information). QHS was developed, for example, to measure the impact of consulting activity on levels of organizational stress, to identify environmental trends in order to target interventions, and to measure EAP resource use and allocation.

The original version of QHS had been brought on-line in 1989 for use by the Health Services Group. Each clinic was fitted with stand-alone minicomputers and self-contained database software operating from a commercially available computer operating system called UNIX, developed by Bell Laboratories. Remote access was possible via modem or hard-wired data lines, for file management between locations. In 1991, the Health Services Group purchased a program called Progress Data Base Management Software, which is scalable to a system's hardware. This facilitated a multitasking multi-user environment for simultaneous use by Health Services' three functions. For example, users can now input data from dummy terminals, desktop personal computers, or laptop computers.

QHS has a password protection system requiring two levels of user identification, with two independent passwords (which users are encouraged to change regularly) at each level. The password protection system grants all medical department staff, including clerical personnel, access to clinic records. EAP records are available only to EAP counselors, with each counselor being permitted entry into other counselors' records. If a non-EAP staff member attempts entry, a stern error message indicates that the user is barred from this sector of the database. When an off-site EAP person makes a note in a client record, the user's identification is automatically recorded, along with a time and date stamp. This allows local EAP staff to see who accessed the record and for what purpose. The EAP is the only function with unimpeded access to all other data, since it maintains the highest standards of confidentiality.

The QHS system also allows EAP and medical staff to select items from predefined "picklists" (to speed up data entry) and to input data into "free-entry" fields. The clinical data entered include severity of psychosocial stressors, global assessments of functioning, and case notes. EAP case notes are unalterable once the field has been exited. Each note is automatically stamped with the user identification and the time and date of entry. The entire information entry process takes five minutes per case contact, on average.

QHS users also have access to personnel department demographic data. Within each geographic region of Bell Laboratories supported by a health services clinic, the QHS database uploads personnel data from computer tapes each month. In New Jersey work sites, for example, data on approximately 50,000 employees are accessible for input. Clinical records can then be created and stored for each employee visiting the medical clinic or EAP. Once created, records are saved to parallel but separate pathways on QHS, requiring the appropriate user identification for entry.

Using QHS Information

The value of a sophisticated MIS lies not in the data themselves but rather in how they are used. The Health Services Group EAP staff decided to evaluate programs through monthly, quarterly, and annual reports. The medical departments produce utilization reports daily. The Quality Healthcare System can also generate ad hoc reports. For example, if a manager from Diversity Affirmative Action requests an audit of EAP activity as it relates to diversity, with a few keystrokes, data on the variables of interest (for example, gender, age, ethnicity) can be accessed, a report format defined, and a final report made ready for presentation, all in under an hour.

Another asset of QHS is its ability to help health services staff identify "pockets of concern" within the company. Because there is so much organizational transformation occurring at Bell Labs, it is critical to be able to feed back to management information about how quality-based work teams are moving through a process, helping management to identify causes of problems and potential interventions that may minimize productivity losses and moderate the effects of change on people.

For example, in a typical month, about 30 percent of cases brought to EAP attention involve workplace problems. During one particular month in early 1994, that percentage approximately doubled, even as the overall caseload increased. More than half of the referrals came from managers who also requested employee fitness-for-duty evaluations, normally an infrequent occurrence. A review of the data set indicated that almost all of the cases were from one particular R&D organization. Furthermore, in their referral of employees to medical and EAP, managers attributed problems to nonperformance, illness, and inappropriate behavior, but did not associate the problems with any environmental causes. Due to these irregular events, a further assessment was done to determine the dynamics occurring within the R&D organization. The onset of the problems, it was learned, corresponded with the onset of organizational change and downsizing in that division. In this way, QHS targeted the problem source rather than the symptoms for intervention.

QHS can also be used by the health services as a surveillance tool to collect data on current environmental and occupational hazards. For example, pregnant employees may visit health services with concerns about potentially harmful exposure to chemicals. Since QHS keeps a registry of all toxins and where they are physically handled throughout the company, it can determine the potential for exposure, with the intent of preventing the occurrence, and retrieve data on any case in the last two years involving actual exposures, with a report of the effect on mother and fetus. The Health Services Group can also work as necessary with Bell Labs' Toxicology Group to take any extra precautions needed, and the EAP can offer the employee personal support and guidance.

As these examples show, QHS efficiently and safely handles detailed information from all of its tributaries. It helps the health services functions accomplish their mission of providing employees with objective information in response to concerns while advancing the risk management and productivity objectives of the company.

How to Avoid Reinventing the MIS Wheel

Information managers who have implemented an integrated health data management system already know the headaches that will be experienced by the BR manager who is trying to implement the same type of system for behavioral risk. First Chicago Corporation, a financial company of 18,000 employees, has created a management information system called OMNI that integrates databases for healthcare costs, occupational medicine, occupational nursing, and behavioral risk.

OMNI was first installed in 1987 in the company's medical department and has been expanding its capabilities ever since. Today, it aggregates data from inpatient and outpatient medical claims, HMO "encounters," disability and absence records, wellness program utilization, laboratory tests (for cholesterol levels, for example), health risks findings (such as high blood pressure and alcohol intake), medical department records, EAP records, physical examinations, handicapped designations, and demographic findings (such as age, sex, job classification and location, and medical coverage).

The system is driven by a "minicomputer" with eighteen workstations (expandable to sixty-four) and has no interface with First

Chicago's mainframe computer. OMNI also accepts data from external services, including the personnel system, but does not export data. It has a scrambling program to ensure the security and confidentiality of medical records.

First Chicago has learned some valuable lessons and managed to sidestep other problems over nine years of implementing, maintaining, upgrading, and expanding its MIS. Medical department staff often share their expertise with counterparts in other organizations so they do not have to reinvent the wheel. Wayne N. Burton, First Chicago's medical director, has overseen OMNI since its inception and knows the pitfalls that can bedevil MIS developers. Considering how many information managers suffer from job burnout owing to the constant headaches attendant on rebuilding systems that no longer meet the needs of their owners and repairing systems that crash due to mechanical failures and overuse, the experiences of successful managers are well worth heeding. The following sections describe mistakes in two MIS areas, implementation and maintenance or upgrading. These mistakes, Burton says, can be avoided with anticipation and planning.

Implementing an MIS

Problems can occur right from the start if BR managers just dive without preparation into the dark and murky pool of MIS issues. The following are pitfalls common to information managers at square one.

Not starting with a vision. BR managers must be able to visualize how they want staff members to use the MIS, what they want to see on the screen, and in what formats they want databases to supply information. Without a clear vision, they may be inclined to buy based on the best sales pitch rather than on the needs they must satisfy.

Not researching software that may presently be on the market. Integrated health data management software is now commercially available and should be evaluated prior to a decision to develop software from the ground up.

Not developing a return-on-investment formula. This is not a reference to the cost-benefit ratio of programs but to the cost-benefit ratio of the MIS. It is determined by observing how much more productive MIS users are than nonusers and weighing that finding against the cost of buying and maintaining the system and the time-cost of training staff. For example, First Chicago determines the time saved by staff use of computerized medical records in place of hard copy files and the results of improved employee (or family member) compliance when staff use MIS state-of-the-art disease management protocols (for hypertension, for example), results measured by reductions in future health and disability costs.

Not communicating the advantages that the MIS provides the company. In addition to performing and publicizing return-on-investment calculations, staff need to promote to others in the organization how the system is being used. Failure to do so may create the erroneous perception that a major investment is being squandered.

Not integrating gradually. A behavioral risk management MIS may comprise a dozen or more databases. Integrating each database with the rest of the system requires troubleshooting in such areas as computer languages, different "fields," and so forth. Therefore, it is best to work from a plan for integrating the databases gradually so as to avoid a massive simultaneous onslaught of problems.

Not heading off turf battles. A BR manager should involve business decision makers from elsewhere in the organization in the MIS planning and development, particularly because the behavioral risk data will flow largely one way, toward the behavioral risk function. A vice president of human resources, for example, may balk at providing personnel files if he or she feels that human resource turf is being encroached on, especially if the BR manager is lower in the corporate hierarchy. Agreement on key issues should be sought during planning and implementation.

Not purchasing a good security system. Several layers of security protection should be provided, but the most important security is the attitude of the behavioral risk management program staff. File security is not possible if attitudes are lackadaisical; it must be a routine part of the daily work of all staff members, who are more likely to continuously protect security if they receive periodic reminders.

Not providing early postimplementation proof of the system's value. Financial and executive officers will want to be shown what the behavioral risk management MIS can do for the company that could not be done before. It must be something more substantial than just linking staff files together. In First Chicago's case, staff showed the ease with which multiple sets of medical and behavioral costs could be tracked and, later, used the information to make better decisions about how healthcare could be gained for less cost.

Maintaining, Upgrading, or Expanding an MIS

The successful implementation of an MIS does not mean that an information manager can kick back and rest on his or her laurels. These are problems that typically occur following initial launch of a system.

Inadequately anticipating hardware and software needs. Once the decision to upgrade or expand is made, BR managers need to anticipate their hardware and software needs for the next two to three years—then double them. If the behavior risk function is successful, the demand for information by the company will far exceed expectations. Further, after BR managers become aware of the range of software products out on the market, they will probably want to expand their MIS capabilities beyond what they originally anticipated. There are products now available to allow managers to do comprehensive spreadsheets, enhance their graphics, perform staff evaluations, do multimedia presentations, create forms, do financial planning, log customer complaints, and even help brainstorm new ideas.

Using rookie consultants. Maintenance of a sophisticated MIS requires someone with more than textbook experience. Hiring a reputable individual or firm with "been there, done that" know-how will save money and headaches.

Encountering problems with HMO cost data. Although the diagnostic codes of HMOs are generally the same as those used by other insurance mechanisms, HMOs may account for costs differently. For example, if the HMO subcontracts the cost of behavioral healthcare to a provider who is at financial risk, the HMO will not be able to provide the actual mental health cost for a particular individual, as a treatment provider could in a fee-for-service financial arrangement. This may require the BR manager to estimate costs instead of using actual figures.

Failing to agree with external service providers on the format of data transfer. Efforts to integrate external data, from, say, the personnel department, a drug-testing laboratory, and a third external source, may be tripped up by files in incompatible formats, for example, some stored on compact disks and some stored on diskettes. Converting files to a compatible format may incur financial costs in any of three ways. First, if the data provider does the conversion, it may try to levy a conversion surcharge. Second, in-house conversion may require additional equipment purchases. Third, the data may need to be manually reentered if it is impossible to download it or if the costs associated with either of the first two steps are prohibitive. Data reentry is a mountain of work for staff, especially when records are very detailed and electronic forms have to be created for the entry process.

Failing to agree on considerations of confidentiality. External providers of behavioral risk services and behavioral healthcare may balk at providing client or patient data, rationalizing that this violates their own confidentiality standards. Therefore, a BR manager should make any contractual agreements contingent upon receiving the client or patient information necessary for case management, auditing, and program evaluation.

Other MIS Hurdles

Even after these major challenges are surmounted, smaller hurdles await. These are likely to occur on a daily basis in accessing other databases, integrating data sets, maintaining legal protections, and so forth. Thomas Amaral, executive director of EAP Information Systems, has catalogued many of them. Among the common ones, which represent decision points in the data management process, are these

Multitudinous categories of lost work time. Payroll databases may have hundreds of categories of lost time. A BR manager needs to determine which ones are relevant to behavioral risk management. For example, vacations, holidays, and personal leave are not relevant (except, perhaps, to identify an absence culture), but absences for medical appointments, paid sick leave, and long-term disability are.

Multitudinous categories of employee injury. An occupational safety and health function may have extensive details of employee work injuries (including ones for which no time off was necessary), especially if the organization has an epidemiology department. A BR manager will need to decide which injury categories have the highest degree of association with behavior, which injuries related to certain environmental factors have no bearing on behavioral risk, and whether the no-time-off injury categories should be analyzed in the event that certain ones are precursors to time-lost injuries later.

Confidentiality concerns if internal MIS staff are used. Normally case files are disguised. However, as a second level of protection when general information systems personnel are involved in behavioral risk management MIS activities, these people should be asked to treat all file information confidentially in the rare event that they inadvertently access files on co-workers.

Problems of communication between behavioral risk management and MIS staff members. Because the working lexicons of these two sets of professionals may vary, when staff are working interdependently having a "translator" who knows the languages of both may be advantageous.

Unreliability and inconsistency of data. When there is a question whether imported data are of limited or no value for analytic purposes, an assessment by the database manager as to the integrity of the information should be requested.

Overabundance of data from individual files. It is common that human resource, healthcare, or other files provide much more information on each employee than is needed. When this happens, either one of two methods can be used to simplify the process of importing and analyzing data. One method is to select the relevant data fields and write a command to download only those onto the behavioral risk management MIS. The second method is to create a customized viewing screen that allows only the information relevant to behavioral risk to be viewed.

Unexpected security and access restrictions. Information on senior managers may not be available without clearances because security breaches could otherwise inadvertently occur. The same could be true of certain categories of personnel information, such as salary grade. In these cases, a BR manager may need to selectively decide which information should be sought.

Trails that can jeopardize confidentiality. When an external database is accessed, audit trails and user log-on procedures leave a record on most mainframes. If confidential individual client records must be sought from a mainframe, the fact that it is the BR manager asking for them must be erased or masked, either by disguising the manager's user name or by imbedding the desired records in a much larger pool of records so that no one else can identify the employees whose records are being examined.

This review of management information systems emphasized the necessity of careful MIS planning, the value of the information that a behavioral risk management MIS produces, and the challenges it presents, including the challenge of maintaining clients' confidentiality. The theme of confidentiality is also an issue in the next chapter, which discusses the third and final special topic: legal and public policy issues in behavioral risk management.

Notes

P. 317, *AT&T Bell Labs:* Behrman, N., Melamed, S. H., and Shoner, L. G. "QHS: AT&T Bell Labs' Two-Gigabyte Solution to Improving Employee Health and Corporate Performance." *EAP Digest* (Behavior Risk Management supplement), 1994, *14*(5), 30–32.

P. 321, *These mistakes, Burton says:* W. N. Burton and D. J. Conti, "Swimming Upstream: How First Chicago Manages Costs While Expanding Behavioral Health Benefits," *Behavioral Healthcare Tomorrow,* 1992, *1*(1), pp. 24–27.

Chapter Twelve

Navigating the Legal and Public Policy Issues

The last special topic in relation to behavioral risk management is a consideration of the relevant legal and other public policy issues. Reflecting behavioral risk management's interdisciplinary nature, a broad band of statutory, regulatory, judicial, and ethical issues can apply to program operation and management efforts to control behavioral risk. The issues include, for example, professional liability, confidentiality, employer negligence, malpractice, employment discrimination, employment at will, employment contracting, affirmative action, employee disabilities, hiring practices, just cause and termination, and others. These issues also define for employers what they can, should, or must do in a variety of circumstances.

Adding to the complexity of public policy issues is the fact that multiple legal remedies are possible for a single exposure. For example, one incident of workplace violence may incur financial and other penalties including workers' compensation benefits paid to the injured employee, fines under the Occupational Safety and Health Act for failing to maintain a safe workplace, tort liability to third-party victims and their families for the negligent acts of people under the employer's control, and perhaps even liability to the perpetrator for defamation or, in the case of a person with a mental disability, disability discrimination.

The list of confidentiality protections and maintenance requirements of employee files quoted in this chapter is reprinted by permission of Jonathan Segal.

In the face of such a large and unwieldy body of public policy, this chapter will be limited to issues that are most likely to influence the implementation and operation of a behavioral risk management function or to affect human resource and other workplace-related policies and practices. The issues are divided into three areas: public policy that protects employees, public policy that regulates employer actions, and public policy that regulates programs, services, and benefits.

Much of public policy cuts across multiple areas, especially that body of law that both protects employees and regulates employer actions. In this chapter, I raise each public policy issue in the behavioral risk area where it has the greatest impact. Later in the chapter, I also consider the role of business and professional ethics, which are also part of public policy and which help to regulate behavior on a moral level and may apply to situations that the law cannot or does not cover.

Public Policies That Protect Employees

Since behavioral risk management defines risk exposures as losses incurred by employees (and family members), an ideal starting point is the laws that protect employee medical and counseling records and therefore affect how behavioral health and life-style claims information is handled. These laws also relate to the confidentiality considerations that surround behavioral risk management MISs, as discussed in the last chapter.

Americans with Disabilities Act

Employees receive protection from the inappropriate handling of confidential medical information under the Americans with Disabilities Act (ADA). The ADA, best known for preventing discrimination against disabled employees and requiring that employers make reasonable accommodations for them, also governs the integration of medical and personnel information. Thus, an MIS that handles multiple sets of confidential employee data raises precarious issues for employers, because the ADA expressly forbids the integration of medical and personnel data in any way that could adversely affect a worker's employment standing. The dangers associated with the information handled by medical departments, managed care providers, and employee assistance programs were brought to national attention by Ellen C. Schultz in the *Wall Street Journal* back in 1994. She suggested that workers' medical privacy is eroding, especially when they file workers' compensation claims for injury or stress-related disability. For example, one consultant she interviewed had called a managed care company to inquire about a beneficiary's records, and the clerk had provided sensitive confidential information about a behavioral health problem without verifying who was calling. Schultz also claimed that some EAPs are pressured by employers for files when an employer wants to take adverse action against an employee. Some employers, if they cannot get confidential information by request, resort to subpoenas (as mentioned in Chapter Eight).

The prevailing issue in integrating medical and personnel data is who has access. The ADA does not explicitly outlaw data integration, but it does specify that the medical condition or history of applicants and employees must be collected and maintained in separate medical files and treated confidentially. Workers' compensation files should be maintained separately from the files of the EAP and other confidential assessment resources, since employers have a need and right to access workers' compensation information but should not see related medical information in that process. As discussed previously, to restrict access to sensitive information on employees, a BR manager also may wish to have data for a behavioral risk audit or Pareto-group analysis integrated and analyzed by an external consultant, who can then provide profiles of Pareto-group individuals so that behavioral risk strategies can be developed, although names of the high-risk individuals would not be provided. This should be sufficient for a BR manager's purposes, since the information cannot be used for intervention with or surveillance of particular high-risk employees. Such interventions or surveillance activities could expose the employer to a discrimination lawsuit under Title VII of the U.S. Federal Code, whether the activities are performed by the BR manager or another manager in the company.

Anonymity, Confidentiality, and Privileged Communication

Anonymity, confidentiality, and privileged communication are of concern to the clinical and work-based problem assessment resource, ombudsman, and conflict resolution specialist. Most executives and managers realize the sanctity of the information a confidential employee workplace resource gains, but horror stories abound among assessment professionals of business managers who felt entitled to confidential information from employee case files. Some workplace professionals have been terminated or demoted because they refused to turn over files on individual employees that management wanted. And some have sued their companies to be reinstated to their former positions.

Most employers are not so nefarious as to want to pry open personal files that are understood to be secret. However, there may be circumstances in which a company needs to defend itself. For example, if a worker sues an employer for negligent retention of another employee following an act of aggression at work, the company might subpoena confidential information to see if the employee filing the suit has a history of confrontive behavior. Or, if a person files a stress-related workers' compensation claim, the company will want to know if that employee has personal emotional issues that could absolve the employer of responsibility for the disability. These examples bespeak the need not for company access to confidential records, however, but for better record keeping on the part of people such as line managers about employee conduct or work performance that warrants adverse company action. However, in an emotionally charged situation with large monetary awards or penalties at stake and a lack of such performance documentation, the employer is likely to pull out all of the stops. For example, an employer even might want personal files revealing an individual's divulgence of private thoughts in an assessment or counseling session if those thoughts corroborate the company view that termination of the employee is justified.

For these reasons, occupational professionals with clinical credentials should know the ground rules about what employee information may be imparted to others and under what circumstances. There are three sets of issues that may come into play: anonymity, confidentiality, and privileged communication. Client anonymity has no independent legal basis, except as an extension of confidentiality rules and regulations and company policy. However, the distinction between anonymity and confidentiality is important because a client may be entitled to confidentiality about the nature of a personal problem but not to anonymity with regard to whether he or she visited a program.

In the following sections, we will look at two sets of confidentiality issues: one relating to program activity, the other relating to integration and maintenance of data sets.

Confidentiality

There is no such thing as a universal "confidentiality law." Instead, the construct for confidentiality is a patchwork of legal and paralegal provisions that may (but not always) hold up in a court of law. They include

- State laws for licensed professionals. These laws provide confidentiality guarantees, usually for specified mental health professionals employed both in and out of the workplace.
- Federal alcohol- and drug-counseling regulations. These regulations provide confidentiality protection to the patient undergoing federal or federally assisted substance abuse treatment.
- Certification and program accreditation codes and professional conduct and ethics codes of professional organizations. These codes represent the collective wisdom and values of organizations and professionals and often hold up under scrutiny in a court of law. Provisos that seek to maintain client confidentiality can be found for ombudsmen, mediators, employee assistance professionals, and such workplace behavioral health professionals as mental health counselors.
- Organizational policy. The aforementioned protections are all subject to circumstances in which confidentiality may not stand up to legal scrutiny, especially if the situation in question is not covered by a confidentiality law applicable to workplace professionals.

Virtually all EAP and behavioral risk management programs have confidentiality protections written into their policies, and many external service providers will not contract with employers without this guarantee. As a practical matter, it is nearly impossible for an assessment program to maintain the trust and credibility necessary for sustained operation without assurances of client confidentiality. Employers considering implementing programs and services to control behavioral risk are well advised to keep this fact in mind.

A person who self-refers to a clinical or work-based problem assessment resource ordinarily receives both anonymity and confidentiality protections. That is, the employer is not entitled to information about the employee's (or family member's) problem or even whether she has visited the EAP in the first place, despite the fact that the employer is paying for the service.

Let's look at some examples in which anonymity and confidentiality are influenced by the specific situation. The first example is supervisory referral of an employee to an assessment resource. If the employee is referred for a conduct or work performance issue, or as a condition of continued employment with the company (say, after a positive drug test), the supervisor or appropriate management representative is entitled to know whether the employee visited the resource. In cases where the employee must visit the resource as a condition of continued employment, the employer is entitled to know whether the client is adhering to the recommended treatment plan. The supervisor is *not* entitled to information on the nature of the problem and specifics of the plan, however, unless the employee has signed a release to divulge information applicable to that circumstance. By the very nature of these cases, there is no anonymity, although confidentiality is still observed.

Other conditions pertain to federal drug-testing and fitness-for-duty laws and regulations, which apply to certain federally regulated industries and require disclosure of employee problems in certain situations where safety or security is an issue. These regulations' disclosure requirements have carved a wedge out of the confidentiality protections offered by employee assistance programs and have prompted many assessment professionals to require clients to sign "limited confidentiality" statements stating that the professional may disclose information to management as required by law or company policy.

When a worker files a stress-related disability claim for a stress-related illness under workers' compensation, the employer is entitled to look for evidence that the behavioral health problems at issue originated outside of the job or that there were significant extenuating circumstances not related to work. In such cases, the information is used defensively by the employer.

Generally, ombudsmen and conflict resolution specialists are not subject to confidentiality protections. Nevertheless, these proceedings are typically treated as confidential (see "Ethical Principles for University and College Ombudspersons" in the Appendix). An example is the situation in which one person alleges sexual harassment by another but wants a peaceable solution to the situation, without the fanfare of an EEO investigation. In such a case, the involved individuals are likely to remain anonymous.

A second type of workplace conflict resolution activity is not anonymous and unlikely to be confidential, either. When work team, manager-employee, and other work-related disputes occur, especially when they impact on productivity and work team harmony, the conflict resolution specialist's role is to help the disputants resolve the disagreement on their own, instead of having management make a decision to resolve the dispute for them, which might lead to lingering hostilities that could arise later. This method is called *passive management*. In these cases, nonprivate meetings will probably be the venues by which the disputing parties seek to reach agreement. There may be other issues that surface during the proceedings, though, such as interpersonal problems not related to productivity, for which a second and this time confidential intervention may be carried out or for which a confidential cross-referral may be made to the problem assessment resource.

As public policy is presently constructed, mental health professionals performing assessments generally must disclose information and records only upon client consent or request, pursuant to court order, pursuant to statutory requirements to disclose information (when there is child abuse or abuse of elderly or dependent adults or when the client lapses into unconsciousness, for example), and upon the discovery that the client might be dangerous toward another individual whom he or she has named.

Because of the complex issues described in this section, it is suggested that a BR manager be a psychiatrist, psychologist, or other mental health professional whose actions are subject to professional conduct or ethical standards. This may provide an extra layer of protection between individual workers and their employer.

Privileged Communication

A higher standard of protection than that just examined applies to communication between a client and a clergyperson, lawyer, psychiatrist, or some psychologists. In these cases, the information is "owned" by the patient and therefore generally not subject to disclosure under any circumstances, unless the patient so permits. An example of privileged communication is the prison discussion that occurred in 1995 between O. J. Simpson and Rosey Greer. It was reportedly overheard by guards, but because Greer was talking as a clergyperson with Simpson, the conversation was deemed not admissible during Simpson's trial for murder.

This area of confidentiality law does not generally relate to behavioral risk activities since most occupational managers are not psychiatrists, but one exception is found in California mediation law. In that state, anything said or any admission made in the course of the mediation is not admissible as evidence in a court of law, and forced disclosure of that information is expressly forbidden. By extension, an employer cannot force a mediator to divulge employee information derived from private sessions. Interestingly, some jurisdictions outside of California have also recognized the California Evidence Code.

Confidential Data Aggregated on an MIS

Confidentiality is increasingly being studied in terms of how it applies to files on management information systems. This area of interest is related to but distinct from confidentiality in program operation. Attorney Jonathan Segal says that employers should observe the following confidentiality protections and maintenance requirements of employee files pertaining to behavioral risk:

- Medical data: confidential and maintained in a separate file.
- Health benefit usage data: confidential and a part of the medical file.
- Work-based problem assessment resource or EAP data: confidential and in a separate file.
- Disciplinary data: personnel file; not confidential per se, although specifics are not customarily disclosed to third parties.

- Demographic data: personnel file; not confidential per se, although specifics are not customarily disclosed to third parties.
- Sickness and accident data: personnel and medical files, although associated medical information should be kept in the medical file.
- Work history data: personnel file; not confidential per se, although specifics are not customarily disclosed to third parties.
- Workers' compensation data: personnel and medical files, although associated medical information should be confidentially kept in the medical file.
- Fitness for duty data (regulated by the Nuclear Regulatory Commission): personnel file; with medical information confidentially maintained in the medical file.
- Drug-testing and medical review officer data: positive results showing illegal drugs that are entered in the personnel file are not confidential; information about prescription drug and alcohol use is confidentially maintained in the medical file.
- Ombudsman data: limited confidentiality, depending on circumstances and policy. The employer may state in written policy that discussions between ombudsman and client are confidentially held except in cases where the employer is legally obligated to remedy a situation (such as sexual harassment) or has a duty to warn (such as threat of violence).
- Conflict resolution proceedings: limited confidentiality, depending on circumstances and policy; the terms may be the same as for the ombudsman.

These maintenance requirements do not apply to the integration of files for analytical purposes but to the integration of data on a behavioral risk management MIS common database. Therefore, data managers need to consider several confidentiality issues as they integrate data on a database. The first is whether the information is collected or aggregated by individual or group. Aggregated data in which breach of confidentiality is not a realistic risk protects all interested parties. However, individual behavioral risk data need to be handled very carefully since, once again, it is illegal to use such data to single out named high-risk and high-cost employees for specific action.

The pivotal issue in the legality of data integration is whether the information is shielded from company representatives who make hiring, firing, and promotion decisions. Confidential information that is nefariously placed or allowed to carelessly drift into their hands breaches confidentiality, regardless of whether that information is to restrict access to benefits or damage the income potential, career, employability, or reputation of the individual. The BR manager also needs to be cautious that not even the *perception* of misuse of confidential information is ever created, as this could damage the credibility of the behavioral risk management function and perhaps invite lawsuits. To control such perceptions, the BR manager should seek to minimize the number of hands that confidential employee information passes through and to regulate information flow through strict and well-publicized protocols that specify the company-imposed and legal penalties for breaches of confidentiality.

Family and Medical Leave Act

Some legislation currently influencing the occupational setting is the result of protections against unilateral employer actions that workers consider unfair. In these cases, statutes and regulations are the functional equivalent of benefits that might otherwise have been gained through the collective bargaining process had a labor union been present. Therefore, like a labor union, this body of law can be considered a behavioral risk exposure, except that it is a blanket exposure applicable to *all* work organizations under a law's jurisdiction.

One such law is the Family and Medical Leave Act (FMLA), which allows eligible employees in companies with fifty or more employees up to twelve weeks of unpaid job-protected leave during a twelve-month period for a variety of family-related reasons. The employee who otherwise would not be granted time off by an employer to attend the funeral of a family member or the birth or adoption of a child can invoke the FMLA for this purpose, even though he may not be compensated for the time off. From a behavioral risk management standpoint, the organizational behavior that

FMLA calls into question is the lack of management action to accommodate employee needs and the resulting collective employee (or public) action to structure a solution.

The family leave legislation is also a nexus between social issues and the workplace that illustrates the relationship between the workplace and society at large. Demographic factors were the precipitants of the FMLA, as the population bulge known as the baby boomers found themselves, for example, responsible for caring for both children and parents, entering a period of high divorce rates, and becoming members of geographically dispersed extended families. Because many employers were slow to respond to employees' needs in these social situations, a remedy has been provided under federal law.

Like many laws, the FMLA has had some unintended side effects that have imposed additional burdens on employers. For example, companies with flexible scheduling policies already in place—and probably already juggling schedules to assure that necessary staff are available to work when needed—may have to deal with even more overtime and staffing issues. Further, one airline found that pregnant reservation agents took advantage of FMLA provisions by taking off four hours for morning sickness, then working four hours at regular pay and four more hours at overtime pay. Some companies' attendance reward programs have been undercut, too, when minor illnesses have been claimed as more serious health conditions.

Occupational Safety and Health Administration Regulations

Regulations promulgated by the federal Occupational Safety and Health Administration (OSHA) and its sister agencies in the states specify minimum standards of workplace safety. The state regulations are more stringent than those of OSHA, which provide a base floor of accountability for employers. OSHA regulations, established in 1970 under the Occupational Safety and Health Act, apply to employers and employees in manufacturing, construction, longshoring, agriculture, law, medicine, charity work, disaster relief, organized labor, and private education.

OSHA regulations address mainly physical hazards, but preventive steps to ensure safety and health are increasingly focusing on behavior-related issues, including stress and mental health and substance abuse issues as well as physical workplace factors likely to contribute to them. While OSHA specifies employer and employee rights and responsibilities for maintaining a safe and healthy workplace, there is little mention in the regulations about employee stress and its relationship with accidents, as it is hard to establish this causal link, and all employees experience some level of stress anyway. However, the regulations do address alcohol and drug abuse—where causal links are more easily established—and many states disqualify employees for workers' compensation benefits when alcohol or drugs have contributed to accidents.

Recent action from OSHA in another area of behavioral risk may provide employers with their best reason to implement a comprehensive behavioral risk management strategy. Amid reports from the National Institute on Safety and Health (a part of the U.S. Public Health Service) that an estimated two million workers are attacked in the workplace each year, OSHA has proffered inspection criteria intended to prevent violence and is issuing citations to employers when acts of violence result in injury or death. Fines of up to $7,000 for a serious violation or $7,000 a day for unabated hazards can be levied. OSHA looks at several factors to determine whether an employer could have prevented workplace violence:

- Whether the employer had direct knowledge of a person's violent tendencies
- Whether there was knowledge of what a reasonable person could have done to prevent a violent act
- What the industry practices are in preventing workplace violence
- Whether the employer took reasonable steps to reduce the hazard

Even though OSHA does not specify actions for employers to take, by examining these factors, it is advocating a preventive approach to workplace violence.

Stress-Related Workers' Compensation

Stress-related workers' compensation has been an area of major preoccupation for employers wishing to diminish their preventable losses. A study by the National Council on Compensation Insurance showed that the cost of an average stress claim was 52 percent greater than for an average traumatic injury claim. This is attributed in part to the fact that stress claims last an average of thirty-nine weeks, fifteen weeks longer than traumatic injury claims.

Stress-related claims are complicated, starting with the fact that they may manifest in any of three ways: as mental-physical claims, in which a mental disorder results in physical injury; physical-mental claims, in which a mental disorder results from a work-related physical injury; and mental-mental claims, in which a mental or emotional stimulus (particularly stress) creates a mental disability.

Mental-mental claims make the most intriguing study, because the employee sometimes totally lacks any physical manifestation of injury while at the same time experiencing incapacitation. According to insurance executive Donald T. DeCarlo, employer concerns are compounded by diverse and ever-changing compensability standards among the states. Each state has its own judicial history with mental-mental claims, fitting into one of four categories:

1.   *No compensability unless a physical component accompanies the injury.* In 1995, states using this standard included Florida, Ohio, Oklahoma, South Dakota, Minnesota, and Kansas.

2.   *Compensability on the condition that the mental stimulus is sudden.* Typically, it applies to mental injuries arising from sudden and violent incidents. An example is the 1992 Maryland case in which a man suffered posttraumatic stress disorder after a three-ton beam crashed through the ceiling of a building and landed beside him. About thirty other states award compensation for mental injuries produced by a mental stimulus reflected in the next two categories.

3.   *Compensability on the condition that the stress is unusual (even if it is gradual rather than sudden).* This standard provides compensation for employees who are afflicted with greater stress than that experienced by other employees. However, there are varying definitions of unusual stress. Wisconsin, for example, specifies that the day-to-day emotional strain of the employee must result from more severe workplace stress than that on *all other employees.* In contrast, Wyoming bases compensability on workplace stress that is demonstrated to be more severe than that of *other workers employed in the same or similar jobs.*

4. *Compensability without regard to whether the mental injury is gradual or sudden and the stress usual or unusual.* There are about eight states whose standards hold that it is enough that stress contributed to the mental injury. Some courts have adopted what is called a "causal nexus standard," meaning that the employee is entitled to recover benefits if, in his or her own perception of reality, he or she believes a work-related factor is causing the mental disability.

There has been a general retraction by the courts of the compensability of stress-related cases in recent years because of concerns that a low standard for compensability invites abuse. As mentioned in Chapter Nine, when California law held that workers had only to prove that their employer was responsible for at least 10 percent of stress-related injury, workers' compensation claims billowed, increasing nearly 700 percent between 1979 and 1988 alone. Since the standard was raised in 1993 to 51 percent— meaning that it now had to be proven that the employer was *predominantly* responsible for the injury—the volume of claims has fallen.

Employers should not assume, however, that if their state workers' compensation system lacks a remedy for stress-related injuries there are no consequences for ignoring stress-producing work cultures, managerial practices, and work environments. Unresolved stress can result in workplace violence, negligence lawsuits filed by employees, higher use of healthcare disability benefits, increased absenteeism and theft, and so forth.

Public Policy That Regulates Employer Actions

Threat of lawsuit is becoming a more compelling reason for employers to look seriously at strategies to control behavioral risk. This is due in large measure to organizational transformation activities that administer workforce reductions and other bitter medicine and lead to employee disenfranchisement, processes that change worker roles, and the litigation frenzy extant in the United States.

Legal awards to employees or customers in compensation for the actions of other employees constitute a growing area of jurisprudence. Employers are held responsible not only for their employees' actions but also for their own *failure to act* when employee behavioral indicators are evident prior to a harmful act, as they might be in cases of workplace violence, sexual harassment, and assault on a customer. Such cases are grist for negligent retention and negligent supervision lawsuits. Negligent retention applies when an employer has retained a worker despite conduct or work performance indicators suggesting he or she should have been discharged. One of the most noted examples is the 1991 case of *Perkins* v. *Spivey,* in which a female employee was repeatedly raped by her superintendent. She filed suit, alleging that the company was negligent because, despite "actual or constructive knowledge," it continued to employ the superintendent and failed to take action against him. Other cases have demonstrated that an employer's liability also extends to the actions of independent contractors as well as employees who attack customers. Finally, negligent supervision lawsuits are related tort actions in which the culpable behavior comes from the supervisor instead of the employee.

In negligent hiring and retention lawsuits, the burden of proof is on the individual filing the lawsuit (the plaintiff). He or she must demonstrate that the employee was unfit for hiring or retention, the employer knew or should have known that the employee was unfit, the employer should have foreseen that the employee would interact with the plaintiff under work circumstances that created a risk of danger, and that hiring or retaining the employee caused the injury to the plaintiff. Some states bar negligent hiring or retention lawsuits, on the premise that workers' compensation laws, whose no-fault provisions specify that employers must provide benefits to injured workers in exchange for employees' relinquishing their right to sue, are applicable. In other jurisdictions, however, courts have admitted these cases.

Employee Retirement and Income Security Act

In 1974, when Congress passed the Employee Retirement and Income Security Act (ERISA), few lawmakers anticipated how broadly the U.S. Department of Labor, which enforces the law, would interpret its provisions. ERISA regulates employee benefit plans, including welfare plans that provide any of the following to participants and beneficiaries: medical, surgical, and hospital care; benefits in the event of sickness, accident, disability, death, or unemployment; and vacation benefits, apprenticeship and other training programs, day care centers, dependent care, educational assistance, and prepaid legal services.

One expanded application of ERISA affects EAP activities. In many cases, EAPs are regulated under ERISA as "defined benefit plans," primarily because these EAPs have taken on the delivery of extended mental health counseling. This definition is consistent with the operating philosophy of these EAPs, which view themselves as extensions of the healthcare delivery system rather than as workplace resources to reduce behavioral risks. Their philosophy is reflected in the fact that they are sometimes sold by healthcare organizations to employers as a free add-on service when the employer is already a customer for healthcare services. Certainly, such programs should be candidates for ERISA compliance review by the Department of Labor.

However, this view of EAPs affects an EAP's ability to deliver workplace services for two reasons: it is a miscarriage of the EAP role, and it has led to several different interpretations of ERISA by the Department of Labor. In particular, the department has been unclear about the criteria it uses to determine whether an EAP should be regulated as a defined benefit plan. One interpretation of ERISA holds that personnel qualifications determine an EAP program's status, even though this interpretation does not specify which credentials make a difference. One could surmise, however, that training in counseling, psychology, social work, or another mental health–related discipline would trigger ERISA, since the prevailing issue is whether the EAP is a healthcare benefit activity.

In another Department of Labor interpretation, however, a determination was based on the range of problems addressed by the EAP. Even though the EAP in question referred clients out for therapy, the department determined that the program provided medical benefits, or benefits in the event of sickness, and was therefore covered by ERISA. Still another opinion stated that because the program was extended to family members, the provisions of ERISA once again applied. However, in a case where the EAP provided a telephone number and employees were referred to an appropriate professional on the basis of the phone discussion, the program was exempted from ERISA.

In the behavioral risk management paradigm, the EAP is primarily a workplace problem assessment resource whose mission is to identify and diminish behavioral risks, not to be a long-term therapeutic tool for resolving behavioral health problems. While the work-based assessment component of EAP practice would probably not position the EAP as an ERISA benefit, except by the most expansionist interpretation, any extended therapeutic counseling probably would make it a benefit, even though counseling is not "employee assistance" in the traditional sense.

Drug and Alcohol Testing

Another body of public policy regulates employer drug and alcohol testing activity. The event that symbolized public outrage about drug abuse was a railway crash in which an Amtrak train carrying over 600 passengers crashed into three Conrail locomotives near Baltimore in January 1987. Sixteen people were killed and another 175 were injured. The engineers of the Conrail locomotives, who failed to slow or stop locomotives at signals before they jumped the switch, were found to have used marijuana before the accident. This was the marquee event amid a swelling series of transportation mishaps that led to tougher drug enforcement laws; passage of the Drug-Free Workplace Act, which requires contractors of the federal government to take certain preventive measures against drug abuse and to take other actions when it is detected, and implementation of federal drug-testing regulations in the transportation industry.

Reasoning that transportation companies are holders of the public trust because of the strong potential for loss of life in transportation accidents, the U.S. Department of Transportation implemented a stiff set of regulations that took effect in December 1988. They mandated drug testing in all six transportation "modes" applicable to the motor carrier, aviation, railroad, maritime, mass transit, and pipeline industries. The regulations require pre-employment, reasonable cause, postaccident, periodic, random, and return-to-work testing, as well as other activities, including policy development and implementation of appropriate employee assistance program elements. Additionally, between 1989 and 1991, drug testing was begun for contractors of the U.S. Department of Defense, companies in the nuclear industry, and contractors working in U.S. Department of Energy facilities.

Some private companies felt the battery of sudden changes in these safety sensitive and security-related industries was ham-handed. For example, a trucking company having small contracts with the Department of Defense and other federal agencies would not have been subject to any federal substance abuse requirements in 1987. By the end of 1989, however, the company would have had to implement random and other forms of drug testing, establish an EAP, sign a statement promising to report to the federal government any employees convicted of drug use, and take other prescribed actions. The regulations also forced the transportation companies to consider how those who test positive would be handled. This was necessary because testing, of course, is only an identification tool, not a solution to the problem. The regulations specified only that employees testing positive must be pulled from their safety sensitive or security-related jobs and that some were not permitted to return to their former classified positions. However, EAPs or, to be more specific, EAP-related activities, were mandated as prevention resources. These activities included the display and distribution of informational material, provision of resources for assistance, and development of a policy on drug use.

The Nuclear Regulatory Commission (NRC) and Department of Defense (DOD) also mandated drug testing, the NRC's program falling under fitness-for-duty regulations. The NRC, it bears noting, has the most expansive definition of EAP among all the safety sensitive industries, requiring assessment, short-term counseling, referral services, and treatment monitoring. The Department of Transportation regulations also created the medical review officer (MRO) function, which reviews positive test results with the donor, verifies the positive result (in order to weed out any extraneous causes), orders retests if the accuracy is questioned, and reports the final result.

Following implementation of the drug regulations, public opinion grew to favor alcohol testing in the transportation industry, too. In January 1995, drug-testing regulations were joined by newly implemented alcohol testing regulations for companies with fifty or more safety sensitive positions. Small employers had until January 1996 to comply. The new regulations created two new occupational functions: the breath alcohol technician (BAT), who administers the tests, and the substance abuse professional (SAP), who conducts face-to-face evaluations of positive test takers to assess the need for and level of substance abuse treatment and who conducts evaluations that confirm employee readiness to return to the job.

Search and Seizure

An employer has a legal right to protect itself from theft, sabotage, and on-the-job drug and contraband activity, three of the most insidious behavioral risk exposures. Thus, a body of public policy pertains to acts of search and seizure by an employer, such as searching employee lockers at work, which must be done in a way that does not intrude on an employee's right to privacy. Judicial precedent seems to be on the side of employers in these cases, because unless the federal government is the employer, federal constitutional law does not apply. State constitutions may apply, however. In a small number of states, employees may be able to bring invasion-of-privacy claims against employers.

It is important for employers to take a reasonable or balanced approach to searches and seizures. For example, random searches are problematic, but reasonable-suspicion searches are likely to be perceived by employees as fair. Also, employers' policies should neither raise employee expectations of privacy too high nor arouse employee feelings of insecurity and oppression. For example, while policy may be worded in such a way that the employer reserves the right to search at will, that statement should be counterbalanced by the tone of the policy and by communication with employees explaining the rationale for the policy and how employee protections will be taken into consideration.

Public Policy That Regulates Programs, Services, and Benefits

Historically, programs and services that control behavioral risk have been implemented either to provide helping services or to serve as a watchdog over employees or those services. Public policy has been developed that puts parameters on the watchdog activities.

Health Benefits

Employee healthcare benefits are regulated by two sets of public policy: one administered by the federal government and generally applicable to self-insured health plans and the other administered by states to specify minimum levels of healthcare benefits when employers offer such benefits. The two sets of policy are generally considered to be mutually exclusive.

Self-insured plans are subject to ERISA, which ensures that healthcare benefits are provided to all employees nondiscriminatorily. In other words, the health benefit plans of self-insured employers must be applied fairly so that lower-paid employees are entitled to the same benefits as are higher-paid employees and officers. These nondiscrimination provisions also specify that interference with an employee's attempts to access benefits to which he or she is entitled is unlawful.

State minimum benefit laws specify that certain coverages must be provided once employers choose to offer healthcare benefits. The most heavily regulated healthcare coverages concern mental health and substance abuse. According to the Intergovernmental Health Policy Project, a Washington, D.C.–based organization that tracks healthcare issues, at the end of 1991, forty-three states had laws regulating behavioral health coverage. Typically, the laws affect group health plans and often HMO contracts. They may mandate certain minimums for inpatient, outpatient, partial, and residential care, and require patient freedom of choice for certain types of providers. For example, in Oregon, a state that has, in effect, been a pilot state for healthcare reform during the 1990s, group contracts must provide coverage for mental illness that includes

- For inpatient care, at least $4,000 for adults and $6,000 for children
- For outpatient care, at least $2,000
- For partial and residential care, at least $1,000 for adults and $2,500 for children

- Benefit caps that are at least $10,500 for adults and $12,500 for children (including treatment for chemical dependency)

  With regard to treatment for alcoholism and drug abuse, coverage must include

- For inpatient care, at least $4,500 for adults and $6,000 for children
- For outpatient care, at least $1,500 for adults and $2,000 for children
- For partial and residential care, at least $3,500 for adults and $2,500 for children
- Benefit caps that are at least $6,500 for adults and $10,500 for children (for chemical dependency treatment only)

Additionally, plan participants must be free to choose among psychologists, psychiatric nurses, and clinical social workers for their behavioral healthcare.

Utilization Review and Drug-Testing Laws

Because laws and regulations reflect public sentiment, they are usually implemented when certain programs and services are thought to affect employees unfairly. This has been the case for laws concerned with utilization review (UR) and drug testing. UR laws can influence behavioral risk if the individual is unable to access benefits necessary to control a behavioral risk exposure. Drug-testing laws may result in individuals' being falsely accused of drug-taking behavior and experiencing negative employment consequences.

Utilization Review

The utilization review (UR) industry has proliferated since the early 1980s, when purchasing UR services to contain healthcare costs started becoming a common employer practice. The subset of the industry that oversees the administration and delivery of behavioral healthcare services has greatly expanded since the late 1980s. Many of these organizations, to their credit, have prudently balanced quality and cost considerations in their precertification and continuing stay activities. Others are best known for their "slash-and-burn" denial-of-care practices.

Even more quickly than the managed care industry arrived on the scene, thirty-three states have passed utilization review laws to contain restrictive UR practices viewed as unfair by beneficiaries and their personal physicians. These states variously regulate appeals and reconsideration processes, healthcare provider credentialing requirements thought to be excessive, public disclosure of review criteria, public disclosure of third-party agents for whom utilization review is being performed, chemical dependency treatment provisions, and licensure and renewal fees. Regulations may also include guarantees of patient confidentiality, requirements of twenty-four-hour availability for emergencies, and prohibition of financial incentives for staff to deny requests for healthcare. Some of these laws apply specifically to behavioral healthcare, while others do not.

In 1995, one UR firm operating in Rhode Island was severely sanctioned by the state for overly restrictive practices. The Rhode Island Department of Health found fifty-five cases in which patients were decertified for continuing behavioral healthcare in situations that could have resulted in harm to these individuals. The department charged the UR firm with the unlawful personnel practice of providing "incentive awards" to staff for truncating treatment episodes, with failure of on-site UR agents to identify themselves as such, with failure to afford patients the complete appeal process, and with other practices that violated Rhode Island's UR law. The firm was required, by consent order of the department, to serve a one-year probationary period subject to compliance with terms and conditions, relieve its executive director and medical director of duties, pay fines of up to $100,000, develop a plan of correction subject to Department approval, and comply with other penalties.

Drug Testing

Drug testing has been a flash-point issue for civil libertarians, labor unions, and others who feel that such testing—or certain aspects of it—infringes on people's right of privacy. Drug testing is one of the activities that most severely tests efforts to balance individuals' rights to privacy with the rights of the public at large to maintain safety and security, since there may be no happy medium that can be struck on this issue. As is the case with environmental laws, drug-testing legalities are likely to be influenced by the ever-swinging pendulum of public opinion.

Today's drug-testing activities can be traced back to the drug-taking behavior of some repatriated solders during and after the Vietnam War. Employers began to look seriously at responding to drug problems during the 1970s, especially as drugs scourged metropolitan areas. Substance abuse treatment proliferated, and alcoholism recovery centers began to treat a wider variety of chemical addictions. In the 1980s, with a conservative White House and a Congress answering to that administration's beck and call, a zero-tolerance mood pervaded the country. Drug testing in many parts of the United States became *the* accepted response to employee drug use. At the same time, laws were passed that provided some protections to employees. Public acceptance of drug testing since then has increased as the risk of false positive test results has decreased due to better controls required by federal law and to improved technology and chain-of-custody procedures for handling of samples by test administrators, laboratories, and medical review officers.

Outside of federal regulations that mandate testing in safety sensitive and security-related industries, public policy now mainly takes the form of state laws that restrict testing. For example, in 1994

- Thirty states had case law.
- Seven states had statutes affecting testing procedures only.
- Eight states and two cities had statutes affecting both the type of test and testing procedures used.
- Five states had voluntary laws affecting drug testing.
- Thirty-five jurisdictions had related workers' compensation statutes.
- Thirty-two states had related unemployment compensation statutes or case law.
- Twelve jurisdictions (including ten states and the District of Columbia and Puerto Rico) had no drug-testing statutes or case law.

State public policy varies considerably. For example, while Florida has no testing restrictions or requirements, it has a voluntary employer law that grants employers a 5 percent discount if they implement and maintain a certified drug-free workplace program. The law requires preemployment, for-cause, periodic announced, postaccident, and rehabilitation testing, and permits random testing. Medical and indemnity benefits are denied if an employee tests positive for alcohol or a prohibited drug.

By contrast, Iowa places restrictions on every form of testing. For example, random testing is prohibited, preemployment testing is permitted only if it is part of a preemployment physical, and for-cause and safety sensitive testing are permitted only when one or more specified conditions are met. Other laws govern testing procedures, serving to protect the employee and giving employees a reasonable opportunity to rebut or explain test results. Workers' compensation benefits may be denied to an employee whose injury is due to intoxication that was a substantial factor in causing an injury.

California's "Knox-Keene Act" regulates prepaid specialized healthcare plans that contract with employers, insurers, and HMOs to provide, among other things, mental health and substance abuse services. This watchdog law is intended, among other things, to prevent fly-by-night providers from deceiving businesses by selling services, collecting payments in advance of service delivery, then spiriting themselves out of town before any services are delivered. Knox-Keene, which requires licensure by the state's Department of Corporations of these healthcare plans, was extended to cover many EAPs in the late 1980s because many EAPs were providing long-term counseling to employees and family members under prepaid contracts with employers.

Knox-Keene has been useful to the EAP field because it has established a regulatory line of demarcation between problem assessment counseling sessions (including sessions intended to motivate the client to accept referral to outside help) and therapy. The cut-off point is three sessions; above that, EAP interaction with clients is deemed to be therapy. Given the fact that there is a limit to the therapy that can be accomplished in three sessions, this would be an appropriate standard for the Department of Labor to use in determining which EAP services in self-insured companies should be ERISA regulated, in place of its present use of sketchy professional qualifications and other criteria.

Duty to Warn

Public policy concerning duty to warn is the flip side of the confidentiality coin. It requires that certain information gained in a confidential or privileged setting be divulged, as appropriate, to management, police, or others when there is a threat of violence against another person or of self-harm to the client. EAPs and other confidential resources in and out of the workplace are understood to be subject to duty-to-warn laws. The landmark judicial test of duty-to-warn laws was *Tarasoff* v. *Regents of the University of California,* whose standard specifically applies to California but is observed in other parts of the country.

In *Tarasoff,* a graduate student at the University of California confided to a psychologist of the university-sponsored counseling service his intentions to kill a female student who did not reciprocate his romantic interest. The psychologist contacted the campus police, who detained the student. The student appeared to be rational and was released. The psychologist reported the events to the director of the counseling service, a psychiatrist, who specified no further action. Neither the woman nor her family were warned of the danger. The student carried out his threats and murdered her. As a result, a lawsuit was filed by her parents against the psychologist, director of the counseling service, police, and university.

The Supreme Court of California determined that a therapist who ascertains during the course of the therapist-client relationship that a patient presents a serious danger of violence to another individual has an obligation to use reasonable care to protect the intended victim against the danger. This may involve warning the victim, notifying the police, or taking other reasonable steps as necessary.

This case is based on California law, so different legal standards may apply in other states. However, other states are enacting duty-to-warn legislation that identifies who is responsible for warning potential victims and specifies legal procedures.

Good Ethics

Much of what gets passed into law and becomes public policy represents an attempt to deter unethical behavior. Ethics apply morals to people's work and personal lives. In the behavioral risk management paradigm, ethics address everything from kickbacks received from a treatment provider for referrals to deliberately skewed decisions or recommendations in conflict resolution proceedings. In the absence of legal remedies for wrongdoing, ethics constitute an honor system used to deter personal (or organizational) behavior that has a negative consequence for another person or entity.

Since it is impractical to attempt to legislate all behavior—because of the vast amount of law that would be required as well as the problems of enforcing it—good ethics are fundamental to maintaining order in business transactions, professional activity, and society at large. Ethical codes can also be used to promote awareness of unethical behaviors born of ignorance. Examples are the ethical guidelines promulgated by professional associations to newer or younger members, and these associations' requirements that those who breach the guidelines undertake education or training to prevent future breaches.

The test of ethical behavior is embodied in four questions:

- Is the action good for me?
- Is the action good for the company?
- Is the action good for everybody affected by it?
- Is the action fair and just?

If a person contemplating a business or professional action can respond in the affirmative to all four questions, there is no ethical problem.

The ethical standards of a community are typically ever changing, though, so ethics are often temporized. For example, whereas a hostile business takeover of a publicly held company would have probably been considered unethical behavior twenty years ago, many stockholders today consider it a fact of business life. The same applies to service providers who, in bidding for contracts, take an initial financial loss in order to undercut competitors and perhaps run them out of business, hoping thereby to come to dominate the market.

Unethical behavior can have deleterious consequences with regard to behavioral risk, though. If a company is known to, say, commit deplorable acts to gain unfair competitive advantage and falls short of the standards in the four-question ethics test, it is likely to lose the loyalty of honest employees, may risk legal consequences, be ostracized in the business community, and lose sales. It may, in short, experience organizational as well as individual risk exposures.

I will give just one cautionary example. Two nationally known heart surgeons in the same hospital system were regarded by hospital staff as demigods. They threw lavish parties, had subordinates (and other doctors!) who assiduously waited on them, and soaked up the media's attention. Then informal partnership between them developed into a competition to see who could acquire the most prestige. They started padding their patient portfolios with the rich and famous, padding their bills, and "stealing" patients from other surgeons at the hospital and throughout a tri-state area. They became at first argumentative then hostile toward each other. Further, both of the doctors seemed preoccupied with the limelight rather than their practices, which began to suffer. Both experienced a fall from grace when they were censured by the state regulatory board for medical ethics violations only a month apart. To the hospital administration, it seemed like the death of their cash cows. After the censure, one of the doctors developed emotional and alcohol abuse problems, which rendered him incompetent to perform surgery, resulting in the loss of his practice. The other lost the respect of his staff (some of whom left the hospital system), and experienced a prolonged (and perhaps permanent) loss of clients and income. He is now in the process of trying to rehabilitate his career.

As this chapter has illustrated, both the federal government and states and local jurisdictions have laws and regulations that impact on behavioral risk. Employers should also be aware that laws and regulations applying to government agencies are often different from those for the private sector. Employers should implement programs and services and make operational decisions based on a knowledge of the full scope of public policy. This will often mean obtaining the advice of legal counsel.

We have now covered the theory and application of behavioral risk management from bottom to top. You now have a complete audit process that you can use to measure behavioral risks, determine the most appropriate individual and organizational interventions, and implement these interventions. You are versed on preemployment activities that diminish behavioral risk. And you are acquainted with management information systems and legal issues. The final chapter will provide you with perspectives on the street-level operation of behavioral risk management.

Notes

P. 327, *one incident of workplace violence may incur:* "Learning the Truth About Workplace Violence." *Pennsylvania Employment Law Letter* (Sample Issue), p. 7.

P. 328, *The dangers . . . brought to national attention by Ellen C. Schultz:* Schultz, E. C. "Medical Data Gathered by Firms Can Prove Less Than Confidential." *Wall Street Journal,* May 18, 1994, p. 1; and "If You Use Firm's Counselors, Remember Your Secrets Could Be Used Against You." *Wall Street Journal,* May 26, 1994, p. C1.

P. 329, *ADA . . . does specify that the medical condition:* Equal Employment Opportunity Commission. "Section VI: Medical Examinations and Inquiries." *Technical Assistance Manual on the Employment Provisions (Title I) of the Americans with Disabilities Act.* Washington, D.C.: Author, 1992, VI-1 to VI-12.

P. 329, *surveillance of particular high-risk employees:* Segal, J. A. "There Are Limits to the Data Mix & Match." *EAP Digest* (Behavior Risk Management supplement), 1994, *14*(5), 27–28.

P. 334, *forced disclosure . . . is expressly forbidden: California Evidence Code,* sec. 1152.5 ("Communications During Mediation Proceedings"), p. 46(a)(1)(2).

P. 334, *observe the following confidentiality protections:* Segal, J. A. "Legal: There Are Limits to the Data Mix & Match." *EAP Digest* (Behavior Risk Management supplement), 1994, *14*(5), 27–28.

P. 337, *FMLA has had some unintended side effects:* "SHRM Testifies on Family Leave Law's Burdens." *HR News,* 1995, *14*(6), 5.

P. 338, *OSHA looks at several factors:* Yarborough, M. H. "OSHA Now Assesses Employer Liability." *HR Focus,* June 1995, p. 7.

P. 339, *the cost of an average stress claim:* National Council on Compensation Insurance. *1993 Issues Report.* Boca Raton, Fla.: National Council on Compensation Insurance, 1993.

P. 340, *factor is causing the mental disability:* DeCarlo, D. T. "Compensability for Stress-Related Workers' Compensation Cases." Paper presented before the International Association of Industrial Accident Boards and Commissions, Workers' Compensation College, Newport, R.I., Apr. 1995.

P. 340, *workers' compensation claims billowed:* "Mental Stress Claims in California Workers' Compensation—Incidence, Costs and Trends." In *CWCI Research Notes.* San Francisco: California Workers' Compensation Institute, p. 1.

P. 341, *1991 case of* Perkins *v.* Spivey: "Negligent Hiring, Supervision, Retention, and Training." In *The 1994 National Employer.* Littler Mendelson Fastiff Tichy and Mathiason, Nashville, Tenn., 1994, p. 434.

P. 341, *negligent hiring and retention lawsuits:* DiLorenzo, L. P., and Carroll, D. J. "Screening Applicants for a Safer Workplace." *HR Magazine,* 1995, *40*(3), 57.

P. 341, *ERISA regulates employee benefit plans:* Coleman, B. J. *Primer on the Employee Retirement Income and Security Act* (3rd ed.). Washington, D.C.: Bureau of National Affairs, 1989, p. 75.

P. 342, *whether the EAP is a healthcare benefit activity:* Fellman, S. J., and Bar, R. B. "ERISA Ruling Penalizes Many EAP Professionals." *EAPA Exchange,* 1992, *22*(5), 25–27.

P. 343, *exempted from ERISA:* Fellman and Bar. "ERISA Ruling Penalizes Many EAP Professionals."

P. 343, *a railway crash:* Stuart, R. "New York-Bound Passenger Train Collides with 3 Conrail Engines Near Baltimore." *New York Times,* Jan. 5, 1987, p. I-1, col. 2; Jan. 15, p. I-1, col. 4.

P. 344, *most expansive definition of EAP:* "Q&A on Federal Drug Testings Regs." *EAPA Exchange,* Feb. 1992, pp. 36–37; 1992, *22*(2), 24–25.

P. 345, *two new occupational functions:* Parker, C. "BATs, SAPs, & MROs: Understanding Their Roles." *EAPA Exchange,* Jan. 1995, pp. 18–20.

P. 345, *feelings of insecurity and oppression:* Segal, J. A. "When You Have to Search or Seize." *HR Magazine,* Oct. 1994, pp. 35–36.

P. 346, *benefits are provided to all employees nondiscriminatorily:* Employee Retirement Income and Security Act, sec. 510, *U.S. Code,* vol. 29, sec. 1140 (19).

P. 346, *in Oregon, . . . a pilot state for healthcare reform:* Intergovernmental Health Policy Project. *State Benefit Mandates for Alcohol, Drug Abuse and Mental Illness (Through 1991).* Washington, D.C.: Intergovernmental Health Policy Project, 1993.

P. 349, *state laws that restrict testing:* de Bernardo, M. A., DeLancey, M. M., and Hahn, B. W. *Guide to State Drug Testing Laws.* Washington, D.C.: Institute for a Drug-Free Workplace, 1994, pp. 9–10.

P. 349, *Florida has . . . a voluntary employer law:* Bernardo, DeLancey, and Hahn. *Guide to State Drug Testing Laws.* pp. 51–52.

P. 350, *Iowa places restrictions:* Bernardo, DeLancey, and Hahn. *Guide to State Drug Testing Laws.* pp. 69–70.

P. 351, *Supreme Court of California determined:* 118 Cal. Rptr. 129, 529 P.2d 553 (1974).

P. 351, *other states are enacting duty-to-warn:* Chapman, C., and Lammond, J. "Ethics: Confidentiality Issues." *The Counselor,* July/Aug. 1995, p. 60.

P. 352, *test of ethical behavior:* Bowie, N. E., and Duska, R. F. *Business Ethics.* Englewood Cliffs, N.J.: Prentice-Hall, 1990, p. 68.

Chapter Thirteen

Behavioral Risk Management at Eye Level

We have looked at the theory of behavioral risk management, at interventions and applications, and at special issues. But what does a behavioral risk management system look like to the employees (and family members) who use it, to managers, and to executives and board members? From these viewpoints, we can see that interventions must vary depending on the particular behavioral risk, on whether the problem is individual or organizational (or both), on the way the problem manifests in the company, on whether resources for helping are internal or external (or both), and on the employment sector or industry of the organization.

The manner in which a system appears to operate depends a great deal on one's vantage point. For example, a spectator watching a professional basketball game from high in the "nosebleed" section sees the patterns in which the players move up and down the court and take their strategic positions. This macroscopic view is also what a senior manager can expect to see in an organization. He or she misses a lot of the bumping and pushing underneath the basket, the communication among players, and the rotation of the ball on a jump shot. However, he or she is also in the best position to understand the tactical dimensions of the game.

The spectator who sits closer to floor level but behind one of the baskets views a sea of raised arms and players trying to circumnavigate this danger in order to position themselves to put up a high-percentage shot. This is analogous to what a manager sees— the intensity, emotion, and determination of the actual people who are playing out a drama.

The employee (and sometimes the manager), like the game participant, has yet another view; he or she is part of the action.

In the design of a behavioral risk management strategy, the perspectives of the people in these three positions are all equally important. If the management system is too unwieldy or complicated, if it is perceived as too far removed from the everyday operation of the organization, or if it is not viewed as a neutral resource, the probability that it will significantly contribute to the organization's business objectives is greatly limited. If the system's credibility with any of these groups is lost, so is its effectiveness.

Seven Case Studies

In Chapter One, I presented seven case studies of behavioral risks that could have been handled better. In this chapter, I offer seven studies of how a well-run system operates.

The first example is an in-depth analysis that includes insights from all three perspectives, while each of the last six examples focus mainly on a single perspective. Together, they present a panoramic view of the behavioral risk management function.

Case Study 1: The Magazine Publisher That Wanted to Avoid Organizational Chaos

Pressform, Inc., is a major magazine publishing company with a stable of forty-five periodicals, operating out of three plants in the southeastern United States, with headquarters located at the largest facility. Over a three-year period, this company of 1,000 employees had become increasingly concerned about reports of "organizational chaos" in some competitors' publishing houses. The industrywide unsettled state was caused by several factors. They included a multiplicity of technological changes such as the rapid transition to electronically formatted rather than typeset magazines, which eliminated the need for composition and stripping departments; a nascent transition to "on-line" or diskette-formatted magazines that subscribers accessed by computer, which involved the use of different technology and would eventually cause the obsolescence of various jobs and skills; and a diversification into new markets in order to beef up thinning profit margins. These factors also underlay some mergers and acquisitions, which were inevitably followed by downsizing.

Executives in the industry privately lamented how employees were "jumping ship," taking expertise and trade secrets to other publishers, complaining about high stress levels, and falling ill with increasing frequency. The executives were also becoming increasingly concerned about such dishonest acts as lying, stealing, and taking credit for others' work. Finally, the industry leaders also sensed that the industry was more susceptible to workplace violence than in the past, which they attributed in part to a protracted period of hostile takeovers and consolidations, plus the lean-and-mean management style to which many of them had resorted.

Pressform, a financially stable, conservative company that had thus far resisted the destabilizing influences that roiled its competitors, nevertheless knew that it would have to begin reorganizing to remain viable in the future. It carried out its reorganization on the following seven fronts:

Strategic development, including setting plans to enter new markets and develop products based on electronic media

Equipment modernization, including upgrading printing operations, acquiring tools for producing electronic media, and providing electronic capabilities for writers and editors

Financial management, particularly using software packages to economize on financial analysis, accounts payable and receivable, and budgeting and projections

Marketing, including making stronger appeals to new and prospective customers

Work team implementation, including arranging teams according to occupational classification in five publication groups and featuring cross-training so that lost work time would have minimal disruption

Management development, including implementing a less autocratic management style.

Workforce stability, including implementing a behavioral risk management strategy

From various data that were maintained or received by the personnel department, the company knew that many of its measures of behavioral risk exposure were at or slightly below average for the industry. It saw the handwriting on the wall, though, when several bouts of employee conflict in different departments occurred within a month's time. Management decided that action had to be taken now to curtail the emergence of more serious problems later.

The company decided to hire a BR manager who could oversee the integration of behavioral risk management programs and services, promote them to management and employees, do behavioral risk training, perform conflict resolution activities with the work teams, and do audits and evaluations. Pressform's competitors, for the most part, had taken none of these steps—the lean and mean management style *was* their solution.

The BR manager was a clinical and organizational psychologist who had expertise in the publishing industry and had consulted to the company from time to time when there were problems between supervisors and among departments. He was given direct reporting responsibility to the company's senior vice president of operations in order to protect the function from managers wanting to tap into confidential information about their employees. Despite this "buffer," he was expected to be highly visible to management and its three plants. To begin the process of creating the behavioral risk management function, the BR manager called two meetings: one with line managers, the other with program managers. He asked the line managers about the kinds of "people problems" they were experiencing on a daily basis, the training they had previously received on managing people, the disciplinary and other types of records they kept on employees, the protocols they used for addressing employee problems, and other matters that would be useful for behavioral risk auditing, training, and interventions.

The BR manager's meeting with program managers included the managers of the human resource, benefits administration, safety, security, health promotion, equal employment opportunity, and risk management functions. The senior vice president to whom he would report also attended. The BR manager inquired about the information that would be available from each manager and described the quarterly reports and analysis of the organization's behavioral risks they would receive in exchange. In this way, he hoped to create and become part of a mutually supportive team. This meeting helped to establish the rapport that would later be useful in making benefit plan revisions, initiating behavioral safety training for employees, intervening with injured workers, devising strategies with security staff to reduce theft, and so forth.

The BR manager also made a change of vendors. Pressform previously used a mental health service provider to do problem assessments, but after a vendor proposal-evaluation process, the BR manager changed to a provider who offered a more comprehensive range of services and had no vested interest in performing long-term counseling. The vendor was paid on a capitated basis for services including clinical problem assessments, wellness activities, work-and-family consultations, critical incident debriefings, and case management of behavioral health. The BR manager himself performed work-based problem assessments upon referrals of employees from supervisors and conflict resolution activities, and collaborated on organizational interventions with a management consultant paid on a fee-for-service basis.

Vendor selection was also based on vendor ability to provide computerized information to management; competencies of the vendor staff; the integration of specialized staff functions, such as problem assessment and wellness; for those cases involving conflict resolution, vendors' willingness to share caseload with the BR manager; vendors' willingness to review case files (especially for cases originating from management referral); and vendor consent to have its files audited by the BR manager on a quarterly basis. The service provider, in return, was given a contract with an incentive. In addition to the capitated rate, the vendor would receive an annual bonus commensurate with reductions in behavioral risk exposure over a contract period of two years. Thus the vendor's income would be linked to organizational performance and the holistic management of behavioral risks, not to a financial formula that discourages the promotion of services to employees, subsequent utilization, and appropriate level of intervention.

What an Individual Experienced

At Pressform, the sales revenue generated per employee had increased 350 percent over the company's last decade, due to labor-saving equipment and new process efficiencies. Recognizing this concentration of revenue-generating capability, senior management felt that it needed to control its behavioral risks better, beginning with hiring practices. So it prepared job analyses, which in turn supported the development of tailored preemployment tests that measured psychological and behavioral traits. Candidates taking the test were informed that it would not query them about highly personal issues and was consistent with the requirements of the job.

One new hire, Carla, received orientation training in a group with five others. The day-long session included a two-hour briefing from the BR manager, who discussed the company's three-sided philosophy of employee empowerment, personal responsibility, and management commitment; the range of services available to employees in dealing with work-related and personal problems; and how to participate in and resolve problems on work teams, with emphasis on interpersonal communication.

After assuming her duties in the bindery department, Carla periodically received additional information on behavioral risk issues, as well as reminders about behavioral risk management programs and services. These came in the form of lunch seminars on life-style, coping with change, and other problems-in-living issues; a peripatetic BR manager who regularly walked the shop floor; posters, mailers, paycheck stuffers, and other literature about the availability of services; a work team training program that included a segment by the BR manager on effective group communication and interaction; and annual work team development refresher training. Additionally, team leaders, appointed each year on a rotating basis, received training on group decision making and mediation.

On three occasions over the next several years, the BR manager was called in to help the members of Carla's work team reach agreement after finding themselves stalemated in conflict. One of the situations involved a conflict Carla had with another employee, Sara, with whom she seldom saw eye to eye. Their disagreement about the scheduling of binding "jobs" did not seem possible to resolve amiably without intervention from outside the work team and department. The team leader was not responsible for settling disagreements, and the department manager felt that siding with one employee or the other would undercut the team process while doing nothing about the underlying personality problems that seemed to beset the two employees. The team leader invited the help of the BR manager.

In the confidential enclave that was his office, the BR manager mediated a solution between the two employees and suggested a process by which they could resolve their own differences in the future. The BR manager also helped both of them understand that more than their personal differences were heightening tensions. Several new magazine launches were adding to their workload and increased their interaction, which, he said, most likely precipitated their current problems. He also encouraged them to visit the problem assessment resource individually. On Sara's visit, during which she filled out a psychological and sociological assessment, the attending counselor determined that her problems were aggravated by the loss of an aunt with whom she had been close and problems with her teenage sons. The counselor provided Sara with information to help her gain a better understanding of how personality, personal life, and workplace issues were interacting to create the state of mind she found confusing. The counselor also gave Sara information on the four stages of the grieving process—denial, bargain, depression, and acceptance—and referred her to a local bereavement support group. The counselor paid her a follow-up call two weeks later to monitor her progress. This holistic approach to resolving behavior-related problems enabled both Sara and Carla to better understand the other and develop a stronger working relationship. A situation that might have resulted in disciplinary action taken against one or the other of these employees was made an opportunity for facilitating their long-term working relationship.

What Managers Experienced

After the conversion to work teams at Pressform, each department had one manager, who oversaw multiple work teams. Therefore, a lot of work was performed by employees without direct supervision. Managers held helping rather than unilateral decision making roles. Some managers had difficulty making this adjustment.

For example, one manager complained to the BR manager about employees who argued over who would be assigned to which publications for the shooting and stripping of negatives and over how work would be divided between day and evening shifts. He did not feel adept at helping employees find a mutually agreeable solution and then develop a technique for resolving future differences. "I never wanted this system in the first place," he said, which revealed his resistance to the work team concept. The BR manager advised the department manager, first, that the new work system was an adjustment for everybody and that the manager should allow himself a year to adjust to it. Second, he suggested that the manager needed to be more patient in listening through problems expressed by employees, to make eye contact, and to nod along to show that he was interested and understood each point. Third, he told the manager that if one employee involved in a dispute appeared to be recalcitrant, the manager should state this—in an inoffensive manner that does not redirect the issue to personality or ego issues—and offer the employee an opportunity to express why he or she holds a particular point of view.

Fourth, in order to avoid larger schisms, the manager was directed to explicitly discourage team members from lobbying other team members for their support. The other team members were to be encouraged to share their own views and, when agreement was not easily reached, to take a vote to decide an issue rather than have a drawn-out stalemate. The effectiveness of this technique (or any other one that suits the work group) should then determine whether or not it is used in the future. Fifth, the BR manager advised the other manager to resist individual team members' solicitations for his support (employees were known to have done this under Pressform's previous operational structure, too, and such solicitation had gratified this manager's ego), as giving in to these requests would undermine the company's team development and the manager's own credibility. Last, the BR manager explained that if problems persisted for which there appeared to be "irreconcilable differences," it might be necessary for him to move one of the employees to another department or, if circumstances warranted, recommend to the human resource department that disciplinary action be taken. Of course, the BR manager would be available to intervene if the manager felt he could not reach a satisfactory solution.

The BR manager also advised the manager to promote the use

of mediation skills by team leaders so that problems had a better chance of being peaceably resolved without involving management. This type of informal and impartial mediation could help teams avoid situations in which some members obstinately dug in their heels. The BR manager further explained that behavioral health problems (such as stress or emotional concerns) can also lie behind team conflicts. For this reason, employees should regularly be reminded of the availability of the behavioral health problem assessment resource.

The line manager recognized that both team members had legitimate arguments. So he told them, first, that there was no "wrong" side to the disagreement. Second, he suggested that one course of action be implemented now, and that the next time around the other be tried. This was acceptable to the team members, and after some negotiation among themselves, it was back to business as usual.

What Senior Management Experienced

Senior management, of course, saw none of these developments. However, in the BR manager's reports to the vice president of operations, senior management received quarterly updates on organizational developments related to behavioral risk. The reports generally concealed the names of particular individuals and teams involved in conflicts unless certain interventions were initiated by senior management in the first place.

The BR manager periodically reported at senior management meetings on developments in training activities, audit results, and current problems and issues. For example, following the implementation of work teams, the BR manager was able to present a concern he had heard in private consultations with managers and during problem assessment sessions with employees that managers were being "spread too thin," which left employees feeling like shoppers needing help in a department store where there are no aisle clerks. He also described how fluctuations in the flow of printing jobs—with a lot of one-time jobs one week and none the next—were causing havoc on many of the teams.

Finally, once a year the BR manager provided executive training on how management decisions can elevate behavioral risk. He incorporated information from the behavioral risk audit, for which objective data were collected quarterly and subjective data prepared annually, following the administration of management and employee surveys.

Case Study 2: The Injured Worker Who Bounced Back

What does a behavioral risk management function look like from the perspective of an injured employee? Consider "Mel," an average worker. He had been a custodian at Metalcast Incorporated for sixteen years. He had ambivalent feelings about his job and, as he grew older, the work seemed more physically demanding. The aches and pains did not go away as quickly as they used to, but he was not sure where else he could get a job.

One Monday, Mel hurt his back. He reported it to his supervisor, who sent Mel to Metalcast's occupational health department. The doctor saw him right away and diagnosed a back strain. He empathized with Mel's complaints of pain and took a few moments to explain the structure of the back, and how and why Mel felt the way he did. He told Mel that simple muscle strain accounts for the overwhelming majority of back pain and that it is a serious condition but one that responds predictably to treatment. He suggested Mel take the rest of the day off and call back the next day. The injury was also automatically reported to the state workers' compensation bureau. Before Mel left, an occupational health nurse questioned him about the accident and his overall health, updated his medical history form, then asked whether any personal factors could have caused or aggravated the condition, such as family problems that could have distracted him from concentrating at work. Mel said only that his wife had been becoming increasingly reclusive and drinking more frequently. Concerned that this might be causing elevated stress for Mel, the nurse suggested he visit the assessment resource, a part of the behavioral risk management function. To increase Mel's comfort level with the assessment process, the nurse and Mel made the initial phone call together. This also ensured that Mel would not simply let the matter drop.

An assessment professional asked to see Mel's wife, Betty, and she received a psychological and sociological assessment. She was experiencing emotional problems and a growing alcohol dependency. The assessment professional precertified Betty for eight weeks of outpatient mental health and substance abuse treatment under Mel's benefits plan, provided by Metalcast. During that time, the assessment function checked on her condition to ensure that treatment was proceeding as expected. After treatment, she was discharged without complication.

Meanwhile, on the day after his injury, Mel was seen by a doctor on Metalcast's workers' compensation medical resource list, who examined his range of motion and functional capability and prepared a description of the physical restrictions under which Mel could work. The restrictions included no lifting over five pounds and no stooping and bending. The doctor recommended light-duty work to Mel's supervisor, who had had experience with such restrictions before and had specific duties that could accommodate the restrictions. After missing only two days of work, Mel went on light-duty activity, dusting, dry mopping, and other simple chores. He did not particularly like it but was capable of performing these tasks. He felt a twinge in his back and a week later visited the doctor, who recommended progressive modification of his restrictions over a two-month period, during which time he was monitored by Metalcast's disability manager. The disability manager also developed a preshift stretching routine for Mel, to guard against future injuries. This, too, was monitored, through a logbook that Mel was assigned to keep. After the two months, Mel was fully recovered and released to full duty.

This case study illustrates how a company dealt with an injured employee forthrightly, which motivated him to achieve recovery, rather than manipulatively in an effort to avoid paying benefits. Second, the employee received coaching and medical advice rather than heavy-handed treatment, which helped him to decide about his own ability to work. This case also depicts how behavioral risk management can be integrated with other workplace functions—in this case, disability management—in order to manage both the physical and emotional health of workers and family members. And it shows why the assessment resource is the centerpiece of the behavioral risk management function. Had the secondary, but vitally important, contributing factor of Mel's wife's problems not been addressed, his back injury might only have been the first of a succession of injuries or other problems arising from personal issues that disturbed his concentration at work.

What if this scenario had been played out in a more adversarial working environment? Mel might have sought to stretch out the period during which he received workers' compensation. He would know how other workers had "milked" the system by feigning continued injury in order to stretch out benefit payments, with no desire whatsoever to return to work. Further, with the passage of several months away from work, Mel would have felt much more isolated, wondering whether his back really hurt. This might have led to more tests, such as a myelogram, in which dye is injected into the spinal fluid to determine whether the spine has an abnormal shape. Psychosomatic symptoms might have interrupted his convalescence, also, increasing his potential for permanent disability. This is quite a different scenario than the successful scenario first described.

In yet another scenario, had Mel's physical injury been more serious, the behavioral risk management function would have become involved in periodically checking on his progress. Mel would have been reminded that his services were missed at the company, that his supervisor and co-workers hoped that he would experience a full recovery, and that his position (or a similar one) would be available upon his return, even if he had to be gradually reinstated. (This case-monitoring activity is the antithesis of case tampering, in which the employer seeks to pressure the injured worker to return.)

Case Study 3: The Law Firm's Drug Abuse Culture

A law firm of seventy-five employees in a small city had a reputation for working hard to win cases for its clients then playing hard at the local country club after the conquest. Through three generations, drinking to excess after victory was the norm for the partners and associates. Generally, this did not pose any performance problems for the firm although, when it did, the partners exercised damage control by severely punishing the malfeasant, if not outright terminating him. The culture of the firm was to restrict alcohol to "its proper time and place," and most times, this was sufficient social policy. However, after a succession of retirements, young lawyers replaced the old, and cocaine started to be used behind the country club and at private parties. A firm that over many years had teetered on the brink of institutional alcohol abuse, lost control in a year's time over drug abuse. Associates started missing work and deadlines, their research was increasingly shoddy and, after they lost a few court cases, business clients noticed.

The senior partners, catching on to the drug problem, immediately implemented random drug testing. Four of the younger lawyers tested positive over six months, and the snap judgement of the senior partners was to fire them, an act that was summarily carried out the next day. One of the senior partners, though, saw that the problems went deeper than a few drug users on staff and that the firm arrogantly and erroneously thought it had a "cloak of invincibility." He argued convincingly that the behavioral standards of the firm needed to be reevaluated, beginning with the partners themselves. With the grudging acceptance of the other partners, he had the associates reinstated, on the condition that they be evaluated for chemical dependency by a clinical problem assessment resource and follow any treatment plan that was prescribed.

The young associates were each referred to outpatient treatment of varying intensities for chemical dependency. Their treatment plans also heavily emphasized drug education. Upon treatment completion, each attended a return-to-work session involving the assessment professional (who did monthly follow-ups to ensure continued compliance with the rehabilitation plan) and the associate's immediate supervisor. One of the young lawyers was terminated for violating his treatment plan, but the other three succeeded. The senior partner who had seen the depth of the problem also suggested that the firm "clean up its house" by introducing conduct standards for its lawyers that specified responsible social behavior (which meant neither public intoxication nor illicit drug use), by reaffirming its ethical standards, by implementing a problem assessment resource and promoting its services; by establishing performance standards for each position; by performing an annual behavioral risk audit; and by training on behavioral risk issues at all levels of the firm. The senior partners also "owned up" to the contributory role they had played in the misfortunes by perpetuating behavior no longer appropriate for the organization.

Instead of creating an oppressive work environment to resolve its problems—which could have led to turnovers and retaliation by the majority of workers, who had done nothing wrong—the firm created a more open and honest work culture that encouraged help seeking where appropriate. Ultimately, the cleanup gave the firm a fresh start which, within three years, restored its good name in the community.

This example shows not only the power that a cultural shift can have in an organization but also the influential role played by the person who champions the development of a behavioral risk management strategy.

Case Study 4: Breaking Through the Law of Diminishing Competence

Weak leadership had condemned one state-government agency to mediocre, and sometimes worse, performance. This leadership had developed as the result of what management consultant Robert N. McMurry calls the "law of diminishing competence," in which each level of management is weaker and less secure than the one above it. This agency's leadership, which fit this pattern to a tee, included an insecure or indecisive boss, who tended to name subordinates who were less competent than he, and seniority-based middle and lower management positions, typically competent in their own areas of expertise but with few leadership skills and a lack of innovative ability. The management levels grew progressively weaker down the organizational chart.

This institutional deficiency was perpetuated for years, until the head of the department in which the agency was housed, a "secretary" appointed by the state's governor, ordered a departmental audit. Because the secretary was an outsider and had inherited great political clout, he was in a strong position to break through the inertia that had plagued this department. An audit firm administered surveys to managers and employees that included many of the subjective questions found on a behavioral risk audit. Survey findings that were particularly insightful pertained to low cooperation between management and employees, poor quality of communication from senior managers to line managers, poor quality of communication from management to employees, high prevalence of rumors in the agency, frequent favoritism displayed by managers, a poor "people orientation" exhibited by the agency toward employees, occurrences of "broken promises" between employees and management, and ineffective resolution of employee problems.

An executive report from the audit firm suggested to the secretary the pervasiveness of the weak management. The findings, substantiated by a review of organizational performance six months later, provided the evidence necessary for the secretary to make managerial changes. The following year, an organizational development firm was hired to evaluate managers' competencies and attitudes and that action broke through the law of diminishing competence that had existed in the agency.

In this way, a behavioral risk audit can identify problems that prevent an organization from achieving optimal effectiveness, even in the absence of behavioral risk programs and services that could otherwise detect them.

Case Study 5: The Company That Planned for Critical Incidents

One insurance company in the midst of transformational change, realizing that it would have to impose a 20 percent reduction in force in order to remain competitive beyond the turn of the century, developed a long-range plan in order to make this a change in a way that it hoped would minimize the amount of pain felt by employees during the uncertainty.

What helped in this process was that the organization had a work culture characterized by open communication between senior managers and line managers, and managers and employees. The company had a high trust level, meaning that managers could literally sit down with employees at the lunch table and openly explain the company's situation, what it was planning to do in the months ahead, and invite feedback from employees. The company assured employees that this would be a fair process by making roughly the same proportion of personnel cuts on all levels of the organization, having no senior executive or external consultant profit at the expense of employees' loss of jobs, offering qualified employees fair early-retirement packages, and providing outplacement services for employees.

On the advice of the BR manager, though, the company knew that it was still at heightened risk for retaliation by disaffected employees when the cuts came a year later. For that reason, the company implemented a critical incident plan. All managers had to participate in a two-hour training session, administered by the BR manager to groups of ten at time. Managers were taught mandatory preventive steps, including

Management referral to the assessment resource of any employee exhibiting bizarre behavior

Management referral to the assessment resource of any employee directly involved in a violent action

Critical incident debriefings, in group format, of anyone indirectly connected with a violent act, including co-workers

Immediate dismissal and legal action against any employee committing a violent act

The assessment resource, which was heavily promoted to employees for purposes of self-referral, also provided the outplacement counseling.

As effective as this prevention strategy was (no violent acts occurred during downsizing), several confrontations between managers and employees did occur. The assessment resource determined that the employees involved were ones who felt highly vulnerable to being laid off. Two of the three employees, in fact, were relieved of duty at that point but were offered outplacement counseling. The third employee was kept but made subject to further evaluation by the assessment resource and to compliance to any treatment recommendation.

Months later, senior management realized that it had "dodged a big bullet" by not having any serious incidents. It attributed this circumstance to the critical-incident strategy.

Case Study 6: The Company That Managed Its Product Liability Risk

A small manufacturer of aftermarket windshields had become concerned about vulnerability to the product liability lawsuits that were becoming common to area manufacturing companies. This increasing potential had already resulted in escalating insurance rates, even though the company, Clearview, Inc., had never lost a lawsuit or settled out of court. Clearview's management, however, was concerned about delayed orders for customers and about manufacturing defects in glass thickness, curvature, and optical clarity. Some flawed windshields not only were manufactured but a dozen times in a three-month period they also had slipped past inspection and into customers' hands, where they were flagged and had to be shipped back to the company. Clearview's owner wondered how many more had been installed, leaving the company vulnerable to lawsuits later.

Meanwhile, on the shop floor, problems were mounting. Employees were habitually absent, slowing production; supervisors "enabled" their employees by covering and making excuses for them, an end product of the company policy of promoting people to management from within; and a lethargy seemed to exist throughout the workforce. The manufacturer, worried that it could not "ride on good fortune," decided to improve its quality assurance process then implement elements of a behavioral risk management strategy. The company took two steps to improve its business performance: give employees a vested interest in product quality and company performance by improving human resource practices—specifically, establishing a bonus program linked to company performance—and set a goal of improving organizational performance by using the following behavioral risk management strategy:

Priority 1. Reduce defects and improve customer satisfaction.

Priority 2. "Professionalize" management. Give managers training on coaching and counseling employees, documenting employee performance problems, using constructive confrontation, and encouraging employees to seek help for personal problems that might be affecting work performance.

Priority 3. Establish employee quality improvement and accident prevention teams, who would observe each other's work in order to foster better work practices.

Priority 4. Encourage employees to take more responsibility for their life-style management and to drink less, by sponsoring lunchtime seminars and wellness activities.

Priority 5. Reduce lost work time by using all of the above strategies.

Once its priorities were established, the company solicited proposals from service providers and listened to four different presentations on how the priorities could be met. The company selected a provider based not on low cost but on the ability and willingness to place a staff member on site one day a week for a nominal cost; to muster the most expertise on management, lifestyle, and behavioral training; to provide regular training; and to link a portion of provider revenues to organizational performance in such areas as accidents, healthcare costs, and attendance.

Management's act of setting priorities and using them to implement the behavioral risk management strategy was providential. Several years later, when the windshield market tightened, and some competitors were knocked out of business, Clearview actually strengthened its market share and revenues.

Case Study 7: The Small Business That Promoted Good Health

A group of three self-professed "workaholics" started a women's casual apparel company called NuTrend Activewear. For the first couple of years, brisk business kept the partners busy manufacturing their line of summer shorts and tops, and twelve employees were hired. When the group decided to design additional products and reach new markets, however, serious disputes developed among the partners and spilled over into the financial management of the business and attacks on each other's personal lives. Fever-pitch disagreements occurred several times a week at work, causing one employee to quit on the spur of the moment.

In order to save NuTrend Activewear, the partners sought the help of a clinical and organizational psychologist, who helped them to sift through their issues as a group and individually. After a series of sessions, one of the partners decided to leave, since she felt her business interests were incompatible with the views of the other two partners. With one-third of the issues instantly resolved, the remaining partners were able to resolve their differences easily, compromising where necessary. Because both of them were sports enthusiasts, they decided to build a distinct work culture that promoted both physical and mental health, use of wellness services, honest and open communication in order to prevent and resolve conflicts, and encouragement of employees to use their personal leave in order to ensure balanced living. Instead of workaholics, they now considered themselves to be "do-aholics," and applied this thought as much to their personal lives as to work.

They decided to contract with an external service provider for conflict resolution, problem assessment, and wellness services. In order to make the services more economical, though, they formed a consortium with other members of a local women's business organization. In that way, the consortium, which had a total of 750 employees, could purchase the services in volume. The consortium found it could purchase behavioral health insurance affordably through the service provider as well, so it contracted with the service provider to form an insurance pool, negotiate an arrangement with an insurer, and then manage the behavioral health benefit. In so doing, several of the consortium members—ones that previously fought with their insurers or health maintenance organizations on behalf of employees or family members restricted in access or denied access to benefits—felt they had gained a measure of control over whether and how benefits could be accessed by employees. The consortium members formed an informal board of directors that oversaw the service provider's activities and set ground rules on how the behavioral health benefit would be managed.

NuTrend Activewear continued to grow over the next five years, and it achieved the internal stability that it previously lacked. Today it has fifty-five employees.

There are as many unique examples of behavioral risk situations as there are work organizations, ineffective management styles, and troubled employees. These cases provide only a glimpse of the versatility of behavioral risk management interventions. What they demonstrate most clearly is that the risk exposures of individuals are best addressed systemically, holistically, and preventively.

Why Risk Ultimately Cannot Be Transferred to the Society at Large

There remain two matters to discuss that are central to any organization's decision to undertake or improve behavioral risk management: risk transfer to society at large and social risks likely to affect employers in the future.

With limited success, employers can transfer behavioral risk onto society by simply "dumping" employees as problems surface and hiring other warm bodies as replacements. This pattern is indicative of an organization without either a behavioral risk prevention strategy or early-stage intervention strategy. It is also a short-sighted tactic, for five reasons.

First, these organizations are likely to be ones that have not considered the full realm of their behavioral costs. If these costs were to be totaled, as they are in a behavioral risk audit, these organizations would be likely to find that paying for a strategy that intervenes early with problems and that also helps to prevent problems from occurring and thus reduces management headaches is a good trade-off for management.

Second, sooner or later these organizations are to lose highly valued employees to behavioral risks. A system that was in place to save lesser-valued employees would have saved the valued ones, too.

Third, if there are systemic problems—such as an addictive organization or a law of diminishing competence among managers—these organizations have no process for identifying their causal factors or for intervening with those factors.

Fourth, there is no such thing as a true risk transfer. The problems are likely to come back later, perhaps in the form of an overall diminution of the work-readiness of the labor pool. While a selective "mercy firing" can be a positive development for an employee needing to adjust his or her work attitude, indiscriminate firing can also create bad public relations, invite retaliation such as vandalism, and in these litigious times, increase the risk of lawsuits.

Fifth, simply "dumping" employees increases the likelihood of unionization or passage of public policy that imposes mandates on the entire community of employers. Once these risk exposures occur, they are almost irreversible.

As in other aspects of life, when the level of pain associated with a particular situation gets high enough, something has to be done about it. Some employers will no doubt continue to consider it more economical to unload employees than to deal with behavioral problems, until they reach the point where getting rid of one set of problems is likely to result in an equally complex new set being hired with the replacement employees.

Why Behavioral Risk Management Will Be More Important in the Future

It is a considerable irony that as employers continue to replace people with machines and other devices to increase output and eliminate employee error, behavioral risk management will become increasingly important.

As computers, robotics, optical fibers, and other technological advances reduce the number of people necessary to perform a certain set of tasks, we might assume that this devalues an organization's remaining human resources. Actually, the opposite occurs. The sales of Fortune 100 companies increased 42 percent from 1984 to 1993, from $1.2 trillion to $1.7 trillion, while the number of employees dropped about 12 percent. The result in terms of the value of human capital is shown in two important statistics. First, sales per employee went from $144,578 in 1983 to $232,877, an increase of 62 percent. Additionally, assets per employee, a measure of the financial and physical resources supplied by the organization per employee, increased from $110,120 to $273,972.

The driver behind behavioral risk management, then, is this: the potential for any single employee to cause productivity and financial losses to an organization has sharply increased.

What behavioral risk management and other workplace strategies ultimately do is help employers attain organizational excellence. Most efforts at excellence are aimed at shortening production cycles, devising space-age production processes that are inherently superior to their predecessors, and implementing other initiatives that have the final result of increasing revenues and earnings.

Behavioral risk management helps work organizations build and sustain a solid foundation on which this growth can occur. As employers move into the next millennium and the era of global competition, behavioral risk management should be universally applied to increase the likelihood that business organizations will meet the challenge.

Note

P. 377, *the value of human capital is shown in two important statistics:* Gubman, E. L. "People Are More Valuable Than Ever." *Compensation & Benefits Review,* Jan./Feb. 1995, pp. 7–14.

Appendix

This appendix contains tools and examples for the behavioral risk management manager and staff. The first item is a complete behavioral risk audit survey for managers and employees. Because supervisors are often expected to be the first to notice specific behavioral risk exposures, the second item is a checklist to help supervisors analyze employee performance and conduct. The final two items are examples of written confidentiality policies and ethical principles.

Behavioral Risk Audit Surveys

The following behavioral risk audit survey for managers and employees corresponds with the subjective behavioral risk indicators described in Chapters Three and Four. This example reflects generic behavioral risks. A company should revise the questions and add others, as necessary, to customize the audit to its own organization and workforce.

Management Survey.

1. The level of stress that I am currently experiencing in my job is:
   ☐ High
   ☐ Moderate
   ☐ Low

2. My current level of stress over the last three months is:
   ☐ Increasing
   ☐ Remaining stable
   ☐ Decreasing

3. Balancing my work and family-life responsibilities is:
   ☐ Extremely difficult
   ☐ Somewhat difficult
   ☐ Not very difficult
   ☐ Not difficult at all

4. The current threat of violence (or physical confrontations) between or among employees and managers at my job site is:
   ☐ High
   ☐ Moderate but increasing
   ☐ Moderate but decreasing
   ☐ Low

5. Employee sabotage and theft in the company are a:
   ☐ Major problem
   ☐ Moderate but increasing problem
   ☐ Moderate but decreasing problem
   ☐ Small problem
   ☐ No problem at all

6. Protections against workplace sabotage and theft are:
   ☐ Very good
   ☐ Good
   ☐ Adequate
   ☐ Poor
   ☐ Do not exist

7. The company has experienced lost sales because of problem behaviors of the organization or employees:
   ☐ Definitely yes
   ☐ In my opinion, yes
   ☐ Maybe

☐ Probably not
☐ Definitely not

8. Rumors in the company are:
   ☐ Common
   ☐ Not very common
   ☐ Do not happen

9. I believe that rumors in the company are:
   ☐ Very detrimental
   ☐ Somewhat detrimental
   ☐ Not very detrimental
   ☐ Not detrimental at all

10. The communications that line managers receive from senior management are:
    ☐ Always clear and concise
    ☐ Usually clear and concise
    ☐ Sometimes contradictory or ambiguous
    ☐ Usually contradictory or ambiguous

11. When I receive feedback from employees, the quality of the information is usually:
    ☐ High
    ☐ Satisfactory
    ☐ Low

12. When management decides on major organizational changes, the amount of lead time it gives employees before implementing the changes or announcing them to the public is:
    ☐ Generous
    ☐ Adequate
    ☐ Too brief

13. I know the company's mission and strategic plan:
    ☐ Yes
    ☐ No

14. The company's mission and strategic plan are:
    ☐ Clear and achievable
    ☐ Clear but not achievable
    ☐ Not very clear

15. The company's mission and strategic plan are well communicated to the workforce:
    ☐ Yes
    ☐ No

Management Survey (*continued*).

16. The amount of cooperation between management and employees is:
    - ☐ High
    - ☐ Moderate
    - ☐ Low
    - ☐ None at all

17. I am able to cope with the pace of work and the demands I receive from higher management:
    - ☐ Always
    - ☐ Usually
    - ☐ Sometimes
    - ☐ Usually not

18. The amount of conflict between line managers and senior management is:
    - ☐ High
    - ☐ Fairly high
    - ☐ Moderate
    - ☐ Low
    - ☐ None at all

19. I believe the demands put on my time by senior management are:
    - ☐ Excessive
    - ☐ Rather heavy
    - ☐ Moderate
    - ☐ Light

20. Supervisors in neighboring departments (or work units) have:
    - ☐ A lot of problems with their employees
    - ☐ Some problems with their employees
    - ☐ Few problems with their employees
    - ☐ No problems with their employees

21. The quality of the management training in handling employees that I receive is:
    - ☐ High
    - ☐ Average
    - ☐ Poor

22. The work relationships in the company are:
    ☐ Harmonious
    ☐ Fairly cooperative
    ☐ Not very cooperative
    ☐ Divisive

23. A lot of managers in the company are "workaholic" (normally working 10 or more hours a day):
    ☐ Yes
    ☐ In some cases
    ☐ No

24. The best way to get ahead in the company is always to work harder and longer:
    ☐ Yes
    ☐ In some cases
    ☐ No

25. I typically work 10 or more hours a day in order to keep senior management happy:
    ☐ Yes
    ☐ In some cases
    ☐ No

26. I believe the safety practices in neighboring departments (or work units) are:
    ☐ Very good
    ☐ Good
    ☐ Satisfactory
    ☐ Poor

27. Disputes between members of my work teams are resolved without interrupting production:
    ☐ Always
    ☐ Usually
    ☐ Sometimes
    ☐ Usually not
    ☐ Never

Management Survey (*continued*).

28. Senior management is prone to knee-jerk decision making:
    - ☐ All the time
    - ☐ Usually
    - ☐ Sometimes
    - ☐ Seldom
    - ☐ Never
29. Crises occur in the company:
    - ☐ All the time
    - ☐ Usually
    - ☐ Sometimes
    - ☐ Seldom
    - ☐ Never
30. Work teams have had to rush through work projects and assignments to meet deadlines, only to have to repeat or fix the product or service later:
    - ☐ Many times
    - ☐ Sometimes
    - ☐ A few times
    - ☐ Never
31. The company lacks long-range planning:
    - ☐ Yes
    - ☐ No
32. Name five major workplace developments in the company over the last three years and indicate whether you believe each one was a positive or negative development.

Development	Positive (P) or Negative (N)
1.	_____
2.	_____
3.	_____
4.	_____
5.	_____

Employee Survey.

1. The level of stress that I am currently experiencing in my job is:
   - ☐ High
   - ☐ Moderate
   - ☐ Low
2. My current level of stress over the last three months is:
   - ☐ Increasing
   - ☐ Remaining stable
   - ☐ Decreasing
3. Balancing my work-life and family-life responsibilities is:
   - ☐ Extremely difficult
   - ☐ Somewhat difficult
   - ☐ Not very difficult
   - ☐ Not difficult at all
4. I am a caretaker for:
   - ☐ Children
   - ☐ Elderly parents
5. I have been a partner in a divorce within the past five years:
   - ☐ Yes
   - ☐ No
6. The safety precautions the company takes are (for response only by employees in hazardous jobs):
   - ☐ Adequate
   - ☐ Not Adequate
   - ☐ Don't know
7. The level of unsafe work practices among my co-workers is (for response only by employees in hazardous jobs):
   - ☐ High
   - ☐ Moderate
   - ☐ Low
8. Co-workers are under the influence of alcohol or drugs on the job (for response only by employees in hazardous jobs):
   - ☐ Frequently
   - ☐ Sometimes
   - ☐ Infrequently
   - ☐ Never

Employee Survey (*continued*).

9. The current threat of workplace violence or physical confrontations between or among employees and managers at my job site is:
   - ☐ High
   - ☐ Moderate but increasing
   - ☐ Moderate but decreasing
   - ☐ Low

10. Employee sabotage and theft in the company are a:
    - ☐ Major problem
    - ☐ Moderate but increasing problem
    - ☐ Moderate but decreasing problem
    - ☐ Small problem
    - ☐ No problem at all

11. Security precautions to prevent sabotage and theft are:
    - ☐ Adequate
    - ☐ Not adequate
    - ☐ Don't know

12. I believe that management treats employees belonging to a racial minority:
    - ☐ Always fairly
    - ☐ Usually fairly
    - ☐ Usually unfairly
    - ☐ Not fairly

13. Management's level of awareness of employee drug and alcohol use is:
    - ☐ High
    - ☐ Moderate
    - ☐ Low
    - ☐ None at all

14. Management always acts when it detects problems of employee alcohol or drug use:
    - ☐ Yes
    - ☐ No

15. I am aware of other employees who injured themselves off the job, deliberately injured themselves on the job, or faked an injury in order to collect workers' compensation or disability benefits:
    ☐ Yes
    ☐ No

16. I am aware of injured employees who sought to increase workers' compensation benefits unfairly or to prolong the period for which benefits are drawn:
    ☐ Yes
    ☐ No

17. The problem of workers taking advantage of the workers' compensation system is:
    ☐ Increasing
    ☐ Decreasing
    ☐ Not a problem
    ☐ Don't know

18. Communications to employees from management are:
    ☐ Always truthful and straightforward
    ☐ Usually truthful or straightforward
    ☐ Sometimes misleading or don't tell the full story
    ☐ Always misleading or don't tell the full story

19. The work directions that I receive from management are:
    ☐ Always clear and straightforward
    ☐ Usually clear and straightforward
    ☐ Sometimes contradictory or ambiguous
    ☐ Usually contradictory or ambiguous

20. Rumors in the company are:
    ☐ Common
    ☐ Not very common
    ☐ Do not happen

21. I believe that rumors in the company are:
    ☐ Very detrimental
    ☐ Somewhat detrimental
    ☐ Not very detrimental
    ☐ Not detrimental at all

Employee Survey (*continued*).

22. The amount of feedback that I receive from management about my work is:
    ☐ Adequate
    ☐ Inadequate

23. The quality of the feedback that I receive from management on the type of work it wants me to do and the quality of my work is:
    ☐ High
    ☐ Average
    ☐ Low

24. When management decides on major organizational changes, the amount of lead time it gives employees before implementing the changes or announcing them to the public is:
    ☐ Generous
    ☐ Adequate
    ☐ Too brief

25. I know the company's mission and strategic plan:
    ☐ Yes
    ☐ No

26. The company's mission and strategic plan are:
    ☐ Clear and achievable
    ☐ Clear but not achievable
    ☐ Not very clear

27. The company's mission and strategic plan are well communicated to the workforce:
    ☐ Yes
    ☐ No

28. My treatment by management is:
    ☐ Always fair
    ☐ Sometimes fair
    ☐ Seldom fair

29. I feel that my job is:
    ☐ Very secure
    ☐ Fairly secure
    ☐ Fairly insecure
    ☐ Very insecure

30. I feel able to speak my mind to my supervisor:
   - ☐ Yes
   - ☐ No

31. The feeling of loyalty I have for the company is:
   - ☐ High
   - ☐ Moderate
   - ☐ Low

32. My wage or salary is:
   - ☐ Satisfactory
   - ☐ Unsatisfactory

33. Managers in my work unit play favorites:
   - ☐ Always
   - ☐ Usually
   - ☐ Sometimes
   - ☐ Seldom
   - ☐ Never

34. The degree of cooperation between management and employees is:
   - ☐ High
   - ☐ Moderate
   - ☐ Low

35. When management makes promises to employees, it keeps its promise:
   - ☐ Always
   - ☐ Usually
   - ☐ Sometimes
   - ☐ Seldom
   - ☐ Never

36. I am aware of stories about the company that make me think it is a "people-oriented" organization:
   - ☐ Yes
   - ☐ No

37. I have a strong advancement potential in the company:
   - ☐ Yes
   - ☐ No
   - ☐ Don't know
   - ☐ Not interested in advancement

Employee Survey (*continued*).

38. The company's involvement in local community affairs is:
    ☐ High
    ☐ Moderate
    ☐ Low

39. If I develop personal or job performance problems, there is a company-provided "safety net" of supportive programs and benefits for me:
    ☐ Yes
    ☐ No
    ☐ Don't know

40. My co-workers and I believe we can trust the company's programs and benefits staff to keep personal information away from management:
    ☐ Yes
    ☐ No
    ☐ Don't know

41. The company has made training or technological improvements that help me to improve my productivity:
    ☐ Yes
    ☐ No

42. I am able to cope with the pace of work:
    ☐ Always
    ☐ Usually
    ☐ Sometimes
    ☐ Usually not

43. The amount of conflict between line management and employees is:
    ☐ High
    ☐ Fairly high
    ☐ Moderate
    ☐ Low
    ☐ None at all

44. When a supervisor finds out that an employee has a problem that makes it difficult for the employee to perform the job, the supervisor typically will:

☐ Address the problem in a timely and satisfactory manner
☐ Put off the problem for a while but eventually get around to dealing with it
☐ Ignore or hide the problem because he or she doesn't want to deal with it

45. When problems develop between employees, management's efforts to settle it are:
☐ Effective
☐ Sometimes effective
☐ Not very effective
☐ None at all (problems get ignored)

46. The work relationships in the company are:
☐ Harmonious
☐ Fairly cooperative
☐ Not very cooperative
☐ Divisive

47. A lot of employees in the company are "workaholic":
☐ Yes
☐ In some cases
☐ No

48. The best way to get ahead in the company is always to work harder and longer:
☐ Yes
☐ In some cases
☐ No

49. I typically work 10 or more hours a day in order to keep my supervisor happy:
☐ Yes
☐ Sometimes
☐ No

50. The work teams in the company:
☐ Always run smoothly
☐ Have disruptions of activity from time to time
☐ Have a lot of disruptions of activity

Employee Survey (*continued*).

51. When we are working together, members of my work team are:
    - ☐ Very supportive
    - ☐ Fairly supportive, but they sometimes doubt the team's effectiveness
    - ☐ Somewhat resistant
    - ☐ Very resistant

52. People on my work team are expected to pull their weight and are held individually accountable for their work and conduct:
    - ☐ Always
    - ☐ Usually
    - ☐ Sometimes
    - ☐ Seldom
    - ☐ Never

53. Rules in my work team are fair and democratic and applied equally to everyone:
    - ☐ Always
    - ☐ Usually
    - ☐ Sometimes
    - ☐ Seldom
    - ☐ Never

54. Disputes between members of my work teams are resolved without interrupting production:
    - ☐ Always
    - ☐ Usually
    - ☐ Sometimes
    - ☐ Seldom
    - ☐ Never

55. The risk of accident or illness faced by my co-workers and me is:
    - ☐ High
    - ☐ Moderate
    - ☐ Low
    - ☐ None at all

56. Senior management is prone to knee-jerk decision making:
    - ☐ All the time
    - ☐ Usually
    - ☐ Sometimes

☐ Seldom
☐ Never

57. Crises occur in the company:
☐ All the time
☐ Usually
☐ Sometimes
☐ Seldom
☐ Never

58. Which of the following most accurately describes the company's operation:
☐ A smooth operation with good planning and realistic deadlines
☐ An operation that is usually smooth but periodically is rushed or has to do things over
☐ An operation that is usually rushed or doing things over
☐ An operation that is always rushed or doing things over

59. Work teams have had to rush through work projects and assignments to meet deadlines, only to have to repeat or fix the product or service later:
☐ Many times
☐ Sometimes
☐ A few times
☐ Never

60. During the work day, I feel:
☐ Always calm
☐ Usually calm
☐ Sometimes anxious
☐ Usually anxious
☐ It varies a lot

61. I feel that I have a good deal of control over my career and work life:
☐ Yes
☐ No
☐ It varies

62. The equipment I use to do my job seems to be made to help me avoid physical strain and injury:
☐ Yes
☐ No
☐ It varies

Employee Survey (*continued*).

63. The company is careful to strike a balance between human and technological resources:
    - ☐ Always
    - ☐ Usually
    - ☐ Sometimes
    - ☐ Seldom
    - ☐ Never
64. Name five major workplace developments in the company over the last three years and indicate whether you believe each was a positive or negative development.

Development	Positive (P) or Negative (N)
1.	_____
2.	_____
3.	_____
4.	_____
5.	_____

Performance and Conduct Checklist

When a worker's performance or conduct deteriorates and fails to show improvement following the discussion between the worker and the supervisor at the corrective feedback and problem-solving stage, the supervisor may want to strongly suggest a referral to the confidential work-based problem assessment resource. The following employee performance and conduct checklist can help the supervisor decide whether to contact the assessment resource for a consultation.

Performance and Conduct Checklist.

HAVE YOU OBSERVED REPEATED AND CONTINUED PATTERNS OF PERFOR-
MANCE DETERIORATION IN ANY OF THE FOLLOWING AREAS?

1. Quantity/quality of work:
   - ☐ Yes ☐ No Gradual reduction in quantity and quality of work over the past year or longer.
   - ☐ Yes ☐ No Quantity and quality of work less consistent and dependable compared with ___ months ago.
   - ☐ Yes ☐ No Work characterized by increased carelessness and mistakes.
   - ☐ Yes ☐ No Frequent errors on routine matters.
   - ☐ Yes ☐ No Details neglected.

2. Job-related awareness:
   - ☐ Yes ☐ No Forgetfulness or lapses in memory.
   - ☐ Yes ☐ No Reduced awareness of what is required to do a satisfactory job.
   - ☐ Yes ☐ No Unable to keep current with information needed to do the job.
   - ☐ Yes ☐ No Unable to identify with and support the mission of the office, work group, or organization.

3. Judgment:
   - ☐ Yes ☐ No Inconsistent in making decisions.
   - ☐ Yes ☐ No Questionable judgments have increased in frequency.
   - ☐ Yes ☐ No Unable to prioritize work and manage time effectively.

4. Initiative:
   - ☐ Yes ☐ No Seldom undertakes anything beyond clearly defined job responsibilities.
   - ☐ Yes ☐ No Often tries to exceed limitations of current job responsibility, and does so inappropriately.

5. Resource utilization:
   - ☐ Yes ☐ No Does not seek support and guidance when needed.
   - ☐ Yes ☐ No Unable to identify and utilize appropriate resources.
   - ☐ Yes ☐ No Does not delegate work effectively.

6. Dependability:
 ☐ Yes ☐ No Overly dependent on others and will encourage others to do his or her work.
 ☐ Yes ☐ No Frequently fails to meet schedules with no reasonable explanation.
 ☐ Yes ☐ No Makes unreliable or untrue statements about events or own capabilities.
 ☐ Yes ☐ No Has poor work habits and is unwilling to take personal responsibility for quantity and quality of work product.

7. Attendance and punctuality:
 ☐ Yes ☐ No Frequent unplanned absences: number in last 12 months is ___; number in last 6 months is ___; number in last 3 months is ___.
 ☐ Yes ☐ No Frequent use of sick leave. If Yes, is major illness present: ☐ Yes ☐ No.
 ☐ Yes ☐ No Suspicious pattern of absenteeism.
 ☐ Yes ☐ No Frequent complaints of vague illness.
 ☐ Yes ☐ No Frequently leaves early for or returns late from lunch: number of times per week is ___; per month is ___.
 ☐ Yes ☐ No Frequent unexplained disappearances from job: number of times per week is ___; per month is ___.
 ☐ Yes ☐ No Bizarre or unbelievable excuses for lateness or absence.
 ☐ Yes ☐ No Spends time on the phone engaged in personal business.

8. Ability to communicate:
 ☐ Yes ☐ No Argumentative or disruptive to the point of reducing unit's productivity.
 ☐ Yes ☐ No Less communicative than in the past.
 ☐ Yes ☐ No Unclear or imprecise written or oral communication.

9. Interpersonal skills:
 ☐ Yes ☐ No Not a cooperative team member.
 ☐ Yes ☐ No Increasingly avoids colleagues and/or supervisor.

☐ Yes ☐ No Complains or is uncooperative with co-workers.

☐ Yes ☐ No Unusually sensitive to advice or criticism.

☐ Yes ☐ No Overly critical of others.

10. Safety conscious:

☐ Yes ☐ No Higher than average number of on-the-job accidents.

☐ Yes ☐ No Disregards safety of others and self.

11. Other behavioral problems:

☐ Yes ☐ No Deteriorating personal appearance.

☐ Yes ☐ No Loss of enthusiasm for job.

☐ Yes ☐ No Impairment on the job.

☐ Yes ☐ No Extreme mood swings.

☐ Yes ☐ No Sleeping on the job.

☐ Yes ☐ No Hostile and confrontive.

☐ Yes ☐ No Inappropriate behavior. Specify:

Source: This checklist was developed by Donald A. Phillips of COPE, Inc., Washington, D.C. Reprinted by permission.

Confidentiality of Employee Assistance Services Record and Information.

As an Employee Assistance Program Provider, we strive to maintain the highest standards of program confidentiality to comply with legal and ethical mandates and meet the needs of our clients. In this regard, we have carefully reviewed U.S. Government regulations pertaining to client confidentiality and canons of professional ethics established by various accreditation organizations concerned with mental health and chemical dependency treatment. As a result of our research, we have established specific guidelines for our own professional conduct with respect to protecting the confidence of client company employees and immediate family members.

Basic Philosophy: Except as noted in subsequent sections, our firm and/or our clinicians, staff, and affiliates will refrain from disclosing or communicating any information identifying and/or describing a user of our services to anyone, including an employee's family, fellow employees or supervisors, or any other persons outside of our organization.

Release of Confidential Information: When assistance for any employee is requested by that person's employer and/or supervisor, we will request that the employee sign a Release of Information Form allowing our clinician and/or consultant to communicate with the company and/or supervisor to facilitate the documentation, assessment, and resolution of work-related performance problems. Such release shall specify the information that may be disclosed, the purpose for such disclosure, and the effective period during which confidential information may be released to a specific party. If the employee declines to sign the Release of Information Form, we cannot confirm that the employee is a client. The company and/or supervisor may request such a release from the employee in conjunction with reviewing the performance-based consequences that will occur if the clinician cannot provide the company/supervisor with reason to expect a realistic improvement in the employee's job performance. We will request from the employee a signed Release of Information Form, which authorizes the EAP to release information to the company and/or supervisor when documentation of work performance or relationships appears necessary for making an accurate assessment or to ensure appropriate action on the part of the employee or supervisor in resolving the problem.

Communication with Treatment Providers: When an employee's difficulties necessitate referral to a treatment provider outside of our organization, the employee will be asked to sign a Release of Information Form allowing our clinician or consultant to share relevant assessment information with the intended treatment provider. If it is not possible to obtain a written release (as in a telephone assessment), the clinician will ask for verbal permission to release the aforementioned information and will document in the employee's record whether permission is verbally granted.

Communication of Aggregate Information: In the case of employees who refer themselves to our firm or who are referred by a family member, we will verify such referrals only through aggregate demographic data reported to the company on an as-needed basis. The same type of information will be reported on employee family members who use our services. This demographic information does not contain data that could be used to identify specific individuals and/or family members.

Disclosure Without a Release: Federal and/or state laws may, in specific instances, require the disclosure of employee information irrespective of a signed and authorized release form. When a clinician has reasonable suspicion that physical or sexual abuse of a child or vulnerable adult has occurred or that there is a threat of harm to oneself or another person by the employee or an immediate family member, then disclosure to the appropriate authorities is necessary and, in many instances, legally mandated. Records may also have to be released, without a signed consent by the employee or family member if subpoenaed by a court of law.

Security Clearance: With client companies whose employees have security clearances, we agree to work cooperatively with security personnel, within established State and Federal guidelines, on medical records and information. We request that the company's personnel and/or department charged with overseeing and maintaining security continue to assume primary responsibility to ensure the integrity of the company security system. Security personnel will need to manage and assess security issues with those employees referred by self or the company for EAP services. If security obtains a signed consent from a referred employee for the disclosure of confidential information to the company and/or security personnel, we will provide the designated information that may be needed by security personnel to assess the employee's risk in this respect. In the absence of a signed and authorized release, the employer must assume the responsibility for monitoring employees deemed to be at risk for breaching security.

With your written confirmation of these guidelines, we will be able to best serve the interest of your company and your employees while meeting our professional ethical and legal mandates.

Authorized Official for the Client Company   Date

For the Employee Assistance Program Provider   Date

Source: "Appendix." *EAPA Program Standards.* Arlington, Va.: Employee Assistance Professionals Association, 1993, pp. 30–31. Reprinted by permission.

Ethical Principles for University and College Ombudspersons.

An ombudsperson is guided by the following principles: objectivity, independence, accessibility, confidentiality and justice; justice is preeminent.

An ombudsperson hears and investigates complaints objectively. Objectivity includes impartial attention to all available perspectives on an issue and may or may not entail support of any particular perspective.

An ombudsperson acts as independently as possible of all other offices and avoids conflict of interest, external control and either the reality or appearance of being compromised.

An ombudsperson is readily accessible to all members of the constituent community, promotes timely solutions to problems and avoids either the reality or appearance of bias toward any individual or group.

An ombudsperson treats with confidentiality all matters brought to him or her. No action is taken on a complaint without the complainant's permission. Information retained by the ombudsperson is kept secure. However, with the verbal or written permission of the complainant, such information may be carried forward by the ombudsperson.

If a complainant reports a serious problem but is unwilling to be part of any steps taken to address it, an ombudsperson tries to find a way to address the problem that is acceptable to the complainant, or that does not compromise the identity of the complainant.

However, if an individual speaks about intending serious harm to himself or herself or others, or if the complainant confesses to serious misconduct or a crime, an ombudsperson must use personal discretion in determining whether or not this information is carried forward. Discretion is likewise required in regard to matters governed by state and federal law.

An ombudsperson is guided by a concern for and commitment to justice. Justice requires that individual interests be carefully balanced with the consideration of the good of the larger academic community. An ombudsperson's commitment to justice includes the understanding of power, identification of the use and misuse of power and authority, and recognition of the need for access to power by the members of the institution.

Other concerns also govern an ombudsperson's conduct. While it is the parties who are responsible for choosing a particular resolution, the ombudsperson attempts to guide them toward options that are fair, conform with institutional policy, and give clear indication of being in their best interest. An ombudsperson remembers, and at all times protects, the right to privacy of all parties, including the alleged offenders. An ombudsperson generally does not act on third-party complaints.

An ombudsperson has a responsibility to maintain and improve professional skills, to assist in the development of new practitioners, and to promote impartial dispute resolution in the institution.

Source: University and College Ombuds Association. Reprinted by permission.

Annotated Bibliography

The following books and other reference materials are suggested reading for understanding the psychological and behavioral manifestations of individuals and work organizations as well as the programs, services, benefits, and other interventions necessary to address these manifestations in the workplace.

Chenoweth, D. *Planning Health Promotion at the Worksite.* (2nd ed.) Dubuque, Iowa: Brown & Benchmark, 1991; and *Health Care Cost Containment: Strategies for Employers.* (2nd ed.) Dubuque, Iowa: Brown & Benchmark, 1993. Describing wellness and health promotion methods, these two books focus on ways management can enhance employee health and improve corporate culture and on cost management techniques for use by middle- and upper-level corporate financial managers.

Fassel, D., and Wilson Schaef, A. *The Addictive Organization.* New York: HarperCollins, 1988. Work organizations often mimic family systems, according to these authors, especially families with active alcoholics and codependents and families in which dysfunctional systems are perpetuated by the adult children of alcoholics.

Fisher, K., Rayner, S., and Belgard, W. *Tips for Teams: A Ready Reference for Solving Common Team Problems.* New York: McGraw-Hill, 1995. Hundreds of solutions are offered for employers wishing to design, implement, and perpetuate work teams. Addressed are the structural, operational, and behavioral aspects that make the work team environment different from the traditional hierarchy.

Glazer, W. M., and Bell, N. N. *Mental Health Benefits: A Purchaser's Guide.* Brookfield, Wis.: International Foundation of Employee Benefit Plans, 1993. A variety of behavioral illnesses are described. Benefit plans and related programs and services, such as employee assistance, are explained.

Googins, B. K. *Work/Family Conflicts: Private Lives—Public Responses.* New York: Auburn House, 1991. This book highlights the strains being imposed on today's American families, evidenced by results of

Boston University's Job and Homelife Study. Work-and-family conflicts are projected into the twenty-first century.

Hirschhorn, L. *Managing in the New Team Environment.* Reading, Mass.: Addison-Wesley, 1991. An overview of the skills and techniques required to manage successfully in team environments is presented along with a discussion of the ways in which the manager's role should change as work teams change.

Kets de Vries, M.F.R., and Associates (eds.). *Organizations on the Couch: Clinical Perspectives on Organizational Behavior and Change.* San Francisco: Jossey-Bass, 1991. Among the informative chapters in this book is one by Donald R. Young and Larry Hirschhorn about the psychodynamics of safety in an oil refinery, based on a clinical organizational intervention following two major accidents.

Nye, S. G. *Employee Assistance Law Answer Book: 1993 Cumulative Supplement.* New York: Panel, 1993. This is an excellent one-volume source of legal information on employee assistance, confidentiality, workplace counseling, and personnel law. The material is presented in question-and-answer format and includes an appendix of case studies and analyses, court opinions, model policies, and forms and contracts.

Quick, J. C., Murphy, L. R., and Hurrell, J. J., Jr. (eds.). *Stress and Well-Being at Work: Assessments and Interventions for Occupational Mental Health.* Washington, D.C.: American Psychological Association, 1992. This book published by the American Psychological Association describes problems in work organizations that have stress as an underlying contributor.

About the Author

Rudy M. Yandrick is a writer and consultant specializing in behavioral risk, human resource, and healthcare issues. He is a contributing author to *Behavioral Healthcare* Tomorrow journal, *EAP Digest,* and other publications. Previously, Yandrick was editor of *EAPA Exchange,* communications director and media relations director for Employee Assistance Professionals Association, and legislative specialist for U.S. Congressman John P. Murtha. He works and resides in Mechanicsburg, Pennsylvania.

Yandrick based the development of the behavioral risk management concept on years of observing changes in American business and on the growth in employee assistance, wellness and health promotion, managed behavioral healthcare, and other occupational programs and services that has occurred as a result of those changes.

About the General Editor

Michael A. Freeman, M.D., is the chairman of the **Behavioral Healthcare** *Tomorrow* national dialogue conference, the editor-in-chief of the *Behavioral Healthcare* Tomorrow journal, and the general editor of the Jossey-Bass Managed Behavioral Healthcare Library. He also serves as the CEO of the Partnership for Behavioral Healthcare and the president of the Institute for Behavioral Healthcare; both organizations are dedicated to improving American and global mental health and addiction treatment benefits, management, services, and outcomes.

Dr. Freeman is a psychiatrist and a member of the clinical faculty at the Langley Porter Psychiatric Institute of the University of California, San Francisco, Medical Center. He is a specialist and consultant in the managed behavioral healthcare purchasing, managed care, and services fields.

Index